The Daily Telegraph
BRITISH BATTLEFIELDS

Also by Philip Warner

The Daily Telegraph

British Battlefields

The definitive guide to warfare in England and Scotland

Philip Warner

WHERE BATTLES WERE FOUGHT

WHY THEY WERE FOUGHT

HOW THEY WERE WON AND LOST

CASSELL

Wellington House, 125 Strand, London WC2R 0BB

This book is a compilation of the four books published separately
by Osprey 1972–5
British Battlefields: 1 *The South*
British Battlefields: 2 *The North*
British Battlefields: 3 *The Midlands*
British Battlefields: 4 *Scotland and the Border*

This edition 2002

British Library Cataloguing-in-Publication Data
A catalogue record for this book is available from the British Library

ISBN 0–304–36332–4

The right of Philip Warner to be identified as author of this work
has been asserted by him in accordance with the
Copyright, Designs and Patents Act 1988

The maps in this book offer a quick, easy-to-use and up-to-date guide
to the location and layout of the battle sites. Readers wanting to make
detailed explorations on and around a particular site may find a
large-scale map of the local area a useful addition.

Maps by Peter Harper

Typeset at The Spartan Press Ltd
Lymington, Hants
Printed in Spain

Contents

The South

Introduction

Very few living men have taken part in a battle, and many must wonder how they would acquit themselves if ever they had to. A medieval battle was a very complex affair; it was far from being a simple matter of kill or be killed. It could be won or lost at any stage; it could turn on the action of one man, and not necessarily a man of high rank either, and it could settle nothing, or alternatively the fate of a nation.

But for the majority, when thinking of a battle, the overriding question would be: how would I behave? What would happen to me? Would I emerge unscathed and join in the celebrations, or would I be left wounded on the battlefield waiting for someone to save me, or for some ghoul to finish me off? Would I lose all fear in the excitement?

In reading the descriptions in this book it may be possible to guess the answers to some of those questions. On some of these battlefields you may feel luckier than on others. When you visit them it is worth bearing in mind that your own relations fought on these fields. This is almost certain. Everyone has two parents, four grandparents, sixteen great-grandparents . . . and so on. If you work this out you may be sure that in any battle described in these books you probably had a number of ancestors fighting on each side. Doubtless they held a wide variety of ranks.

What were your chances? Battles are very strange. A wise commander does not give battle till he is sure he can win; some do not do so until they feel they have won already. Even today your estimate of why a former battle was won may be as good as anyone else's, for it is a strange fact about battles that often men do not know why they were won. The fact that one side had more casualties than the other means little. Most of the slaughter took place when one side had decided all was lost. The number killed when the battle was being fought may be small.

In examining these battlefields, and assessing the general situation, you must put yourself in the position of one of the senior commanders. You must remember how many troops you have and consider their quality. Are they well-trained, and well-armed? If not, are they well led? Do the junior commanders know their job? Will they keep their heads, take their men to the right objectives, control them in apparent victory, rally them in apparent defeat? Are they all going to be in their right places at the right time? What are their weapons like? Are the men skilled in their use? Many hundred years ago, in the declining years of the Roman Empire, a strategist wrote: 'A handful of men inured to war proceed to certain victory, while on the contrary numerous armies of raw and undisciplined troops are but multitudes of men dragged to slaughter.' It is as true today as it was then.

There were fashions in warfare, just as there were fashions in everything else, and sometimes a military fashion could be as impracticable as any other. On occasion armies were defeated because their commanders were relentlessly obstinate about moving with the times. In the first battle of this book we shall see how cavalry and bowmen won a battle against infantrymen but this led to an over-emphasis on the value of cavalry and neglect of infantry.

The axe was despised by the Normans because the Saxons used it, but became a very fashionable weapon for Normans later. The doom of the armoured knight eventually came from the longbow which was in use at the time of Hastings but in remote parts of Wales only.

Whatever plans commanders make for battle they are – as often as not – thrown into disarray by unpredictable happenings on both sides. Confusion soon settles down on a battlefield and it is the commander who in that fast-changing, dangerous situation can think constructively and clearly who wins. The atmosphere of muddle which settles on to a battlefield is known as 'the fog of war'.

The terms 'strategy' and 'tactics' are used loosely nowadays, and applied to so many non-military matters, that their proper meaning tends to be blurred. Strategy means the overall plan of a campaign for the defeat of an army, nation and people. Strategy requires you to mobilize all your resources, not only of people but also of food and weapons and equipment. It involves organizing the use of land, sea, and air transport, the use of propaganda, the preparation of detailed plans for a campaign and the provision of contingency plans against the unexpected. Just as it tries to organize its own resources it will try to disorganize the opposition. Nowadays, propaganda designed to upset enemy morale can be disseminated through radio, press and television. In the past it was done by spreading rumours through infiltrators. Rumours – particularly of bad news – spread very rapidly. The most morale-destroying rumour is that the commander-in-chief has prematurely departed from the field. In at least two of the battles described here commanders killed their horses at the outset with a view to showing that they themselves would stay to the end, whatever the probable result.

Strategy might or might not be influenced by the nature of the ground; tactics undoubtedly would be. Tactics is the science of the layout of troops in the face of the enemy and their use in action. Minor tactics deals with the problems occurring to sub-units, which maybe of patrol strength. However, it must not be thought that minor tactics are of little account. Skill in minor tactics is vital to success in a campaign. Strategy and tactics were not invariably the reason why battles were fought, for some occurred by accident; but strategy, if not tactics, brought the opposing armies to the point at which battle was joined. Both were in turn influenced by the physical features of the countryside. Very often these might be overlooked. It is obvious that armies have to take into account mountains, hills, rivers, roads, swamps, forest, or very rough ground. What is less obvious is the influence of much smaller physical features. The battle of Poitiers in France 1356 was won by the Black Prince because the English could not be dislodged from a twenty-foot high hill protected by a hedge and a ditch; at the battle of Agincourt in 1415 the French lost because they tried to advance over newly-ploughed fields which were sodden from the recent rains. But battles may be lost for even less obvious reasons. A tree might serve as a rallying point, as an observation post, or as the cause of the split in the advance of an army; a stream might enable an army and its horses to refresh themselves, or might lead to its defeat. When on a battlefield it is advisable to look for every tiny rivulet and patch of marshy ground. As that rivulet was trampled in and clogged with bodies it could soon become a marsh, and then a miniature lake. Woe betide anyone who was pushed back into it, particularly if he was wearing heavy armour. On some battlefields you will find a site marked 'Bloody Meadow'. A glance at the surrounding topography will show how it obtained its chilling name.

A stream might have been damned before the battle began in order to make the enemy advance on a very narrow front. This would nullify an advantage in numbers. During the Zulu wars in the nineteenth century a handful of Dutch held back thousands of Zulus because the latter could not reach them; the place was subsequently known as 'Blood River'. Kenilworth Castle, which does not look particularly formidable today, was once made impregnable by the damning of two small streams; it was then surrounded by 111 acres of water.

Control of an area is made effective by a commander being able to move forces rapidly from one part to another. Thus you will find battlefields near roads or rivers, or *nodal points* as junctions of either are called. For the same reason you will find the entrance to valleys, or passes, or bridges and fords, all bear traces of nearby fortifications. It is all too easy to underrate these fortifications because many people merely see them as inert defences which would be dangerous within arrow range only. On the contrary they were bases, and although built to give a good account of themselves if besieged, would mainly be used to house fighters who would tackle the opposition just as they emerged out of the river or perhaps before they were in sight of the fortification. The problem of a fortification, however small, to an advancing army, was that it would be too great a threat to be left untaken, yet might take time to reduce. And time might be a vital commodity. Delay might prevent an army reaching a vital river crossing before it was strongly defended, might prevent it from capturing a town which held vital stores, or might prevent a link-up with other forces, converging from different directions.

The sites of battles are then anything but haphazard. But before being able to predict why and where battles must have been fought you need to investigate what changes have taken place in the countryside between the date of the battle and today. It may surprise you. What is now dry ploughland may once have been wet tussocky scrubland, the battlefield may perhaps have a town built on it but even then there are probably tell-tale signs. But even if the surface of the battlefield has been largely obliterated the surrounding area will do much to explain it. You will soon learn to recognize the importance of certain features – or 'develop an eye for ground'. With a little practice you will be able to estimate where the attack came from before even looking at the detailed map. You will make mistakes. You will perhaps forget the time it takes to move men over encumbered ground; it is no good saying 'he should have attacked on the flank' if the approach would have been thick with bodies and abandoned equipment. You will probably try to squeeze too many men into too small an area – as many a commander has done before you. You will perhaps neglect your cavalry, or your artillery. In assessing what you yourself might have done you must accept completely what the enemy did do. Your version of the battle may prove more successful than your predecessor's – or less.

Battles, in the times we speak of, lasted but a day. Pursuit and slaughter may have taken longer but the decision would be reached in a matter of hours. Siege battles were, of course, a different story.

The explanation of the shortness of early battles lies in the weapons they used. Draw a bow a hundred times and see how much longer you want to go on for. Take a sword, or a billhook, and try hacking a way through a copse for an hour. Better still, pad yourself up with protective clothing before you begin and move rapidly from place to place. Even then you will lack the noise, the effect of cavalry changes sending a shock through the ranks, and the bruises that often came from the weapons of friends as well as foes. But you will be getting the feel of a medieval battle.

The Battle of Hastings

14 October 1066

Most people have heard of the Battle of Hastings, and know that it was fought in 1066. What is known beyond that usually tends to be wrong or, at least, misinterpreted. The general impression is that the true Englishman King Harold was defeated – somewhat unfairly – by a foreigner who had no right to be in England at all.

The facts are as follows. The Battle of Hastings was not fought at Hastings but at Battle, which lies six and three-quarter miles to the north-west. The site is also known to some as Senlac, which means 'a sandy brook'; the term Senlac Hill which is sometimes used is therefore confused.

The Normans who conquered the Anglo-Saxons[1] at Hastings were not, as is generally supposed, the first Normans to set foot in this country. Edward the Confessor, who reigned from 1042 to 1066 was almost more of a Norman than an Englishman. He himself came of the Anglo-Saxon family descended from Alfred the Great but as the Danes had overrun the country Saxon heirs to the throne had to live in exile or lose their heads. When the last Danish king died in 1042 Edward was brought back from Normandy, where he had virtually forgotten the Anglo-Saxon language, and made king.

1 The Anglo-Saxons will henceforward be referred to as 'Saxons' in this account of the battle.

Edward then became an ineffective king at a time when the country was desperately in need of firm government. For most of his reign he was either overawed by the powerful Saxon Earl Godwin or duped by his own Norman favourites. When Godwin died his son Harold took over his posts and his influence. Harold was a brave and able governor of England and also made himself well-respected in Scotland and Wales. The story of Macbeth is well-enough known; it was Harold who organized his defeat and the restoration of the true heirs to the Scottish throne. In Wales Harold personally led an expedition which chased the Welsh king to the heights of Snowdon; there he was decapitated by his followers and his head brought to Harold's feet. This was the type of man Harold was: awe-inspiring, brave, experienced, and respected.

William was no less of a warrior. His upbringing had been harsh and dangerous. He was the bastard son of the Duke of Normandy by a tanner's daughter; it is said that his father first saw his mother when she was washing in a stream. Later she was married off to a suitable husband and had other distinguished sons. Bastardy was no hindrance to succession in Norman law, and William succeeded to the dukedom of Normandy at the age of ten; that he survived and grew to manhood and great power was due to a large measure of luck. Much of his childhood was spent in avoiding being assassinated; much of his early maturity was spent in desperate fighting to obtain a grip on his dukedom, and protect it from his ambitious neighbours. His claim to the throne of England was marginally stronger than that of Harold, who had no blood connection. However, when Edward the Confessor died the Saxon Council (the Witan) had no hesitation in electing Harold as their king. He was on the spot, he had virtually ruled the country for the last fourteen years, and he was apparently recommended by the dying Edward. There was, in fact, another candidate in Edward's great nephew Edgar Aetheling – but as he was only ten nobody paid any attention to his claim.

The situation was further complicated by the fact that under duress Harold had been tricked into swearing he would support William's claims.[1] Yet another problem for Harold was the fact that he had much jealousy to contend with in the north of his kingdom.

Harold was not a 'lucky' commander. He won battles by courage and technical brilliance; the succession of events which brought his death at Senlac would not have happened to a lucky man.

The first piece of bad luck was the broken oath to support William. Although an oath under duress it was an oath none the less. This meant that the force which William brought to England had a papal blessing and his men believed they would win because they were fighting a usurper and an oath-breaker. Morale has always been a vital factor in battles but never more so than in medieval warfare; on this occasion morale was boosted by the religious nature of the invasion, but also by the thought of the magnificent plunder which success would bring.

The battle took place on 14 October 1066. Six months earlier William had begun assembling an invasion army and the fleet to carry it. Harold was well aware of these preparations and had maintained a coast watch throughout the summer. Military service was then supplied by the 'fyrd' system, by which men were called up for two months at a time. In September the weather was cold and blustery; it looked as if winter would soon make invasion impossible. The most critical time for a country fearing invasion is when the harvest has been gathered and before winter has set in. Readers may recall that 'Operation Sealion', the German plan to invade Britain in

1 He had once agreed to support William, when, after a shipwreck, he had fallen into William's power in Normandy.

the autumn of 1940 was cancelled by Hitler on 12 October; this was because the German Air Force had failed to establish air superiority before rough weather made the crossing of the Channel with invasion barges impracticable. Unfortunately for Harold, on 15 September 1066, the King of Norway made a surprise landing in Yorkshire. (On 15 September 1940 the Battle of Britain was won in the air.)

Hardrada, King of Norway, also had a claim to the English throne although neither he or anyone else took it very seriously. However, in the previous year, Harold had made an unfortunate diplomatic mistake. His younger brother, Tostig, had been made Earl of Northumbria by Edward the Confessor. It was a bad appointment, based entirely on a personal whim, and this was shown when the district rebelled against the new earl. Harold, having looked into the matter, advised Edward to banish Tostig, and in his place approved the appointment of Morcar. Northumbria was then much more than Northumberland is today and comprised roughly what the name suggests – the district north of the Humber. This substantial favour in no way diminished Morcar's envy and jealousy of Harold, and eventually contributed to the loss of the Battle of Hastings. Morcar's feelings were shared by his brother Eadwine, who controlled Mercia, as the central provinces of England were then called. This feeling of jealousy and antagonism was eventually expressed by the brothers' failure to hurry support to Harold against William's invasion. Five years after the conquest they received their just reward; one was killed in a skirmish and the other was imprisoned for life.

But in 1066 the nemesis of Eadwine and Morcar was far distant. As Harold was waiting for the inevitable invasion from Normandy he suddenly heard that a more immediate danger was present in the north. Tostig, raging at the loss of his earldom, had gone to Norway and enlisted the aid of Hardrada the King of Norway. The Vikings were a formidable people; they fought for the pure love of fighting, fear did not exist for them, and they took no heed at all of the occasional disasters which overtook them on land and sea. But of all the Viking raiders – and there had been many – none was so famed and feared as Hardrada. He was reputed to be seven feet tall – and this could have been true, for some of the Vikings were veritable giants – but whatever his stature there was no question of his ability. Tostig had no difficulty in enlisting his aid; it was a fight with the plunder of the kingdom to follow. They embarked in 300 ships.

Morcar and Eadwine were the first to meet the onslaught but their forces were brushed aside with wholesale slaughter, at Fulford, near the gates of York. Morcar and Eadwine did not stay to see the eventual results of the fight, which would doubtless include the capture and sacking of the city; they had previously moved out of the danger area. However, in this case, the early departure of the chiefs from the battlefield probably did not demonstrate lack of personal courage but merely a frantic desire to rally other resistance. Among the qualifications for military command, at any level, complete absence of fear was always assumed. Even if the fear was not absent – and it seldom is – the commander would never show it. This assumption is as marked and important today as ever it was. In previous centuries this absolute freedom from fear has always been considered a natural prerogative of the aristocracy, a man-at-arms, or a peasant might be as brave as his lord, but none could be braver. Then, as now, good units had both individual and collective courage. As Napoleon said of his veterans at Waterloo 'They will not run away and it will take a long time to kill them all.' The Vikings, and their descendants the Normans (originally 'the Northmen') probably felt no fear, only excitement. They were possessed with 'berserkgangr' – joy in battle, which made them at their happiest when fighting; they probably approached a bloody conflict with the same feelings which modern man does a game of football.

The battle for York had taken place on 20 September and the disastrous news was brought promptly to Harold; even more promptly he acted. Having heard of the landing a day or two previously he was already on his way to the north but time prevented him from collecting more than 3,000 men against the invaders' 6,000. He reached York on 25 September and pushed on to meet the invaders in the dawn of the next day at Stamford Bridge, seven miles from York. Hardrada and Tostig were caught unprepared for the sudden onslaught and hardly had time to take up their proper fighting formation. There was a dramatic 'Horatio holds the bridge' scene when they had retreated across the Derwent, for the single bridge was held by a formidable Viking. Unlike Horatio, this intrepid warrior who was holding up the entire Saxon army, did not save the bridge; he was stabbed from below by an equally hardy Saxon who had floated himself under that part of the bridge on which the Viking was standing.

The battle of Stamford Bridge lasted for a few hours only and it must have been one of the bloodiest of all battles. Apart from the shield wall favoured by Saxon and Viking alike there seems to have been little in the way of tactics. Hardrada and Tostig were both killed and the remnants of the force which had required 300 ships to bring it in was glad to slip away in twenty-four, possibly some 500 men in all. It seems unlikely that the rest can all have been killed in a few hours' battle but fugitives would have had short shrift in those times.

However, the day after Stamford Bridge saw the Norman invasion force cross the Channel. It had been held up for a month by contrary winds, a circumstance which caused William much trouble and anxiety. But with the change of wind William's star was undoubtedly in the ascendant: the fyrd had been disbanded, Harold's own fleet had just put in to London for a refit leaving the crossing unopposed, and Harold and his army were in the middle of Yorkshire.

Harold did not, in fact, learn that the Normans had landed until 2 October. But again he lost no time. The southern fyrd was called up and began to move towards Pevensey, which was where the Normans had landed. Harold set off south on a forced march with his army. They were an elite force. The housecarles were a personal bodyguard, and the officers were thegns – that is, landowners who were men of substance, rank, and responsibility. Unfortunately, as a fighting machine it was slightly out of date.

The Norman force which had established itself in Sussex was a better balanced and more modern army. In quality it was probably inferior to Harold's Saxons but it had two useful assets which the Saxons lacked; it had cavalry and it had archers. In all the army probably numbered 9,000, of which one-third were armoured knights or mounted troopers. Transporting the horses had been a considerable problem; some had not stood the journey well, and if William had not been extremely fortunate in the weather there is a strong chance that his cavalry would have lost him the battle before it even began. It was not a very sophisticated army for they had little idea of manoeuvre. Their general technique was to charge their opponents, lay about them with sword and mace and hope to make a breach in the line which could be exploited by foot soldiers. The latter carried a variety of lesser arms which included spears, slings, swords and bows. The bowmen were not very highly rated; they had short bows which they drew to the chest; these were in no way comparable to the formidable crossbows and longbows of later years. Still, anyone who has ever used a bow – and most people have – know that it does not require much of a weapon to send a sharp arrow a distance of some seventy yards. Later bows managed five or six times that distance.

It is believed that here were a few archers among the Saxons too, but not enough to have much effect. Most of Harold's army were armed with axes, which they used with fearful strength and precision. They could split an adversary to his chest or lop off a limb with easy skill. Some had short-handled axes which they might throw – in the Frankish tradition, and there was a wide variety of crude but deadly implements, a scythe, a billhook or a spear are formidable weapons in the hands of an experienced and skilled user. However, if you are handling a weapon which you swing, and which depends very much on the velocity of that swing, it means that your body armour must be light, flexible, and therefore not a great protection. By contrast, the Normans could wear chain mail and carry long shields. The chain mail was simple, consisting of rings sewn on to leather but it kept its wearer out of much trouble. There was always a delicate balance in these matters. Either you fought with light weapons and minimal armour, relying on speed and agility for effectiveness, or you transformed yourself into a sort of land battleship, heavy, slow, difficult to conquer, but by no means invulnerable.

Having heard the bad news of the Norman landing on 2 October Harold set off south with a substantial contingent immediately. He arrived in London by nightfall of the sixth, a journey of just under 200 miles in six days. This was an excellent but by no means exceptional achievement. In medieval warfare men were often required to make forced marches, and were well-accustomed to long and awkward journeys. The powers of endurance of the medieval soldier have been scarcely recognized but they were obviously almost superhuman by many modern standards. However, in World War II, the Special Air Service, which sent raiders deep behind the German lines in the desert, achieved similar standards. As an example one man walked 180 miles alone, without food and with very little water, and part of the way without boots (Private Sillito in 1942). There were other performances hardly less remarkable. Doubtless many medieval soldiers would not have found them remarkable at all.

The general impression that Harold marched north to defeat Hardrada, and then promptly marched straight back to Hastings where he was defeated because of exhaustion is incorrect. He spent four days in London collecting his forces and arranging his army. He should have waited longer, for Morcar and Eadwine had not yet joined him because of jealousy and stupidity, and the western contingents had not had sufficient time to march in. But Harold would not wait. It was said that this was because he did not like the reports he heard of Kent and Sussex being pillaged by the Normans but it is more likely that he was over-confident and longing to get to grips with William. On the eleventh he left London.

The site he chose for the battle cannot be faulted. In order to reach London William would have had to march along a ridge which extends nearly seven miles north-west of Hastings. Just before the ridge reaches Senlac it drops; the traveller therefore has to cross a valley and climb a steep slope on the farther side. On that slope Harold deployed his army. It was broad enough to make a flank attack difficult, and had the added advantage of a wooded region in the rear in case the Saxons were driven back from the slopes. The

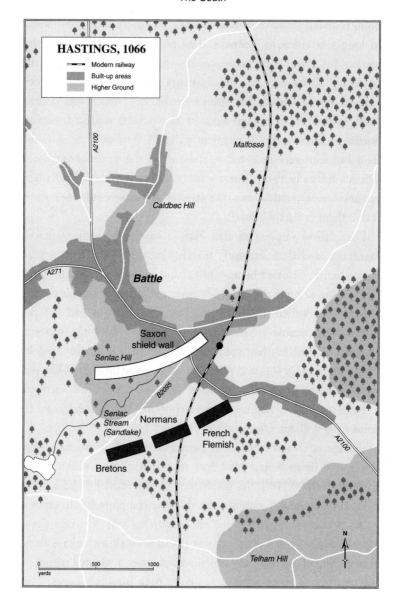

HASTINGS, 1066

Modern railway
Built-up areas
Higher Ground

A2100

Malfosse

Caldbec Hill

A271

Battle

Saxon shield wall

Senlac Hill

B2095

Senlac Stream (Sandlake)

Normans

French Flemish

Bretons

A2100

0   500   1000
yards

N

Telham Hill

bottom of the valley was marshy, from the Senlac stream. Senlac or 'Senlache' meaning 'sandy stream'. The point was apparently marked by a 'hoar apple tree' but subsequently William established an abbey on the spot, placing the High Altar on the place where Harold was killed. The hill itself is 1,100 yards long by 150 yards wide. It was clearly a point of great strategic importance and had doubtless been known as such for centuries. It is fifty-seven miles from London and Harold had covered the distance in three days. As a march it bore no comparison with the trek up north and back again but fifty-seven miles in three days in full battle kit scarcely leaves a man at his freshest. As the battle took place on the fourteenth it was obvious that Harold had to occupy the site or subsequently fight in a much less favourable situation.

One point will never be resolved. Harold may have been pressing forward to destroy the Normans around Pevensey and Hastings but might have halted for the night in a good defensive position. Alternatively he may have been warned that the Normans had abandoned their destructive activities in Sussex and were now marching towards London; if so he had to meet them in a defensive position which was ideal for the purpose.

Today the upper part and crest of the hill is occupied by Battle Abbey but it is possible to walk over most of it. There are a number of guides who will give a full account of 1066 and subsequent history. It is possible, without too much walking to view the battlefield from both Saxon and Norman positions. The local museum, in the middle of the town and almost opposite the Abbey

The battle site is partly built on by Battle Abbey (which provides excellent guides). The Norman viewpoint is best seen from the B2095 road. The main features of the battlefield are clearly discernible. (East Sussex)

gateway, has an excellent relief plan of the battlefield with the disposition of the opposing troops.

It was said – by the Norman chroniclers – that the Saxons spent the night before the battle in feasting, and the Normans spent it in praying; neither seems particularly likely. One account says that the Saxons dug themselves in with a trench protected by stakes, but this may have been a misunderstanding of what was meant by the 'shield wall'. Whatever their nocturnal activities it seems that it took a considerable time for them to get into battle array on the fourteenth, for the battle does not seem to have begun till 9 a.m. – or perhaps even later. The numbers were probably approximately even, about 9,000 each. On the Norman side about 3,000 were mounted, armoured in chain mail. There was some chain mail among the foot soldiers also.

The Saxon army comprised an élite force of housecarles, probably numbering 2,000. These held the centre, and fought with axes. On the flanks were the less well-armed levies of the *fyrd*. The latter had a wide assortment of weapons, including spears and bows. The Saxons possessed horses, and often rode them to battle but would fight dismounted. They were in a good position on top of the ridge; they were blocking the road to London at a point where either side was marshy, where the slope was steep enough to take the edge off any cavalry charges, and where any retreat would draw the invader into a particularly dangerous piece of forest. However, Harold never contemplated retreat or luring the Normans into an ambush. He planned to fight it out where they stood, and in fact came very close to victory by that method.

The Norman army was drawn up in the pattern which became standard practice later, that is, in 'battles', which were oblong divisions. Each battle was made up of a front of archers, a centre of foot soldiers and a rear of armoured knights. Anyone who changed his mind about wanting to be in the hottest part of the battle would have little scope, for if he turned to flee he would be chopped down by his own side. Once a man was committed to a medieval battlefield it was undoubtedly 'death or victory', unless he was of such high rank that his ransom would be so valuable that the enemy would do their best to take him alive. William arranged his army with Bretons on the left, with Normans under his personal command in the centre, and with French and Flemings on the right. William had surveyed the position from Telham Hill, behind his centre, and perhaps retired to that observation point at intervals in the battle. Harold's command post is marked today at Battle, and is a few yards from the spot where he finally fell.

As the Norman army moved forward a jester named Taillefer rode out in front, anxious to strike the first blow. He succeeded, but in a few moments was killed. The armies paused for a second to watch, then set-to themselves. The Norman archers launched off a few flights of arrows but these inflicted very little damage. As they came close together there was a shower of spears from either side but these too had slight effect; the Saxon shield wall remained unbroken and the Normans still pressed forward. When they came to close quarters the real bloodshed began; the Normans hacked away with sword and lance while the housecarles swept their formidable axes like flails and cut through armour and man. The tremendous power of the Saxon axeblows sliced cleanly through the Norman mail and took off an arm or leg in a blow. The charges of the Norman cavalry were perhaps more of a novelty than a threat, for their horses were light, and there was little tactical plan, so after a while they fell back and let their infantry get on with the work; their own time would come later. William had three horses killed under him during the battle, though at what stage is not known, and there were doubtless other Norman knights who were equally surprised at their reception. The Normans hoped to batter holes in the shield wall; the Saxons on the other hand were prepared to chop all comers to pieces. The slaughter at close quarters was a little too much for the Bretons on the Norman left and they fell back. In doing so they exposed the left flank of the Norman battle in the centre, and this column too began to retire. In the confusion William was lost to sight and the rumour – quick to spread in such circumstances – was that he was dead. He was equally quick to dispel it and pulled off his helmet as he stood up in his stirrups and shouted angrily at those around him. They steadied, and as soon as they did so William and his half-brother, the notorious and warlike Bishop Odo, put in a cavalry charge on to the Saxons who had come down the slope in pursuit of the Bretons. For a while all was confusion and then it was seen that the Saxons were giving way under this unexpected onslaught. As we see in other battles in this book there were few incidents more destructive to morale than a heavy cavalry charge on their flanks just when men thought they were proceeding to victory. Well-organized infantry with pikes, and training in handling them, would be a match for cavalry but on disorganized troops the effect of cavalry can be devastating. Some of the Saxons fought to the death on the mound to the left; the remainder straggled back up the hill to their comrades. It had been an ugly moment for both sides and it came after continuous fighting when neither side was in a fit state to take proper advantage of the situation. There was a lull while both sides recovered breath and prepared for the next grim onslaught.

When it came the Normans were committing their whole force and tried time and again to break into the Saxon line. But the line held and as the bodies mounted it was the Normans who at times fell back. Clearly they could not have fought continuously, and as the Normans occasionally withdrew the Saxons pushed forward in spite of their earlier experience. Subsequently the chroniclers described these minor retreats as tactical devices to break up the Saxon formation but this is unlikely.

But the Saxon line was shrinking. Perhaps they should have gone on to the attack and driven at the heart of the Norman position. As it was they stood on the defensive, which is never very helpful to morale. It is said that some of the fyrd were losing heart and slipped away. Whatever the reason, the line of housecarles became shorter and became a semi-circle around Harold.

At that moment the Normans, who had sent back to Pevensey for more arrows, had a stroke of luck. Knowing that the arrows could not penetrate the shield wall they sent them high in the air from close range. Whether one hit Harold in the eye or not is not known. A piece of the Bayeux tapestry, on which much of our knowledge of the battle is based, gives the impression that an arrow is either passing Harold's head or penetrating it. His brothers were already dead; his faithful thegns were close around him but they must have been few in numbers. The chances are that most of the fyrd had fallen back to lose itself in the shelter of the trees in the gathering dusk, and the housecarles, who had borne the brunt of the battle, were fighting almost alone. But they fought on, even when Harold was wounded. Finally a party of Norman knights broke through the last cordon and stabbed the dying king. One, in fact, stabbed him after he was dead, and was disgraced for what was considered a coward's blow. Harold was heavily cut about and his corpse was so disfigured that it could only be identified by his mistress – Edith Swan-neck. Those thegns who were not killed fled overseas. Their possessions were forfeit if they had been at Hastings and many of them joined the Varangian Guard, the élite corps at Byzantium.

Even when the battle was over the Normans nearly met disaster.

Pursuing the remaining Saxon, some of the cavalry had ridden on recklessly in the dusk. The ground behind the Saxon position is rough today, and then would undoubtedly have been more so, as well as being covered with trees. At some point behind the Saxon position, mentioned in the chronicles as 'Malfosse' (the evil ditch) the Normans ran into disaster. Probably some of them broke their necks on the steep slopes of Caldbec Hill, or were ambushed in the forest. In any event some of them panicked and were fleeing back to Senlac until they were once more rallied.

One day's battle had won a kingdom, for there was no other major battle; and London surrendered after William had made an encircling movement. Afterwards he held down the land with motte and bailey castles, with sheriffs, and laws, and feudal obligation. By parcelling out the land into manors, and making the owners rent it by military service he gave himself an army with a vested interest in his survival. When the conquered gave trouble – as they did in Devon and Yorkshire – he destroyed them, their horses, and their crops. Appropriately he met his own death twenty-one years later when his horse trod on a burning beam in a French town he was sacking, and fatally injured him by throwing against the high pommel of his saddle.

The Normans who won the Battle of Hastings had short hair and shaven faces; the Saxons had long hair and moustaches. Before many years, however, the Normans were also growing their hair long and appearing with moustaches, although much criticized by their priests and leaders for doing so. The controversy about hair is as old as the British nation.[1]

After William had won the battle he took a vow to build an abbey

1 It is often thought that the Anglo-Saxons were a brutal and uncivilized people and that the Normans were culturally far more advanced. Archaeologists have evidence which refutes this.

with the High Altar on the spot where Harold fell. He honoured his oath, and the foundations may be seen to this day, although the abbey which now stands on Senlac Hill is of much later date. The tree known as Harold's oak (actually a beech) is, of course, later still.

Unfortunately, few other traces of the battle remain for the surface has risen. Perhaps one day deep excavation will bring relics to light.

The battle inspired many Normans to lyrical prose but some of their description may owe more to enthusiasm than to fact:

There was a French soldier of noble mien, who sat his horse gallantly. He spied two Englishmen who were also carrying themselves boldly. They were both men of great worth and had become companions in arms, and fought together, the one protecting the other. They bore two long and broad bills, and did great mischief to the Normans, killing both horses and men. The French soldier looked at them and their bills, and was sore alarmed for he was afraid of losing his good horse, the best that he had; and would willingly have turned to some other quarter, if it would not have looked like cowardice. He soon, however, recovered his courage, and spurring his horse gave him the bridle and galloped swiftly forward. Fearing the two bills, he raised his shield, and struck one of the Englishmen with his lance on the breast, so that the iron passed out of his back. At the moment that he fell, the lance broke, and the Frenchman seized the mace that hung at his right side, and struck the other Englishman a blow that completely broke his skull.

On the other side was an Englishman who much annoyed the French, continually assaulting them with a keen-edged hatchet. He had a helmet made of wood, which he had fastened down to his coat, and laced round his neck, so that no blows could reach his head. The ravage he was making was seen by a gallant Norman knight, who rode a large horse that neither fire nor water could stop in its career, when its master urged it on. The knight spurred, and his horse carried him on well till he charged the Englishman, striking him over the helmet, so that it fell down over his eyes; and as he stretched out his hand to raise it, and uncover his face, the Norman cut off his right hand, so that his hatchet fell to the ground. Another Norman sprang forward and eagerly seized the prize with both his hands, but he kept it little space, and paid dearly for it, for as he stopped to pick up the hatchet, an Englishman, with his long-handled axe struck him over the back, breaking all his bones so that his entrails and lungs gushed forth. The knight of the good horse meantime returned without injury; but on his way he met another Englishman, and bore him down under his horse, wounding him grievously, and trampling him altogether under foot. (Wace: Roman de Rou)

In one day the pattern of England was established. But as Guizot, the French historian, put it 'England owes her present liberties to being conquered by the Normans.'

The Battle of Lewes

14 May 1264

After the Battle of Hastings the Normans established an iron grip on the country which they had conquered in one battle. William I died in 1087 and was succeeded by his dissolute son William II (Rufus the Red). William was a fighter, as a king in those days had to be, but his court, full of homosexuals and harlots, was as corrupt as this country has ever seen. William II was succeeded in 1100 by his brother Henry I, who was noted for lechery, parsimony, and cheerlessness. When Henry died in 1135, leaving a daughter as his heir, anarchy broke out and for nineteen years the country was torn by a civil war in which robber barons did exactly as they pleased to the distress of everyone else. It was known as 'The nineteen long winters when God and his saints slept'. Stephen was eventually succeeded by Henry II, who once more established an iron grip on the country. He is, however, mainly remembered for the careless remark which led to the murder of Thomas à Becket in Canterbury cathedral. Henry II was succeeded by his warlike but absentee son Richard Coeur de Lion, but Richard was killed by a gangrenous arrow wound in 1199 after a ten-year reign, and was succeeded by his brother John. John is one of the most vilified kings in English history but although not an estimable character was probably not as black as he was painted. His reign came to an end in 1216 when he was succeeded by Henry III, who reigned for fifty-six years. Both the beginning and the end of Henry's reign saw trouble, the earlier ones being none of his own fault (he was only nine when he succeeded), but the latter ones entirely due to his own stupidity.

The reign began in civil war because the barons who had rebelled against John had brought over Louis of France to be their potential king. Now that John was dead, and the new king was merely a young boy, there was little point in this rebellion against a tyrant king. But the war was still on and did not come to an end until two considerable battles had been fought; its effects lasted much longer. The country was full of mercenaries and foreigners who had been brought over by John. There were many problems to be resolved, and they were dealt with by Hubert de Burgh until 1227. But after that year Henry was an adult and ruled unadvised except by those who flattered him. He found most of his support in the foreign relations and friends of his wife, Eleanor of Provence. Naturally generous beyond his means Henry went to absurd extremes with these foreign favourites. He even made his wife's uncle, Boniface of Savoy, the Archbishop of Canterbury. Boniface was a young man of no recognizable merit and the appointment was one of extreme irresponsibility. Unfortunately it was typical of many of Henry's actions. He engaged in two futile foreign military enterprises, squandered money recklessly at home and abroad, and appointed foreigners to English posts. (There were 300 Italian priests in lucrative English benefices.) Eventually, when he summoned the Great Council in 1257 and told the barons he needed an enormous grant he found a degree of opposition he had not bargained for. Curiously enough the strength of the opposition was largely due to the personality of a man whom Henry had originally brought from France. This was Simon de Montfort, whose grandmother had been heiress to the earldom of Leicester. The de Montforts were out of favour and had never been allowed the Leicester estates until Henry patronized Simon, married him to his sister, and made him his counsellor. But Henry was too fickle to maintain a long friendship; he soon tired of de Montfort, and sent him abroad to be governor of Guienne. There de Montfort had to use most of his own money in crushing a rebellion and was not reimbursed by Henry. By 1258 de Montfort was an implacable opponent of the English king. As de Montfort was sober, sincere, and competent, he attracted widespread support. The result was that Henry was bound by the *Provisions of Oxford* (where the Great Council had met and earned itself the name of 'The Mad Parliament') to govern by the advice of three committees, and to adhere to the principles of Magna Carta. In the ensuing four years Henry tried to strike off baronial control, and eventually was absolved from his oath by the Pope. He then persuaded the barons to accept the King of France as an arbitrator. The latter, in the *Mise of Amiens*, declared he should no longer be bound by the *Provisions of Oxford* although he must act in accord with Magna Carta.

This decision precipitated a civil war for the barons refused to accept the abolition of the restraints imposed by the Provisions. However, their refusal caused some conflict of loyalties and this shifting allegiance would have some influence on the two bloody battles which ensued.

The first of these took place at Lewes on 14 May 1264; the second, which reversed it, was fought at Evesham on 4 August 1265.

In the early months of 1264 when it was obvious that a civil war was impending, both sides were organizing their support. Henry had the great earls of Norfolk and Hereford, as well as his own son Prince Edward (who would be the architect of victory at Evesham), about fifty barons, and most of the minor aristocracy. De Montfort had the support of most of the major barons, and probably mustered a greater and better equipped force than his king, though it was not available at Lewes. However, among them were the citizens of London whose indignation at unjust taxation was greater than their military prowess; they were slaughtered wholesale at Lewes. The Londoners had had a fairly good run for their money in the previous five years. They felt that supporting the cause of de Montfort gave them authority to pillage foreign property and massacre Jews. In 1264 they had plundered and destroyed a number of royal possessions. Prince Edward's reckless conduct in pressing on and destroying them at Lewes may well have stemmed from the fact that they had terrified his mother and threatened to drown her as a witch.

Henry began his preparations at Windsor and then raised his banner at Woodstock. He ordered Oxford to be cleared of students; some say it was for their own protection but others think it was because he distrusted their anti-authoritarian attitude. De Montfort planned to muster at Northampton but before he had left Peterborough Prince Edward took the town by a combination of daring on his side and treachery on the other (5 April 1264). Forty royalist knights slipped into the Cluniac priory through a convenient breach in the wall, and the castle was occupied by a subterfuge. The hero of these activities was one Philip Basset, who also distinguished himself at Lewes later by being the last to leave the field although wounded in twenty places. Some of the strongest opposition at Northampton[1] came from the ejected Oxford students who displayed a skill with crossbow and sling worthy of the great classical generals they would otherwise have been studying; they did so much damage that they

1 Northampton Castle, once one of the most impressive in England, was mainly destroyed by the greed of railway speculators in the mid-nineteenth century.

were lucky not to be put to death in the general massacre which followed the capture of the town. De Montfort's son was taken prisoner as were many other valuable supporters. The earl relieved his feelings by returning to London and letting loose a massacre of foreigners and Jews. Meanwhile Leicester and Nottingham surrendered with minimal resistance.

After having left London with no doubt as to who was in control he set off to capture Rochester, which was a royal castle. Rochester had been the scene of a notable siege in the previous reign, and this one looked like being as murderous, for de Montfort employed unusual siege engines and a fireship, but the news that Henry's army was now approaching London caused de Montfort to abandon the attack, leaving a small force to prevent ingress or egress at the castle. But the threat to London had been over-estimated for it was only a probe by Prince Edward, who was very skilled at these alarming opportunist moves. Having set London buzzing, and upset de Montfort's plans, Prince Edward pushed ahead to Rochester and disposed of the small force still investing the castle; he chopped off their hands and feet. Henry could probably have occupied London at this point but instead decided to capture the powerful baronial castle at Tonbridge. Having now got a firm grip on the midlands and the south-east Henry decided to move to the west and demolish baronial support on the way. Finally, no doubt, London would be pleased to surrender.

In the event, it did not work out like that. Henry's army had a very trying time from Welsh archers whom de Montfort had thoughtfully sent to harry them. The Welsh, who were the inventors of the longbow, which would win great glory later, were swift, active, and born guerrilla fighters. Using the plentiful cover on the way they did considerable damage to the royal army. Henry was glad to halt at

Lewes where the town and castle belonged to John de Warenne, Earl of Surrey. De Montfort, following up, camped some nine miles away and sent a message saying he did not want war but he did require the king to accept the *Provisions of Oxford*. The king did not see this so much as an olive branch as an insult. His rejection said as much. De Montfort, reluctantly, decided to put the issue to battle. He gave orders for the march to Lewes to begin. At Offham village, two miles to the north-west of Lewes he turned off the road and took up position on the hill. Having made an early start he arrived in the early morning and set out his army in three battles with one in reserve. It was a small army in numbers but not in experience; most of his commanders had had experience in French wars, and some in the Crusades. Owing to the disaster of Northampton it was short of cavalry. The Londoners, being of known lesser quality, were mainly in reserve. Three who seemed in need of restraint were locked in a carriage pending disciplinary action. In all probability the opposed forces were roughly equivalent in numbers to those at the Battle of Hastings – 9,000 a side, although de Montfort's army may have been a thousand or two less. Its arrival seems to have taken the royal army by surprise but the latter soon turned out and fell into battle array. Henry commanded the centre, his brother, Richard, Earl of Cornwall took the left wing, and his son, Prince Edward was on the right, which also included the experienced John de Warenne; the latter however lacked the fighting quality of the other members of his illustrious family.

Tactics showed no improvement on those of Hastings, nearly 200 years before, although military science had improved greatly in the meantime. One account says that de Montfort advanced at a walk until within a hundred yards of the royal force, then ordered a charge. Not wishing to be caught standing when the rebel army

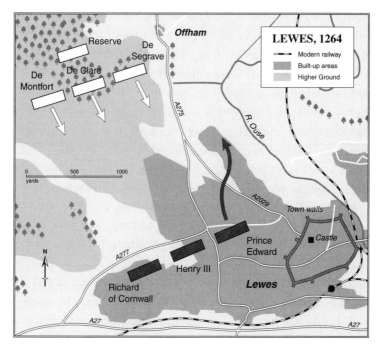

The Royalist view of the battle may be seen from the ramparts of Lewes Castle; the rebel position by climbing the footpath from Offham village. (East Sussex)

had gained momentum the royal army responded with a similar order; the two forces therefore met with a splintering crash. Prince Edward's force on the right soon pushed ahead. The troops opposing were mainly London citizens with no military experience; finding the situation too arduous for them they turned and tried to get out of trouble. Some tried to cross the river (Ouse); others sought shelter in the trees where they felt the royal cavalry would not, or could not, follow. But they were mistaken. Edward and his subordinate commanders, who included a number of Frenchmen

41

who knew themselves to be heartily detested, never let up. The unfortunate prisoners in de Montfort's carriage were killed before they could explain themselves. Those Londoners who tried to escape across the river were either killed or drowned. As always happened there was a 'bloody meadow' on the river bank where men had hoped to find a ford. Other would-be escapers were slaughtered in Cooksbridge and Halland, and even today it is easy to see why these places proved to be such death traps. It is said that some of the fugitives reached Croydon, some forty miles away, where they had the misfortune to run into another royalist force, and be slaughtered.

But the casualties were by no means all on one side. While Edward rushed on in reckless pursuit, much as Prince Rupert did at Edgehill some four hundred years later, a very different story was unfolding elsewhere. De Montfort's centre column was pressing forward steadily towards King Henry's banner, and getting the best of the encounter. Henry, although fifty-six, and not a soldier by inclination, fought well. He is said to have had two horses killed under him and had been battered by sword and mace. Eventually he withdrew from the battle and took shelter in St Pancras priory, which had been founded by the wife of the first Earl of Warenne, soon after the Conquest. His brother, Richard of Cornwall, performed less well. On leaving the field he hid in a windmill where he was surrounded by scoffing de Montfort supporters; however, unlike many, he was allowed to surrender and save his life. Even if you were rich and worth a good ransom in a medieval battle you might not always get away with your life. Tempers ran high; you might be decapitated by an equal in rank or stabbed by some churl who thought he was doing his duty. Fighting went on in various parts of the town but eventually the remnants of the royal army were pursued into the marshes to the south. The river is tidal at this point and when men and horses tried to cross they sank into the soft ooze. They reappeared the next day when the tide receded, making a macabre sight, dead yet still sitting erect on their horses, held upright by their saddles and armour. By the time Edward arrived back from what he had thought was part of a glorious victory de Montfort had won the battle and was besieging the last remnants of resistance in the castle.

The casualties in this battle were quoted by the Abbot of St Pancras as 2,700 which probably represents those found and buried in and around the town. Several hundred more found other resting places. A reasonable estimate of the total would be four thousand, perhaps one out of every five engaged. However, the battlefield was in a confined area, being bounded by a town, a river, and a steep slope, and, once the fighting began, survival was more a matter of luck than of skill.

In the nineteenth century various burial pits were discovered by builders. Some were found in 1810 and others in 1846. On the latter occasion a railway was being made through the Priory. The bones were simply thrown into the embankment, a typical example of the material outlook of the age.

The battlefield as a whole is best seen today from the ramparts of Lewes castle, where there is an arrow pointing towards it. The perfect death trap of the meadows may be clearly appreciated.

De Montfort's masterly handling of the battle is best realized by climbing the hill to his initial position. It is not possible to walk over the entire battlefield for Lewes gaol is on a part of it but a clear enough picture may be obtained from various viewpoints without ever leaving the roads. Whether de Montfort so shrewdly judged Prince Edward that he planned to remove him from the battlefield entirely by offering him an easy and tempting target will never be known, but it may have been so. Rash though Edward had been he was prepared to continue the fight when he returned, and make up for his impetuosity, but he was unable to rally adequate support at that late stage. It is said that if Edward had not fallen into de Montfort's tactical trap the latter could have achieved as good a result by setting fire to the town and then attacking from behind the royalist position. Finally, Henry, with his army dispersed, had no alternative but to surrender, and was kept under arrest for the next fifteen months.

It was a fierce, bloody, and interesting battle. As at Hastings the right wing of the more numerous army pushed ahead and won a temporary victory but by becoming separated from the main body weakened the total effort. At Hastings however the right wing suffered heavy casualties through pressing forward, which did not happen at Lewes. At Edgehill an over-enthusiastic charge took most of the royalist cavalry off the field of battle; when they returned it was too late for them to have any effect on a battle which had gone badly for their side.

The length of the battle is not known but in all probability it was over by midday. There have been a number of theories about it. One makes an even closer parallel with Hastings in that it suggests that de Montfort remained on the defensive at the top of the hill. This seems highly unlikely for Henry's army had nothing to gain and everything to lose by storming a hill position which the rebels could not live on for more than a day or two. There was no food to be found in that area and an army of several thousand could never afford to stay long in one position in the Middle Ages, unless local food supplies were exceptionally plentiful.

Apart from the battlefield and the castle (with an adjoining museum) it is also possible to visit the ruins of the Cluniac Priory of St Pancras, just south of the town. It was founded by William, the first Earl Warenne, whose coffin was dug up in the nineteenth century, and now lies in Southover Church. He was one of the most powerful of the Norman barons who came over with the Conqueror but although a fearsome man in battle was given to pious works when not wielding his sword.

As we have noted, the majority of the battle was probably fought close to the castle. De Montfort probably drew up his front between the Chalk Pits and the Racecourse grandstand. He had marched that night from Fletching and caught Henry's look-out on Offham asleep. Doubtless the sentry was persuaded in a medieval way to give as much assistance and information as he could to the rebel earl. De Montfort may have planned to let the king attack him in this strong position, and then perhaps use his reserve in an encircling movement but seeing Prince Edward disappear from the battlefield probably caused him to change his plan and to charge on to a much diminished and disorganized royal army. As in many medieval battles the general outline is well known but the details are obscure. The modern visitor may perhaps come as near to guessing the truth as the expert.

The peace terms after the Battle of Lewes were of considerable importance for they set the stage for the return match which would be at Evesham fifteen months later. They were known as the *Mise of Lewes* but unfortunately no written record of them survives. The gist of them was that Henry was bound to act on the advice of his counsellors and dismiss his foreign favourites and that Prince Edward, his son, and Prince Henry, his nephew, should be hostages for his good behaviour. The two princes apparently did not have too dull a time for they were moved from one castle to another, Dover, Berkhamsted and Wallingford being mentioned. At Wallingford there was a chance that they might be released by royalist supporters but this possibility was discouraged by Edward when he was told that any rescue attempt would merely cause him to be launched from the castle by siege catapult. Eventually he was sent to Kenilworth.

The Battle of Evesham

4 August 1265

In the year following Henry III's defeat at Lewes conditions in England deteriorated generally. Parts of the country were still royalist, and among them were the Cinque Ports, which was inconvenient for commerce. In the uncertain conditions lawlessness increased; it was illegal to bear arms without a licence but the law was often flouted. As trade flagged and prices rose there was a general restlessness through the country that operated against honest work and effort. There was also general uneasiness at the knowledge that the lawful monarch was under continuous arrest, and that his son was in confinement as a hostage. However irritating Henry may have been as a monarch it seemed quite wrong that he should be dragged around the country as a prisoner. There was discontent with de Montfort for other reasons too; he was pious but his supporters felt that he had gained too much from military success, and they themselves too little. High-minded people are especially irritating when their lofty principles cause them to withhold rewards from others if at the same time they confer substantial benefits on themselves. There were doubtless good military reasons for his acquiring eighteen confiscated baronies, and the royal castles which had been captured, but they were not apparent to those less well-rewarded. By the spring of 1265 he had alienated such powerful supporters as Gilbert de Clare, Earl of Gloucester, and Roger

47

Mortimer. A strong opposition began to build up in the west country and was soon joined by barons who had fled overseas after their defeat at Lewes; among them were John de Warenne, of Surrey, and William de Valence, Earl of Pembroke. De Montfort set off to Hereford to crush this growing threat. But the danger was much more widespread than he realized at first. An army was being mustered in Pembrokeshire, there was incipient rebellion in Worcestershire, and royalist supporters were bearing arms openly and defiantly in the north. De Montfort may have been haughty and overbearing but he was no fool and knew when flexibility was the best policy. He promptly sent a letter to the King of France requesting him to act as arbitrator and reconciler between himself and his discontented supporters. If it gained nothing else it would gain time for his opponents to begin quarrelling among themselves. Unfortunately for this astute appreciation Prince Edward managed to escape at the end of that month while on a little hunting party he had persuaded his guardians to arrange, while confined at Hereford. He soon outstripped the rest of the hunt and reached safety at Wigmore castle (the main stronghold of the Mortimers).

After this there was no chance of reconciliation. De Montfort still had the king in custody and claimed that he was ruling with royal consent, but this in no way impeded Prince Edward from strengthening his position by taking in the north-western counties. De Montfort, who was a man of action as much as a diplomat, moved through Gloucester to Wales where he tried to make an effective alliance with Llewellyn. His journey into Wales was not a success and he retired to Newport waiting for supplies and reinforcements. He was disappointed. The supply fleet was engaged and wrecked by the royalists. There was no point in remaining. With a greatly dispirited army de Montfort moved north again to Hereford. It was not a pleasant journey, but it was a very necessary one, for de Clare and Prince Edward were now on the Severn and it was essential to move quickly if he was to get back across again. He had sent instructions to his son Simon to collect an army and take it up to Kenilworth, which was the principal de Montfort castle. Simon de Montfort the Younger took unduly long over his task but for all the good he did on arrival he might just as well have taken longer. On arrival at Kenilworth, which was a very strong castle surrounded by 111 acres of water he very unwisely quartered his army in the town instead of the castle. Prince Edward, who was an early pioneer of army intelligence, knew all about de Montfort the Younger and the movements of his army. Acting on the knowledge his spies and scouts brought him he made a forced night march and caught the rebel army just before dawn. The surprise was so complete that there was virtually no resistance and young de Montfort himself escaped naked into the castle. This was 1 August.

During the previous weeks de Montfort had been looking for a place where he could cross the Severn. Knowing that the rebel earl needed to do this urgently and return to England at the earliest opportunity Prince Edward and his allies had destroyed all the bridges and deepened all possible fords. Furthermore, they had kept careful watch along the eastern bank; some of the watching had been done by the earl's discontented former supporters. However, at last de Montfort found an unguarded crossing place at Kempsey, four miles south of Worcester. Once across, he planned to march straight to Kenilworth and join up with his son's forces, but to do so he needed to keep well clear of Worcester, which was in royalist hands. Accordingly he took the Pershore road to Evesham, a distance of fifteen miles; at the latter he would turn north to Warwick and Kenilworth. Both armies were now very weary, de Montfort after

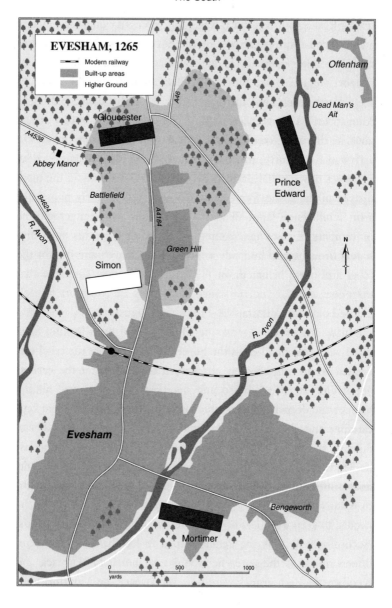

EVESHAM, 1265

Modern railway
Built-up areas
Higher Ground

A46

Offenham

Dead Man's Ait

Gloucester

A4538

Abbey Manor

B4624

Prince Edward

Battlefield

A4184

R. Avon

Simon

Green Hill

R. Avon

Evesham

Bengeworth

Mortimer

0   500   1000
yards

scanty feeding in Wales and a night crossing followed by a swift march, Prince Edward after a forced march, a lightning victory, and a swift counter-march. Although knowing he would now get no support from his son, Edward was determined that de Montfort should not reach the safe haven of the castle, where he could reconstruct his plans at leisure. Although utterly weary, the prince put his army on the road again to head the earl off his objective.

It was a masterly and decisive move, fully worthy of the great strategist the young Edward would become later. To block every path open to de Montfort, he took the risk in dividing his force, and split it into three 'battles'; he commanded one himself, gave one to de Clare, Earl of Gloucester (who had fought valiantly for de Montfort at Lewes) and the other to Mortimer. He himself came from due north, Gloucester from the north-west, and Mortimer from due west.

The key to the disaster which then overtook de Montfort is the situation of Evesham. At this point there is a loop in the river Avon, and Evesham lies at the southern end of it. On the morning of 4 August de Montfort had reached the abbey and was resting there, possibly in consideration of his royal burden, who at the age of fifty-seven was probably feeling and showing the effects of the long marches and privations. He did not know exactly where Prince Edward was and would not suspect that his son's army had been already destroyed. He might have hoped that the young man would send out a supporting force down the road from Kenilworth and

There is a memorial obelisk in the grounds of the Abbey Manor. The battle took place on the slopes below. 'Dead Man's Ait', the meadow where most of the slaughter took place, is opposite the Bridge Inn (known as The Boat) at Offenham. (Worcestershire)

might appear from the north, or east over Offenham bridge (which no longer exists). When he heard that a large army was moving down from the north he believed that this was what was happening, particularly as a look-out reported seeing de Montfort banners in the van; he was correct, they were banners captured by Prince Edward at Kenilworth. Soon, however, the look-out saw less welcome sights, Prince Edward's banner following close behind the captured standards and far worse still, Gloucester banners were to be seen on the road from the north-west, and Mortimer banners to the south – behind him. Had he wished he could still have escaped on a fast horse over the bridge but his army was doomed and he knew it. The only words of despair he uttered were 'Now God have mercy on our souls, for our bodies are theirs.' He urged others to leave, among them Philip Basset, who had done so much for his cause, but no one would desert him.

As the enemy approached, the old earl marshalled his army in battle array, and with himself at its head launched it at Prince Edward's advancing army. If by some wild stroke of luck he could kill the young prince he might – it was a very slender chance – so discomfort his opponents that they would come to terms. He nearly succeeded, for he hit them with such a shock that they had to be steadied by Warine of Bassingbourn. Already outnumbered by three to one de Montfort's army took another shock when Gloucester's army came on to their flanks and rear. But they fought on. The only supporters they had lost were Welsh archers who had already begun to slip away as he marched to meet Prince Edward's army; they failed to escape and were mostly killed on Dead Man's Ait (or Eyot), another bloody meadow just opposite the Bridge Inn at Offenham. The battle degenerated into slaughter, and the chronicler (Robert of Gloucester) recorded it as 'the murder of Evesham for battle it was not'. De Montfort, who had his horse killed beneath him, and saw his son being killed next to him, grasped his sword with both hands and tried to hack a path into the centre of the royalist force. He fell under a dozen strokes. So great was the hatred that had been aroused that his body was mutilated and his head stuck on a pole. In the heat of the fighting the captive Henry was knocked to the ground and nearly killed, being thought to be a de Montfort supporter. It is said that he only saved his life by calling out: 'Do not kill me, I am Henry of Winchester, your king.'

In spite of this crushing victory the war dragged on for a further two years in desultory sieges.

The battlefield is badly marked and difficult to access. Above the slopes on which the battle was fought is a monument hidden in the trees but approachable by a footpath from the road. It bears the inscription:

On this spot in the reign of Henry III the Battle of Evesham was fought August IV, 1265 between the King's forces commanded by his eldest son Prince Edward and the Barons under Simon de Montfort, Earl of Leicester, in which the Prince, by his skilled valour, obtained a complete victory. The Earl with his eldest son, Henry of Montfort, eighteen barons, one hundred and sixty knights and four thousand soldiers were slain in the battle.

The battle itself was fought in a thunderstorm, and at times the field was so dark men could scarcely distinguish friend from foe. Montfort's remains, or what could be found of them, were buried in Evesham Abbey. His tomb became a place of pilgrimage and it was said that many people were cured of ailments by praying there. The abbey and tomb were destroyed in the reign of Henry VIII.

The obelisk, which was erected in 1845, is said to mark the spot where de Montfort was killed but this is unlikely; it was probably put in that conspicuous position to enable visitors to survey the battlefield from the best vantage point. Nowadays the obelisk is completely obscured by trees, although it can still be reached by an overgrown path. 'Dead Man's Ait', where the Welsh and many others were slaughtered, may be reached by ferry from the Bridge Inn at Offenham. The inn is known locally as 'The Boat'. Up till two hundred years ago there was a narrow stone bridge there and a usable ford.

The wholesale and merciless slaughter at Evesham was partly in revenge for Lewes. Welsh archers were probably employed by both sides and would have no compunction about slaughtering each other for there was bitterer hatred and rivalry in Wales than anywhere else in the British Isles. All guerrilla fighters have a hard time when they are eventually trapped by their opponents.

The main battle is said to have lasted less than two hours, but the hunting of fugitives doubtless went on all day.

The Battle of Pilleth

22 June 1402

After the Battle of Evesham there were no other major disturbances in Henry III's reign. Towards the end of it Prince
Edward went off on a crusade, where he distinguished himself, as
might have been expected. In 1272 when Henry died he succeeded
and England was ruled for the next thirty-five years by her most able
warrior-king, now known as Edward I. His greatest memorial is
probably the great castles he built in Wales: Harlech, Conway,
Caernarvon, and Beaumaris are excellent examples. He was equally
forceful in Scotland and France.

When Edward I died his son Edward II proved to be completely
unlike him. Though idle, irresponsible, and cowardly, he lasted
for twenty years before being murdered at Berkeley Castle. His
son Edward III who followed him to the throne was the complete
opposite, and much like his grandfather Edward I. He was only
fourteen when he succeeded but by the end of his fifty-year reign he
had won battle after battle, notable among them being Halidon Hill
(1333), Crécy (1346) and Poitiers (1356). His son was the famous
Black Prince but the latter had died before him, and the throne went
to the Black Prince's son, Richard II. Richard II came to the throne at
the age of ten and reigned for two more years than his notorious
grandfather Edward II, whom in many ways he resembled. It is, of
course, unwise to be too critical of events which happened so long

ago, and there may be more in Richard's favour than history has so far brought to light. But the general verdict is that his reign was a wretched and unsuccessful tyranny, which was only brought to an end when the throne was usurped by his cousin Henry of Bolingbroke, whom he had treated unwisely and perhaps unjustly. There was no battle involved. Richard's supporters fell away, and his cousin had no difficulty in taking the crown. How Richard's life ended is not known. He was sent to Pontefract castle and no story ever emerged to tell of his fate, although he was certainly murdered. The secret was well-kept.

The new king, who became Henry iv, had a difficult reign of fourteen years, before he died of leprosy. Needless to say there were plenty of his subjects who were shocked by the fate, unknown but suspected, of Richard ii, and plenty more who were prepared to pretend they were if they could turn the circumstances to their own advantage. Civil war broke out within two months of his accession but he was quick to act and some vigorous head-chopping stabilized his position again. But this was a domestic matter and did not involve more than a few discontented and badly-organized earls. A rebellion which broke out in 1400 was a far more serious affair. Owen-ap-Griffith (ap = son of) of Glendower had been one of Richard's squires and had a respect and liking for him. He was also a genius at guerrilla warfare. As a descendant of Prince Llewellyn, of Welsh royal blood, he could claim that he was ruling Wales by appointment from Richard ii whom he claimed was still alive but living in exile in Scotland. Glendower captured a number of English-held castles in Wales, though some defeated him; and he made nonsense of Henry iv's attempts to apprehend him. He proclaimed himself Prince of North Wales, and there was nobody who could deny his de facto right to the title.

The task of suppressing him was given to Edmund Mortimer who came of a family with generations of border fighting experience. As he was closely related to Richard ii it may seem surprising that he should be assisting his murderer but the explanation is that he and his tenants felt they might lose their lives and property in the next raid if Glendower was not checked. Glendower had recently beheaded the entire garrison, sixty men in all, of New Radnor castle when he had captured it; he buried heads and bodies separately. Mortimer, therefore, had little difficulty in raising an army from people who were tired of having their property plundered by raiders from Wales, and from others who thought a little Welsh rape and pillage would be most acceptable, and set off to teach Glendower a lesson. The people in these areas had fought each other so often that there was virtually a D.S.[1] solution to every problem. In this situation experience had taught invaders that it was unwise to move up the valley which was marshy and difficult; a sudden attack might send the entire column floundering into a morass. Just beyond Whitton the invaders came to Pilleth where many years before the Normans had built a motte and bailey castle blocking the valley; the wooden ramparts and tower have long since disappeared but the formidable earthworks remain. Further along the valley are tumuli which tell of more ancient wars.

Mortimer was not going to be caught in the marsh like many of his predecessors had been. He therefore kept well to the right and moved on to a spur, which was separated by another valley from the next ridge. It was the sort of choice you had to take in war, risky and unpleasant because the lower part of the hill was covered with bracken and the upper part with gorse but it was the sort of gamble

---

1 D.S. Directing staff. The D.S. solution is the Instructor's view. The Instructors at Staff Colleges and military training establishments are known as the Directing Staff.

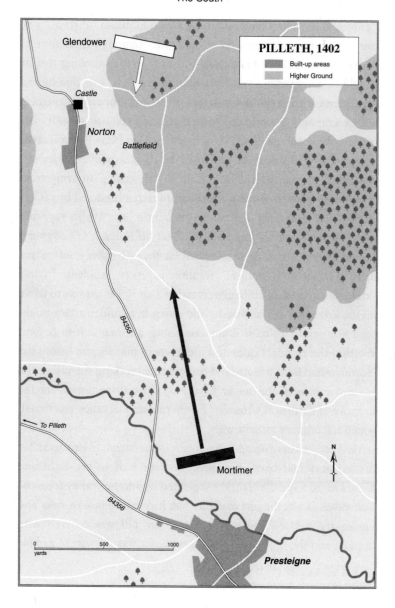

PILLETH, 1402

Built-up areas

Higher Ground

Glendower

Castle

Norton

Battlefield

B4355

To Pilleth

Mortimer

B4356

0   500   1000

yards

N

Presteigne

they had taken a dozen times before, and been none the worse for it. But on this occasion they were up against the astute military brain of one of the greatest of guerrilla fighters, Owen Glendower. Colonel Topham Hood, who as the tenant of the battlefield had plenty of time to reconstruct the events, considers that Glendower must have been watching Mortimer all the time he advanced up the valley. At the top of the ridge Glendower was in a perfect position to observe his enemy advance, then launch a frontal attack down the steep slope or – if Mortimer persisted in keeping to the valley – come in on his flanks just where he was threading his way through the marsh.

Doubtless Mortimer sent scouts up the slope to make sure all was well. They did not report any unusual occurrence, which is not surprising, for they would all be lying with their throats cut in the bracken where they had been swiftly and silently ambushed.

Halfway up the hill Mortimer realized his terrible mistake. The Welsh poured on to his army, first smothering them with arrows, then bearing down the hill in what seemed an endless rush. The slope is like the roof of a house and as the English forced tired men and horses up it the Welsh hurled them or their corpses down again. Mortimer was singled out to be taken prisoner but others were not so lucky. The Welsh were too excited to give much thought to the possibilities of ransoms, and the fighting was altogether too fierce and bloody for nice considerations of rank and precedence. Today in the middle of that field is a grove of trees which were planted on a pit of bones. Perhaps the pit did not need to be dug but was a natural hollow which filled up as men encountered it unawares. According to local report the Welsh camp followers of Glendower shamelessly

Take the road from Presteigne, and Pilleth will be found just past Whitton. The battle site may be seen clearly from the road. (Powys)

mutilated the corpses of the dead English; perhaps it seemed an appropriate revenge for the treatment they had often received from invaders for their principal activity was castration. No one troubled to bury the dead for a long time and the reek of the hillside of decaying corpses caused the area to be shunned for months. The hill was called Bryn Glas, and the battle is sometimes known by that name.

All that needs to be seen of the battlefield may be seen from the road which approaches it and runs alongside. The hillside is now bare of gorse and bracken, and is covered with close-cropped turf. The little churchyard where some of the most important personages were buried has no record of them.

The battlefield was doubtless plundered immediately afterwards, before the corpses began to rot; the only relic which was subsequently discovered was a pair of revolving spurs, wicked enough but not unique.

Among the many killed that day was Sir Walter Devereux of Weobley, and Sir Robert Whitney, who was Knight-Marshal to Henry IV.

Mortimer, very soon afterwards, married Glendower's daughter, and announced to his own followers that he was now in alliance with the latter to restore the rightful line to the English throne. The rightful line was his own nephew, the Earl of March, who certainly had a better claim that Henry IV, but as a mere boy could only be the pawn of greedy and power-seeking barons. It is said that Henry had refused to ransom Mortimer. Subsequently, when Glendower's army had been scattered Mortimer died at Harlech castle which was then under siege (1409).

The Battle of Shrewsbury

21 July 1403

After Pilleth there was little that Henry IV could do to restrain the Welsh for he had too many other troubles on his hands. Norman privateers crossed the Channel and raided the south coast, Scots under the redoubtable Douglas crossed the border and harried the northern counties. At Homildon Hill, on 14 September 1402, two miles west of Wooler, he mustered a reputed 10,000 Scots. On the English side, inevitably, was the chief enemy of the Scots, Earl Percy, of Northumberland. It was a victory for the English archers, for the longbow so outdistanced the Scottish short bow that the Scots were nearly annihilated before they could get to close quarters. When they did the odds were in favour of the English who completed the carnage with charges. Always in the forefront of the battle was Harry Percy, the Earl's son, who was known as Hotspur from his activities in the forefront of battle. Among the Scottish prisoners they took on that day were Murdoch of Albany, Earl Douglas, Earl Moray and Earl Orkney. The ransoms of these powerful noblemen were worth a fortune. To the disgust of the victors they were required by Henry IV to hand over the prisoners so that he could use their ransoms to bolster his own sagging finances. Earl Percy took it very badly for he had previously been Henry's main support and felt that at the very least he should be allowed to profit from his own successes.

Henry would not hear a word of it. Rewards would come from him later, if and when he chose. It was not a very intelligent message to send to a border chieftain flushed with victory and power. Northumberland's reaction was entirely predictable; he decided that Henry IV had become unreasonable, and should be dethroned at the earliest possible moment. To that end he began negotiations with Glendower, who in turn brought in the French. Northumberland also released Douglas who rallied a Scottish force. The plan was that after having deposed Henry they would instal the Earl of March (cousin of the Mortimer captured at Pilleth) who was next in line to the throne, in his place, while dividing the kingdom between them.

By July 1403 they felt ready to act. On the ninth Hotspur marched into Cheshire by the side of his traditional enemy, Earl Douglas. From Cheshire after brisk recruiting he moved to Stafford, where he was joined by his uncle, the Earl of Worcester; all three then set off to Shrewsbury where they had arranged to meet Glendower with a substantial force from Wales. To do so he needed to reach the town before Henry IV, as whoever held Shrewsbury commanded the passage of the Severn at that point. Once the alarm was given in medieval warfare the rival armies raced to the vital nodal point, knowing that 'history repeats itself because geography remains a constant'. Henry reached the town on the night of the twentieth; Hotspur reached it on the Saturday morning. The key to the king's success seems to be that he had marched from Lichfield in a day – a distance of forty-one miles. Hotspur could probably have made the effort and beaten him if he had realized the urgent necessity of the task although he had already marched nearly 250 miles but he did not and the rebels' fate was thereby sealed. When Hotspur arrived he found the gates locked and Henry's banners on display; this was ominous because Henry's army was considerably larger than the rebels'. There was no sign of Glendower who was reputed to be on the way from Oswestry. According to his own story he had been delayed by floods and had made the best haste he could; according to his critics he had dawdled along and then watched the inevitable battle from a convenient tree at Shelton, a mile or so away, prior to declaring his allegiance to either party; the latter view was somewhat unfair to a great guerrilla leader, although it must be admitted that for him to be on the losing side would be as disastrous for his country as himself, and whatever else the Welsh might be accused of it could never be lack of courage. In fact Glendower was still in Carmarthen. Denied entrance to the city, and short of expected numbers, Hotspur fell back and took up position on a site he had surveyed the day before. He knew that Henry must come out and attempt to destroy him, for in medieval warfare when the time to give battle came it must be taken or your own side might accuse you of cowardice and melt away to join the opposition. Hotspur's position was on a slope about three miles along the Whitchurch road. He probably felt that it was good enough for his purpose but if he had known the country a little better he could have taken up a greatly superior position two miles to the south-east on Haughmond Hill. However, it is not possible to be dogmatic about the choice of medieval battlefields. Low ground could be marshier; high ground could be more difficult to access. For his purpose the area known as 'Battlefield' was entirely adequate. Hotspur, who was thirty-nine and by no means the hot-headed youth depicted in Shakespeare, had won many a battle and had every intention of winning this one. He required a ridge from which his bowmen could survey the advancing army, and a few hazards at the bottom of the slope. The battlefield has probably not altered very much since his day, although now there is a church in the middle of it. One of the best places to survey

The South

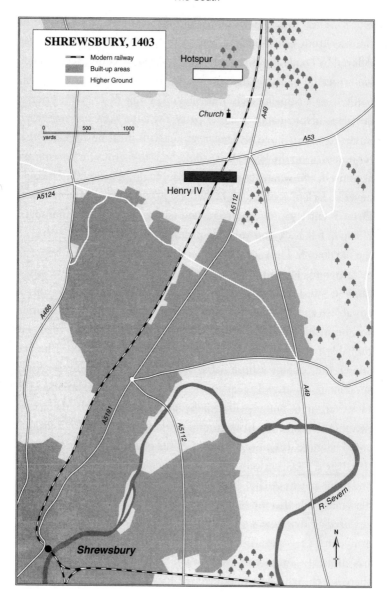

64

it is from the bridge over the railway line. Hotspur seems to have positioned his army along that ridge behind the old track through Allbright Hussey. On his immediate front there was a field of peas, and ahead of that were ponds. As the enemy funnelled past the ponds and advanced with difficulty through the tangle of fully-grown peas they would make useful targets for the bowmen he had recently recruited in Cheshire. This was the great age of the archer. Nearly sixty years before they had cut the French to pieces at Crécy; now two well-matched armies – the smaller with an advantage of ground – were going to fight one of the greatest of all longbow battles.

The longbow, which both sides would be using with deadly effect, was reasonably accurate at 240 yards. At shorter distance it could be as deadly as a rifle; at longer ranges, particularly if aided by wind or slope it could blanket a target like a creeping artillery barrage. A trained archer – which means a man who could send off up to a dozen arrows a minute – was an invaluable asset but he had to be kept at fighting pitch by constant practice. The bow had a seventy-pound pull, and there was considerable skill in reloading at speed. Five thousand archers averaging a mere ten shots a minute could cover the target with arrows coming from every level. They would have a devastating effect on horses and their riders, however well-armoured both might be. In the twelfth century there was a revealing story of a knight who was caught by an arrow which went through his mailed skirt, his leg, his saddle, and into the horse. He turned to ride out of battle and have it attended to, and as he did another arrow did exactly same for the other leg. It was

The battlefield lies just off the A49 road three miles out of Shrewsbury. (Shropshire)

recounted not because of the power of the arrow but because it was an unusual occurrence like a man having a rifle bullet pass right through his chest without touching a vital organ. That first shower of arrows was something you merely hoped to live through; if it missed you, you would be on to the archers to cut them to pieces before they could recover or obtain fresh supplies. But if the shock sent your army staggering those same archers would be among you with hammers to crack open your armour and long daggers to push through the cracks. A medieval battle might sometimes be delayed by parleying – as on this occasion – but once the first arrows sped away there was no drawing back.

The ponds which are mentioned in some accounts, but which can no longer be seen, were perhaps marshy patches, but probably something much deeper. The disappearance of any holes on a battlefield is easily explained; the casualties from both sides were rolled in and earth thrown on top. Who would dig a hole big enough for a mass grave if he could roll the corpses into something put there by nature; in all probability it would be half full of corpses already.

It seems that on this occasion Hotspur's bowmen may have been deceived over the dispositions of the advancing royal army, which had probably fanned out more than expected. Prince Henry (later Henry v) commanded the left wing while the king commanded the right. Neither seems to have received the full benefit of the opening archery volleys, which must have concentrated on the centre, for both were able to put in powerful attacks making a pincer movement by oblique approaches into the rebel centre. As Hotspur's army was drawn up in line, and would be in three battles, the pincers would close at the divisions, and, as every soldier knows, there is no better position to put in pressure. If the battles, regiments, or combat teams have never fought together before, and if they come from different parts of the country – or even different countries – there is remarkable confusion, probably misdirected effort, and a feeling that others are letting you down. In times like that, good leaders rally their men and try to get them moving forward. This is what Hotspur and Douglas did. They knew by long experience that at this point in the battle victory hung in the balance and depended on morale. With spearmen, archers, and cavalrymen milling around in a tangle of personal combats the only way was to drive a path through the confusion and kill someone important on the other side. Prince Henry had already received an arrow in his face, which had sent him to the rear, so it was the king or nothing. In the event it was nothing, for Hotspur received a fatal jab in the general press, and when he fell the rebel spirit began to crumble. The rebel army fell back on to higher ground but there was no one capable of rallying them and turning defeat into victory. Back they went, and finally broke and fled. Douglas, seeing all was lost, decided to leave and fight another day. He broke from the fight, spurred his horse towards Haughmond – where he could have obtained sanctuary in the abbey but fell before he reached it, and lay on the ground with a broken knee-cap. But he was much too valuable as a potential ally to be killed. He was given treatment and then set free by the king. Others were less lucky. Worcester and most of the other rebel leaders were beheaded, and Worcester's head had the honour of being impaled on a spike on London Bridge.

Hotspur's corpse had even more humiliating treatment. It was buried honourably, then exhumed, displayed in Shrewsbury and finally quartered. In the medieval custom a limb was sent to each town from which he had drawn support.

Most of the fighting settled down to the point on which the church now stands. It is said to be built on a pit of bones but bones do not make the most secure foundation and it probably stands alongside the biggest burial pit. It was not built by a grateful King Henry IV but by a neighbouring rector (Roger Ive, of Allbrighton Hussey) on a site given by Richard Hussey in 1406. The place now known as Battlefield was then Haytelfeld. The original name of a battlefield often helps to tell us more than all contemporary accounts for it often gives us the reason why events occurred as they did. Here there is a choice. Haytelfeld may have derived its name from 'hay' meaning grass of the variety which would grow long in a marshy area, or from 'haies' the old Norman hedges which could afford shelter or cover. The ground today is not too difficult, although there is a sunken road which could have been a death-trap – or perfect cover – and some sudden changes of level which would play havoc with a charge.

A disconcerting feature of this battle was that Henry IV took the precaution of having several of his retainers dressed as royalty while he himself wore inconspicuous clothing. Doubtless he had no difficulty in obtaining 'volunteers' for this dangerous task. It was a sound plan economically for most of them were probably killed and did not need to be paid – let alone rewarded. And it was very disconcerting for the rebels. Deception did not occur often in medieval warfare but here was used with considerable success. Few things can have been more frustrating than to reach your chief opponent only to discover it is not him after all as the real man is, apparently, two dozen yards away.

The numbers on the battlefield are not precisely known but it seems probable that there were 14,000 on the king's side and about 11,000 on the rebels'. Estimates of 20,000 a side are obviously too high, for such numbers could never have found a space on the battlefield. Even the smaller, more feasible figure was probably not committed all at once. It is thought the duration of the battle was four hours but the aftermath would go on most of the day.

The battlefield is easy to find, and survey. The church was long since robbed of its commemorative glass but has the coats of arms of the victors inside; gargoyles, which are supposed to represent the rebels, are on the gutters outside. The gargoyles are lifelike and were probably recognizable likenesses.

Although the result was doubtless regarded with mixed feelings by many, it left the country in a more stable position than if the rebels had won. Militarily it was a triumph for the better tactician, and in view of the experience and power of the rebels was a remarkable achievement. Henry IV was probably one of the greatest of the warrior kings. If he had ever been able to set out on a path of foreign conquest his successes could have been dazzling.

After the battle Henry's army moved west and confronted Glendower's at Leominster. Glendower summed up the situation, decided there was no gain to be made from a fixed battle, and slipped back into Wales. Henry was too wise to follow on that occasion.

The First Battle of St Albans

22 May 1455

After winning the Battle of Shrewsbury Henry had only a temporary lull before other troubles came his way. The source of most of them was Hotspur's father, the Earl of Northumberland. In 1405 he managed to stimulate another rebellion, in which the Earl of Nottingham and the Archbishop of York were leading figures. However, these two were duped into coming to a conference with the royal commander (the Earl of Westmorland), arrested, and executed. Northumberland had been too wily to come to the conference but had to make a quick departure and hide away in Scotland for two years. Two years later he was back and making a quick drive on York. Unfortunately for his plans he was caught at Bramham Moor where he put up a tremendous fight before being killed; he was seventy.

Two years later, Henry met another trouble, and one which he could not shake off. It was leprosy, and in 1413 he died of it. England was lucky in that neither Scotland nor France were in a position to give much trouble at this time. When his son Henry v came to the throne he was permanently on the offensive and in his nine years reign won his battles with devastating ease. His first great triumph was Agincourt in 1415, and from this he went on to conquer most of northern France. The French were assisted by Scottish troops but it made no difference to the result. Henry died in the hour of his triumph, in 1422, at the age of thirty-four. His successor Henry VI soon managed to lose all the French conquests of the previous reign, and through no fault of his own, plunged England into suicidal wars which lasted for thirty years.

The key to the tangle of battles which are known as the Wars of the Roses was the usurpation of the English throne by Henry IV. As we saw in the previous chapter, Henry IV never succeeded in enjoying the throne he had gained by murdering his cousin Richard II, and subsequently Henry V's path of conquest so occupied men's minds that they had little time to reflect on whether the true heir sat on the throne or not. When Henry V died it was a different story. His son was under a year old on his succession. That in itself was not too serious for he had an able guardian for his early years: this was the Duke of Bedford. However, the good effect of Bedford was largely offset by the follies of the Duke of Gloucester which largely contributed to the loss of France. An even greater contribution to disaster was made by the Duke of Somerset, but unfortunately Henry VI favoured him and made him his counsellor. A far more suitable choice was the Duke of York, but both Henry and his French wife, Queen Margaret, suspected (wrongly) that the duke might have designs on the crown, as he was a closer relative of the murdered King Richard than Henry himself was. York became the head of what became known as the Yorkist faction in the ensuing wars. Their badge was the White Rose and they numbered among their supporters the enormously wealthy and powerful younger branch of the Nevilles (the Earls of Salisbury and Warwick; the latter who changed sides later became known as the 'Kingmaker'). The younger Nevilles hated and opposed their cousins, the family of the Earl of Westmorland. All had the advantage of hosts of experienced soldiers who had fought in the French wars and these supporters often proved so obstreperous and turbulent that it was necessary to keep them employed before they found some private objective of their own to fight for. Supporting Henry VI were the Lancastrians – the party of the Red Rose (although the badge was not assumed at first) and they included such powerful and aggressive noblemen as the Duke of Somerset, the Percys of Northumberland, and the Staffords of Buckingham. How venomously the protagonists hated each other will be seen in the aftermath of the battles we shall describe. In one sense the war was regional, for the north, the west, and Wales adhered to the king while the Midlands, south, and east were Yorkist. Much blood would be spilt before this conflict would be resolved, and the end only came when most of the leaders of either side had been killed off. On the few occasions when it seemed that the bitter blood feuds might calm down, Henry went mad. However, the madder and more hopeless Henry became, the more relentlessly ferocious his Queen Margaret became.

The first battle took place not because Henry went mad but because, after eighteen months of insanity, he became sane again. While he was mad two interesting events had occurred. One was that York became Protector and ran the country to everyone's satisfaction – except the hard-core Lancastrians, the other was that Queen Margaret gave birth to a son after nine years of unsuccessful matrimony. It was suggested that Henry had had his husbandly efforts supplemented during the period of his madness but this was never proved, and the heir was regarded as legitimate. However, when Henry recovered, and at the instigation of the young mother dismissed York from his post, while restoring the hated and incompetent Somerset, the stage was set for the first battle.

York was not normally an impatient man but this was a little too much for him: he gathered his army of some 3,000 battle-experienced supporters and set off for London. He had no ambition to secure the throne but he was not prepared to see Somerset run and ruin the country, so he had prepared to see Somerset run and ruin the country, so he had prepared an ultimatum demanding that the latter should be tried. His move took Henry and his friends by surprise but they managed to muster an army of about 2,000 to intercept York at St Albans. St Albans is one of those few towns which has not so far been replaced with grim concrete blocks and the visitor today can still trace the battle. (There were in fact two battles of St Albans, the second taking place in 1461 when the Lancastrians won. By that time there had been many other bloody encounters.)

The First Battle of St Albans had an indecisive beginning but once it began was ferocious enough to satisfy the most bloodthirsty. York had hastened down from Yorkshire, knowing that he had supporters in the capital and that the nearer he got the better it was. Henry on the other hand wished to fight as far from London as possible. They met at St Albans which is twenty-one miles from London and on the top of a hill. Henry arrived first and was able to throw up a few barricades; York arrived on the eastern outskirts at approximately the same time, that is 7 a.m. But instead of pushing on to defeat the smaller army before it could receive reinforcements, York waited. Reinforcements were not in fact available but York would not have cared greatly if they had been, for his aim was not so much to defeat the king in battle as to demonstrate that his policy was provoking determined opposition. For three hours the armies waited while a few vague messages passed back and forth. Finally York stated his terms as bluntly as he felt diplomatic; he required that the Duke of Somerset should be handed over to be executed.

Henry would have none of it. The battle was now inevitable.

Its course is easy to trace. Henry held the middle of the town with

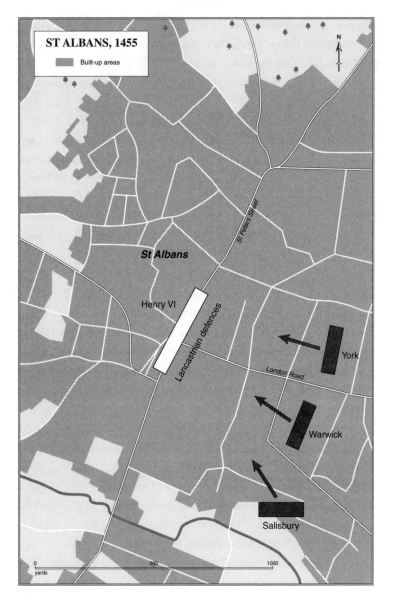

ST ALBANS, 1455

Built-up areas

N

St Peters Street

St Albans

Henry VI

Lancastrian defences

York

London Road

Warwick

Salisbury

0   500   1000
yards

his H.Q. in St Peter's Street, almost opposite the National Westminster Bank, which was the site of the old Castle Inn. The Yorkists left their halting place (Key Field) and moved in two columns up Sopwell Lane (halfway down the hill) and Victoria Street (this was then called Shropshire Lane). Both these were barricaded close to the point at which they emerged into St Peter's Street and Holywell Hill. At the other end of these roads was the Town Ditch, which was not as well defended as it should have been. The Yorkists had little difficulty in crossing the ditch which was thinly defended, partly because it was 1,000 yards long and partly because some of its defenders had left their posts during the parley, under the impression that there would be no fighting to do. When battle began the dispositions along the line were not good enough to stop determined threats by the Yorkists. In the streets, by the barricade, it was a different story and it looked as if the struggle would be long-drawn, if not entirely inconclusive.

The deadlock was broken by Warwick, who gave a taste of the drive he would later show in other battles. He was already twenty-five so the popular story that he was little more than a headstrong boy belongs to romance not reality. The route he took is over the London road.

Warwick took a look at the houses on the inner side of the ditch and decided he could get through them. These, and all the other buildings which backed onto the ditch were known as the 'Town Backsides'. He crossed the ditch and began to batter a way through the not very substantial medieval walls. Probably the royal forces

The best way to see the battle site is to start in St Peter's Street; most of the roads retain their fifteenth-century alignment, as indeed many of the buildings retain their character. (Hertfordshire)

were too occupied with street fighting to be alert to what was happening, for their first intimation of his activities was when he broke through the walls of an old house into St Peter's Street right in the middle of the Lancastrian position. The rest of the Yorkists were quick to follow and in minutes the roadway was full of men hacking, stabbing, and slashing at each other. Those behind loosed off arrows into the tightly packed opposition. The slaughter was concentrated, and contemporary accounts leave none of the details to the imagination. Henry himself was wounded by an arrow and might well have been killed in the general excitement had he not been taken away to a tanner's cottage. The battle lasted half an hour only, but inevitably St Albans suffered from the exuberance of the victors *after* the conflict. Somerset was killed in the battle so, with his war aims achieved, York was able to come to Henry – in the tanner's cottage, go down on his knees, and beg forgiveness. Henry granted it.

It is said that the principal casualties were all among the nobility; it seems improbable. Undoubtedly noblemen were killed but it is naive to accept the frequently made assertion that the higher ranks were singled out and the remainder were left untouched. What is more likely is that the slaughter was heavy enough among the men-at-arms but on this occasion the knights in armour had to fight dismounted, were in the thick of it with no avenue of escape, and were not spared for their ransom value. However, it was reported that not more than a hundred were killed. In the press it would be difficult to do more than lunge, hack and stab at heads and shoulders. It would look spectacular enough from the roofs of the nearby buildings but could not, in the circumstances, have been as murderous as battles in which there was more room for action.

Medieval battles had different types of casualties from modern warfare. Then, they had open gaping wounds; today many wounds are not so spectacular as they are lethal. Then, wounds tended to be on the upper part of the body; today many are in the legs and lower abdomen. Then, it was a disgrace – or took some explaining away – to be wounded from behind; today it is a frequent occurrence.

The Battle of Northampton

10 July 1460

Within a year Henry had reasserted himself as a monarch and dismissed the Yorkists from the posts they had assumed. York himself did not greatly care, for his arch-enemy Somerset was dead, and he had no personal ambition for the throne. But there were other forces at work. There were the powerful barons who needed to act to demonstrate their own importance to themselves and their followers, and there was Queen Margaret, who hated York and saw him as a threat to the chance of her own son succeeding to the throne. For three years she spent most of her time travelling and campaigning for support in the next, inevitable, clash.

Bloodshed began again when Margaret tried to have Warwick, the architect of victory at St Albans, assassinated in a provoked incident when he was visiting London. During the years after that battle she had won over a number of supporters, in Hereford, Gloucester and Cheshire. She had conferred on them the badge of Prince Edward, which was a silver swan, and it is said that many were so beguiled that they would have accepted the young prince as their monarch in place of his father. As York himself lived at Ludlow, Shropshire, and she had concentrated her energies on to the adjoining counties, notably Chester, this was carrying the war into the enemy's country and giving a challenge that would not be ignored. Warwick's father, the Earl of Salisbury, set off with 3,000 men to join the Duke of York at Ludlow. Henry and Margaret heard of it, and called on their supporters to counter the threat. The king's representative was Lord Audley and he intercepted the Yorkists on 3 September at Blore Heath, two and a half miles east of Market Drayton. It was a grim and bloody battle, in which Lord Audley was killed, and – it was said – caused the stream to run red with blood for three days. The Yorkists were outnumbered but must have handled their forces with greater skill than the Lancastrians.

This was all that was needed. England was once more plunged into civil war. The Yorkists centred on Ludlow while the Lancastrians assembled their army at Worcester. This was apparently the first and last time that Henry looked and behaved like the son of his famous warrior father. Nevertheless he did not lose his diplomatic or compassionate quality and gave his opponents every chance to avoid the next battle by offering free pardons to all his would-be opponents. The Yorkists, well aware of Queen Margaret's probable clemency to those in her power, shifted their feet uneasily, and said they had no quarrel with his royal personage but they would like other assurances before they disbanded their army. Henry was not pleased and set his own forces marching forward. Intelligent though he was he could not appreciate that his particular circle of advisers was so hostile to the Yorkists that unless he dismissed half of them and replaced them with nominees from the other side, peace was impossible.

Surprisingly enough the ultimate defeat of the king was obscured and delayed at this point. There was still uncertainty in the Yorkist ranks and when the news circulated that they could go home with a free pardon, rather than try conclusion with a force which was said to outnumber them by ten to one, many of them slipped away during the night. This was the Battle of Ludford, the battle which was not a battle. The Yorkist army dispersed. York fled to Ireland; Warwick, Salisbury, the Earl of March (York's eldest son) and Sir John Wenlock, who will figure spectacularly, but not fortunately, in a later battle, rode desperately to Devonshire. From Devon they had a most difficult journey to safety at Calais, and would not have reached it at all had Warwick not taken the tiller personally.

The Yorkist rout looked worse than it was. Warwick controlled Calais and a useful fleet; York was supreme in Ireland. In terms of real power they were far superior to the king for they controlled the trade routes in and out of the kingdom. Meanwhile Henry's army made itself vastly unpopular by sacking Ludlow, and followed this by the sacking of Newbury for no better reason than that it was supposed to favour the Yorkists. Henry held a form of Parliament at Coventry which merely seemed a legislative device for oppressing those of his opponents who had a legitimate grievance.

The news of what was afoot was not lost on Warwick and the other Yorkist exiles. At the first moment which seemed opportune Warwick landed at Calais and moved swiftly inland, but not so swiftly that he did not recruit numerous supporters in Kent. Support in London was excellent and Warwick marched in to the capital unopposed. The swift and successful Yorkist return was a shock for the Lancastrians but they were not too disconcerted, nor too unprepared. They still had loyal supporters even in predominantly Yorkist areas. In London Lord Hungerford and Lord Scales retired with their forces to the Tower of London and blazed away in all directions with their cannon. However, possession of the Tower was not vital to Yorkist success and Warwick's army did not pause long. Victory and a change of government could come by pitched battle only, so he lost no time in setting out to confront the royal army, and its adherents.

The Lancastrians were strong in the Midlands, and had supporters they could rely on in the north and west. Nevertheless, when
Warwick set out marching north-west from London on 5 July
rumours were flying ahead that his force was unbeatable. The
foundation for this overstatement seems to be that they had obtained
the support of the Papal Legate and also the Archbishop of Canterbury, as well as a number of other religious leaders. It is said that
Henry, who was now going through one of his periodic lapses, was
too feeble in mind to grasp the extent of the physical and spiritual
power arrayed against him but many of his supporters did and a
number found their consciences so disturbed that they slipped away
to become neutrals, holding themselves in readiness to join the
winning side.

Northampton is sixty-six miles from London so without much
pressure the Yorkists were able to reach it by the ninth. Thirty-two
miles north-west of Northampton lay Coventry, which the Lancastrians had used as their Midlands seat of government. The Lancastrian army had moved south-east out of Coventry to confront the
Yorkists but had prudently sent Queen Margaret and her young son
back to Eccleshall in Staffordshire, thereby placing them about
seventy miles behind the danger zone and in a district where they
had numerous friends.

The Lancastrian strategy was partly intentional, and partly forced
upon them. It was their ambition to confront the Yorkists and defeat
them, but as there was by now a disparity in numbers (the Yorkist
army being given as 7,000, and the Lancastrian as 5,000) as well as a
considerable advantage in morale on the Yorkist side, the Lancastrians decided to take up an entrenched position. If the Yorkists now
attacked they would be at the disadvantage of attacking a prepared
defence, which normally requires a three to one superiority (if

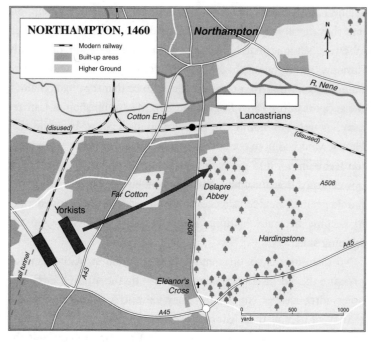

NORTHAMPTON, 1460

- ▬▬ Modern railway
- Built-up areas
- Higher Ground

Northampton

R. Nene

Cotton End

Lancastrians

(disused)

(disused)

A508

Delapre
Abbey

Far Cotton

Yorkists

A508

Hardingstone

A45

rail tunnel

A43

Eleanor's
Cross

A45

0   500   1000
yards

It is advisable to go along the A508 road and inspect the meadows on the
Delapre Abbey side. (Northamptonshire)

success is going to be likely). If they did not attack the royal army
they would leave it between them and the capital, and would be
caught between it and other Lancastrian forces which would now be
marching from the north and west. The royal army therefore took
up a position inside a bend of the river Nene, which was a broad
river in those days. (The Nene, up till recently, was known as the
'Nen'.) The exact position is not accurately known for it is said that
the river has changed its course a little since those days, but is
sometimes identified as the site of the Avon factory.

However, when we reflect that 5,000 men were in the entrenched position it is obvious that the royalist army could have occupied not merely one but several bends. In medieval warfare a man needed at least a yard and a half of frontage, perhaps even two yards, if he was not to do more damage to his own side than the enemy while swinging his weapons. The reader may prove this to himself by simply swinging a tennis racket and seeing how much ground he requires if he is not to injure the nearest person. So if the royal army was five deep it could still have required a frontage of a mile. In fact, it was probably ten deep and extended over half a mile.

The exact date of the Lancastrian army's arrival in Northampton is not precisely known but it seems that it was in sufficient time to make a considerable defensive position, with banks and trenches. We may have some doubts about the depth of the trenches for the area is wet and marshy today, and was undoubtedly much worse then. The fact that the ensuing battle was fought in pouring rain cannot have added to the value of the trenches as fire points although it certainly helped to impede the advancing Yorkist infantry.

The choice of position had considerable advantages but substantial liabilities. It was a tactical position the French had frequently used in the late wars and the English had reason to respect it but such a site requires some luck if it is going to be successful. And Henry was not a man to create luck.

An interesting feature of this battle – and many other battles of the Wars of the Roses – was that non-combatants rarely became involved. Law and order had to a large extent broken down but both sides had the sense not to involve merchants and trades-people in their quarrels. The Lancastrians could – had they wished – have occupied and defended the town, which had a very strong castle, but this would have involved hardship and bloodshed among the innocent; and as it was not the policy of either army to alienate civilians, on whom they relied for supplies, the battle was fought outside the town. It could easily have taken place on Hunsbury Hill, an old Danish camp, but the Lancastrians preferred the river site, and Hunsbury was left for Warwick to occupy as his headquarters on the night of the ninth. The following morning he made a tentative attempt at a negotiated peace by sending the Bishop of Salisbury to see Henry but it was obvious to both sides that this was an issue which could only be settled by battle. Salisbury returned without speaking to the king. Warwick therefore led out his army along the old drove road towards Hardingstone Meadow (or Newfield – or Cow Meadow). They skirted the grounds of the Delapré Abbey and came down towards the entrenchments by the river. On their way they passed the Queen Eleanor Cross, which Edward I had put there when his wife's coffin had rested at that spot on the way to burial in Westminster Abbey in 1290. (Charing Cross was the last of the long line of Eleanor Crosses). It is said that the Archbishop of Canterbury and the Papal Legate stood together on the mound bearing the cross and watched the battle. Today the cross is surrounded by trees, and it is impossible to test this interesting claim, but it seems unlikely that they could have had much of a view over several fields in pouring rain. What they may have seen was some of the outlying skirmishes.

It seems that owing to the rain, the marsh, and the perimeter defences which were by now ditches filled with water, the main attack did not begin till 2 p.m. The assault may not have been intended at all for it must have seemed to the Yorkists impossible to break through the watery defences which during the Middle Ages had over and over again proved themselves better than any stone and mortar. But inevitably there were the probing frontline troops who were inspired by the thoughts of reward as well as threats from their captains immediately behind. The Lancastrian archers had a fine time with the Yorkist mounted troops, whose horses stuck in the mud; those armoured men who reached the rampart found it impossible to climb the slippery sides. Honours were still even, for the handguns – and larger guns too – which the Lancastrians had relied on to terrify any Yorkists who came to close quarters had become wet in the rain and would not fire. For half an hour the battle hung in the balance, then, as often happened in these wars, treachery led to the decision. The right of the Lancastrian position was commanded by Lord Grey. His efforts had not been very striking but had at least been adequate; on the left Buckingham was going much better and it looked as if he might soon make a sally and begin to slaughter the floundering Yorkists. Suddenly – although it must have been by prearranged signal – Grey's men were seen to be assisting the Yorkists into their lines. Baron Fauconberg, who commanded the Yorkist left wing, then ensured that Warwick, commanding the Yorkist centre, and the Earl of March (later to be Edward IV) would soon follow.

It is said that Warwick gave orders that the nobility only were to be killed, and the rank and file should be spared. This was not a time in which men gave much heed to promises, and the Lancastrian soldiers mostly decided to take their chance of crossing the river. This, of course, was in flood, and as many of them were forced to chance the passage by the mill where the current was swiftest, many were drowned. Nevertheless the casualties seem surprisingly light in relation to the numbers involved. The figure of 300 is given but this can hardly include those drowned trying to cross the river. But the roll call looks impressive enough for it included Buckingham,

Shrewsbury, Beaumont, and Egremont. Henry, again, narrowly escaped injury, and was taken into custody by a Yorkist archer. He was subsequently treated with courtesy, but kept under surveillance in London. When he arrived the Tower was still holding out but surrendered two days later (18 July).

Lord Scales was released, and promised a safe passage but was murdered while in a boat on the river; the war had by now become bitter and treacherous, and no one trusted promises whether by his own side or the enemy's. Scales' body had apparently lain on the ground in a Southwark cemetery 'naked as a worm'. Warwick had not ordered the murder but is blamed for not having issued firm orders to prevent it. One of Scales' custodians had been Sir John Wenlock, and this incident may well have been remembered on the battlefield at Tewkesbury (see page 114).

Northampton seems to have been an occasion when men settled a few private scores. A contemporary writer described how Sir William Lucy, who lived near the battlefield, came to see what assistance he could give to the royal party as they seemed to be in trouble. He was promptly killed by John Stafford, a Yorkist who was in love with Lucy's wife, whom subsequently he married.

On hearing news of the disaster Queen Margaret fled for safety to North Wales. She had a difficult journey. Near Malpas castle in Cheshire she was intercepted by a Yorkist but escaped. Later her own servants turned against her and robbed her of her money and jewels but she was rescued by a fourteen-year-old boy John Combe of Amesbury who took her to safety at Harlech. Subsequently she moved to Denbigh Castle where she had the protection of the Earl of Pembroke, and was able to begin rebuilding her forces. Many of her most powerful supporters had not been at Northampton and she was still able to call on such formidable allies as the dukes of Somerset and Exeter, the Earls of Wiltshire and Northumberland, and 'the butcher', Lord Clifford.

Attempts were made to lure the Queen out of her fastness in order to visit King Henry but she was not deceived. Towards the end of 1460 she went by ship to Scotland where she betrothed her son to the daughter of the Scottish queen,[1] and handed over the town of Berwick in return for Scottish support in her forthcoming struggles.

Meanwhile the Duke of York, who had been in Ireland since the fiasco at Ludford, now returned and laid claim to the throne. His bid was not a success. Although Henry was known to be mad, and his supporters had made themselves thoroughly unpopular, he was still considered the rightful king. The Duke of York had a slightly stronger claim in that he was the nearest living relative to the murdered Richard II, but that event had happened over sixty years ago and nobody had disputed the Lancastrian title since. Furthermore the Lancastrian title to the throne had been confirmed by Act of Parliament, and any fresh contender had to obtain its consent before he had any status in the eyes of the country as a whole. As a state of war still existed, and the crowned king was still alive, even if mad, it was unlikely that there could be much enthusiasm for the Duke of York. He recognized the fact himself and although Parliament accepted that he was now the de facto king he had the sense to style himself Protector.

However by this time York had made the fatal mistakes which led to his ruin. Instead of driving north after the victory of Northampton he had wasted valuable time. When he moved in December it was too late; the Lancastrians were now reorganized and in great strength. On 30 December just outside Sandal Castle, Wakefield,

1 The king, James II of Scotland, had been killed when one of his cannons burst while he was besieging Roxburgh Castle on 3 August.

York's army was massacred, and he himself was killed. Two thousand five hundred Yorkists were killed for the loss of 200 Lancastrians. Queen Margaret had the heads of the leading Yorkists set above the gateway to York with the Duke's head in the middle wearing a paper crown.

The war had now become revengeful and bitter, far removed from the courtesy of the first Battle of St Albans. And there was worse to come.

The Battle of Mortimer's Cross

2 February 1461

Wakefield, though a disaster to the Yorkists, was not the end of their hopes. Although York would be difficult to replace, for he was moderate and statesmanlike, there were other good men on the Yorkist side, and plenty of supporters who believed England had a better future with the Yorkists than with mad King Henry and his embittered wife. Now that York was dead the next heir to the throne on the Yorkist side was the Earl of March, who had commanded the right wing at Northampton, and his brother Richard of Gloucester. The Earl of March would become Edward IV and Richard would become Richard III, the alleged murderer of the princes in the Tower.

The Earl of March, who will from now on be referred to as Edward, was at Shrewsbury when the Battle of Wakefield was being fought; he was waiting there to forestall any attempt the Earl of Pembroke might make to make a swift drive into England. On hearing the news of Wakefield and realizing that the Lancastrians would waste no time in following up their victory with a march to London, he increased his army to set off to intercept them. If he linked up with Warwick's forces he would probably be able to cripple the Lancastrians, and slow them down, if not actually to defeat them. But when he reached Hereford he was overtaken by other more serious news. The Earl of Pembroke had now begun to

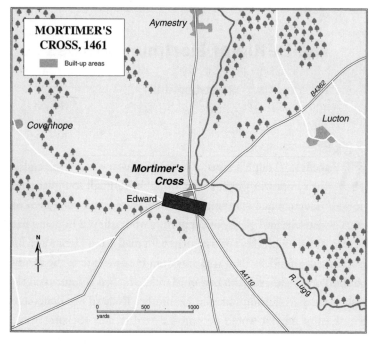

This battlefield is very easy to find. Go to the junction of the A4110 and the B4362 roads. (Herefordshire)

march, in company with the Earl of Wiltshire and a strong supporting army of Irish, Bretons, French, and Welsh. Edward turned back. If Pembroke's army reached the Midlands the Yorkist cause might be as good as won. Edward was not the man to flinch from the right decision, however upsetting it might be to his former plans.

The ensuing battle took place at Mortimer's Cross, Herefordshire. Edward's force was not one to inspire great confidence for it had nothing comparable in battle experience to the opposition. He made his dispositions in Wig Marsh, close to what is now known as Mortimer's Cross. In the inn at the crossroads there is a map of the battlefield, and this is by no means the only asset to recommend it.

It is said that Sir Richard Croft, who lived in Croft Castle nearby, advised Edward how to make his dispositions, and advised the future king to let the Lancastrians attack. As Edward's army was now skilfully disposed in what was then marshy ground, but which is now meadow, this was reasonable enough. Nevertheless Edward's position seems to have some liabilities and he appears lucky to have got away with it. All his forces were to the west of the river Lugg which was some twenty feet across at that time of the year. Edward himself commanded the centre battle which held the bridge. The explanation of the tactical dispositions – and the reader may have a better one – seems to be that Edward wished to block the Lancastrian advance and was prepared to expend some of his troops in doing so. As he had greater numbers, though they were less well-equipped than his opponents, he could afford to be lavish in expending them.

The battle was preceded by a remarkable omen, or so it must have seemed. By some meteorological phenomenon the sun appeared as three suns. Edward decided it was a favourable auspice, which represented both the Trinity and success to his own side. He knelt down and said a prayer of thanksgiving. As he rose to his feet the Lancastrians approached and the battle began.

It lasted all day, although the decisive point had been reached long before darkness, and the later fighting was only that of desperate men trying to escape. Edward commanded the centre of his own army and confronted Pembroke. There is very little information about the course of the battle but it is not difficult to reconstruct. It seems highly likely that apart from his dispositions in the marshy area Edward would have stationed bodies of archers on the high ground behind, where they had ample cover until they wished to declare themselves. It seems that Pembroke kept a portion of his force confronting Edward in the centre while the wings tried to find a way around and over the river. Such a manoeuvre would be highly dangerous with badly trained and ill-disciplined troops for they would quickly become scattered. Edward, with Sir Richard Croft to guide him, would know the best crossing places and would have archers positioned to rake them with fire. He could afford to sacrifice his wings for this would encourage the Lancastrians to press forward and sway from the critical point of the battle. When he judged that the Lancastrian centre had been sufficiently weakened by converging arrow fire, by casualties sustained in trying to push forward through treacherous marsh onto prepared positions, and by detachments sent to assist the flanks, Edward would press forward and begin the massacre of his heavily outnumbered opponents. When the Lancastrian flankers returned, well satisfied with their progress they would find the situation which we have already seen at Lewes and in other battles – while the wings were winning the centre was being defeated. The Yorkists would spend most of their time trapping and killing small parties of Lancastrians. Many of those who managed to escape from the immediate area of the battlefield would have short shrift, for this was a Yorkist area, and small wonder that the number of Lancastrian dead was given as 3,000; this may have been over half their army. Doubtless they had set out in smaller numbers than was safe, confident that all that was required of them was to join up with the victors of Wakefield, and take part in the general plundering and massacre. They could hardly have imagined that Edward, with his father so recently killed, and the Yorkists in disarray, would be able to recruit a large and enthusiastic army. They were also, had they but known it, confronting one of the great military tacticians of the century. Not least of the reasons for their defeat would be surprise at finding their way blocked by so large a force.

After the battle no mercy was shown to the defeated leaders. The most spectacular killing was that of Owen Tudor, father of the Earl of Pembroke. After Henry v had died, Tudor, who was then a Welsh country squire, had married his widow. His son had been created Earl of Pembroke and his most famous descendant would be Henry Tudor, who would become Henry vii. But all that was of little avail after the battle of Mortimer's Cross. He was taken to Haverfordwest market place and beheaded. Haverfordwest is the place given in a contemporary account, and as it is in Pembrokeshire it would appear to be eminently suitable for the public execution of the father of the earl, but other accounts give the scene as Hereford, which would certainly be more convenient, through being nearer. Haverfordwest or Hereford, it made no difference to Owen Tudor. He did not believe he could be beheaded until he saw the axe and the block, and even then he had doubts, thinking that perhaps it was all a device to frighten him, and there would be a last minute reprieve. But when his executioner ripped off the collar of his red velvet doublet, so that it should not deflect the axe, he realized it was all over. Philosophically, he said 'That head shall lie on the stock that was wont to lie on Queen Catherine's lap.' After his death his head was put on the market cross, but it was taken down by a woman, said to be mad, who washed the blood off the face, combed the hair and surrounded it with more than a hundred lighted candles.

Today the battlefield of Mortimer's Cross is easily recognizable, although there are now hedges which did not exist when it was fought. The best starting point is at the intersection of the A4110 and the B4362. If the reader comes down the road from Presteigne he will realize how great was the shock to the Lancastrians. Either they had to press on and cross the river, or turn right and move along the old Watling Street and Leominster road. Either way they were at a disadvantage. They had one other course but no one seems to have thought of it. Perhaps the reader will see this, and others.

Edward, although only eighteen years old, was experienced enough in battle to know that one victory was not enough and there were other urgent tasks on hand. Nevertheless, on this occasion he seems to have displayed a little of that lethargy which sometimes affected him. In a crisis he could drive himself and others like a superhuman but once the immediate danger was passed would waste time in dissipation. By the time he displayed his next burst of energy another disaster had overtaken the Yorkists. This was the Second Battle of St Albans.

The Second Battle of St Albans

12 February 1461

After Wakefield Queen Margaret had rewarded and reorganized her forces; she had not hurried matters, possibly because the near disastrous defeat of Northampton was still present in her mind. The victory at Wakefield had been due to careful preparation and planning; the question now was what was the best course of action.

The king, although useless as a warrior, was still in Yorkist hands, and could perhaps be used by them in bargaining. It was therefore expedient to rescue him as quickly as possible. Once the decision was taken there was no delay. With a large army, which was said to contain Scots, Welsh, and French, she set off south.

This march of the Lancastrians was one of the few occasions when the war really affected the civilian population. Possibly her motley force was out of control, possibly she was letting them do as they wished on the principle of terrorizing the countryside and softening up the opposition with fear and rumour. When the English armies had fought in France during the Hundred Years' War the policy of 'havoc' – that is, to devastate the countryside and spread terror, had been frequently followed. Each town the Lancastrian army passed through had good reason to remember the experience: Grantham, Stamford, Peterborough, Huntingdon and Royston were especially mentioned. At Dunstable they clashed with a party of Yorkists, said to have been commanded by the town butcher. The Lancastrian army was too much for it; the Yorkists had 200 killed and the butcher hanged himself for shame.

Meanwhile Warwick was arranging for their reception, and doubtless hoping that Edward would come up to assist him. In the event, matters turned out slightly differently.

The battle which is known as the Second Battle of St Albans is of great interest and complexity. The first battle, described earlier, was straightforward, though interesting enough. The second is full of puzzles.

The Lancastrian army was advancing down the route of the A1 but for some unknown reason Queen Margaret turned west and came on to what is now the A5. In all probability she realized that her coming and her likely route into London would be anticipated. This swerve would have an element of surprise.

Warwick, however, was not deceived. Doubtless his scouts were keeping him well-informed. When he knew the Lancastrians were swerving left he realized they were sure to come through St Albans. A victory there would wipe out the former defeat of the Lancastrians when Henry had been wounded and taken prisoner. Warwick was fairly confident of victory and took the king with him to St Albans. The widow of the late Duke of York was less confident and she sent her two younger sons to Holland. These were George, Duke of Clarence, later to be drowned in a butt of Malmsey wine, and Richard of Gloucester, who later became Richard III.

It has been said that Margaret's tactical manoeuvres on the road to St Albans were unique for the period but this is not by any means true. There were, however, two features which made her man-oeuvres more effective. One was that she swerved across the front of the enemy position, and then doubled back; the other was that to double back she made a night march, and followed it with a dawn attack. Night marches are an attractive idea, as are night attacks; the problem with a night march is that men can go astray, desert, or injure themselves on rough ground; and the hazard of a night attack is that an army may well attack some portion of its own side by mistake in the darkness.

However, events went well for Margaret. Her army completed the twelve miles from Dunstable to St Albans without mishap and it is said that they reached their destination well before dawn. As they came to the town they crossed the site of the old Roman city of Verulamium and came up George Street. It is probable that they fanned out and came in on each side of the abbey but after the first surprise they were confronted with deadly arrow fire and could get no further. For the second time in this war the narrowness of the streets was proving a decisive factor, for the Lancastrian advance was funnelled into a perfect killing-ground for the Yorkist archers. Checked and dismayed the Lancastrians fell back. Their beautiful flanking move had achieved initial surprise but now seemed to have been checked.

As the Lancastrians very well knew, the main Yorkist army was not in the town at all but spread thinly as a screen to the north. Warwick's front line was nearly four miles long, but he had strong detachments on the main roads. Not surprisingly he took advantage of the old Belgae ditch defences that had been constructed in pre-Roman times. Along this he had laid various devices of the type that were well enough known in close defences but had rarely been used in open warfare. Among them were caltraps, which were four spikes jointed together so that however they fell on the ground one would be pointing upwards. They were cheap and easy to make and could be sown in thousands. They were deadly to men but especially disconcerting to cavalry. They also laid cord netting with spikes at

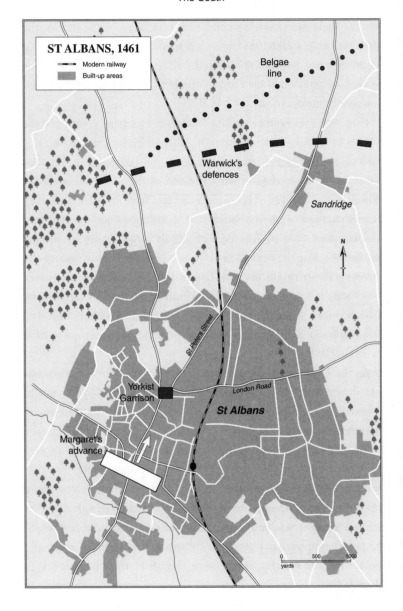

ST ALBANS, 1461

Modern railway
Built-up areas

Belgae
line

Warwick's
defences

Sandridge

N

St Peters Street

Yorkist
Garrison

London Road

St Albans

Margaret's
advance

0   500   1000
yards

each corner which could be concealed under leaves in pathways, or gaps through hedges. Another feature was the use made of pavises. A pavis was a wooden or hide shield carried on a crossbowman's back. He would shelter behind it while winding up his crossbow, and also, sometimes, use it for a guard when shooting. On this occasion the pavises were studded with sharp protruding nails so that when the archer had fired off all his bolts (or quarrels as they were often called), he could lay down his pavis and make walking very hazardous for his opponents. (There are some pavises in the Fitzwilliam Museum in Cambridge.)

The Yorkists also had handguns. These were carried by Burgundian mercenaries, and were meant to shoot darts and arrows. However they were more of a morale-raiser than an effective weapon. Rain would put them out of action, a stiff breeze would blow away the powder, they might discharge unpredictably if badly packed; and loading took the best part of half an hour. Two shots an hour against a longbow which can manage twelve shots a minute is not effective for long. Eighteen were said to have been burned to death by flames from their own guns. The Yorkists also had some cannon but these again were less effective than intimidating. For the moment, however, the main Lancastrian force was not engaged.

By now the tactical dispositions had become a commander's nightmare. The Yorkist detachment in the centre of the town – in St Peter's Street – had Lancastrians on both sides of it, some from George Street, some from Folly Lane. Equally the northern group

It is best to begin the battlefield tour in the town and then move out on the Harpenden road. Sandridge, Beech Bottom and Wheathampstead are easily found, and it is possible to follow the course of the old Belgae line. (Hertfordshire)

of Lancastrians had Yorkists on each side, and as Warwick sent some of the outlying defenders back to the town the situation looked unhealthy for the Lancastrians.

At this point the Lancastrians nearly lost the battle. Their proper course was to leave a small detachment engaging the Yorkist garrison, thus preventing it linking up with the vanguard under Warwick. But – possibly because their minds were dull after a night march and a dawn attack – they played for apparent safety, and concentrated on eliminating the town garrison. This provided a situation in complete contrast to the First Battle of St Albans. Then the Yorkists were trying to capture the Lancastrian-held centre with an attack from the south; now the Lancastrians were trying to defeat a Yorkist-held town with an attack from the north. Another contrast between the two battles was that in the earlier one the twenty-five-year-old Earl of Warwick had shown great fire and initiative, possibly because he was keen to attack and make his name; now at thirty-two he seemed to have lost his impetus in the complexity of making an elaborate defensive plan. It may of course be borne in mind – but not by misogynists – that Queen Margaret was a first-class general, better than Warwick and all the other Yorkists except Edward. Undoubtedly she was the architect of the surprising Lancastrian victory at Wakefield, and the fact that her armies were beaten at Towton and Tewkesbury seems more a matter of bad luck than bad judgement.

As may be expected the Yorkist garrison did not submit to elimination very easily or quickly. As the holders of the town they had cleared fields of fire from the windows of the houses overlooking the street, and their archers were able to do a vast amount of damage before they were killed. Medieval St Albans offered excellent facilities for the stubborn defenders of doorways, passages and staircases. Even today, with the aid of grenades and other forms of explosives, clearing a street of snipers and others is by no means a simple and quick procedure. By the time the last Yorkist had been slaughtered it was midday.

Warwick, as the Yorkist commander, was in an awkward position. He could of course have sent a detachment to harass the Lancastrians before they killed off the Yorkist garrison in the town. But if he did so he would be weakening his already dispersed and scattered force. There was no doubt that by coming up on the flank, and surprising him both in timing and position, Margaret had sent his plans staggering. He therefore had to regroup before his detachments were overrun. His careful defences were now likely to be a bigger hazard to his own side than to the enemy. His whole army, once collected, had to be turned round to face in the opposite direction. Hastily they moved the nets, and pavises, though there was nothing they could do about the caltraps.

When the armies met again the fighting was stubborn and bloody, though showing signs of weariness. Some of the vaunted Yorkist handguns blew up in their users' hands, and some incendiary arrows came back to their own side, but they were intimidating to the Lancastrians for all that. It began to snow. The scene on the battlefield was now indescribably confused, but more and more Lancastrians were coming up with a taste of success on their lips, and more and more Yorkists were getting lost in the general disarray. To add to Yorkist discomfiture Captain Lovelace changed sides at the critical moment and took his Kentish men over to the Lancastrian side. This and other actions – such as that of Grey at Northampton – made this a war in which a man could hardly trust his neighbour. Finally the Yorkist left wing gave way and fled. It was a chilling sight for the remainder but Warwick then showed something of his true quality. He rallied his own centre column, collected what was still left of the right wing, and held a ridge until dark. Once night fell it was almost impossible to tell friend from foe; he managed to extricate 4,000 of his followers and march them to Chipping Norton, Oxfordshire. The king was not with him. Once again Henry vi was sitting by himself, smiling patiently and uncomprehendingly. He was taken to St Albans Abbey.

The numbers engaged in this battle are given as 10,000 on each side. It sounds a suspiciously round figure but may not be far from the truth. When medieval chroniclers wished to indicate huge but unknown numbers they would describe them as 60,000 men, and this had much the same significance as the modern '64,000 dollar question'. The Yorkist casualties were undoubtedly heavy, and it seems unlikely that Warwick could have got away with 4,000 unwounded men; for that number the Yorkist army would probably have needed to have been over 10,000 strong at the outset. The probable figure is that there were 2,000 Yorkists left on the field and about another 2,000 accompanied Warwick. Some perhaps went home and decided they had had enough of battles and fighting.

The young Prince of Wales, aged seven, was knighted on the field. By all accounts he was an unpleasant child, doubtless made so by his embittered mother. He was given the task of deciding how captured Yorkists should die, and happily assigned this one to the axe, this one to the hangman, and that to the sword. Not surprisingly when his own turn came ten years later he received no mercy either.

A more commendable record was that of Andrew Trollope, who was also knighted. He had stepped on a caltrap early in the fight and been somewhat inconvenienced. As he put it, 'he had only managed to kill fifteen men'. Trollope was an old soldier who had originally been a Yorkist but who had joined the Lancastrians after Ludford.

The visitor to St Albans will need plenty of time if he is to walk both battles. The second is clearly the more complicated and he will need to move well out to Barnard's Heath (sometimes called Barnet Heath) to Beech Bottom, and to Sandridge. The centre of the town has, like many others, changed in appearance in recent years but it is still possible to obtain a clear idea of the battles as they were fought 500 years ago.

The Battle of Barnet

14 April 1471

The Lancastrian victory at St Albans, described in the last chapter, could have ended the war if it had been followed up. It is said that Henry VI prevailed on Margaret not to let loose the wild northerners on the capital. The Lancastrian army included in its ranks fighting men from the depths of the Highlands, and Borderers who spent their lives in fighting, and it was felt, and not only by Henry, that once they were inside the city walls there would be no end to their plundering and destruction; it was feared that the city itself might be burnt to the ground. Also the city was already hostile and might put up a fierce resistance, enabling Edward to come up with his army.

But the decision was fatal to the Lancastrian cause. While Queen Margaret's army waited at St Albans, and the city was sending delegates to negotiate its surrender, Edward arrived on the scene. Having delayed a little after Mortimer's Cross he had now made up for it. A forced march brought him to London and completely transformed the military situation. Instead of facing an apparently defenceless city the Lancastrians were confronting a victorious army, which had already been supplemented by the forces Warwick had extricated from the recent battle.

Once the opportunity had been lost there was no point in staying at St Albans. There was no food for an army, and the northerners were already making their own arrangements by plundering far and wide. Had Edward driven forward immediately he could have reversed the previous decision; Margaret who was only too alert to swift vicissitudes from triumph to disaster was not to be caught. Gathering up her forces, who seemed to regard the entire country south of the Trent as enemy territory, she fell back towards York. This move led to the greatest battle of the Wars of the Roses. Edward pushed up north after her as fast as he could, and eventually overhauled her army at Towton near Tadcaster. That great and bloody battle is described in the second book in this series. At the end of it 35,000 dead were said to be left on the field. The real figure may be one-third of that number but there can be no doubt that the slaughter was enormous. For once, almost everyone concerned was on the field, and the winner took all. Subsequently there were, of course, pockets of resistance which had to be crushed, and there were two sizeable battles in 1464 but the Lancastrians seemed crushed for the time being. Although Henry VI was still alive – he was not murdered till 1471 – Edward IV became king and his title was recognized by Parliament. It seemed that all was set fair for the Yorkists.

But, as often happens, the great military commander was not really interested in the problems of peace. When not fighting he merely interested himself in clothes, women and drink. His capacity for women and drinking was phenomenal, although it seems to have led to an early death at the age of forty-one. A night's carousing with Edward – now Edward IV – was a prospect which would make the hardest drinker blench. What his numerous mistresses thought of his amatory prowess is not recorded, but at least ten of his children were legitimate.

Fortunately, again as often happens, there was someone at hand who enjoyed the work which Edward detested. This was Warwick, now known as 'the King Maker'. He was immensely rich and fond of power; in fact he was richer than the king himself. One of the factors which contributed to the long continuance of the Wars of the Roses was the enormous wealth possessed by certain families. The reasons lay far back in time and do not concern us but the effects, of course, do.

Warwick, of course, had good reason to think highly of himself. He had been consistently loyal and more often than not had helped to turn the scales in Yorkist favour. But when he attempted to crown his efforts by marrying Edward to a suitable bride he was surprised and disgusted to hear that the king was married already; in secret, so as not to arouse the animosity of his family, he had married the widow of a Lancastrian. When Warwick showed indignation Edward laughed at him. His bride's family (the Woodvilles) were flaunted and loaded with titles and honours. It was meant to show Warwick that he was not indispensable but it had a greater effect than intended.

Warwick's reaction was to plot with the Duke of Clarence, Edward's brother. Clarence was a dubious character who seemed to like nobody, but he was jealous of his brother and was happy to plot with Warwick. Eventually their efforts brought open war and at the Battle of Edgcote Field, near Banbury (1469) Edward was beaten and taken prisoner. Later he was released on the assurance that he would rule according to the wishes of Clarence and Warwick.

It was an unlikely possibility. Edward was given permission to raise an army to deal with Lancastrian rebellion but then turned it against Warwick and Clarence. Caught unprepared they were lucky to get out of the country.

'Hell hath no fury like a woman scorned' unless perhaps it be a disgruntled King Maker. Warwick promptly set off to treat with Queen Margaret, and restore Henry to the throne. Henry was by now a poor wretched thing, but no matter. Margaret hated and distrusted Warwick but after much hesitation she agreed to her son being betrothed to Warwick's daughter. Once more Edward was caught unawares, although again he would be quick to recover. When Warwick and Clarence landed in 1470 the tide of Lancastrian support rose so quickly that Edward had to escape to Flanders. Henry vi, said to be as animated as a sack of potatoes, was taken from his dungeon and made king. The Lancastrians had triumphed again.

But Edward had not been beaten, only discomfited. Having raised money and men on the Continent he landed at Spurhead in Yorkshire in 1471. He moved swiftly to London in one of his now famous marches. Clarence, who should have intercepted him from the west, decided instead to betray his father-in-law, and joined his brother. Edward marched into London and Henry vi was once more his prisoner.

Warwick's conduct during Edward's march south had been vacillating and surprising. Twice he could have confronted him and given battle, once with superior numbers. Possibly he felt that if Edward marched around enough he would lose more supporters than he gained; or perhaps he hoped to cut him off in the south. Unfortunately for the Lancastrians, when Warwick took action it was too little and too late.

On 12 April Edward, who was now in London, heard that Warwick was approaching with a huge force. Edward wasted no time. On the thirteenth he was setting out north to meet Warwick, and the unfortunate Henry was taken along with him.

The Battle of Barnet which took place on 14 April is usually dismissed as a chapter of accidents. In fact it was exactly the sort of

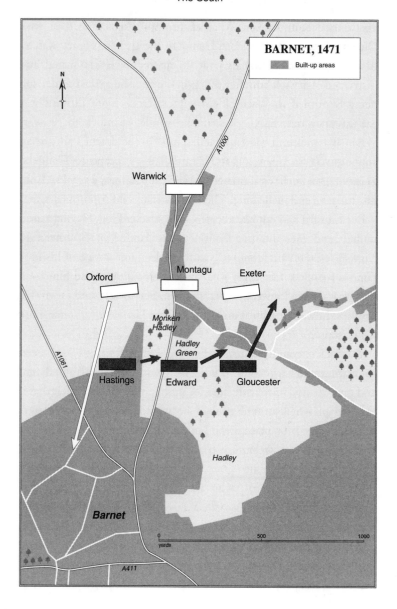

BARNET, 1471

Built-up areas

N

Warwick

A1000

Oxford

Montagu

Exeter

A1081

Monken
Hadley

Hadley
Green

Hastings

Edward

Gloucester

Hadley

Barnet

0   500   1000
yards

A411

battle that could be expected at this stage in the wars. On 13 April the vanguard of Warwick's army was already in Barnet but shortly after their arrival Edward's leading troops also reached the town. There was a brisk encounter, of which the details are unrecorded but the upshot of it was that Edward's men had the best of it and the Lancastrians retired.

At that point Edward could have occupied Barnet. However, memories of St Albans and the hazards of fighting in narrow streets seem to have deterred him and so he sent his vanguard right through the town to establish contact with Warwick's forward position with the rest of his army close behind. Warwick was disconcerted at this probing move and ordered his artillery to fire into Edward's lines all night but his enemy was much nearer than he realized and most of the shot passed harmlessly over their heads. Unlike many armies, earlier and later, Edward's army was instructed to do nothing to give away its position. Doubtless they shivered in the chill of an April night through not being allowed to light fires, and it must have been irritating to be under artillery fire and not reply, but Edward stood no nonsense; an order was an order.

The next day was Easter Sunday and Edward was up at 5 a.m. It was foggy, as might have been expected in that area at that time of the year. Edward's force was inferior in numbers but was drawn up in three 'battles' with himself in the centre, Hastings on his left, and Gloucester on the right. Their position, as will be seen from the

Travel up the A1000 from Barnet to Hadley Green. Turn right at Hadley Green for the line of Yorkist positions along the Enfield road. The obelisk where Warwick was probably killed is just north of this. To the east of the A1000 is the hollow known as 'Dead Man's Bottom' where much of the slaughter of the Lancastrians took place. (Greater London) sketch map, was directly north-south in line with the Barnet-Hatfield road. The visitor will notice how marshy the ground is and how ponds produce unexpected hazards. The ground is still fairly open, although there are now a few buildings, but it is easy to visualize what the battlefield looked like, and entailed, in 1471.The opposing armies faced each other across the Enfield road, although in that light and fog they had little idea of what their opponents were doing. It is said that the armies were not quite square to each other, being aligned slightly to the right but there is no proof of this. Subsequently both wheeled to the right, but this was for a different reason. It was, of course a tendency for armies, before the days of good maps and binoculars to swing to the right, and this fact had interesting and usually predictable consequences – as we have already seen in other battles.

Both armies fought on foot, and this extended to their leaders. Nevertheless the leaders would travel on horseback to the battlefield and tether their mounts at some convenient point. This fact often led to criticism by the rank and file who suspected – often with good reason – that the horse had been well placed for the owner to make a quick getaway if the need arose. At Towton Warwick had slaughtered his horse in view of his army in order to dispel that impression; at Barnet he did not repeat the gesture, and few would have seen if he had, but he left it well to the rear; in the event his action proved fatal for he was killed trying to reach it.

There were of course other reasons for not leaving a battlefield prematurely. The principal one was the ring of knights behind, waiting in reserve perhaps, but always on hand to cut down a man who decided to take to his heels once the battle had been joined. It has a very steadying effect on a man's mind if he knows that he merely faces possible death if he moves forward but certain death if he drops to the rear. Medieval leaders had no compunction whatever about taking the sword to their own troops if they thought their efforts were not strenuous enough.

The battle began with a Lancastrian success on the right flank. Oxford drove forward on the right wing and scattered Hastings' troops. The latter were partly outflanked but quickly panicked and ran for it. So rapidly did they depart that Oxford's men streamed out in the pursuit – we have seen this happen in so many other battles – and were extremely difficult to rally. It is said that many of them were enjoying themselves looting in Barnet when they were summoned back to the battlefield. Only about one quarter of the original force were recoverable, but in the event it would have been better if they had not returned at all.

While the Lancastrians were enjoying this initial success, the remainder were making little headway against each other. The Yorkists seem to have been content to hold their own till the fog cleared, for they had fewer men than the Lancastrians, perhaps 10,000 against 15,000. Edward was, of course, an opportunist who could sense the precise moment in a battle to attack, to swerve, or to split his force. His chance came soon enough on this occasion.

As Oxford made his way back to the Lancastrian position, with as many of his troops as he had been able to recover, he had to pass through a hedge which still exists. After he had left, his former position had been taken over by Somerset's men who did not like to leave their flank 'in the air'. When therefore Oxford's men returned, they were mistaken by Somerset's men for Yorkists. It was a natural enough mistake; no one could have expected that Oxford's men would now come straggling back, and to make matters worse the Oxford badge of a silver star was mistaken in the fog for the white rose of York, as worn by Edward's men. Not surprisingly Oxford's men were welcomed with a shower of arrows; not surprisingly either Oxford's men called out 'Treason' and retaliated. Oxford had had enough; his reward for victory was apparently treacherous ambush; he left the field. But more damage than that had been done. The word 'Treason', so deadly because so vague, spread quickly through the Lancastrian ranks. On both sides there were men who had fought against each other in earlier battles and trusted neither themselves nor the men standing next to them. On the Yorkist side Edward was keeping a very close eye on Clarence who had deserted Warwick a few days before and was clearly capable of further treachery at short notice.

The fighting that broke out between those of Oxford's men who could not disengage themselves and Somerset's, caused more than local damage. Many of Somerset's men began to fall to the rear, being afraid they were going to be cut off by a flanking attack. On the left of the Lancastrian line Exeter was gradually being pushed back by Gloucester. Edward saw his chance. One desperate push into the centre and the whole Lancastrian force would disintegrate. He took that chance.

Warwick too realized this was the critical moment but with both wings gone and enormous pressure from the Yorkist right and centre there was nothing he could do. The ground to the left of the Lancastrian centre drops away sharply, and when his troops took the full crunch of the Yorkist charge that slope was their undoing. Significantly the area below is still known as 'Dead Man's Bottom'.

Warwick too turned to flee, but he had left it too late. He would have done better to have died fighting but he attempted to escape and was caught in Wrotham Wood. While trying to force his way through a tangle of thicket he fell, was overpowered, and was killed methodically and in cold blood. His body was taken to St Paul's and displayed for three days before being buried at Bisham Abbey. It is possible that the monument at the present fork in the road at Barnet marks the spot where he died.

The Battle of Tewkesbury

10 May 1471

On the day that Warwick was killed and the Lancastrian army was scattered at Barnet, Queen Margaret landed at Weymouth. For several weeks this indomitable, though not necessarily admirable, woman had been gathering an army. She knew that she could count on plenty of support when she landed, for the Duke of Somerset had been organizing an army in Devonshire, and there were plenty of other sympathizers. She was met at Cerne, near Dorchester, and learnt of the disaster of Barnet. However, all was not lost. Somerset and Courtenay (the Earl of Devon) had now raised substantial forces in the west country, and Fauconberg had a substantial fleet which was threatening London.

As both Edward and Margaret knew, from the previous experience, all the latter needed was time. With time she could raise sufficient forces to win another victory like Wakefield or the second St Albans. What Edward therefore decided was that she must not have time. But it was not easy.

For the first two weeks after the landing neither side was in any condition to give battle. Edward's army had to have some rest and reward after the Barnet victory; much of it had been dispersed. It had to be recalled; there were casualties to be replaced, a new pattern of command to be installed, and more supplies to be found. It is rarely difficult to find recruits for a winning side but the problem of sorting out the good from the bad, the useful from the opportunists, is more difficult than if the army is having a difficult time, then at least you know that your men have their hearts in their work.

While Edward was resting and regrouping Margaret was vigorously recruiting. Support for the Lancastrians had always been good in the west country and now she planned to take a substantial army from that area, march it north, cross the Severn at Gloucester or a little further up, and link up with an army raised in central and south Wales by Jasper Tudor. From there she could combine forces with an army from Lancashire.

Edward realized only too well that if Margaret was not checked before she had finished her recruiting drive his tenure of the English throne would soon be over. At this point he displayed his greatest ability as a strategist and tactician. The first need was to stop Margaret crossing the Severn at the nearest possible point, which was Gloucester, and Edward therefore sent soldiers to Richard Beauchamp, the Governor, with an urgent message to close the gates and man the defences of the city. Beauchamp, with a small force could probably hold the city till Edward himself arrived. In any event he would delay the Lancastrians, and cut them off from valuable supporters and supplies in the town. Margaret realized at this point that she had delayed a little too long in the west country and on the second and third of May made a forced march to Gloucester. She arrived at 10 a.m. on the morning of the third but it was too late. Beauchamp had already organized the city defences, and with Edward hastening up to support him Margaret dared not delay to take the town. Had she tried but been repulsed she could have been attacked from behind by Edward's army which was now not far away, having come up close through one of his astonishing forced marches.

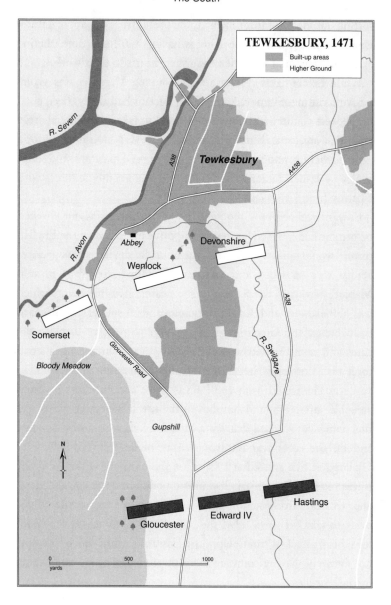

TEWKESBURY, 1471

Built-up areas
Higher Ground

R. Severn

A38

Tewkesbury

A438

R. Avon

Abbey

Devonshire

Wenlock

Somerset

A38

R. Swilgate

Bloody Meadow

Gloucester Road

Gupshill

N

Gloucester

Edward IV

Hastings

0   500   1000
yards

It is impossible not to feel sorry for Margaret, making her desperate last throw. Doubtless she should have risked everything at Gloucester but it must be borne in mind that her army was tired, was untried in battle, and not by any means ready to take on Edward's experienced and well-equipped force. Even so, Edward's army cannot have been feeling too fresh either and might well have been delayed long enough for Margaret to get the majority of her army across the river.

Margaret, however, had decided this was no time or place to give battle. She decided their best course of action was to push on to Tewkesbury which was ten miles up the river. Although there was no bridge at Tewkesbury the river was at least fordable and a further seven-mile march would take them to Upton-on-Severn where the bridge was entirely adequate but could be destroyed after their passage. However, after the night march it took the Lancastrians another six hours to reach Tewkesbury, from which it is possible to deduce that there were many stragglers and formation had been lost. Edward's army was in considerably better shape although he had forced it along and refused it a rest in Cheltenham (described as 'a village'). His army was in battle formation with screens of mounted scouts or 'scourers'. From these he learnt that the Lancastrians had now reached Tewkesbury. He pressed on another five miles, and halted three miles from the Lancastrian position as night fell.

Margaret had not wasted her time on arrival, desperately weary though she, her commanders, and the men must have been. Many of

The battlefield is easily found. 'Queen Margaret's Camp' is nothing to do with King Henry VI's wife but is an earlier earthwork. The Gupshill Manor Inn on Gloucester Road was the centre of the start of the battle. 'Bloody Meadow' is marked, and there are various memorials in the Abbey. (Gloucestershire) them would have been too tired to eat what little food they managed to lay their hands on in Tewkesbury. The next day they were up before dawn, and ranged in position to meet Edward's onslaught.

The battlefield is easily found; its centre was the Gupshill Manor Inn, which was then a farmhouse. It is said that Margaret slept that night in Gupshill (then called Gobes Hall) but that seems unlikely as it was the front line of her dispositions. The earthworks up the slope to the east of the inn are sometimes misleadingly called Queen Margaret's Camp but these belong to a different era, and are probably prehistoric, though perhaps used by the Normans as the site of a motte and bailey castle.

The Lancastrians had chosen a good defensive position, a fact which is usually attributed more to the Duke of Somerset than to the Queen. It was one mile south of the town with the river Severn on the right, and the Avon, which joins the Severn here, running behind the Abbey. In front of the Abbey is another stream which runs into the Avon but curves around to the left of the ridge known as the Gastons. The Lancastrians therefore were on a ridge with the Severn protecting their right and the Swilgate stream offering an obstacle on their left. The Swilgate provided a death trap for many Lancastrians later when they fell back and tried to find sanctuary in the Abbey grounds. In the event they might just as well have been killed trying to cross the Swilgate as trust in Abbey sanctuary, for Edward's Yorkists paid no heed to religious restraints and were quite prepared to slaughter within the Abbey itself if needs be. In front of the Lancastrian position was very rough ground. Both armies had marched nearly sixty miles in the last three days and it was hoped that the rough ground would take its toll of Edward's men as they came in to attack, as they were bound to do.

On the right of the Lancastrian position the 'battle' was commanded by the Duke of Somerset, the centre was nominally in command of Prince Edward but in fact under Wenlock, who had been a Lancastrian first, then a Yorkist and was now a Lancastrian again. The left was commanded by the Earl of Devon. In the Yorkist army the Duke of Gloucester (later Richard III) commanded the left, which was slightly overlapped by Somerset's 'battle' opposite. On the left flank of Gloucester's position running up till it joined the Avon was a brook, now more of a ditch, which made the surrounding ground wet and marshy. The results of this will be seen later. The centre of the Yorkist position was commanded by Edward himself and the right by Hastings. Edward had, however, made an astute tactical move by detaching 200 'spearmen' – which means mounted lancers, and placing them in the wood to the left of his army's position. There they were obscured from view by a hillock. This would not seriously weaken his main front although with a probable 5,000 in his army he was outnumbered by about 1,000 Lancastrians.

The battle began with an exchange of arrows and it would have suited the Lancastrians very well for it to have continued that way. However, in a battle, as in a game, you perform as well as your opponents allow you to perform. Gloucester, wishing to get inside the artillery and the shower of arrows falling on to his position, and also perhaps with the intention of splitting off Somerset from Wenlock, pushed forward in a brisk attack. The going was slow on the very rough ground and Somerset realized that there was a good chance to outflank Gloucester's toiling battle and to come around to attack the Lancastrian rear and Edward's flank.

This, of course, was what Edward had been expecting, so when Somerset's men were stealthily moving around the hillock to the Yorkist rear they were suddenly startled and confused to find themselves charged on their right flank by the 'spearmen'. In all battles, ancient or modern, surprise has always been effective when it has been achieved. Surprise is particularly devastating when the recipient thinks he is himself giving a surprise; this accounts for the disruption of Somerset's men.

It had already become apparent to Somerset that he had his hands full with Gloucester's frontal attack, for the latter was coming over the ground faster than expected. The Lancastrian artillery, which had been dragged along from Bristol, was proving too little to check the Yorkists, who were much better served in that arm. There was apparently a plan for Wenlock to follow up the flank attack on Gloucester with a tremendous assault on Edward, or more probably, on the division between the two 'battles'. But the attack never materialized. Somerset had the mortification of seeing the main part of his 'battle' pushed back and then soon after joined by fugitives from his brilliant flank manoeuvre, which had now been cut to pieces by the 'spearmen'. To his horror and fury he saw the whole of his 'battle' disintegrate, some trying to cut right and get into the obscurity of the trees, some coming straight back through the lines and others veering back along the line of the Coln brook with the probable intention of putting first the Avon and then the Severn between them and their grim adversaries. But few, if any, succeeded. That long hollow today is still known as 'Bloody Meadow' (there is a sign at the roadside) and it needs little imagination to visualize what it must have looked like by the evening of 4 May 1471.

Somerset did not stay to witness the slaughter of his infantry. Instead he rode back to the centre where to his astonishment he found Wenlock calmly inactive. Somerset was so angry he could hardly speak but when he did find words and asked Wenlock what he thought he was doing he did not wait for a reply. Instead he raised the battle-axe that hung by his saddle and scattered Wenlock's brains with it.

Whether in fact Wenlock had decided to change sides again is a matter which has caused some speculation. His record was not one to allay Somerset's suspicions but it seems unlikely that he would have received much reward from Edward even if they had already plotted it together. The chances are that he was waiting for orders. It must be remembered that the nominal command of the 'battle' had been given to the young Prince (also called Edward) and any action likely to hazard the life of the Lancastrian heir to the throne, on whom all hope rested, would probably incur equally summary treatment from the Queen. However, right or wrong, Wenlock was dead.

What is surprising at this point is that Somerset did not take over command of this battle and drive forward. He could at this stage have sent Prince Edward to join his mother, who, by all accounts, had already left the battlefield. The Lancastrian position was bad but not irretrievable. Doubtless Edward was now pressing in the centre, and Hastings would be at grips with Devon but the Lancastrians still held the ridge – the Gastons as it is known – and the battle was by no means over. In fact the wild irrationality of Somerset's conduct at this point suggests that he had lost whatever grip he had on the day's events. He had virtually lost the battle on his own, much as the Earl of Oxford had done on the right wing at Barnet; furthermore he had strayed from a vital position. Wenlock would clearly have been at fault if he too had pushed down the slope in partial support.

However, once morale began to crumble in the Wars of the Roses, men fled while they could. These were no battlefields where the victor would behave chivalrously, where the helpless would be spared, or terms would be offered to save slaughter. The fight when it was joined went on to the bitter end. Too much hatred, too much revenge, had already gone into previous battles. The battle cry was 'kill them all'. Nobody wanted prisoners. The opportunities were there for plunder and it was easier to plunder a corpse than a living man.

The Lancastrian dead seem to have amounted to 3,000. Many were drowned trying to cross the streams and river, and once a few bodies blocked the channel the waters rose, and made room for others. There were many bones found centuries later at the corner of land where the Swilgate joined the Avon. Doubtless many of them belonged to the Lancastrian left wing who after giving a good account of themselves found the rest of the army had disappeared and they were the last to try to escape. It was no good their trying to go east, they had to find a way west across the river before the confusion of battle was over. But unfortunately for them it was sufficiently over for there to have been no chance of escape.

The aftermath of the battle was as grim as might have been expected. Prince Edward, aged seventeen, who as a child of seven at St Albans had chosen the forms of death for the captured Yorkists, now met his own fate. It is said that he was killed on the field of battle but nobody really believes this story. It is more likely that he was offered sanctuary in a house, then betrayed to Yorkists who murdered him. Until recently there was an old house in Tewkesbury, with a stain on the floor said to be from royal blood. The stain might be dubious but the house and the circumstances could have been genuine enough. He was buried in the Abbey and a small stone marks the spot in the floor. His young wife, daughter of Warwick the King Maker, was pardoned. Eventually she married Richard of Gloucester who became king for two years.

Those who thought they would find sanctuary in the Abbey

proved to be mistaken. It was not officially a sanctuary but even if it had been it is doubtful if that would have prevented Edward from removing his intended victims. However the Abbey had to be consecrated the following month presumably as a result of the desecration which had taken place during and after the battle.

Two days later the surviving Lancastrian leaders were taken from the Abbey and beheaded in Tewkesbury market place. Somerset was clearly the most important, but there were many others. (His brother, and the Earl of Devon, had already been killed on the field of battle.) Among those 'decapitatus' were a number of civilians whose crime was, presumably, supplying materials and munitions to the Lancastrians. Those fortunate enough to be pardoned were for the most part imprisoned and heavily fined. Queen Margaret was captured soon after the battle but pardoned and allowed to return to France. With the death of her husband in the Tower, doubtless at Edward's orders, and of her son after Tewkesbury, there was no more danger to be expected from the Lancastrians in the foreseeable future. There was – although Edward probably thought it of no account – a line of Lancastrian descent from Henry IV's brother, although one had to go back seventy years to trace it, and it was now a connection through the female line only. Nevertheless this threat had already produced Henry Tudor and Henry Tudor would in another fourteen years become Henry VII. He would also marry Edward IV's daughter and bring the Wars of the Roses finally to an acceptable close.

But all this was far removed from the blood-soaked meadows of Tewkesbury. Like Prince Edward, the most important of the Lancastrians were now buried in Tewkesbury Abbey, but there were areas where resistance would smoulder on. Jasper Tudor, Earl of Pembroke, and uncle of the future King Henry VII was still at large in Wales, there was a rising in Yorkshire and Fauconberg was threatening London. Of these the last was the most effective. Three days before Tewkesbury Fauconberg had led an army – raised in Kent – to the south of the city of London. Only unexpectedly strong resistance stopped him from entering the city and capturing Edward iv's own wife and son, as well as Henry vi who was in the Tower of London. Had he succeeded the entire situation would have been changed, Tewkesbury notwithstanding. But when he was repulsed he lost heart, and dared not wait outside the walls to be pulverized by Edward's victorious army. He returned to Sandwich, and was there allowed to surrender honourably. Five months later he attempted to escape custody and was beheaded. But by then Edward's victory was complete.

There are certain contradictions in accounts of the Battle of Tewkesbury which make an interesting study. There are also certain features of the preliminaries which have not been discussed earlier but which deserve a place in this narrative.

When Margaret landed at Weymouth (some say at Portland) Edward was taken by surprise. He had already told his victorious army it could disperse after the Battle of Barnet. He reassembled it at Windsor, but the process took a week. His great advantage was that he had good firearms, and started out well-provisioned from his base. His first need was to ascertain Margaret's intentions, and this was not easy for she sent some shadow patrols towards London to give the impression she was heading in that direction. However, Edward was not deceived for long and he set off via Abingdon to cut her off near Bristol. He reached Cirencester on 30 April, which was also the day on which Margaret reached Bath. Edward was then dangerously close, perhaps closer than Margaret realized, but she had to delay further by calling at Bristol, and collecting much needed arms and stores. Fortunately Bristol was friendly and gave her all the aid she needed. Edward heard of this move, and turned south. At this point he could have intercepted her army anywhere between Bristol and Cheltenham. However, he did not, for the following reason.

Margaret, now forty-two, was an experienced general and a woman as well. A little deception came easily to her. The only way she could keep Edward out of her path north was to give him the impression she had abandoned her original plan and was now making a dash south-east to outmarch him to London. If, in fact, she had done so she would have linked up with Fauconberg and won the war.

Instead she made a feint move to Sodbury Hill, some twelve miles north-west of Bristol. This swing to an obviously strategic point – there was a hill fort there – was picked up by Edward's scouts, and in consequence the vanguard of his army probed ahead to Sodbury. There, to their surprise they found a Lancastrian detachment and were mostly killed or taken prisoner. Those behind took back the news and Edward, deciding the Lancastrians were now about to give battle, paused and rearranged his army after the long forced march.

But Margaret had no intention of giving battle at Sodbury. With extraordinary coolness she marched her army within three miles of Edward's position and headed north for Berkeley. That night the Lancastrians slept in the shelter of Berkeley Castle and were on the road to Gloucester before dawn. By the time Edward learnt what had happened – and had doubtless finished cursing his scouts for their ineptitude – the Lancastrians were a good fifteen miles ahead.

But Edward was not to be put off easily. Guessing that she was heading for Gloucester he sent messengers ahead to the governor of the city, with the results which we already know. It is said that on the last phase of the desperate march north Edward's vanguard was overlapping Margaret's rearguard. It was apparently a boiling hot day, and they had troubles enough from nature without considering the enemy. It is said however that on the last stages the Lancastrians abandoned some artillery and this fell into the hands of Yorkist reinforcements from Gloucester who were following directly behind the Lancastrians.

Sites of medieval battles are known from contemporary chronicles or grave pits; however in the absence of either it is not impossible to trace out the probably course of the action. Few grave pits have been found at Tewkesbury, and it may of course have been that many of the dead were too scattered to make it worth the trouble of burying them at central points.

However, there is one theory of the battle which might be considered. It is that the Lancastrians drew up their lines much closer to the Abbey than is normally thought. This would mean the Yorkists would have to attack up the slopes from Bloody Meadow. If Somerset then charged down on them he could still have been caught in a flanking movement by spearmen. Edward might conceivably have made this move in order to cut the Lancastrians off from any possibility of reaching the ford. The reader, walking over the ground, might like to consider this theory; it does at least account for the concentrated fighting in Bloody Meadow.

The Battle of Bosworth Field

21 August 1485

When the Lancastrians were being defeated at Tewkesbury, Henry Tudor, Earl of Richmond, the future Henry VII, was a boy of fourteen. Age alone did not bar him from high rank or efficiency in holding it. Boys were accustomed to the battlefield from an early age, and took to it like a modern child does football. Sometimes they were unlucky, as was the twelve-year-old Earl of Rutland, killed in cold blood at Wakefield, and Prince Edward at Tewkesbury, but the young Black Prince had successfully held high command in the previous century, and both Gloucester and Edward, commanding 'battles' of the Yorkist army at Tewkesbury, were only nineteen. Nevertheless, without backing, Henry Tudor was too young to be a threat. His uncle, Jasper Tudor, Earl of Pembroke very wisely took him off to Brittany to acquire years and experience in safety.

Edward's reign was not an unsatisfactory one, for most of the bigger names in the field of dissent had been beheaded, and the smaller fry had been massacred in the blood baths after Wakefield, Towton, Barnet, Tewkesbury and the like. The middle classes had tended to stay out of trouble and it is interesting to note that, whenever possible, in the Wars of the Roses, battles took place outside towns, and armies interfered as little as possible with normal commercial activity. Edward IV was therefore able to succeed to the throne of a reasonably prosperous country. His record is by no means bad although he is criticized for having had his treacherous brother George, Duke of Clarence, put to death. Clarence was said to have been drowned in a butt of malmsey in the Tower of London. Clarence was undoubtedly a nuisance; he was always involved in some intrigue or other, but his sudden and mysterious death was thought by many to be unnecessary. Some suspicion fell on Gloucester, who, it was said, had encouraged Edward to take this extreme step. Gloucester later became Richard III and was said by many to have made preparation for that event long before. However, Gloucester, whatever his faults, and much has been made of them, was absolutely loyal to his brother Edward in his lifetime, and was a most capable soldier.

When Edward died, at the age of forty-one, in 1483, he left seven living children. The two sons were Edward, aged twelve, and Richard, aged nine. This of course meant a Regency. There were two candidates for the position, one the family of the late king's wife, the other Gloucester.

The situation was soon resolved. As the young king was coming to London for his coronation he was met by Gloucester, and taken into 'protective custody'. During the next few months a number of the young king's potential supporters were sent to the block on one pretext or another; one of them was Hastings who had commanded the Yorkist right wing when Gloucester had commanded the left at both Barnet and Tewkesbury.

Gloucester's next remarkable discovery was that Edward IV's marriage had been invalid, and had not taken place in a church at all; this meant his entire family were bastards. Confronted with this surprising discovery Gloucester saw no way out but to take the throne himself, and as London was packed with his armed retainers, nobody was prepared to suggest alternatives. Shortly afterwards the two young princes, who were now lodged in the Tower for their own safety, disappeared without trace. Nearly two hundred years later their bones were discovered under a staircase (which is still there to be seen today).

In recent years it has been suggested that Richard III's character has been made out to be far worse than it really is. This is possible but does not seem particularly likely. In his two years' reign, opposition to him mounted steadily in spite of his own skill in putting down rebellions. By 1485 most of his real or potential enemies had found their way to Henry Tudor. One who had not was Lord Stanley, who, in spite of once being arrested by Richard III, was now in a position of great power in the north-west.

By August 1485 Henry Tudor decided the time was ripe to return. He landed at Milford Haven on 7 August. His army was small, numbering little over 2,000, but he was soon, joined by a number of useful supporters. He had a promise of support from Lord Stanley but the latter did not dare to come into the open for fear that his son, who was in Richard's hand, would be executed. Nevertheless, by the time he reached the Midlands he had about 5,000. In spite of the smallness of his numbers Henry had the heartening experience of a trickle of supporters continuing to join him. Nevertheless he appears to have been an inept commander, and a contemporary account states that at one point he lost contact with his army and spent a night away from them; they were greatly relieved to see him again in the morning.

Richard had an army at least twice the size of Henry's; it may perhaps have numbered as many as 15,000. Unfortunately for him, his commanders' hearts were not in their work, as we shall see. Initially he had positioned himself at Nottingham, ready to move in

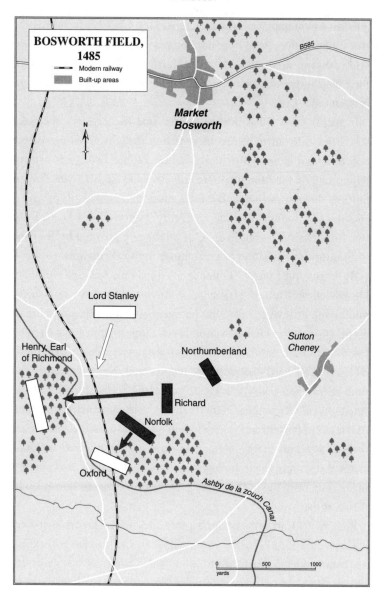

BOSWORTH FIELD, 1485

Modern railway
Built-up areas

N

Market Bosworth

Lord Stanley

Henry, Earl of Richmond

Northumberland

Sutton Cheney

Richard

Norfolk

Oxford

Ashby de la zouch Canal

0   500   1000
yards

B585

whatever direction was necessary to confront Henry. As soon as he learnt that Henry was moving across the Midlands he marched his army to Bosworth, and set out his troops in an excellent battle position on a long ridge running between Sutton Cheney and Shenton. Each army contained about one-third bowmen. By this time artillery (of which Henry had very little) was just becoming effective but the main brunt of the attack fell on the archers. Armour was by now highly complex; knights had well-made plate armour with elaborate jointing; men-at-arms had good plate armour, but the jointing was less efficient and gaps were filled with chain-mail or boiled leather. Henry had 2,000 French mercenaries in his army and these would doubtless have had the latest form of handgun.

So efficient had armour now become that it was the custom for almost everyone to carry a hammer. The flat side of this would be used to crack arms, whereupon it would be turned round and the point used to finish off the now vulnerable adversary.

At the Sutton Cheney end the ridge is about 400 feet high; at the other tip it is 390 and is known as Ambien Hill. The slope and surrounding grounds are wet; it was therefore a good position on which to await the enemy's attack. The crest was clear of trees, vegetation or hedges but there must have been tangled undergrowth in the marsh. Ambien Hill was clearly the key point at this stage and Richard got there first although he was not a little nettled to find that Stanley did not join him. Stanley's excuse was that he had been delayed by 'sweating sickness' a mysterious epidemic which affected England that summer.

Henry, being less experienced in war, was slower off the mark.

The battlefield is two miles south of Market Bosworth near the village of Sutton Cheney. (Leicestershire)

Richard watched him come into range but held his fire for a moment. Then as if by a starting signal both armies loosed off the opening rounds of cannon shot and a few flights of arrows.

From then on it was almost a chess game in treachery. Further along the ridge lay Northumberland's 'battle'. Northumberland was determined not to commit himself till he saw which side Stanley was going to fight on. Once he discovered that he could join in and be on the winning side. Stanley had 2,500 mounted infantry under his own command and his brother had 3,500 foot soldiers, so whichever side they fought for was likely to be the winner. The only man showing any real enthusiasm for the battle was the Duke of Norfolk who was pushing hard against Henry's centre with 3,000 men. Henry's centre was commanded by the Earl of Oxford, whom we last encountered fighting at Barnet when he allowed his battle to run away with him and largely contributed to the defeat of his own (Lancastrian) side. There was no question of that piece of history repeating itself. They were now in tight formation, held in by marshy land and pressed in front by Norfolk's men. Bit by bit they were forced back, mainly by sheer numbers. Henry himself had placed his command post well to the rear, and had taken no part in the fighting so far. Rather ill-advisedly he had remained static and the rest of his army had pulled away from him. Richard, watching the battle from the hill, heard this tempting news. It is said that it was too much for him to resist and that he plunged through the battle to find his Lancastrian challenger and kill him. This may be true. It may also be true that he saw the Stanleys come into the fight on the other side and decided to die in battle rather than be captured. Certainly it was at that moment that the Stanleys showed their hand. Apparently Richard hurled himself right into the middle of the Lancastrian army, which closed around him as he moved forwatd and swung his axe like the great fighter his record showed him to be. Unfortunately for him – though it made no difference to the ultimate result – his horse rode straight into the marsh and could not get out. He leapt out of the saddle and gazed wildly around. He may well have said 'A horse, a horse, my kingdom for a horse!' as he is said to have done, before being cut down by a dozen Lancastrians.

Northumberland, seeing the way the battle had gone, did not need to enter the fight at all. Norfolk went on to the bitter end, and died fighting. Stanley, the architect of victory, was said to have picked up Richard's crown from beneath a thorn bush and put it on Henry's head. As subsequent history was written by people who had opposed Richard III his character was not shown in its best light. Whether he was more or less unscrupulous than other leaders of the Wars of the Roses is conjectural but no one can deny that he was one of the greatest of the soldiers.

There was no massacre after the battle; there was no point in it. The battle had lasted little more than an hour, and half those on the field had never been engaged at all.

The surrounding towns were not without their part in the battle. Near the battlefield was Atherstone on the Watling Street, Tamworth, where there was a sizeable castle, and Leicester, and of course, Market Bosworth. Henry is said to have camped at Atherstone on the night before the battle on the site known as Royal Meadow; he is also said to have acquired useful arms from Tamworth.

There is no difficulty in identifying the ridge and there is a notice by the roadside which refers to the probable site of the battle. Some say that the fighting took place around Ambien Hill; this view seems to be based on the position of the marsh. However, if the visitor follows the path behind the notice he will soon find ample evidence that the marsh could have extended along most of the base of the ridge; today, even with deep drainage ditches the ground can be very wet in August.

In Sutton Cheney church there is a plaque to the memory of Richard III put up by the Richard III Society in the last decade.

There is some mystery attached to this extremely important battle. Perhaps it was appropriate that the vital battle of the Wars of Roses should be won by wholesale treachery. Perhaps Richard was the sort of soldier who makes a first-class second-in-command but lacked the ability to be a successful commander-in-chief.

It has often been stated that the armies of the Wars of the Roses were for the most part of untrained ill-armed men. This does not seem likely. The enormously rich and powerful barons had their own contingents and they could hardly fail to train and arm them adequately. Even the marching alone would have produced a degree of battle-fitness. Knights' armour in the fourteenth century was complicated, effective and expensive, but that of their men-at-arms would not have been cheap. Good examples of both, as well as weapons, including crossbows, may be seen in the Fitzwilliam Museum in Cambridge. It is sometimes said that the longbow was outmoded by the pistol because the latter could penetrate armour but the arrow could not. This view does not take into account the variety of arrow-heads available, some of which were as effective as a bullet. The reason why the longbow was prematurely discarded was that it required endless practice, and although this could be enforced by powerful barons – or in successful foreign wars, it was altogether too time-consuming in peacetime for all but a minority.

The Battle of Stoke Field

16 June 1487

The last battle in this series took place just south of the Trent, which many southerners will think of as part of the north, though the opinion will not be shared by northerners or midlanders. It is a much neglected battle but is of particular interest to those who have followed the battles of the Wars of the Roses, for it was the very last round of that bitter and bloody struggle.

After Bosworth Henry VII found himself in a powerful yet precarious position. His victory had been won for him by an extraordinary combination of allies, some of whom had fought for the Yorkists in the past. He was a most unlikely champion for the aggrieved and wronged but curiously enough that was what he was, and what proved to be his strength. Six months after Bosworth he married the daughter of Edward IV thus uniting the claim of Lancaster and York by marriage. Bosworth had not been followed by a massacre of the helpless – as had happened so frequently before, and although opponents who had been absent from Bosworth Field were indicted, they were not executed. Henry was a curious mixture: he was sober and restrained, intelligent and parsimonious, a little devious, but liable to act viciously and without restraint on occasion. This last may well be the behaviour of a frightened man rather than the sign of a sadist. There was, however, little attractive about Henry although there was no doubt that he was the right man in the right place, at the right time.

The early months of his reign saw little trouble, and his subjects seemed content to accept a rest from the bitterness and bloodshed of the past. But there were a few hardy spirits, and until they exterminated themselves in facing impossible odds there was bound to be conflict.

Notable among them was Lord Lovell. He had been a favourite of Richard III and was lucky not to have been executed after Bosworth. But Lovell was not a man to sit idle if there was any chance of winning or losing in desperate stakes. His first move against Henry VII was an attempt to kidnap him when the latter was visiting York. It failed, but Lovell was lucky and got away to France. There he was welcomed, sheltered, and encouraged by Margaret, Duchess of Burgundy, who was the sister of the late King Edward IV. Together they plotted a more thorough rebellion, and brought in John de la Pole, Earl of Lincoln. The latter had been declared heir to the throne by the late King Richard III but even if Richard had not died at Bosworth the chances of Lincoln ever succeeding him would have been slight, to say the least. It was decided – with good reason – to set on one side any claims Lincoln might have on the throne and instead put forward those of the son of the Earl of Clarence. Clarence, it will be remembered, had been drowned in a butt of malmsey in 1478 on the orders of Edward IV. His son was Edward, Earl of Warwick, and this young man seemed as good a figurehead to put forward as heir to the throne as the conspirators were likely to find. But Henry was too seasoned an intriguer to have this obvious incentive wandering around at large and had prudently put him under guard in the Tower of London. This was a problem for Lovell and his friends, but not an insuperable one. They resolved to find a suitable impersonator, parade him as the real Warwick, win battles in his name, and – when the time came – discard him and install the real Warwick, whom they would then release from the Tower. The anarchy which the success of this scheme would let loose, would of course make the recent wars look like a childish game, but this was of no consequence to the conspirators.

The plot was organized with a skill that made it almost admirable, if not commendable. Ireland had always been a Yorkist stronghold – and had served as a refuge at difficult moments such as the time after the rout of Ludford. The chosen pretender, Lambert Simnel, the son of an organ-maker in Oxford, was therefore sent to Ireland to arouse sympathy and support. It was said that he had just escaped from the Tower, and the deception worked like a charm. The Irish welcomed him as the true heir to the English throne and rallied in support. Lord Thomas Fitzgerald raised 4,000 men to support the impostor's claim, and these were joined by 2,000 German mercenaries. As Henry had secured his throne with the help of 2,000 French mercenaries it seemed propitious that 2,000 Germans were now going to be used by the opposition. The combined force landed in Lancashire on 4 June 1487 and were joined by a number of disaffected Englishmen; the final strength of the rebel force was little short of 10,000. Their first move was to get to York but after crossing the Pennines through the Aire Gap they changed course and began to move south. In the event they would probably have been wiser to have pressed on and captured York, which should not have been difficult with their numbers. Instead, they came south, possibly with the intention of capturing Nottingham. Their route is almost an exercise in strategic geography. Having crossed the main east-west obstacle of the Pennines at the best available point, they now had to cross the second great obstacle between them and London, the river Trent.

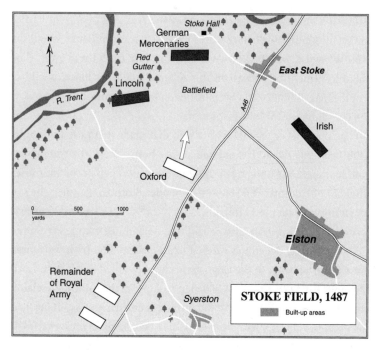

East Stoke is three miles from Newark on the A46. There is a road which leads past Stoke Hall to the battle site. (Nottinghamshire)

The best crossing places were at Nottingham and Newark but both were strongly garrisoned by loyal troops. Clearly, with an army such as Lovell had assembled a commander had to act or lose troops by desertion. Accordingly Lovell decided to cross the Trent at Fiskerton, four miles south of Nottingham. It was not a good or an easy ford, but it sufficed.

Meanwhile Henry had not let the grass grow underneath his feet. When he heard the news of the invasion, probably on the seventh of June, he was at Kenilworth. Hastily collecting as many troops as he could muster he moved north via Coventry and Leicester. After some difficulties over map reading he arrived at Nottingham on the twelfth and was very pleased to meet a strong contingent of loyal Derbyshire troops who had been brought to Nottingham to meet him; they numbered 6,000. This reinforcement brought Henry's forces up to 12,000 but, of course, numbers are by no means everything in a battle though they are a help. Henry was an astute politician but not in the category of generals such as we have seen earlier, e.g. Warwick the King Maker, Edward I and Edward IV. But, in his favour, it must be said that he lost no time in getting his troops to the battlefield at either Bosworth or Stoke. Wisely, he allowed the Earl of Oxford to make the pace and to take up a station in front of the battle. The rebel army, although undoubtedly surprised at the speed at which the royal army had come up, had chosen a reasonable position. Lincoln had placed his battle with its right on a hillock but also had the Trent partly covering the rear; the German mercenaries held the centre, almost immediately south of Stoke Hall; and the left was made up of the Irish.

The battle was a curious one. In view of its importance, for it finally established the Tudor dynasty, it was scantily recorded, and there are contradictions in the different versions. However, it seems probable that the version given here is correct, though the reader may care to consider the account given in Polydore Vergil.

Oxford in his usual forceful manner, so clearly shown at Barnet and Bosworth, pressed forward until he was well ahead of the rest of the royal army. In consequence he took the full onslaught of Lincoln's battle and the German mercenaries unaided. It was more than his troops could sustain and a portion broke and fled after about two hours' fighting. However, this apparent victory with the opposing forces slightly out of alignment, spelt disaster for the rebels, for the Irish contingent, who had so far had to do little fighting, poured forward in the jubilation and carelessness of victory already won. Their awakening was a rude one. As they swept forward on to what they thought was the wreck of Henry's army but which was, in fact, only Oxford's badly mauled 'battle' they were hit by the second and third royalist contingents almost immediately. Luck, deception, and surprise were playing their usual part in warfare. The Irish, whose courage and dash might have won the day if they had been properly used, now found themselves hammered by well-disciplined, well-armed fresh troops. Inevitably they began to fall back but what began as an attempt to re-group soon became a wild dash to get out of harm's way. Safety lay on the other side of the Trent – although even that would not have helped for long – but few enough of them reached it. Many were caught in what became known as 'Red Gutter', named doubtless because it became a veritable river of blood that day.

This was a far greater battle than Bosworth had been. Casualties were heavy on both sides, partly because Oxford's 'battle' had been nearly wiped out and partly because the slaughter of the vanquished was so thorough. A broad river is a fine protection against enemy attack from flank or rear but a deadly hazard when an army is making a hasty departure from the battlefield. Usually the casualties are not so evenly distributed between the opposing sides. The joint total on this occasion was said to be 7,000, approximately one third of those engaged. Many of them were the German mercenaries, who fought with a dogged persistence which impressed even those who had little wish to admire them.

Some of course escaped over the river, and found a long and difficult way home. Lovell was one, but his fate was sealed. Whether he died at Minster Lovell, which was later to be renowned for the macabre 'mistletoe bough' story of the bride who was trapped in the chest with the spring lock or whether – as seems more likely – it was at Rotherfield Greys, near Henley, we do not know. But it is said – and there is little reason to doubt it – that he was concealed in a secret underground room and that his guardian was killed or captured in a search; Lovell therefore starved to death, sitting at a table waiting for the helper who never came again.

Lambert Simnel was luckier. Henry realized that there was no point in victimizing him so he made him a cook in the royal kitchens. Apparently he enjoyed the position and thrived; he was a good cook.

Lincoln, Schwarz (the leader of the German mercenaries) and Fitzgerald were all killed on the battlefield.

Subsequently a few other conspirators to the throne met their deaths, deserved or undeserved. Among them was Perkin Warbeck, a young Frenchman who pretended to be the younger son of Edward IV; Stanley, who had betrayed Richard III at Bosworth but felt disgruntled at not receiving an earldom as a reward, and had supported Perkin Warbeck in his futile rebellion; and last but quite unjustified, Edward, Earl of Warwick (son of the Duke of Clarence) who had been a prisoner in the Tower for sixteen years, which was most of his lifetime.

Thus were the last threads of the Wars of the Roses cut off and destroyed. With them went an age which would not appear again. There would be battles in plenty, and even another civil war, but nothing again in English history would match that period when all the great families in England slowly and remorselessly tore each other to pieces.

The Battle of Sedgemoor

6 July 1685

For the last battle to be described in this volume we go to the west country, and two hundred years on in time. Many other battles took place in the period between Stoke Field and Sedgemoor, and as many of them were fought in the north of England they are described in the second volume of this series. Most of them occurred in the Civil War of 1641–9.

The details of the history of the period between the Wars of the Roses and Sedgemoor do not concern us here but it is useful to appreciate the main events and changes during that time. A brief summary is as follows.

Henry VII, after Stoke Field, was able to settle down to curbing the nobility and refilling the Exchequer – tasks which he managed to combine. His son Henry VIII was considerably more bellicose and fought with varying success in Britain and abroad. In his reign, however, England came as near as she has ever been since Hastings to being conquered by the French.

Henry VII's son, Edward VI, was a sickly youth but his supporters won battles for him. Mary, who followed, was less fortunate; her supporters lost battles. Elizabeth had no trouble at home which could not be dealt with by an astute counter-intelligence department, and although at times in great peril finished her reign triumphant over all her foreign enemies. With her death the Tudor line came to an end and the Stuarts of Scotland – heirs by tracing the line back to Henry VII – came to the English throne. James I was not a success, and his son Charles I took the country into civil war. After Charles I's execution there was an interim period of Parliamentary government which soon became a dictatorship. It will be remembered among other things for Cromwell's victories abroad, particularly in Ireland where his name is still mentioned with hatred. In 1660 the Stuarts were restored with Charles II who had had enough of being an unwelcome guest at foreign courts and did his best to keep out of trouble. Even so, his attempts to make England Roman Catholic, and to once more put the throne above Parliamentary control, took him very close to disaster. The former ambition started a movement which was to have its full effect in the succeeding reign and cause the Battle of Sedgemoor. It was well-known that when Charles II died he would be succeeded by his brother who was an even more ardent Roman Catholic than Charles was, but considerably less flexible about achieving his ambitions. With this in view, the Protestant opposition to Charles II became sufficiently alarmed to back a rival candidate for the throne. This was the eldest of Charles II's illegitimate sons, the Duke of Monmouth. His mother was Lucy Walters, and in order to make his candidature more credible the story was put about that she had been secretly married to Charles. Apart from being a personable young man who looked the part of a suitable heir-apparent, Monmouth was also an able soldier who had performed very well in defeating some Scottish Covenanter rebels at Bothwell Brig in June 1679. The plot to make Monmouth king made little headway during Charles II's lifetime, but when it ended more rapidly than anyone had supposed, at the age of 55, the situation became quite different. Charles, although authoritarian and Catholic at heart, had lasted for twenty-five years; his successor lasted three.

James II succeeded in February 1685, and in view of his professed Romanism it seemed clear to Monmouth and his allies that the new king could have little support. In the event, they turned out to be grievously mistaken. At the time Monmouth was living abroad, in Holland, but as the time seemed ripe he landed at Lyme (Regis), Dorset in June 1685. His principal supporter was the Earl of Argyle, who had landed in Scotland a month earlier.

Both men arrived with inadequate forces but retribution was swifter in overtaking Argyle. He raised the Campbells but found no one else willing to join him. His army melted away and he himself was beheaded.

Monmouth was more fortunate, or, at least, lasted longer. To his astonishment and discomfiture few people of any standing came to join him; the story that his mother had really been married to Charles II was a little too hard to swallow. From the beginning his enterprise seemed ill-starred. It should have arrived earlier when it was hoped that the government would be sending troops north to fight Argyle. Monmouth was delayed by a variety of reasons and was lucky to avoid interception at sea. Soon after his arrival one of his chief supporters, Thomas Dare, quarrelled with the most experienced soldier, Andrew Fletcher, who promptly shot Dare dead. So great was the local indignation that Fletcher had to be sent abroad at once.

On 15 June Monmouth had a local victory at Axminster and if he had followed it up could have captured Exeter, which would have given him badly-needed supplies. Instead he went to Taunton, where he was persuaded to proclaim himself king, a step which he had not so far taken. When he moved on towards Bristol he had a force of about 6,000 but most of them were rustics whose total arms consisted of scythes, picks and home-made weapons. The force was notably deficient in muskets. The cavalry were mounted on cart horses. The opposition was not very formidable but had experience and discipline. It was commanded by Lord Feversham; his second-in-command was John Churchill, later Duke of Marlborough who would subsequently show himself to be one of the very greatest of British generals. In numbers it was little over half that of the rebels but it had seventeen useful guns to set against Monmouth's four.

Monmouth appears to have had very slight idea of strategy but eventually decided he must capture Bristol. He therefore set off north-east, moving through Glastonbury (where he camped), Wells, and Shepton Mallet. However, he understood that Bristol was much more strongly defended on the Somerset side than the Gloucester-shire side, and decided it would be better to cross the Avon at Keynsham, prior to making an attack on the north-eastern side of the town. When he reached Pensford, about five miles from Bristol, he heard that Keynsham bridge had been broken down, and waited while it was being repaired. It seems likely that if he had pressed forward direct to Bristol he might have captured the town, as he would have found supporters as well as opposition inside the walls.

When he reached Keynsham on 26 June the bridge had been repaired, and with a little forcefulness he could have crossed it. However, he was much set back by a charge of one hundred Life Guards under Oglethorpe, which scattered some of his cavalry. Showing even more uncertainty than ever he began to fall back to Bridgwater and during this march a number of his supporters decided to slip away and return to their farms.

Various courses were still open to him but none of them looked particularly hopeful. He could march north and hope to pick up support from Wales and the north-western counties; to do so he must first avoid Bristol and flank attacks; he also needed to arrange to feed, clothe, and supply his army with footwear if his soldiers were going to stay together on the march. Bath therefore became his next objective but Bath proved no less disappointing than Bristol, for with the knowledge that the royal army was close at hand, the city showed no wish to surrender. Monmouth retired without firing a shot. On 26 June he quartered himself at the village of Norton St Philip and was lucky to avoid being killed by an enemy snipe who shot a silver button at him while he was standing at a window.

Norton St Philip saw a lively skirmish. Realizing that Feversham might try to attack the village Monmouth placed a barricade across one of the approach roads. As the royalists approached the barricade they were caught in a brisk crossfire from Monmouth's musketeers, few in number, but effective enough. The Royalists lost about a hundred before they withdrew, and it seemed for a time that as both armies deployed there would now be a serious battle. Curiously enough the battle never took place. After a few shots Feversham withdrew the royal troops, and Monmouth made no attempt to pursue; instead he fell back to Frome.

At Frome he met two further disappointments. First he found that a small rising meant to help him had been suppressed a few days before, and all arms removed from the town; secondly he heard that the Scottish rising had failed and Argyle had been captured.

So bad was Monmouth's situation that apparently he considered fleeing overseas, and leaving his supporters to their fate. Had he done so their fate might have been better than what eventually befell them; it could hardly have been worse. However, he was persuaded by Grey, his cavalry leader, that this idea was monstrous; and in consequence he moved towards Bridgwater. Once again he passed through Wells, and on this occasion his rabble army – which included a number of Puritans – damaged some of the ornaments in the Cathedral and stripped the roof of lead to make bullets. They reached Bridgwater on 2 July.

Much had been hoped from Bridgwater; it was reported that the town was full of well-armed and eager recruits. It turned out otherwise. There were indeed supporters but they were few in numbers and their arms were primitive in the extreme. Once again the idea of a march to Cheshire was mooted but once again vacillation prevented any forthright action being taken. As the town was completely unfortified a few ditches were dug but that was all. Most serious was the fact that so many of his men had now deserted that he now only had about three thousand seven hundred men, scarcely a thousand more than the much better-armed and trained opposition.

The very desperation of his plight now goaded Monmouth into action. If he delayed longer he might even become outnumbered. On the evening of 5 July he was told that the King's army could be seen – through glasses – from the top of Bridgwater church. Monmouth himself went to look; it was true. Feversham had brought up the royal army and it was now encamped at Sedgemoor, three and a half miles away.

Sedgemoor in 1685 was a wide plain which was only partly drained; that sort of countryside is particularly treacherous after rain. The drainage – such as it was, was effected by three main dykes, the Blackmoor Dyke, the Bussex Rhine, and the Langmoor Dyke. There was a triangle of villages at points where the ground rises slightly – they were Chedzoy, Middlezoy, and Westonzoyland. 'Zoy' is derived from old English and means an island.

The main part of the Royalist army was encamped behind the Bussex Rhine (the word 'rhine' in old English signified a large open ditch). Most of the regular Foot were stationed next to Chedzoy, and

147

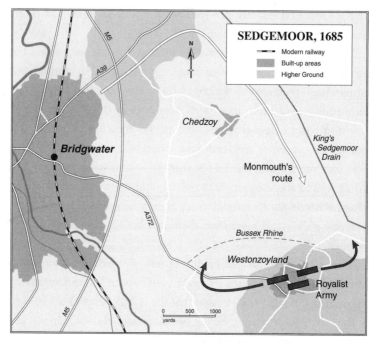

Take the A372 from Bridgwater and the battlefield is reached after three miles. The ditches are now different but the course of the Bussex Rhine, now filled in, can be traced. (Somerset)

the marks on the north buttress of Chedzoy church are said to have been made by them sharpening their weapons. Similar marks are however to be found on many churches up and down the country. They were made by medieval archers who were compelled by law to practise after churchgoing on Sundays, and sharpened their arrows on the stones so that they would stick in the targets. Feversham set up his headquarters at Westonzoyland, where their cavalry, the Blues and Life Guards, were stationed. Middlezoy was occupied by the Wiltshire Militia, who were apparently of uncertain quality and uncertain loyalty. In the event they were kept out of the way of the battle.

Monmouth, now, at long last decided on action. He would attack at night and by force and surprise, scatter the royal army. It showed immediate spirit; unfortunately for him he made one appalling error.

Night attacks are, of course, always a hazard. You may lose your way, you may attack your own men; it is almost impossible to know whether you are winning or losing until the issue is decided and it is too late to change your tactics. However, in Monmouth's desperate situation it was not a bad plan to adopt. And if he won there was nothing to stop him marching on London and being crowned.

Silence was vital, and in order to ensure it an order was issued that any man speaking or making any noise should be stabbed by his nearest neighbour. Silence was maintained, except for the whispered recognition word 'Soho' – reference to Monmouth's London residence.

The route was north-east from Bridgwater to the Black Dyke, which would then be followed (the Black Dyke is now the King's Sedgemoor Drain). Then by turning sharply south-east they would infiltrate inside the Langmoor Rhine. It was foggy, and much time was lost.

This was hardly surprising. The weather had been very rainy, many of the tracks were very muddy, and the moor itself was not so very different from the refuge area which had sheltered the local inhabitants from invaders in the past on account of its tangled impenetrability. It was a major achievement for the rebel army to have travelled so far and so fast in the dark. But when they came to the Langmoor Rhine some confusion developed. As the vanguard was trying to find the appropriate crossing point (a causeway of stepping stones) the centre and rear moved up closely. It was impossible – with the order for silence – to prevent it. Some confusion developed as men stumbled into each other in the dark. It is more than likely they made a noise. It is said that a treacherous officer then gave the alarm by firing a pistol; he was certainly accused of it afterwards. A more probable story is that a trooper in the Blues heard the noise, suspected a surprise attack was afoot, and loosed off his pistol to give the alarm. He then rode back to the Bussex Rhine and yelled the alarm some twenty times before notice was taken of him. But at last it was and the royal troops stood to, lit their matches, and provided Monmouth's men with a superb target.

There are conflicting versions of what happened next. Some accounts say that the rebel army pressed forward during the delay in the royalists' acting on the alarm and were making good headway when they were staggered to find an unsuspected stretch of water ahead of them – the Bussex Rhine. Other versions say that the Bussex Rhine was no surprise and in any case was nearly dry at the time but the forthright attacks of the royalist cavalry cut the rebels to pieces before the foot soldiers got to grips at all. Whatever the details the main effects were clear enough. Once vital surprise had been lost rebel morale fell. On the other side the cavalry reaction was much better and more vigorous than might have been expected. The Royalist artillery also began to play its part. The rebel 'cavalry', surprised and disappointed at the failure of their manoeuvre, refused to advance, and no amount of cajoling and cursing would make them move. It would have been better for them if they had, for at the first volley from the royalist foot the cart horses took fright and became uncontrollable. Their panic spread to other parts of the rebel army but not all. Monmouth, once the battle was joined, made heroic efforts, but to no avail. Nevertheless many of the rebels were now fighting with the desperation of men for whom all is lost, and life can mean little. Their greatest handicap was shortage of ammunition but when that ran out they gave the royal troops a hard time with their scythes and home-make pikes. The miners from the Mendips would neither surrender nor run away, and died to the last man. The battle lasted three hours.

The concentration of the fighting in the final stages was shown by the placing of the grave pits, the main ones being near Weston-zoyland and Chedzoy.

When, soon after dawn, Monmouth saw that the battle and his cause was lost, he abandoned his efforts to drive his men forward, and himself took to flight. He was captured half-starving three days later, and six days after that was executed on Tower Hill. It is said that he pleaded for his life but when he realized it made no difference what he said or promised pulled himself together and behaved with impressive courage and dignity. His execution was bungled and the executioner took at least five strokes to chop off his head.

Monmouth's venture, which, as we have seen, was an extra-ordinary mixture of half-heartedness and briskness, cost the lives of 1,000 of his followers killed at Sedgemoor. The Royalist losses were 300.

The horrors of this particular battle were not restricted to the battlefield for it was followed by Judge Jeffreys and the Bloody Assize. Jeffreys held a mockery of a trial at Taunton as a result of which 230 suspected sympathizers were hanged and 800 deported. Neither women nor boys were spared, and the number of those killed 'resisting arrest' by 'Kirke's lambs', the troops of Colonel Percy Kirke, went unrecorded. 'Kirke's lambs' had recently been in Tangier, where they had acquired some unpleasant methods.

Unfortunately the details of Sedgemoor are not easy to trace today, although enough remains to make it well worth a visit. The churches still stand but the Black Dyke is now part of a wider drainage complex. The Bussex Rhine and the Langmoor Rhine were filled in long ago.

The battlefield is signposted, and there is a monument, but it is not easy to trace out. There is a map in Chedzoy church.

The 'last battle on English soil' is often dismissed as being the rout of some half-armed yokels by a small efficient band of regular troops. It is more than that. It is a tribute to the courage and stubbornness of the west countrymen who, in spite of vacillating leadership, could manage a perfectly disciplined night march and then fight a far better equipped force. It is also a tribute to the efficiency of a small regular army which, though surprised and outnumbered, recovered and won a victory in the confused conditions of fog and dark. It is also a tribute to the generals, Feversham and Churchill, who handled their troops with skill and resource. Lastly, although this may seem strange, it is a tribute to Monmouth's tactical ability for he nearly won by a desperate and difficult manoeuvre when all was seemingly lost.

BOOK TWO

The North

Introduction

The battles described in this book occurred between 1066 and 1648, and they took place in the area between Cheshire and Scotland.

Usually battlefields are a complete mystery to the visitor, for even if he knows when and where they were fought he rarely knows why, nor how they were lost or won. Still less does he appreciate how they may have hung in the balance or might have had a different result. The author of this book has vivid memories of the frustration of visiting battlefields in early youth without any clear guidance on the techniques of the period, nor the background causes which brought men to battle at that place at that time, nor the ultimate result.

The pattern of this book therefore is to fit each battle into the background of the time, to describe it and explain it; and then to bridge the period to the next northern battle. The battles which occurred elsewhere in the British Isles are mentioned and detailed descriptions of them are given in the other books in this volume: the South; the Midlands; Scotland and the Border. Each book is self-contained and adheres to the main principle that a reader can grasp the sequence of events leading to a battle in his own area. Two of the most confusing periods in English history are the Wars of the Roses and the English Civil War. It is hoped that, by following the events and battles as described in this volume, a reader will not only understand these eventful campaigns but also derive great enjoyment from visualizing those battles and considering what sort of a commander he himself would have made at the time.

The period covered in this section is almost exactly six hundred years. Enormous changes took place at that time, not least the introduction of the longbow and, later, of gunpowder. The first battle in this book was a contest of immensely strong, adventurous men who wore little armour and hacked their way to victory with spear and battle-axe. Their weapons and strategy may seem crude and facile to modern eyes but the weapons, at least, required great strength, agility, and skill. The medieval warrior was an athlete of no mean ability.

Seventy years later the bow was coming into use, and contributed largely to the winning of the Battle of the Standard. Propaganda, too, played its part here.

At Boroughbridge in the early fourteenth century the longbow was then as established a weapon as the automatic rifle is today. Ground was surveyed and ranged to a yard; and the whole of a target area was blanketed with missiles.

Otterburn at the end of the same century was that most unpredictable of occasions, a night battle. All the usual mistakes were made.

Wakefield, in 1460, was almost a modern battle, certainly in a tactical sense. It had deception, surprise, and well-timed, concerted flank attacks.

Towton, the greatest and bloodiest battle ever fought on English soil, began with the longbow but soon became a vast personal combat, fought to a bitter end with no mercy shown by either side.

Hedgeley Moor and Hexham, although different battles, were so much part of the same campaign that they are treated together. Hexham had some interesting tactical aspects.

Flodden, although a medieval battle, in some ways resembled later, more modern battles. Readers will see some parallels with Marston Moor.

Winceby was essentially a cavalry engagement and was the fore-runner of many a similar encounter. It was one of the smaller battles of the Civil War but had an importance which went far beyond the numbers involved.

Newark was a touch-and-go battle. It could easily have been a crushing defeat for Rupert but instead became a spectacular victory. By now guns and gunpowder were regular features of battles.

Marston Moor began in the evening in a thunderstorm and finished an hour or two later by moonlight. For most of the battle, the eventual winners thought they had lost and the losers thought they had won. With the dark, the rain, and the gunsmoke rolling over the battlefield, the confusion is not surprising.

Rowton Heath saw the end of the Royalist hopes in the first stage of the Civil War. Here again was a small battle, but its result was crucial.

Preston, which lasted for two days and part of a night, was the decisive engagement in the second stage of the Civil War. It was handled ineptly by the Royalists but brilliantly by Cromwell. Its redeeming feature was the courage and endurance shown in an otherwise not very creditable campaign.

The battles described, therefore, include most forms of possible tactical manoeuvre, and encompass a whole era of changes in weapons and armour. The English and Norsemen at Stamford Bridge wore boiled leather jerkins but little armour. Bows were few. Gradually the body became more protected, and shields became more cumbersome. A hundred years later the axe, once despised by the Normans, had become a cherished weapon, but for the next two hundred years infantry were considered vastly inferior in every way to cavalry. With the advent of the longbow in the thirteenth century infantry suddenly became extremely important and we find that, as archers, not only could they destroy cavalry at long range by pouring arrows on to them at about ten shots a minute, but they could also receive them with pikes and destroy them that way. But throughout the Middle Ages the knight, with his heavy complicated armour, and his magnificent expensive horse, was socially, if not militarily, supreme.

In the Civil War all the heavy armour was discarded, and horse and foot were scarcely hampered by the light body protection worn. Headgear, however, was still heavy. The Civil War produced excellent infantry, notably pikemen, but was essentially a cavalry war. Surprisingly, the Parliamentarians got the better of most of the cavalry battles.

A feature of medieval warfare not generally realized is the large number of foreign mercenaries who took part. But equally, there were numbers of English mercenaries serving in armies overseas.

The strategic geography of England played a very considerable part in the campaigns described in this book. Students of military history will be well aware of the importance of roads, ports, hills, and rivers. The fundamentals of strategic planning require roads for the movement of armies and their supplies: large numbers of men cannot move in cohesion over roadless country; they need ports for supplies and sometimes for tactical manoeuvres; they must avoid hills and marshes and therefore travel *via* the gaps, which thus become strategic points themselves; and they must be able to cross rivers by bridges and fords, use them for transport, and deny them to the enemy. Warfare, therefore, even in its crudest and bloodiest medieval form, was not haphazard but an elaborate form of chess with troops as the pieces upon a highly complicated board.

The Battle of Stamford Bridge

25 September 1066

The Battle of Stamford Bridge was as important as Hastings – which took place less than three weeks later – but, because Harold won the former and lost the latter, Stamford Bridge has been relegated to the list of minor battles. But, if Harold had lost Stamford Bridge, Hastings would not have been fought, and when the Normans eventually came to grips with the Scandinavian invaders a very different line-up of forces might have been seen; William's invasion army would have been dispersed over the countryside and he could well have been fighting at a considerable numerical disadvantage.

Stamford Bridge is eight miles east of York, and there, in the middle of the village, is a stone which commemorates one of the bloodiest fights in English history. It is inscribed in English and Norwegian:

> The Battle of Stamford Bridge was fought in this neighbourhood on 25 September 1066 – *Slaget ved Stamford Bruble utkjempet idisse trakter den 25 September 1066.*

Even today, with a picturesque water-mill on one side of the river, and a caravan camp on the other, it is not too difficult to visualize that scene a thousand years ago. One can picture the long, desperate, bloody conflict. Less easy to comprehend are the extraordinary

160

jealousies and motives that caused this battle and made it so envenomed. Ironically, the losers had their revenge when their conquerors were themselves beaten and destroyed at Hastings so soon afterwards. But if ever there should be a haunted battlefield it would be this one.

For nearly four hundred years the inhabitants of these islands had suffered invasion and attacks from the north – mainly from what is now Scandinavia. In 787 the Anglo-Saxons – themselves once intensely warlike but now more settled – had suffered their first raid from the Vikings. This wild, adventurous, relentless Nordic people, who later became Danes and Norwegians, first terrorized by raids, then later invaded and settled in England. At times they were defeated – as by King Alfred in 870 – but eventually much of the North and Midlands was in their control. Gradually, however, they became absorbed into the English kingdom. Events were far from peaceful but, on the whole, the country was settled until, at the end of the tenth century, a fresh wave of Nordic invasions began, this time mainly by the Danes. Ultimately, a Danish king, Canute, ruled all England and Denmark and Norway as well, and, because he was supreme, gave his realm nineteen years of peace. After Canute's death it was a different story, and England was torn apart by the quarrels of his two jealous sons. When they both died within a short time of each other the new king was the ineffective Edward the Confessor, but the real ruler was Godwin, Earl of Wessex. When Godwin died, his son Harold, later to win Stamford Bridge and be killed at Hastings, took over Godwin's position and influence. This was 1054, and for the next twelve years Harold ruled England – though without a royal title – and ruled it extremely well. As a measure of Harold's fighting skills it should be remembered that he organized the conquest of Macbeth, the murder of Duncan, in

Scotland, and also crushed a Welsh rebellion by chasing the rebels to the crest of Snowdon where they beheaded their leader, and brought his head to Harold's feet. He was said to be a small man, and modest; he was, in spite of his defeat at Hastings, a superb fighter and tactician.

But Harold had formidable problems. Some of them stemmed from his own lenience, for when he was defied by Aelfgar of Mercia, who twice brought the Midlands out in rebellion against him, he forgave him and let him hold the powerful earldom of Mercia. But another, more dangerous, problem arose from his trusting nature. Harold's younger brother, Tostig, was Earl of Northumbria, which then comprised most of the area north of the Humber. Tostig ruled his earldom so badly and unjustly that the people rose in rebellion, and in his place installed Morcar, the younger brother of Aelfgar of Mercia, who, as we saw above, had no love for Harold. When the rebellion was investigated, Harold recommended (to the king, Edward the Confessor) that Tostig should be banished and that Morcar should retain the earldom. It was a remarkable decision, kindly and statesmanlike, but disastrous folly for those times. By it Harold had made a bitter enemy of his evil younger brother, and put into powerful league – with over half the country at their disposal – two brothers who were united in their hatred and jealousy of himself. Harold had, of course, other troubles (from William of Normandy)[1], but these did not affect him at Stamford Bridge. The northern troubles came to a head when Edward the Confessor died, and the Saxon Council (the Witan) had to choose between appointing the late king's ten-year-old great-nephew, or Harold, the man who had effectively ruled the country for twelve years. They had no

1 See *British Battlefields: The South.*

hesitation over choosing Harold but immediately the appointment was announced it set loose a storm of troubles. William of Normandy felt that his own – admittedly dubious – claim should be admitted. Morcar and Eadwine felt that they could now exploit the power he had put into their hands, although he attempted to gain their allegiance by marrying their sister, Ealdgyth. But the real threat came from a totally unexpected quarter. Tostig, burning with rage in his exile, had gone to Norway and persuaded Harald Hardrada to espouse his cause.

Hardrada was a formidable figure by any standards. He was generally considered to be the greatest Viking who had ever lived. As the Vikings had produced generation after generation of fearless, skilful, immensely strong, and unwaveringly determined fighters, this was praise indeed. 'Espousing Tostig's cause' meant that Hardrada was prepared to bring to England an invasion force that would defeat the English and install Tostig – and perhaps Hardrada himself – in Harold's place. And, as many countries already knew, when Hardrada set out on the path of war, terror preceded him, and victory with appalling slaughter was inevitable.

Tostig had been anything but idle in his exile, for already, with a fleet of sixty ships, he had been ravaging the English coast, beginning with the Isle of Wight, which he had sacked with impressive cruelty, and then moving up the coast to Yorkshire leaving a trail of slaughter and destruction. He had landed in the Humber but been driven back to his ships by Eadwine and Morcar. As soon as he was at sea, he had been intercepted by a fleet Harold had sent up after him, and in the ensuing battle lost nearly fifty of his sixty ships. The remnants of Tostig's fleet had then fled to Scotland where Malcolm, who owed his throne (after the death of Macbeth) to Harold, somewhat ungratefully gave Tostig refuge and allowed him to accept Scottish volunteers. Malcolm was probably glad to see some of his more turbulent subjects find themselves dangerous employment some distance away, instead of making life unbearable for their neighbours and their overlord, but it caused considerable bitterness between the two countries for many years.

The strength of Tostig's refitted fleet is not known but the general consensus of opinion is that Hardrada's numbered three hundred. This joined up with Tostig's force at the mouth of the Tyne, and together the combined fleet sailed for the Humber. Viking boats were renowned for their penetrative powers. When there was wind they crowded on every available inch of sail and drove before it – sometimes to spectacular disaster in storms – and when it was calm their crews rowed day and night on a shift system. The shallow draught of their ships enabled them to sail (or row) up narrow streams or creeks; they would be seen far inland one day and at a point along the coast 100 miles away the next. On 19 September most of Hardrada's vast fleet had sailed up the Humber, then slipped up the Ouse and disembarked at Ricall, some ten miles south of York. Swiftness and deception had enabled them to land unopposed, but Eadwine and Morcar were only too well aware of the threat, and had collected a substantial force at York. But it was in vain. When the two armies met at Fulford, two miles south of York, in a battle of which we have few details, the fighting was prolonged and bloody, but provided a devastating victory for the invaders. It was said that a hundred York clergy accompanied their army to the field to encourage them against the heathen invaders, and that they too fell in a general slaughter. But Hardrada did not sack York. For some unknown reason he merely demanded provisions and took hostages. He also left Norwegians to see that dead Vikings were buried with the correct warrior ritual. Possibly he thought that York would be his capital if he went on to take the English throne. The battle of Fulford had taken place on 19 September and the settlement of York on the 23rd. Now a further arrangement was made to exchange yet more hostages at Stamford Bridge. The choice of this venue seems to have been based on the fact that it was a nodal point – a crossroads and a river-crossing combined. Even so, it seems a curious point to have chosen – well away from his base camp at Ricall and also from his new acquisition, York.

The invasion was well-timed. In Anglo-Saxon England the army was called up under the *fyrd* system which produced a rota of men-under-arms. At the end of the 'invasion season' – which was during the summer months – the *fyrd* was disbanded. Harold therefore had a difficult enough task in keeping the *fyrd* mobilized when he knew William was waiting with an invasion army in Normandy and the invasion did not come (it was delayed by contrary winds). Now a fresh threat developed in the north. At the best of times he would not have had enough men to meet the two threats simultaneously but now he was faced with a very difficult decision. Should he wait in the south for the greater threat from Normandy, which might arrive at any moment, but might, perhaps, be indefinitely delayed, or should he take a calculated risk and move up to the north where the invader was already on English soil? He decided on the latter. Hastily recalling as many as possible of his disbanded *fyrd* he rapidly organized his army. Then he set off north. On the way he heard of the disaster at Fulford and realized that there could now be no hope of a northern army to help him. He may well have suspected that his 3,000 would be numerically smaller but he could scarcely have expected they would be outnumbered two to one by the northern host. He was himself, apparently, by no means physically well at the time.

On 24 September Harold reached Tadcaster. This small, attractive town on the Wharfe, famous for its brewery, has seen many armies, and the fugitives from many battles. Here Harold found his northern ships which had slipped out of the way of the Vikings. They would have been rapidly annihilated if they had tried to check Hardrada's fleet, but if the forthcoming battle went well for the English they might play a useful part when the Vikings tried to move away. Here, too, Harold was joined by other supporters. Morale, after the disaster of Fulford, would be at the lowest ebb, but the quiet, confident resolution of Harold – who always won – would be sufficient to send a surge of new hope through the fugitives. Harold wasted little time at Tadcaster. He had come to defeat the invaders, and the sooner he did it and went back to the south the better it would be for all. He marched straight to York, which, as we have seen, held only a token force of Vikings. It was a mere ten miles away, not much for an army which has already marched 200. He knew Hardrada had moved off eastwards, and doubtless suspected some cunning move to bypass him – and perhaps re-embark and land further south, possibly at London. But, to his astonishment he learnt that the Viking host was only a mere eight miles away, and apparently quite unsuspecting of his arrival. It was a golden opportunity – he would take them by surprise, for they clearly had no idea of his nearness. There would be a little murmuring from his men who had looked forward to a night or two in York, with its attendant pleasures, but there was no arguing with Harold's orders, nor any audible muttering either.

Surprise it was. Hardrada's army was scattered on both sides of the river, quite relaxed, and, as is the custom of an army in camp, quite unaccourtred for battle. Even the sight of the English vanguard did not at first cause alarm, for it was thought to be a

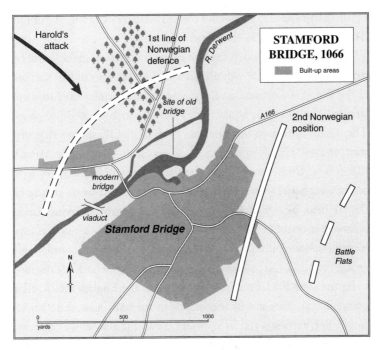

Harold's attack

1st line of Norwegian defence

R. Derwent

STAMFORD BRIDGE, 1066

Built-up areas

site of old bridge

A166

2nd Norwegian position

modern bridge

viaduct

Stamford Bridge

N

Battle Flats

0   500   1000
yards

The battle site is eight miles to the east of York on the A166. The course of the battle is easy to follow as the main features are largely unchanged, although the present bridge is 400 yards downstream from the original one. (East Riding of Yorkshire)

contingent from York with news about the hostages. When the significance of the situation was grasped, Harold was less than a mile away. For a moment all was confusion, then it began to sort itself out. There was no time for proper deployment, and Tostig – with the bitter memory of two recent defeats – was not keen to invite a third; his suggestion was that they should fall back to Ricall. This, however, was not a policy to appeal to Hardrada. If Harold had never been defeated, he was not the only one; neither had Hardrada. The order was given to stand and fight.

The ground over which the battle was fought is easily discernible today, but the bridge which played a vital part in the conflict was not at the site of the present one, but was approximately 400 yards upstream. The river was about forty feet wide in 1066, and was deep. The visitor will note that the east bank is slightly higher than the west, and will readily appreciate the river for the formidable obstacle that it was. Unfortunately for Hardrada, many of his soldiers were on the west bank, so even if he had wished to retreat down-stream on the far bank he would have had to fight a lengthy delaying action before that could be accomplished. The bridge was a wooden one, placed on stone pillars in the stream, and was apparently only wide enough to allow the passage of two men at a time. Hardrada decided to let the west-bank army take the edge off the English attack, then gradually fall back across the bridge to the east bank. The bridge would not be destroyed as it would be an ideal means of filtering the English army through to the slaughter. It was an excellent plan tactically, but it did not work out so well. The English attack was certainly blunted by the semicircle of Viking defenders. They stood like a solid wall, sometimes locking their shields like a barrier, at others, when the attack fell back, swinging their deadly axes in blows which went through arm, armour, and body. But the English were just as good, often better. This swinging of a razor-sharp, two-headed axe had more of the gymnast than the traditional soldier to it. The axe could be used as a boxer uses his fists, a short jab, a slippery parry, and an occasional full swing like a boxer's right cross. The strength, dexterity, and skill which was shown with ancient weapons, whether broadsword, axe, or pike, is difficult to comprehend today, but a hint of it may be gained from watching a modern woodman (who can cut and trim logs at a speed which makes a chain-saw seem slow, and who maintains an edge that you could almost shave with).

Hardrada's tactical plan went awry for two reasons. One was that his west-bank army were caught *in situ* without being aware at all that they were part of an intelligent withdrawal exercise. To them it must have seemed that they were merely the unfortunates caught on the far bank while their luckier comrades watched them fight it out. They were, of course, hopelessly outnumbered by Harold's army, who probably had a very fair idea that on the other bank the position would be the exact opposite. But fighting men fight, and that is it. They do not, however, fight any better for feeling that when their more important leaders decide the time is ripe they will skip back over the bridge and give the order for it to be demolished. Even if a man would die rather than retreat it is not encouraging to think that he has no choice in the matter. Doubtless the English were taunting the Vikings by telling them to get back while there was still time. And then, because there is a bend in the river at that point, the English broke through as the Vikings were manoeuvring to close a sudden gap. Suddenly the English were at the bridge and the half-circle of defenders was defending nothing of importance. Orders to retreat were shouted across the river. It is not, however, easy to retreat if you are under heavy and skilled attack; if you turn to look behind you to see where you might go that is when the spear comes through your guard, and you have no need for retreats. As the Vikings fell back they tried to cross the river with their weapons and armour, but the Derwent is deep here, and has steep banks. Many Vikings scrambled ashore but many were undoubtedly drowned in the way that always happened on these occasions – by others leaping down on top of them and treading them under, before perhaps suffering the same fate themselves.

But the bridge had not been destroyed. It is not, of course, easy to destroy a solid bridge instantly, particularly a bridge which is built on stone pillars in the stream. Even unhampered, such a task can take a considerable time, and the Vikings, who were in easy missile range, were anything but unhampered. While attempts were made to destroy the bridge one man leapt forward to hold it. This latter-day Horatius was no ordinary man. Nowadays if you are a superb athlete you win titles, become a national boxing champion perhaps, or achieve worldwide fame in one sphere or another. Then, your only arena was battle, and, scornful of death, you showed your prowess. When your moment came you took it. And what better fate could a warrior wish for? As Macaulay put it, referring to Horatius who held the bridge over the Tiber against Lars Porsena:

> *For how can a man die better*
> *Than facing fearful odds,*
> *For the ashes of his fathers,*
> *And the temple of his Gods?*

But this Norwegian holder of the bridge was defending no city against the invader. He was a soldier who liked a fight and knew a good cause when he saw it. His name is unknown, and his feat is unrecorded in his own country – as might be expected in a lost battle fought far overseas. Doubtless there were others like him. But to the English, trying to cross that bridge, he was memorable enough. He did not trouble to stand in the middle or at the east end of it but, scornfully discounting all the advantages he might have had, stood at the entrance. Had the story come from his own side it would have been difficult to believe that one man could have held up an army, dodged all the missiles which were thrown at him, and remained unscathed. Had he held his position for a moment or two, then given way it would have been credible but he did more – he held it for a considerable time. One chronicler stated that he held it for nine hours; possibly he meant against nine men in succession. At all events he caused the battle to pause. It is clear that there were no archers in the English army or his fate would have been swift.

But in the end it was subterfuge which destroyed him. An Englishman, realizing that this was going to decide the outcome of the battle, and perhaps the fate of the nation, obtained a boat in which he floated downstream. Doubtless the Vikings were unaware of what he was doing till it was too late. Once the boatman was under the bridge he was able to stab a spear through the crevices in the logs. A lucky jab drove the spear into the Viking's leg and as the man staggered he was overwhelmed. It was said that the boat was a swill-tub and that for many hundreds of years afterwards there was a pie-feast each September at Stamford Bridge, in which the pies were made to look like old-fashioned swill-tubs.

As the English army poured across the bridge the Vikings made little attempt to restrain them. Instead they deployed for battle on the rising ground behind them, doubtless intending to drive their foes back into the river wholesale. But the mastery did not lie with the Vikings. Foot by foot they had to give way until the last phase took place on 'Battle Flats' – it still keeps the name – and it was a simple matter of skill, endurance, and determination. Perhaps, at this point the contrasting experience of the two armies told against the Vikings. Their mode of warfare was the fast-moving, intense terror-raid – at which they were superb. Now they were caught in a different mode of warfare – dogged, static, attrition fighting. It was not that they had no stomach for it – they had no experience or flair for it. But to the English it was meat and drink as would be seen on many another battlefield. At last the protagonists were almost face to face. Legend has it that Tostig was killed by Harold himself. At one stage in the battle – some say before it – Harold offered his brother a pardon and an earldom if he should lay down his arms. Tostig is reported as asking what Hardrada would receive and being told 'Seven foot of English earth, for he is taller than most men.' And that was what Hardrada did receive, for he was killed in the battle, possibly by a chance spear.

It was, by any standards, a bloody and heroic battle. The army which had needed over 300 ships to bring it in was able to leave in 24 – 500 men, perhaps, from 6,000. Many of the Vikings were drowned in the last stages of the battle as they tried to leave a lost field, but the fate of the fugitives in that countryside can have been little less preferable, if at all. Harold burned most of their boats at Ricall but, once the fighting was over, was remarkably lenient to the defeated. Prince Olaf of Norway (the son of Hardrada) and the Earl of Orkney were both taken prisoner but both released and sent home. The dead were too numerous to be buried, and most were left to rot where they lay, but a few of the higher ranks were put in a tumulus nearby. Later, when the fields were cultivated, many of the other bones were collected up and interred.

It may seem curious that so much depended on a single wooden bridge. The explanation is soon obvious from a glance at the river. Not only are the banks steep but the bottom is muddy. A few optimistic warriors no doubt tried fording or swimming but their fate was soon a warning to others. The bridge was all important, but Hardrada – unused to that type of tactics – failed to appreciate the fact and lost the battle.

For the English it was a remarkable victory, won against overwhelming odds, for they were outnumbered, far from fresh, and attacking a difficult position. There was no opportunity for tactical skill, only for sheer bloody fighting. Probably they won through endurance and stamina. The Vikings had arrived by sea, where they had had all their exercise at the oars. Since landing they had had an easy battle and little marching. By contrast the English were as hard as nails, capable of marching 200 miles, then doing another eighteen in the space of about twelve hours. Stamford Bridge was, above all else, a lesson in the importance of battle-fitness.

The Battle of the Standard (Northallerton)

22 August 1138

The Battle of the Standard, which took place just three miles north of Northallerton, Yorkshire, was one of the most extraordinary battles in English history. It occurred near the beginning of the most anarchic reign England has ever seen, for though the Wars of the Roses and the Civil War both tore the country apart, neither caused the widespread misery and dislocation of King Stephen's reign, aptly called 'the nineteen long winters when God and his saints slept'.

The battle at Northallerton was a contest of English against Scots but it was related to causes other than border warfare. In common with many battles and conflicts, the root causes were very simple and can be described briefly.

They originated when William the Conqueror brought over a host of self-seeking adventurers in 1066 and won the Battle of Hastings with their aid. He himself was strong enough to control his followers and wise enough to reward them with estates and tasks which would keep them out of mischief. His successor, William Rufus, achieved much the same stability by spectacular debaucheries during his short reign (1087–1100). The new occupant of the throne – a grasping opportunist – was Henry I; and he was shrewd enough to keep his barons in order, although at that time, some fifty years after Hastings, they were sufficiently stable on their estates to be ambitious and greedy. And in an age when boredom was the greatest enemy, and warfare was the only form of recreation, outlet for ambition, and admired activity, it was inevitable that there would be immense turmoil if ever there was any relaxation in the strong grip of the monarch. That grip might be exercised by a combination of terror, blandishment, and bribery but it needed to be strong in all three of them. When Stephen came to the throne he was in the unfortunate – thus, weak – position of being an elected king. His claim was as good as Henry's daughter, Matilda – to whom he had been preferred in spite of Henry I's dying wish – but the fact that his right to the throne was arguable gave a semblance of justice to the manoeuvrings of every self-seeking baron in the land. The full horrors were not seen for some time, but later in the reign we have a gruesome chronicle of murder, torture, and general brutality. All this could have been checked had Stephen been firm, but he was generous to the point of idiocy, extravagant to the point of bank-ruptcy, and naïve beyond all recognized standards. His only saving grace was his outstanding personal courage.

Matilda, Henry I's daughter, whose claim to the throne had been set on one side in favour of Stephen's, had formidable allies. One was David, King of Scotland, the other was her half-brother, Robert, Earl of Gloucester. Both were undoubtedly honest, which is more than can be said for many of those who fought with them.

David crossed the Tweed and headed south in the summer of 1138. He had a large, wild army, and his ostensible reason for the expedition was to make Stephen restore to him the counties of Huntingdonshire and Northamptonshire which his family had forfeited in William the Conqueror's reign. The claim was some-what tenuous but doubtless David thought he could honour a bond to see Matilda on the throne and also acquire handsome slices of territory for himself. The reaction of the north country to the arrival of thousands of marauding Scots was predictable; they had seen it all before and did not believe the invaders had any war aims except plunder. This cynical view was soon shown to be only too correct; the Scots ravaged Northumberland and north Yorkshire so savagely that it was obvious to all that this was yet another border raid on a massive scale, lasting longer, and better organized than most. If it were not checked, however, it could well become something more serious, that is a wild, undisciplined host of invaders who would eventually move south and create such a wave of destruction that the whole country would be set back several hundred years. Nothing so dangerous had ever been seen in England, not even with the Saxons and the Vikings; to estimate its effects one had to look to the invaders of the Dark Ages in Europe.

Fortunately for England there was a man available to check the onslaught, unsuited though he seemed for such a task. This was Thurstan, Archbishop of York. He was a man of advanced age, crippled, and ill at the time of the invasion. Nevertheless he would have taken part in the actual fighting if he had been able to force his deformed limbs into a suit of armour. Apart from his archbishopric he held the title of Lieutenant of the North, and, as the King's deputy by virtue of this appointment, he soon set about his task. With astonishing speed – possibly because bad news travels fast – he recruited an army from everyone in the immediate neighbourhood and from many further south who knew that their fate too was at stake. It is said that he enjoined his village priests to preach that this was a holy war; the appeal of a holy war is that if you fight in it you obtain remission for sins. Men fighting in holy wars tend to win or are defeated only at great cost. Many of the barons who rallied to Thurstan's side bore names renowned in warfare. They included

Albemarle, Ferrers, de Lacy, de Mowbray, de Courcy, and two names more famed in Scottish history than English, Bruce and Balliol. The rallying point was York and there Thurstan, a master of the whole art of war if ever there was one, provided a remarkable banner for them to carry into action. This was the redoubtable 'standard' which gave the battle its name. It was mounted on a four-wheeled wagon. At the top of the mast was a pyx containing a consecrated wafer, and from the two arms of the cross hung the banners of St Peter of York, St John of Beverley, St Wilfrid of Ripon, and St Cuthbert of Durham. A host of clergy accompanied the army.

Thurstan's cavalcade moved northwards from York like an avenging crusade. It halted at Thirsk, and Bruce and Balliol went out to parley with the Scottish king, and to offer him the earldom of Northumbria, which he had already claimed as his right. It is said that David, who knew that the north of England was in terror of his army, merely laughed scornfully. Bruce and Balliol were not impressed, and before they left to return to the English lines formally renounced their fealty to the Scottish king. When they arrived back with their bad news, Thurstan's army was neither surprised nor discomfited, but promptly set off towards Northallerton, marched through the township, and arrived at Cowton Moor three miles north; at the time the Scots were approaching the same area.

The battlefield is easily reached, for the A167 runs through it, and there is a monument to the right of the road. It covers a considerable area, as would be necessary with the numbers involved, perhaps 15,000 Scots and supporters, possibly a thousand or so less English. Naturally enough, some of the details of so ancient a battle have been lost in the ensuing eight hundred years but it is not difficult to

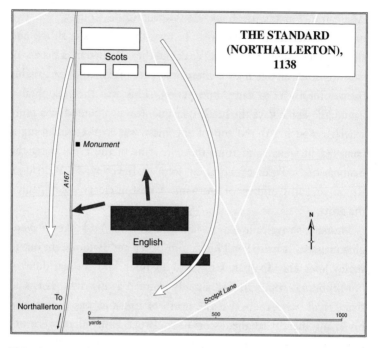

Take the A167 from Northallerton and after three miles the battle monument can be seen on the right of the road. By turning right at the top of this road you can make a complete circuit of the battlefield. Scotpit Lane runs east–west across the southern end of the battlefield. (North Yorkshire)

reconstruct the sequence from an examination of the battlefield. The Standard was placed on the hill to the north-east of the monument. As the battle is described as having taken place 'early in the morning', this would probably be soon after first light, perhaps between 5 and 6 a.m. Doubtless each side heard the other was on the move and both moved early to obtain an advantageous position in the coming conflict. In the event, there was little advantage to either side, but the Standard was placed at a conspicuous point, and was an encouragement to the English.

Both sides adopted the same formation; the front line were archers, who would discharge their arrows and then resort to other weapons; the second row consisted of spearmen; and the third rank was made up of knights and dismounted men-at-arms. In the first instance, David had wished to put armoured knights among the archers in his front line but his dispositions were wrecked by the men of Galloway who insisted on taking the foremost point in the battle, ahead of the Scottish centre. These Galwegians were a fearsome sight; they fought nearly naked, and their ferocity was proverbial. On the right of the Scottish line was a mixed force commanded by Prince Henry of Scotland, and on the left, a contingent commanded by Earl Alan of Percy. King David, of course, took the centre.

The battle was crude in the extreme. There was no kind of strategy or tactics. As the two armies rushed at each other the English archers discharged point blank into the oncoming Galwegians. The effect of this was almost as severe as a volley of rifle fire. It seemed to be utterly unexpected by the Galwegians who had expected to come to close quarters and hack their way to victory.

The effect of this volley went far beyond what might have been expected. The Galwegians, checked by fearful slaughter in their ranks, but unable to come close enough to the archers to stop them, resorted to trying to fall back out of range. Unfortunately for their efforts, their leader, the Earl of Lothian, was killed in the hottest part of the fire and the leaderless division staggered and plunged backwards in hopeless confusion. Although unaccustomed to such intensity of close-quarter arrow fire, they knew that if they retired fifty yards or so they would be out of its range. But, as so often happened on other battlefields, as the front line staggered backwards it tangled itself with the second line and the two, hopelessly confused, presented a superb target to the advancing English. The result, in a short space of time, was that an enormous hole had been punched in the Scottish centre and only the third line, which had a stiffening of French and English knights in it – mercenaries, of course – stood firm. The Galwegians are said to have fled from the battlefield, but if so they must have got out to the flanks for they would certainly not have been able to break through their own rear lines.

But the Scots were by no means finished. Prince Henry, seeing the confusion in the centre, rallied the best of his army and charged down the slope on to the left wing of the English army. The ground he covered – the visitor will note – is low-lying and wet, and by the time the impetus of the charge was exhausted he and his men would be ripe for slaughter. There were, of course, well over 20,000 men on the battlefield and it must have been impossible to know at the time which way the tide was turning. Seeing the Scots advancing again, many of the waverers would come back in, some from the flanks, some from behind. The English centre, fresh from its initial victory would turn to its left flank and follow Prince Henry's charge. The Scots, blocked at the front, floundering on wet slippery ground – even in August – would then be attacked from flank and rear. This accounts for the slaughter which took place in Scotpit Lane, where bones and pieces of weapons were to be found many years afterwards. The Scots, now outnumbered, were hopelessly trapped between the two halves of the English army. The Scots were almost their own worst enemies, for wherever there was fighting they plunged in, regardless of whether they were outnumbered or outmanoeuvred. So fierce was the fighting that King David and Prince Henry were able to slip away back to their horses and leave the lost battle. Only a few of their followers attempted to emulate them; the most part were content to carry on fighting in a lost battle for the sheer joy of combat. It is said that 10,000 men were killed that day, most of them Scots, but in addition fifty Scottish knights were taken prisoner. The only notable Englishman to be killed was de Lacy.

This battle has been regarded as somewhat of a mystery for centuries, and this is because the main grave-pits are behind the English position, although the English won. As we have seen, the explanation is simple enough. Scotpit Lane was probably a sunken road. As such, it may have been used as a defensive ditch by the English, or it may have been left for the Scots to fall into on their charge. Undoubtedly it played a bigger part in the battle than being a mere cemetery. Even today it has a slightly macabre look.

The Battle of Boroughbridge

16 March 1322

The years between the Battle of the Standard in 1138 and the Battle of Boroughbridge in 1322 saw many other conflicts at home and abroad, but at the beginning of the fourteenth century we find the same problems unsolved. Eight years before Boroughbridge the English army had been cut to pieces at Bannockburn, an event which would have seemed unthinkable in the previous reign (that of Edward I). There was no real threat to the throne from Scotland yet, but there was more than a hint that the anarchy which had not been seen for two hundred years in England might now be at the point of returning.

Over and over again in English history a pattern of events repeated itself. Whenever there was a strong king there was military conquest and firm government; but also a depleted treasury; and inevitably that strong king was followed by a weak one whose reign verged on anarchy. In the twelfth and thirteenth centuries strong King Richard I, who spent nine-tenths of his life fighting futile wars abroad but ruled over a stable country by sheer prestige, was followed by vacillating King John whose inconsistencies brought chaos. In the fourteenth century strong Edward I was followed by his weak son, Edward II, and later the country would see the might of Edward III dissipated by Richard II. The most dramatic events in this sequence occurred in the fifteenth century when the great conqueror Henry V left an infant son who grew up as Henry VI and was murdered in the Wars of the Roses.

Edward II, who reigned from 1307–1327, would have been a most unsuitable occupant for any throne. His father had exemplified all the military skills and virtues, his mother was a paragon among women. Edward II, however, was idle, obstinate, and feckless, sometimes cruel, homosexual; and attracted to friends who went out of their way to make enemies out of potential allies.

Boroughbridge was the result of one of the few occasions when the king showed any real purpose. His motive was purely revenge. His first and most irritating favourite had been Piers Gaveston, who had a trying habit of applying appropriate nicknames to leading nobles. The Earl of Lancaster was called, not inappropriately, 'the Actor', the Earl of Pembroke, 'Joseph the Jew', and the Earl of Warwick 'the Black Dog of Arden'. However, the three earls had the last laugh, for Warwick and Lancaster had Gaveston beheaded without any pretext but revenge. Edward II was compelled to pardon his friend's murderers for he had other and greater troubles on his hands at the time. All was in vain, however, for sheer incompetence caused him to lose the battle of Bannockburn although his army outnumbered the Scots two to one. But even the humiliation of Bannockburn did not cause him to forget his craving for revenge. To some extent it fostered it; it certainly aided him in achieving it. After Bannockburn Edward was virtually dethroned, and put under supervision. Lancaster, who had not even accompanied him to the battle, was put in charge of the administration. In his seven years of almost absolute power, Lancaster inevitably made many enemies. Nevertheless, it was not until 1320 that the lethargic Edward saw his opportunity. It occurred when Baron Baddlesmere refused Edward's wife, Queen Isabella, entrance to Leeds Castle in Kent. (The castle has no connection with Leeds in Yorkshire but both places derive their name from the Anglo-Saxon word for a stream.) Isabella, who later connived at Edward's murder and lived in open adultery with his supplanter, had appeared one night at the castle with an arrogant retinue and demanded entry. Admission was refused by the castellan, and the Queen gave orders to attack. The attack was repelled. (Centuries later a body was dug up near the entrance to the castle. Although the feet were missing it still measured 6ft 3in.)

Edward stirred himself to action, raised an army and forced the very strong castle to surrender in eight days. He was now full of confidence. Realizing it was now or never if he was to regain power, he set out to capture Lancaster and his friends. The barons were not, however, prepared to be an easy prey and called up their own supporters. Almost immediately there was a state of civil war.

But the initiative, the power, and the luck lay with Edward. He captured Hereford and Gloucester, which were centres of baronial power, and called out a royal muster at Coventry. Lancaster, however, knowing that he had everything to gain and nothing to lose, assembled an army at Doncaster and set off south. He did not get far. First he lost most of his baggage in a flooded stream (a disconcerting event, as King John had found just over a hundred years earlier), then he was by-passed at Burton-on-Trent, where he held the bridge, but overlooked the ford. Realizing that he was outnumbered at this point as well as outflanked, Lancaster hurried back north in search of reinforcements. His hasty move was criticized, for it caused the prompt surrender of Kenilworth and Tutbury castles and so alarmed one of his most valued supporters, Robert de Holland, that he changed sides and joined the King's army at Derby. Lancaster's position was weakening daily. His confederates were undisciplined but self-opinionated. It is said that

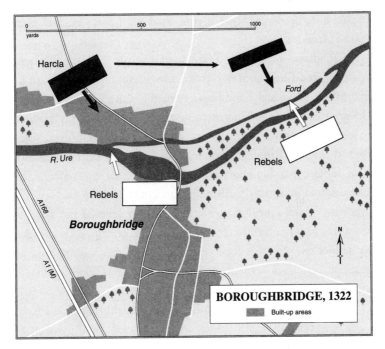

Boroughbridge is seventeen miles north-west of York on the A1. Visitors to the battlefield should not miss the opportunity to look at the old Roman city of Aldborough. (North Yorkshire)

one of them drew a knife on him in one of their 'councils of war'. Lancaster himself wanted to make a stand at Pontefract, where there was a strong though by no means impregnable castle, but his supporters all urged him to fall back to Dunstanburgh, which he owned, and where they might be joined by the Scots, who would be very happy to embarrass the English monarch by supporting a rebel faction. Reluctantly, and against his better judgment, Lancaster agreed. His army crossed the Aire at Castleford, and the Wharfe at Wetherby. It was then *en route* to cross the Ure at Boroughbridge.

Meanwhile, however, other events, fatal for Lancaster, had been taking place.

Sir Andrew de Harcla, Warden of Carlisle and the Western Marches, remained loyal to Edward. On receipt of the royal writ he had called out an army and began to march south with it. He heard the news of Lancaster's northern march but at first merely planned to join the royal army and take orders. On 15 March however, when he had reached Ripon, he learned that Lancaster's army was now close by and was heading for Boroughbridge, six miles away. The Ure was said to be sixty yards wide at this time, and the road lay over a narrow wooden bridge, so the opportunity seemed too good to miss. There was a ford to the right of the bridge, which also needed to be blocked. Not the least of the effects of this move would be surprise, for Lancaster had no idea that Harcla was opposing him at all, let alone with such skill.

Although, like every town in Britain, Boroughbridge has altered with the years, it is still sufficiently unchanged for the visitor to visualize the battle clearly. Just under a mile east of Boroughbridge lies Aldborough, the old Roman town of Isurium, and this too had its influence on the battle, for the Romans had used the Milby ford to the east of Boroughbridge.

The extent of Lancaster's surprise may be gauged from the fact that his men were already finding billets in the town before they (and he) realized their onward path was blocked. The outlook for his army was ominous; not only was the way ahead full of enemy, and his force partially surrounded, but he knew only too well that Edward's other loyal supporters, the Earls of Kent and Surrey, were close on his rear. His immediate reaction was diplomatic rather than military. He sent a messenger to Harcla and met him for a lengthy discussion. In the past they had been good friends, and Harcla had benefited from the friendship. Strong inducements to change sides were offered to Harcla, but in vain. Harcla was no staunch loyalist – for a year later he made a fatal mistake which led to his somewhat barbarous execution – but at this moment he was not prepared to take the risk of joining an obviously losing side.

At the end of the conference, Lancaster cursed Harcla for a traitor and foretold that he would have an appropriate death. As Harcla was subsequently hanged, drawn and quartered, the prophecy proved correct but whether the prophecy was ascribed to Lancaster before or after the event is doubtful. With Lancaster's curses ringing in his ears, Harcla then returned to his own side of the river; hardly had he crossed than Lancaster's men tried to follow. But Harcla's archers were alert to this possibility, and though there was a brisk exchange of arrows it seemed that there was now a stalemate.

But Lancaster could not let such a position last. He needed to cross the Ure before Kent and Surrey closed on his army from behind. The initiative was taken by Humphrey de Bohun, Earl of Hereford. He led a charge across the bridge but was killed by a spear-thrust from underneath. The spearman was a Welshman who had doubtless never heard of Stamford Bridge nor his Saxon predecessor some three hundred years before. Next to fall was Clifford, and, somewhat disconcerted with two of its foremost leaders gone, the rebel army fell back from the bridge. Meanwhile Lancaster had turned to the ford where he hoped to force a passage. But here again the odds were against him. Harcla had anticipated the move and positioned his archers to cover every inch of the crossing. As the first party of Lancaster's men reached the river every arrow found a target. It was said that not a single horse managed to wet its feet in the river before it or its rider was hit by the deadly Welsh bowmen. Many of Lancaster's most valuable and influential supporters fell here, men like Lovell, Ellington, and Bernefield, whom he could ill afford to spare. But Lancaster was no coward, nor novice. Once again he threw his army at the ford, this time more widely dispersed and with a different timing. It made no difference. The bowmen had the whole area ranged to a yard; their bows might have been zeroed to their targets, so deadly and accurate were they. Lancaster's men began to waver, and some had clearly deserted: they had little wish to face that suicidal river crossing and then try to force their way up a bank protected by Cumbrian pikemen. But, by some unknown means, Lancaster was able to obtain a truce from Harcla and the following night it was Harcla who remained on the defensive while Lancaster's men slept peacefully, though perhaps apprehensively, in the town. During the night Harcla received further reinforcements from Yorkshire, brought in by the High Sheriff of that county, and the next day the two crossed the bridge and called on Lancaster to surrender. It was a bitter pill for a man who had ruled England like a king for nearly eight years, but there was no visible alternative; there was no fighting in which he could die spectacularly. He did not give in immediately for he thought he could find sanctuary in the chapel. Sanctuary was not, however, obtainable in every religious building, as Lancaster abruptly realized; and he was taken out and was soon on his way to Pontefract. 'The richest man in England' now dressed in an old gown was given a summary trial and, having been led to his execution on a 'lean white jade', was beheaded. Had he been less well-connected – for he was Edward ii's cousin – he would probably have been drawn and quartered in public. Harcla did not survive him long; for he changed sides unwisely in the Scottish wars and met a traitor's fate. But whatever his morals, Harcla was a tactician of the highest class, as Lancaster saw only too well at Boroughbridge.

The battle was commemorated by a stone pillar which stood for many years in the main street of Boroughbridge. In 1852, for some unknown reason, the monument was removed to Aldborough, where it still stands. Visitors to the Boroughbridge battlefield should not miss the opportunity to look at the old Roman city of Aldborough.

The Battle of Otterburn

19 August 1388

In a long series of desperate border battles one of the most renowned was that of Otterburn. It was described extensively by Sir John Froissart, the French chronicler, who had spoken to many of those who had fought on each side; it was also the subject of heroic ballads. A number of these ballads were collected up in the mid-seventeenth century, and were published a hundred years later by Bishop Percy in 1765 as Percy's *Reliques of Ancient Poetry*. Two of them are 'The Ancient Ballad of Chevy-Chase' and 'The Battle of Otterbourne'. Both describe aspects of the same battle. Sir Philip Sidney, who lived between 1554 and 1586, knew them well and wrote 'I never heard the old song of Percy and Douglas that I found not my heart moved more than with a trumpet; and yet is it sung by some blind Crouder, with no rougher voice than rude style; which being so evil aparalled in the dust and cobwebs of that uncivil age, what would it work trimmed in the gorgeous eloquence of Pindar.'

For this encounter to be celebrated in verse and song several hundred years later it must have been an outstanding piece of bloody warfare even for those days and for that area. It is not perhaps generally realized that when the border Scots and English were not fighting each other they were usually fighting equally fiercely among themselves. The picture of a peaceful countryside stirred to arms by an invader was less true than quarrelsome families having temporarily to forget their enmities and unite against a foe who might exterminate them all. The dirk – known very appropriately as 'the widow-maker' – would merely be turned towards a different target till the greater danger was past; the English, of course, were no less fierce and turbulent than their foes across the border.

However, Otterburn was also part of a wider conflict, which may be outlined briefly. We described how, at Boroughbridge, Edward's supporters were victorious and restored him to power. This state of affairs did not last long, and through apathy and stupidity he soon fell victim to the treachery and ruthlessness of the other side. Eventually he was murdered in Berkeley Castle. His son, Edward III, was of a very different character, and proved as great a warrior as his grandfather, Edward I. Edward III won the great battles of Crécy and Poitiers, but fell into premature senile decay. His son, the Black Prince, had predeceased him, so the next king was Richard II, a boy of ten. He, too, would be murdered after reigning twenty-two years, and the details of this crime, which took place at Pontefract Castle, would be a better kept secret than Edward II's death at Berkeley. But in 1388, when Otterburn was fought, Richard was far away and having his first brush with his rebellious subjects. The news of the internal troubles of England had reached Scotland and it seemed an ideal time for a border foray, if not for a full-scale war. The Scots, of course, would have been extremely unwise if they had not seized every opportunity to improve their military position against the English, and were always delighted to do so.

The Scottish army was mustered at Jedburgh on 5 August 1388. In order for the war plans to be kept entirely secret, the leaders resorted to a nearby church to confer. However, the English were not unaware of the preparations going on on the other side of the border and sent along a squire to obtain what information he could. The squire, who had disguised himself suitably, entered the church with the Scottish chieftains, and heard all their plans, but, when he returned to where he had tethered his horse, found it had been stolen. Naturally enough, he did not wish to draw attention to himself by making vociferous enquiries so instead he set off for England as he was. However, the spectacle of a man in boots and spurs setting off to invade England on his own was a little too obvious, and in a short time he had been overhauled, brought back, and questioned. In the persuasive way which medieval interrogators had, they encouraged him to confide in them the English plans. The English, he told them, had only a small army, and did not therefore wish for a straight confrontation. Instead, they planned to let the Scots move first, then by-pass them, and wreak havoc in Scotland behind. This policy would doubtless bring the Scots headlong back, and give the English time to collect a larger army against further trouble. It was, however, vital to the plan to know the Scottish invasion route; if they came through Cumberland the English planned to invade by Berwick, but if the Scots chose the eastern route the English would head up through the western side.

Greatly pleased by this information about the English strategic planning, the Scots resolved to thwart it by splitting their army in two and invading on both sides simultaneously. One half therefore set off for Carlisle, led by the Earl of Fife; the other, which consisted of 3,000 men-at-arms and 2,000 infantry, set off towards Durham. This eastern army was led by the young Earl of Douglas. Both Scottish armies were very well equipped and armed, having just received a large consignment of arms from France. Young Douglas's army pushed rapidly through Northumberland, scarcely pausing to destroy, but, when they reached the outskirts of Durham, it was a different story. There the Scots slaughtered, burned, and pillaged, and then returned towards Scotland with their spoils. The raid had succeeded brilliantly. The English, thinking this was the vanguard of the entire Scottish army, had planned to check them at some point in south Durham or north Yorkshire, and were taken by surprise by the tactics pursued by the Scots.

So far the Scots had all the initiative, and, on the way back, although burdened with loot and spoils, decided to take Newcastle. Newcastle was lightly held, although its commander, Sir Henry Percy, had hastily put it into a state of defence. The Percy family of Alnwick Castle were old rivals of the Douglases, and any encounter between the two countries was almost certain to bring these two antagonists face to face. This happened at Newcastle where the Scots failed to take the town but where Douglas succeeded in capturing Percy's pennon. The pennon was a long triangular flag carried on a lance; it served as a rallying-point for a knight's followers. If he was promoted on the field of battle, the point would be cut off, making it a banner, and he would become a 'banneret'.[1] The loss of a pennon was a serious matter, as Douglas well knew, and in a spirit of chivalry which was more often talked about than seen, he decided to give Percy a chance to regain it. He did not therefore hurry back to Scotland but instead paused at Otterburn and attacked the castle. His attempt was futile, for Otterburn Castle required proper siege equipment; but even then Douglas did not move on. Instead, he cut down trees and made a camp.

The site of Douglas's camp was just to the north-west of Holt wood, on a hill containing some ancient earthworks.

Douglas's delay may have had more to it than chivalry. Possibly his great burden of plunder was impossible to move quickly; perhaps

---

1 There was no connection with baronet, which was a rank invented several hundred years later.

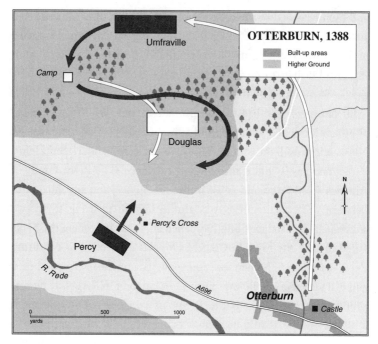

OTTERBURN, 1388

Built-up areas
Higher Ground

Umfraville

Camp

Douglas

N

Percy's Cross

Percy

R. Rede

A696

Otterburn

Castle

0   500   1000
yards

Otterburn is thirty-two miles from Newcastle on the A696. The battlefield is marked by Percy's Cross. (Northumberland)

he decided that if Percy wished to catch him up he could lose more than a pennon. Probably, too, he was reluctant to leave England without having one more good wholehearted fight.

Percy seems to have behaved with unexpected wisdom and caution. Perhaps he thought he was being drawn into an ambush; perhaps, however, he was merely waiting to assemble an adequate number of troops. He was apparently surprised to find the Scots had made so little progress.

By now the armies on this side were evenly matched numerically, though the Scots had the advantage in equipment.

Percy, once he had decided the time was right, hesitated no more. He arrived at the Scottish camp towards evening on the 19th. It was well-concealed in the woods and he did not realize how close he was to it till the alarm was given. According to Froissart, Percy did not reach the camp till after sunset and first saw it by moonlight; this is unlikely, as medieval armies, like campers, usually liked to settle down for the night while there was still light enough to see what they were doing, unless there was some good reason to do otherwise. Percy, however, took an unusual step in that he decided on a night attack. Night attacks can be devastating to the opposition when they are accompanied by surprise, but they can be disastrous to the attacker who may fall into unseen natural traps, and also do as much damage in the dark to his own side as to the opposition.

Percy, perhaps because he was not entirely confident that Douglas might not receive reinforcements if the battle was delayed, decided on the somewhat ambitious plan of a two-pronged attack. One wing went round to the rear of Douglas's camp, led by the Umfravilles, the other, led by himself, attacked from the front. Unfortunately, the camp Percy attacked was not the main one at all but a baggage pound. Its occupants were soon slaughtered but in the time this took Douglas had led a large detachment round to the English right, skilfully avoided the Umfravilles who had circled too far to the north. Just when it seemed that the English were winning, Douglas hurled himself on to their flank. The fighting now became bitterer than ever, but the English, although now hard pressed, fought with relentless courage. The sudden appearance of armed men, gleaming in the moonlight as they emerged from the trees, must have been an awesome sight, but a ghostly look is no proof against a sword-cut. Owing to the Umfravilles' error, the English were probably out-numbered in the main fight but soon the Umfraville party corrected its bearings and came to the Scottish camp. It was, by now, empty, so they left a guard – all of whom were slaughtered by the Scots later – and tried to find the others in the darkness and general confusion. Again, however, they took a wrong direction and instead of coming on to the rear of the Scots he arrived on the right of the now much-battered English. The only time there was a pause in this bizarre conflict was when the moon was clouded over. But, in the brighter intervals, the English numbers were now beginning to tell. Douglas, however, at this point showed what a leader can do. Swinging his battle-axe he carved a path into the English army. He fell from four wounds but the inspiration was enough to set the Scots surging forward and the English reeling back. Sir Henry Percy and his brother, Sir Ralph, were both wounded and taken prisoner. The fighting still went on, but in small groups only.

The battle continued for most of the night and the next day the victorious Scots were hunting the English for prisoners worth a ransom. It was said that the poorest were allowed to go free which, if true, would make this unique in medieval battles.

Percy had attacked too soon, for the next day the Bishop of Durham came up with several thousand reinforcements. However, with their leaders captured, the heart had gone out of the English army and after a few manoeuvres the Bishop retired, leaving the Scots unmolested.

Various explanations are given for the English defeat, and all are credible. One was that after a march of thirty-two miles they had not the strength for a prolonged night battle; another is that they could not use their longbows in the dark; yet another is that the Scots had better armour and equipment for hand-to-hand work. But the most probable reason was that in an indescribably tough battle the better-trained army won. The Scots had been in the field for most of

August, constantly fighting and on the move; the English in contrast were partly hastily-summoned levies. Froissart said of it: 'Of all the battles and encounterings that I have made mention of heretofore in all this history, great or small, this battle that I treat of now was one of the sorest and best foughten without cowardice or faint hearts.'

Otterburn, as Percy's army knew, is thirty-two miles from Newcastle (on the A696). The 'Percy Cross', a monolith, marks the battlefield. Perhaps it should more appropriately have been called the Douglas stone for he must have been killed close by.

The Battle of Wakefield

31 December 1460

The Battle of Wakefield was an unexpected, but extremely important, victory of the Lancastrians over the Yorkists in the Wars of the Roses. The term 'Wars of the Roses' refers to the series of increasingly bloodthirsty battles which took place between 1455 and 1485. Even after 1485 there were attempts to keep the conflict open.[1] Many historians consider that the Wars of the Roses were really over by 1471, for after that year there was an interval of fourteen years till the next major battle. However, the contest was not resolved in 1471; but for the time being no one was strong enough to challenge the holder of the throne.

During the first part of the wars, battle succeeded battle with steady frequency, and when one side was victorious the other knew its turn would come before long. The explanation of these extraordinary vicissitudes lies in the background to the conflict. Although with surprising consistency a strong king had been succeeded by a weaker one – often the former monarch's own son – the situation had never been as disastrous as when the warrior king, Henry v, died on a campaign in 1422 and the next heir was less than a year old. Worse was to come, for when the new king, Henry vi, came of age he was already showing signs of the insanity which was later to

1 As described in 'The Battle of Stoke Field' in *British Battlefields: The South.*

dominate his life. He was undoubtedly murdered at the end of his chaotic reign but the secret of how and when it happened was well kept. But it was not the folly and insanity alone of Henry VI which caused the disaster of the Wars of the Roses; it was also the underlying weakness of his claim to the throne. This stemmed from the deposition and murder of Richard II by his cousin, who became Henry IV. Richard was a fool, and also arrogant, but can scarcely be said to have deserved his mysterious fate in Pontefract Castle. However, when his cousin took the throne there was bound to be a challenge to the line sooner or later. It did not come in Henry IV's reign, although he had other troubles to contend with, and it was smothered during Henry V's reign, for he was a brilliant and successful warrior king; it was even delayed in the reign of Henry VI for over thirty years, but when it came it tore England apart, and exterminated the leaders of many powerful families.

As well as the disruptive effect of weak sons following strong fathers, there was the even more disturbing factor of the weak sons choosing unsuitable friends. People are prepared to put up with a monarch's weaknesses but they are not so ready to accept the activities – and insults – of his cronies. As Henry VI's favourites had apparently contributed to the loss of France, it would have been wise for him to have chosen differently when their incompetence was brought home to him. But Henry, like many a weak man, was also obstinate. In 1453 he was loyally adhering to the Duke of Somerset although a wiser man would have replaced that unpopular but successful figure. In 1453, however, the king went mad. It seemed almost too good to be true – and it was. Henry VI's cousin, the Duke of York, who might be said to have had a better right to the throne than Henry, was promptly elected Protector of the Realm, the unpopular Somerset was put in prison, and it seemed as if all would be well, as York would soon succeed to the throne. Unfortunately for these hopeful thoughts, two things upset the prognostication. One was that Henry's wife, Queen Margaret, produced a son after nine years of barren marriage; the other was that Henry recovered his sanity after eighteen months' madness. Now, the position was worse than ever. Prompted by Margaret, who had an almost psychopathic hatred for the well-meaning York, Henry dismissed the Protector from office, and in his place put Somerset, who had been incarcerated in the Tower of London during York's period of power.

York was slow to anger but this was too much. He conferred with his friends and marched towards London. At the first Battle of St Albans he was completely victorious, and Somerset was killed. This, however, was not the end of the matter but only the beginning. Margaret was determined to remove York and his line from the scene so as to ensure that there could be no obstacle to her own son's taking the throne when Henry vi died. Battle then succeeded battle, but on 10 July 1460 the Yorkists won a crushing victory at Northampton which seemed to put the issue beyond doubt. Many people now felt that the country should be stabilized by York taking the throne. It was said, in support of this policy, that Margaret's son had been fathered by someone other than Henry vi, and that York would have to succeed sooner or later.

This was all very tidy and neat but it reckoned without Margaret who, after Northampton, had fled to the north where she knew she had friends. They included notable fighting names already mentioned elsewhere on other pages – the Percys, the Nevilles, the Cliffords, Dacre, and lesser fry. The army she assembled was said to number 10,000 (some gave it nearly twice that number), and it should be borne in mind that these northern soldiers had spent most of their lives fighting in one war or another. The problem was not how to make them fight and win, but how to control them when they were not so engaged. Their great asset seems to have been dash and mobility, and, though their opponents were by no means sluggish, it was Margaret's ability to exploit these qualities which brought her victory on several occasions. Margaret had an interesting combination of characteristics: she was French, she was a young woman, she had an astute tactical brain, and she was relentlessly and ruthlessly determined. Although not a very attractive character, she earns our admiration for her physical stamina, and unstoppable determination. When Margaret was finally beaten, eleven years later, it was because she had played every card in her hand but lost every trick.

But Wakefield was the hour of her triumph. Six months before, she had been fleeing for her life; now she had an army, perhaps 2,000 stronger than York's. York had, in fact, badly miscalculated. He should have gone on after the victory of Northampton and led the armies himself to the north. There a few minor battles would probably have finished the Lancastrians for good. Instead he dallied in London, trying to legalize his position in Parliament. When he decided he must move he made the mistake of under-rating his opponents. His eldest son was occupied in North Wales, where Welsh Lancastrian sympathizers were becoming active, but would have been better employed with the main force. York appears to have been very careless – or perhaps preoccupied – for a large contingent of Lancastrian supporters from the West Country marched right across the West Midlands to join Queen Margaret's army at Pontefract. Margaret was quietly optimistic about the result but after her unfortunate and dangerous experiences following the Lancastrian defeat at Northampton she decided to stay in Scotland until results were announced.

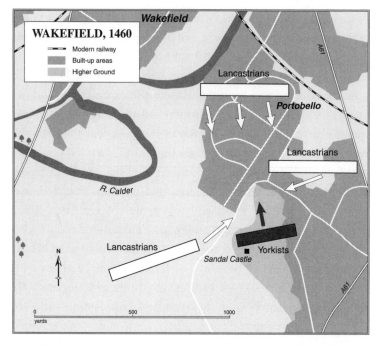

The battle took place under the shadow of Sandal Castle, two miles south of Wakefield. Visitors should turn off the A61 at Castle road. The best view is from the castle mound. (West Yorkshire)

York set out north on 9 December. On 16 December his vanguard brushed with the West Country army at Worksop. York's men were apparently taken by surprise, for many of his troops were killed. However, even if York had known the West Countrymen were marching to Pontefract he could hardly have expected to meet them in Worksop. His own destination was Sandal Castle, two miles south of Wakefield. This once powerful castle is now an earth mound, but excavations are now bringing to light some of the stonework which has been obscured for centuries; it is an impressive sight. Sandal

Castle was destroyed by the Roundheads in 1643, after surrendering, and its former glories are not easily visualized. But in 1460 it was immensely strong and when York reached it he may have been glad of the fact; when he sent probes towards the Lancastrian camp they had the worst of it in an encounter with the Lancastrians and were pursued right up to and into Sandal Castle. York therefore decided to take no immediate action but to sit tight and wait for reinforcements.

But the Lancastrians had sized up the situation well, and also knew the character of the men they were opposing. Sandal Castle was not provisioned to victual an army some 8,000 strong and the Lancastrians had ensured there would not be much gain in foraging in the countryside. However, they had not the siege artillery to break a way into the castle, and if they waited to starve it out, even if only for a few days, half their unpredictable army might wander off elsewhere. Then, when York's son, Edward, brought up reinforcements from the Welsh border it might be the Lancastrian turn to be well outnumbered. They may not have known how short of provisions York really was but they probably hazarded a useful guess.

The battle took place on the open space between the castle and the River Calder which slopes fairly gently. This was then known as Wakefield Green.

The surrounding ground was heavily wooded, and this fact enabled the Lancastrians to practise a very simple deception. They split their army into two halves and set one marching towards the castle as if prepared to make an all-out assault. The other was concealed in the surrounding woods, where it took up positions unobtrusively.

The arrival of a much smaller Lancastrian army than he had

expected was a welcome sight to York, and without delay he decided to demolish this threat to his comfort and stomach. The Lancastrians seemed to show no great appetite for a fight, relying on defensive work by the archers, and giving way as the Yorkists approached. York's army was, of course, being drawn further and further from the castle. Then at last the Lancastrians stood. As the two armies became locked in combat the rest of the Lancastrian army suddenly appeared from the flanks and rear, and hurled themselves on to York's surprised and outnumbered army. The timing was apparently perfect, and the battle was over in half an hour.

Tactically, this was the most unusual battle for medieval times. Its techniques were almost modern. They included subterfuge in luring the Yorkists out of the castle into an ambush, surprise and perfect timing in the flank attacks, and concentration of force at the right place and the right time.

York was killed, but whether in the battle or after it is not known. The story which evoked the most horror was the death of the young Earl of Rutland, who was killed in cold blood by Clifford. Apparently Rutland knelt and begged for mercy but Clifford replied, 'Your father killed mine so now I shall kill you'; and did so. Equally chilling is Margaret's treatment of York. His corpse was beheaded and his head displayed at the gate of York wearing a paper crown; it was flanked by those of the old Earl of Salisbury and the young Earl of Rutland. Wakefield was a bitter and revengeful battle and then and afterwards many old scores were settled by both sides. The pity of the Battle of Wakefield was that the best man of the Wars of the Roses was outwitted and killed halfway through the conflict. That was the Duke of York, who was the most stable, restrained, and statesmanlike figure of the period.

The Battle of Towton

29 March 1461

The Battle of Towton was the bloodiest and most bizarre battle ever fought on English soil. Contemporary accounts gave the casualties as 28,000. This may well have been accurate for killed and wounded, and it is worth while bearing in mind that in a battle of this nature only the lightly wounded would be likely to recover. The number killed on the battlefield itself was probably not less than 10,000, which is a staggering enough figure, for in those times – with the exception of a man caught by a cannon ball – killing was a laborious process. Most of the combatants were protected by some form of armour, and mortal wounds were not easily inflicted.

One of the bizarre features of Towton was that it was fought from dawn to dusk in a snowstorm. It took place on Palm Sunday, 29 March, on a bleak upland and in a sodden valley; on this occasion men did not merely fight men; they fought the elements as well.

Visitors to Towton and the neighbouring village of Saxton today need little imagination to visualize the scene. Everyone of note was there on that battlefield, and brought to it the feelings of hatred, ambition, and revenge which had been stored up for the previous five years. Many battles have been fought without great feeling on either side; the armies of two separate interests clashed and there was a battle. Men were killed and wounded, issues were settled, and increase it. When therefore the order 'No Quarter' went around, as it sometimes did – and certainly did at Towton – it was welcomed as it was always assumed that the opposition would be the ones to be slaughtered and lose their goods. Edward arrived at Pontefract just before 25 March, and camped at Bubwith Heath. There he paused and organized his army which had been greatly augmented by recruits, and numbered at least 25,000; some sources gave a suspiciously exact figure of 40,660.[1] The Lancastrians were now at York but had no desire to be besieged there. The fashion of the day was to confront the enemy in the open field or on ground of your own choosing. This, of course, is when your own superior handling of troops would tell, when you could outmanoeuvre your enemy, break up his formation, and demolish his forces piecemeal. If you are going to do this it will be as well if you have made the right calculations and have made every gain possible before the battle. A man who chooses to give battle at a certain place and time needs to be very sure of his estimates and troops, otherwise he may well find he is commanding a beaten army which should have avoided battle altogether on that occasion.

The Lancastrians had the advantage of choosing the ground and selected Towton Heath, two miles south of Tadcaster, twelve miles from York. It is easily found; the A162 skirts one side of it and the B1217 runs through it. Lord Dacre's monument on the side of the latter road serves as a battlefield monument. To the left, as you face north, is the River Cock, which will be noted as a fast-flowing stream between steep banks. The banks are deceptive and anyone trying to cross would be suddenly precipitated into much deeper water than he had anticipated. This would play a significant part in the battle.

1 At the same time the Lancastrians were quoted as numbering 60,000.

Without knowing exactly where the Lancastrians were going to stand, but knowing it could not be far off, Edward sent a small force up to Ferrybridge, two and a half miles north-east of Pontefract to hold the ford over the Aire. Twenty-four hours later this force was surprised by a Lancastrian raid commanded by Lord Clifford. The Lancastrians killed both the commanders and most of the garrison. Clifford, who led the raid, was nicknamed 'The Butcher' on account of his cold-blooded killing of Rutland at Wakefield. The news of this reverse came as an unpleasant shock to the Yorkists and many began to regret joining the army. However, two dramatic incidents served to check this sag in morale and restore confidence. Warwick killed his horse and said that henceforth he would fight as a foot soldier; this removed the unpleasant suspicion that if the Lancastrians looked like winning the Yorkist leaders would be the first to leave the field. Then Edward announced that if anyone wished to leave the army he could do so now, though not later. It is said that no one accepted the offer, and doubtless everyone was subsequently glad of the fact.

Nevertheless, even with high morale, matters did not go well for the Yorkists. An attempt to retake the ford was flung back with heavy casualties. However, Edward as not to be deterred and sent a detachment to cross up stream, which it did at Castleford. Once Clifford learnt the Yorkists were across the Aire and his retreat to the main body of the Lancastrians could be cut off he fell back rapidly. Unfortunately for him, he did not fall back fast enough and, as he reached Dintingdale, was caught in an ambush the resourceful Fauconberg had quickly prepared for him. Clifford was caught by a chance arrow and killed, and the ambush closed in on his force. Only two or three escaped. The ruthlessness of Towton was already foreshadowed. Clifford's body was never discovered; possibly it was hacked to pieces by vengeful Yorkists, for not only was he credited with the murder of Rutland but was said also to have decapitated the dead body of York. Soon the remainder of the Yorkist army was passing through Dintingdale (which is eight miles north of the Aire). It was then late afternoon on 28 March. They marched forward whilst it was still light and took up battle formation at Saxton. On the other side of the valley were the Lancastrians who had what seemed a very good position with the left flank on the ridge close to the Tadcaster–Ferrybridge road, and the right flank on the shoulder where the hill drops away to the valley of the River Cock. They were large armies and they covered a lot of ground. The night of the 28th was bitterly cold. Doubtless both sides made fires where they could find enough fuel. Some men would stand around them; others would huddle themselves in their cloaks and pack tightly together, getting some sleep; for they were tired, and a hard man can sleep in almost any conditions, even in torrential rain, if he is weary and accustomed to such rigours. When they woke up, many of them were covered with snowflakes, and they would stamp around to get warm.

There was probably little food, for both armies were large, and the fact that we know next to nothing of medieval commissariat arrangements suggests that they were fairly scanty. But even with empty stomachs and cold hands morale on both sides was still high. It may seem strange that it should be so, but in medieval battle a man had the great comfort of seeing his own side, and its apparently superior numbers; and if he did not already believe the enemy were outnumbered and outclassed his commanders would undoubtedly tell him that it was so. It was only when he found later that the enemy also seemed to have unlimited numbers that he began to feel less confident. But then it was too late to think about it. There was no retreat. All he could do was to try to kill as many of them as he could, and hope his comrades were being as successful. Once the battle was joined he would not have time to be afraid. Neither side could see much of the other as they deployed at Towton. The snow was now blowing in gusts. Even if visibility had been good it is unlikely that either would have taken much note of the shallow gully in the ground separating the two armies. It sloped towards the River Cock and, later, when the armies were surging crowds of fighting men, it gradually tilted them towards the river itself.

Both armies were drawn up in two parallel lines on a wide front – some said it was as long as a mile, though this seems unlikely – with the archers to the fore and the infantry and men-at-arms behind. Command of the Lancastrian army was given to the Duke of Somerset; unlike his unpopular ancestor, he managed to survive a crucial battle. He also commanded the centre, which included Lord Dacre, who was less lucky. The Lancastrian right wing was commanded by the Earl of Northumberland; subsequently he escaped from the battlefield but died of his wounds at York. Exeter, who commanded the Lancastrian left, escaped and survived. However, it was clear from subsequent events that the left flank was badly positioned.

Opposite, the Yorkist left was commanded by Edward. Although only nineteen he was six foot four, and strong in proportion. He was untiring, and moved over the battlefield constantly encouraging. The centre was commanded by the resourceful Fauconberg, and the right by Warwick. Who would have thought that day that ten years later Warwick would lose his own life fighting for the opposite side at Barnet, and would lose it because once again he had abandoned his horse to show that there was no possibility that he would leave the field prematurely?

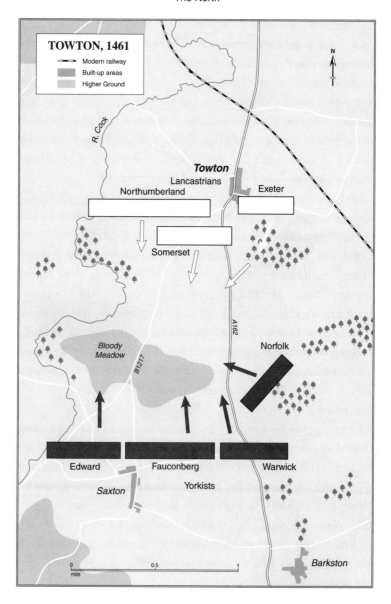

TOWTON, 1461

- ⊟ Modern railway
- ▨ Built-up areas
- ▨ Higher Ground

N

R. Cock

Towton

Lancastrians

Northumberland

Exeter

Somerset

A162

Bloody
Meadow

B1217

Norfolk

Edward

Fauconberg

Warwick

Saxton

Yorkists

Barkston

0   0.5   1
mile

The Yorkists, as the challengers, advanced slowly to give battle. The wind was behind them and the snow over their heads was blowing into the Lancastrian faces. As the Yorkists came into range they loosed off the first flights of their arrows. They flighted them high into the wind and they flew over a broad front among Somerset's men. There would have been no chance of avoiding them even if they had not been obscured by the snowstorm but the fact that the snow was full of arrows was disconcerting. The Lancastrians replied hastily but as they launched their arrows blindly into the oncoming snowflakes the Yorkists had begun to fall back. Luck favoured the Yorkists for they were at extreme range when they loosed their arrows and now the Lancastrian arrows were falling short in no-man's land. It was a typical Fauconberg manoeuvre. He was a tactician to his finger-tips, a soldier who had learnt from every moment of battle experience. As the Lancastrian arrows fell short he ordered his men to gather them up and send them back. By this time the Lancastrian arrows were running short and it must have seemed as if they were facing an army of archers. Arrows were a great asset but were soon gone; when that had happened an archer became a lightly-armed foot soldier, and highly vulnerable unless he was following up a successful arrow attack. However, the Lancastrians were not easily upset, and when the two sides began close-quarter fighting the slaughter among the lightly-armoured archers was very high indeed. Here men fought as they had fought at Agincourt, climbing over piles of dead bodies to get at the enemy. It

The A162 skirts one side of the battlefield and the B1217 runs through it. The visitor will note Lord Dacre's monument. His tomb is in the Saxton churchyard just to the south. An easily visited and most memorable battlefield. (North Yorkshire)

was kill or be killed, but more often kill *and* be killed. This was one of several 'bloody meadows' which marked the battlefield. Local names usually show the more intense areas of fighting and 'bloody meadows' and 'red pieces' are found on many an ancient map. Towton seems to have had at least two: one where the two forward lines clashed in the hollow, and another to the left where the fighting swayed down towards the flooded river. The fighting in this quarter went on relentlessly all through the morning. Clearly there must have been pauses for breath but these did not last long. When a party of men from either side were victorious they looked around for fresh victims. The battle was not now being fought on a basis of tactics ordered by commanders, but was a huge desperate horde of men, fully committed to battle, past fear but not past revenge and hatred. Victory, they knew, would come only when the other side had been killed or had fled. The armies were so huge, and it was so difficult to get at the other side that large numbers still remained uncommitted as the battle continued hour after hour.

The turning-point seems to have occurred in the early afternoon, and, ironically, because the latecomers put in their appearance. It seems that Norfolk, who had been sent to collect his retainers and make them into an army when Edward was still at London, had at last caught up with the battle. He arrived along the Ferrybridge road and charged into the struggling mass which the battle had now become. It seems doubtful whether the Lancastrians can have recognized Norfolk's men as fresh troops but the shock of their charge into the right flank of the battle must have gradually pushed the whole conflict down the slope towards the River Cock. That slope is very steep in parts and once a man found himself on it he would not be able to check himself until he reached the bottom. And at the bottom were the flooded meadows of the river. Many

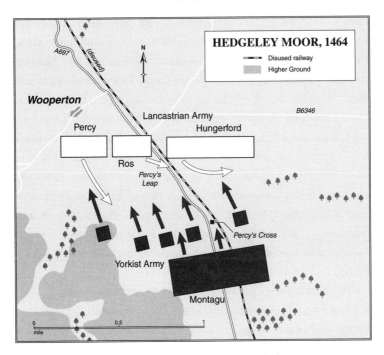

Take the A697 south of Wooler for seven miles. Insufficient detail has been recorded to make it possible to reconstruct the exact sequence of this battle. Percy's Cross is at the south-eastern end and Percy's Leap at the north-west. (Northumberland)

Lancastrian resistance, the Lancastrians had their own plans, and they boded ill for Edward. In April 1464, the Lancastrians mustered two small armies in Northumberland, where they still held the vital northern castles. Their number was not large but, as Edward very well knew, if they had a few initial successes recruits would pour in and the result of Towton might be reversed. The situation therefore looked ominous when the Lancastrians seized two vital strategic castles: Norham in Northumberland, and Skipton in Yorkshire. Unfortunately for the Lancastrians they did not then push ahead with recruiting fast enough. Montagu therefore reached Durham without serious check, although Sir Ralph Percy tried to ambush him. Montagu heard of the plan and changed his route. Then, having obtained reinforcements at Newcastle, he set out to confront the Lancastrians. The battle which followed, vital though it was in this Northern campaign, has been very scantily chronicled but we know that Montagu had a well-balanced force of about 2,000 and met the Lancastrian army at Hedgeley Moor, south-east of Wooler. The Lancastrians were in slight disarray at his sudden arrival. Apparently, supreme command had not been allotted, but the various detachments were under Lord Hungerford, Lord Ros (or Roos), and Sir Ralph Percy. The two former, realizing they were heavily outnumbered, soon saw excellent reasons why they should leave the field and fight another day, but Sir Ralph, as became a Percy, was made of sterner stuff. The Lancastrians then closed around Percy, whose force consisted mainly of his own tenants and retainers, and attempted to kill or capture all of them. Percy, however, thought otherwise and made a spirited charge at what seemed the weakest part of the Yorkist line. At this point his horse made a tremendous jump – at what subsequently became known as 'Percy's Leap' – but was wounded shortly afterwards. Percy, too, received a wound and died quickly. His dying cry was 'I have saved the bird in my bosom' which is interpreted as meaning he had died for his lawful monarch, after temporarily deserting him when pardoned by Edward iv. His soldiers were methodically despatched by the Yorkists, mainly on the marshy part of the battlefield.[1]

---

1 The 'cross' is merely a stone column today. It is engraved with the arms of Percy and Lucy.

A point, which brings out the complexity and folly of these wars, was that Percy's mother was a Neville. He was the seventh of her nine sons. The elder branch of the Neville family, who held the title of Earls of Westmorland, were staunch Lancastrians, and had always been so since Henry IV had taken the throne from Richard II. But the younger branch of the Neville family, which was the line of the Earls of Warwick and the Earls of Salisbury, were equally staunch Yorkists (until, of course, Warwick 'the Kingmaker' changed sides shortly before his death in 1471). Whether the older and younger branches of the Neville family fought on opposite sides because of political sympathies, or whether because they were intense and bitter rivals and could not possibly have supported the same cause, is not known, but the latter seems more likely than the former.

So Percy was dead, and that was a bitter blow to the Lancastrians, but they had endured bitter blows before and still come back. Hope now resided in the Duke of Somerset, son of the unpopular minister who had been killed at the first battle of St Albans. Doubtless Montagu would have proceeded to battle straight away if he had known where to find the Lancastrians, but he did not. For the moment he could only move tentatively towards Bamburgh; then suddenly he heard that Somerset was with a substantial force at Hexham. Where Montagu himself was at the time is not precisely known but it was probably well to the north, for he did not reach Hexham till 14 May.

Somerset, who would be executed after this battle, had done everything to deserve it. After Towton he had been pardoned and then much favoured by Edward. He was made custodian of Bamburgh Castle and captain of the royal guard. Edward gave him money, though he had not too much himself, and saw that Somerset's titles and estates were restored to him. Somerset was less popular with others and, when the two had visited Northampton, Somerset had nearly been killed; Edward saved his unpopular friend's life only by distributing so much wine that the crowd of would-be assassins were too drunk to know where to look. He then sent Somerset to North Wales for his own safety.

But Somerset had wearied of the royal friendship and seemed hell-bent on his own destruction. First he assembled as many Lancastrian supporters as he could find in North Wales and then rode with them one night through the Yorkist lines to Newcastle. Edward reacted much more quickly than Somerset had expected, seized Newcastle, and executed Somerset's men. Somerset had meanwhile moved to Bamburgh.

In hindsight it is all crystal clear. When not fighting, Edward was so casual, debauched, and apparently incompetent, that no one could believe he was secure on the throne. The incident at Northampton must have convinced Somerset that Edward was only hanging on to his power by a mere thread. He was not the only one to make such miscalculations. In peace, Edward was a self-indulgent fop; in danger, he was alert, indefatigable, and brilliant at both strategy and tactics. Somerset was soon to learn this at the cost of his own life.

Hedgeley Moor had been a setback but, owing to their prudence – or cowardice – in leaving the field early, the Lancastrian strength had not been greatly diminished. In the ensuing three weeks Somerset busied himself with enlisting every possible Lancastrian supporter; doubtless the promise of rewards did not err on the side of restraint. On 14 May he arrived at Hexham and pitched camp at Linnels, on the banks of the Devilswater. It was a good place for a camp but a bad place for a battle. Somerset's army had its backs to a curve in the stream at Hexham Levels, his front was screened by a wooded hill. It was unlikely that he could be surprised, for the Devilswater was a fast stream and just to the right of his position it was joined by the West Dipton Burn which would be very difficult to cross. It was as snug a camp as you could wish for, and well protected by natural features. However, it was distinctly less satisfactory when an army approached, as Somerset soon found; but he had the sense to dispose his forces well forward in the face of Montagu's oncoming army, and thus gave himself some space to manoeuvre on either side. He had also been wise enough to leave Henry at Bywell Castle and not to risk such a valuable hostage – or encumbrance – on the battlefield.

Montagu, once he learnt of Somerset's position, came up at great speed, hoping to pin the Lancastrians against the river and cramp any possible manoeuvres. This type of tactic is excellent provided your own men are going to be superior in the inevitable close-quarter fighting. If, however, the opposition fight with the desperation of the doomed, it may be necessary to order a fast retreat and quick regroup, for the battle may be lost on minor tactics. In the event, Montagu was lucky, for the Lancastrians were on a broad front, and the wings, seeing the centre yielding, did not reinforce it but themselves took to flight. In the general confusion of Lancastrians fanning out in several directions at once, some men from the centre had the time necessary to cross the Devilswater and escape. As was seen at Towton and elsewhere, crossing a stream was a possibility, if you had time and were unhampered, but was a death-trap if the pursuers were close at your back. Somerset was wounded, was slower at getting away than some of the others, and was captured about a mile from the battlefield. He was taken into Hexham and executed with the greatest indignity. His spurs were struck off by a common servitor, his coat of arms was torn off, and

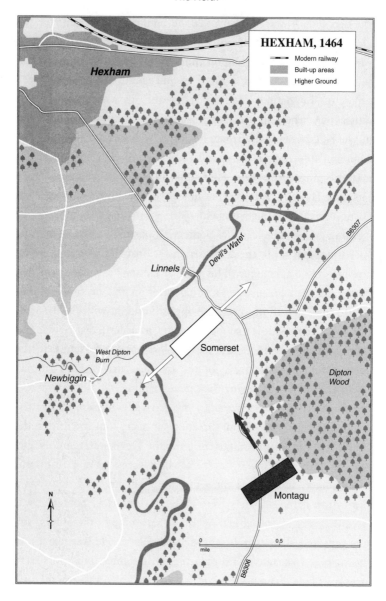

HEXHAM, 1464

- Modern railway
- Built-up areas
- Higher Ground

Hexham

Linnels

Devil's Water

B6307

West Dipton Burn

Somerset

Newbiggin

Dipton Wood

Montagu

N

0   0.5   1
mile

B6306

he was strapped to a hurdle. Then he was dragged to the scaffold and beheaded.

It was only one of many executions. Ros and Hungerford were also captured and were beheaded at Newcastle. Other Lancastrian leaders were executed at various points, some as far south as York, to convince potential Lancastrian supporters that allegiance to Henry VI and Queen Margaret was a quick way to the scaffold. However, Henry had been warned, and had escaped, though leaving all his personal possessions behind him, including his sword. The great northern Lancastrian strongholds, Alnwick, Dunstanburgh, Norham, and Bamburgh surrendered soon afterwards, though the last-named required gunfire to make it haul down its flag. With that the Lancastrian cause in the north was ended for the time being.

Take the B6306 from Hexham. The battlefield lies between Linnels and Newbiggin. (Northumberland)

The Battle of Flodden

9 September 1513

The last chapter ended with the complete defeat of the Lancastrians in 1464. In this account we describe a devastating victory in the reign of a king who was born of the union of a Lancastrian king and a Yorkist queen. The intervening events and reasons may be sketched in very rapidly. More detailed accounts of the battles involved are to be found in the other books of this 'British Battlefields' volume but, as they did not take place in the north, can be treated only incidentally in this section.

All would have been well for Edward if he had not rather foolishly married a Lancastrian widow, Elizabeth Woodville, and made no attempt to mollify those of his supporters who felt affronted by the match. Chief among the aggrieved was Warwick, but Edward's response was only to try to humiliate the great 'Kingmaker' who seemed to him altogether too powerful and influential. Warwick thereupon allied himself with Edward's younger brother, the Duke of Clarence, and organized a rebellion in 1469 which resulted in the Battle of Edgcote and the capture of Edward himself. Edward was subsequently released on parole but, inevitably, took the first opportunity to raise an army and chase Warwick and Clarence out of the country. Burning with humiliation and rage, Warwick offered his services to Margaret who was then living in exile in France. But this uneasy alliance caused nothing but further bloodshed. Warwick himself was killed at Barnet (1471) and, in the same year, Margaret was imprisoned after the Battle of Tewkesbury where her son and heir had been killed (or perhaps murdered after the battle). Henry vi also died mysteriously at this time, in the Tower of London, probably with the assistance of his gaolers.

However, after twelve years, Edward's way of life had changed him from a superbly fit young man into a debauched invalid; he died at the age of forty-one. By then he had had ten children by his lawful wife and an unspecified number by mistresses.

The new heir was Edward v, who subsequently became one of the two princes who disappeared without trace in the Tower of London. The next king was Richard of Gloucester, who became Richard iii. His reign was short; having taken the throne in 1483 he was killed at Bosworth in 1485.

Henry vii, who had an extremely easy and lucky campaign to obtain the throne in 1485, married the late King Edward iv's eldest daughter. At long last the rivalry between the factions of Lancaster and York was now dissolved by a dynastic marriage. What was rather more to the point was that nearly all the potential trouble-makers had killed each other or been executed during the previous thirty years. Furthermore, the country was as anxious for peace as Henry was to provide it. This did not entirely prevent battles, as was seen at Stoke Field in 1487, Britanny in 1491, and Blackheath in 1497, but it did eventually produce stability, a full treasury, and a docile aristocracy.

But Henry vii's successor was of different mettle entirely. The young Henry viii – he was only eighteen when he succeeded – was very able, quite ruthless, and a heavy spender. Furthermore, he was always anxious to prove that he was better than others. Success seemed to come naturally to him, and he was also very lucky. In 1513 he landed at Calais with an army of 25,000 men. After capturing two towns with very little effort he won the 'Battle of the Spurs'. The battle took its name from the haste with which the French knights urged their horses from the contest.

While Henry was thus engaged, the Scots, who were distinctly fonder of the French than the English, decided that the time was ripe to settle a few outstanding military accounts. Fortunately for England, Henry had left the country in charge of Thomas Howard, Earl of Surrey. Howard was no youngster; he had even fought for Richard III against Henry VII at Bosworth. Subsequently he had been pardoned and proved a loyal servant of the new king, who had appointed him Lord Lieutenant of the North. Surrey did not at first realize that this was to be full-scale war but after a very large raiding party, under the Earl of Home, had been ambushed, it seemed to him that the Scots were intent on more than border raiding. He therefore briskly set about the organization of a suitable defensive army. This was early in August 1513. The muster point was Newcastle. There converged an interesting motley of forces, and Surrey took to it the banner of St Cuthbert which was alleged to be the one carried against the Scots at Neville's Cross 167 years before, and was doubtless believed to be the same one that was taken by Thurstan to Northallerton in 1138, 375 years before. Like Thurstan, Surrey was too crippled to take part in the fighting – he was over seventy – and travelled to the battle by coach. However, Surrey scarcely needed propaganda to boost his efforts; he was well-experienced in the art of war and had the measure of James IV. On being sure that James was intent on full-scale invasion he sent him a challenge. The significance of a challenge went back to medieval times, and its chivalric implication was that the acceptor would fight at the date and place named. Surrey hoped that this challenge would cause the Scots to fight on ground unsuitable to them. It did not, however, work out quite as well as that, for James was no fool and had taken up position at Flodden Edge. It was said that he had 100,000 men. The number was probably a third of that amount. James had plenty of men and some useful arms, including 600 hand culverins[1] and 400 arquebuses, but his force was undisciplined and insufficiently trained. His men also had 6,000 pikes, but handling a pike, which can be up to eighteen feet long, in formation requires time and practice. An untrained pikeman is a bigger danger to his own side than to the enemy.

Heavier artillery consisted of five large cannon, each of which required a team of oxen (seven) to draw it, and twelve culverins of varying sizes. Cannons were very effective, when they functioned properly, but usually produced endless problems. In 1460, at the siege of Roxburgh, James II of Scotland had been killed when one of his own cannons bursts, and at all times early cannon were unreliable. Their explosive charge was usually too violent, which made them dangerous and erratic, or too slow-burning, which made them ineffective. Ammunition was a problem, too, for whereas the old siege catapults had been highly effective with almost any lump of stone, and quite accurate as well, cannon-balls had to be carefully shaped, and therefore took time to prepare. This could rarely be done near the battlefield; there was therefore the need for an enormous ammunition train. Nevertheless, when the cannons and culverins started peppering castle walls the effect on morale was even greater than the effect on the masonry. Thus Wark, Norham, Chillingham, and Etall castles surrendered to the Scots much more quickly than they needed to have done, particularly the last.

1 Culverin is another name for a cannon and derives from the French word coulevrine (=snake).

Surrey took his army to Wooler in two divisions. It numbered approximately 25,000 but there were another 50,000 available in the midlands and south who might come up and join him if for some reason it was decided to delay the confrontation with the Scots. Larger numbers in that area might have proved more of an embarrassment than an asset, for food supplies were distinctly meagre in the border area. Surrey had less artillery than the Scots but more archers. He also had 1,000 marines brought in by his son Admiral Henry Howard, who was his second-in-command. At Wooler the English army was only six miles from the invader.

However, it would have been extremely foolish of Surrey to have challenged the Scots in their strong position. It was a pity that they had refused his challenge and declined to face him on ground of his own choosing; this unsporting, unmedieval decision was blamed on the French who were present with James and undoubtedly advising him. However, this being so, it was necessary to tempt or frighten the Scots out of their position if that were possible.

With extraordinary boldness (or rashness, depending on how you look on these matters) Surrey ordered his army to march due north from Wooler on 8 September. It was pouring with rain at the time and the tracks were full of water and mud. Surrey was taking almost every risk it is possible to take. He was presenting a long flank to the enemy, and at the end of his march, although he would be between the Scots and their homeland, equally well he had placed his own army between a large invasion army and its hostile motherland. The journey involved his crossing the River Till, using the bridge at Twizel and the Milford ford. Although it is not exactly known it seems likely that they moved dismounted, as under those conditions the horses would have been too much of a liability. Apparently they had had no beer for days and they accomplished that march

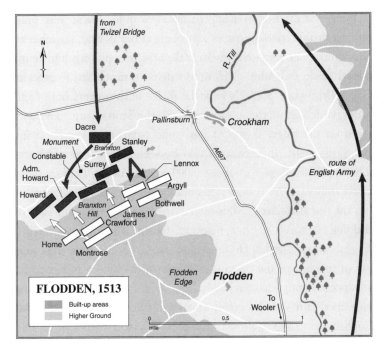

The following labels appear on the map: from Twizel Bridge, R. Till, Crookham, Pallinsburn, Dacre, Monument, Stanley, Branxton, Constable, Surrey, Lennox, Adm. Howard, A697, route of English Army, Argyll, Howard, Bothwell, Branxton Hill, James IV, Crawford, Home, Montrose, Flodden Edge, Flodden, To Wooler.

FLODDEN, 1513

■ Built-up areas
▨ Higher Ground

0   0.5   1
mile

Turn off the A697 to Branxton. The monument is approximately in the centre of the battlefield. (Northumberland)

without food either. Once across the river the army veered back to the south.

The move took the Scots by surprise but did not have precisely the effect intended. Instead of descending to the plain the Scots moved north to the other edge of the ridge, which is known as Branxton Hill, and took up positions facing northwards. The slope is steep here, being about one in five. The highest point is Pipers Hill and at the bottom of the slope lies a boggy area known as Pallinsburn. Like many bogs this varies somewhat in firmness from one year to another, but extends over approximately a mile. There were only two reasonable crossing-places, one being at Branx Brig, the other at Sandyford. The English army had taken the precaution of obtaining a local guide and Admiral Howard's division proceeded to cross at Branx Brig while Surrey's took the ford. As they came out of the water, which lay on the surface, they saw the Scottish army ahead of them on the ridge. It was in four solid detachments, each about 200 yards apart. In between could be seen the Scottish artillery. The entire frontage was about 2,000 yards. As the English came closer they came into range of the heavier guns – about 1,500 yards – but the few shots fired at this stage buried themselves harmlessly in the bog. It was a delicate moment, for the two divisions of the English army, Admiral Howard's and the Earl of Surrey's, were well out of touch; had the Scots charged down the hill on to Howard's advance column Flodden might have had a very different result. However, James iv had no information about the disposition of the English army, and could scarcely guess it was in such a vulnerable state. Meanwhile, Howard halted and Surrey was able to close up. The opportunity was lost. Nevertheless, no one could blame the Scots for not abandoning such an excellent position. The Admiral must have sweated gently as he realized that about a mile separated the two sections of the English army. However, he was not too apprehensive to note that the Scottish army was in four columns, while the English was in six. Should one or more of those columns come down the hill they might punch a hole in the English front which would be irreparable. It was now the afternoon of the 9th, and the English spent it in reforming so that the Scottish squares opposite were as nearly matched as the disparity in numbers allowed. And it was still raining.

As the two armies faced each other, now only 600 yards apart, the artillery opened up. Visibility was naturally very poor, and as a result the Scottish artillery over-ranged. The English artillery, inferior in size and numbers, were fortuitously presented with an advantage. Having no facility of range they simply discharged point blank into what was their only possible target area. It was, of course, crowded with Scottish infantry. Goaded into desperation, the left flank of the Scottish army, on to which most of the rounds were falling, decided to charge forward. These were not disciplined troops, accustomed to holding their effort till the last moment; they were wild Borderers, second to none in offensive spirit, but completely unaccustomed to fighting in an army with an essential pattern of disciplined commit-ment. As they came down the hill they looked even more formidable than they were. But they were powerful enough, too, and they tore through Howard's division, killing many and putting more to flight. It was a fine start to the battle from the Scottish point of view but not quite as good as it looked. The English right had not been entirely demolished; it only seemed to be so. But to James IV, seeing it from the top of the hill it looked like the prelude to absolute victory: up to this point the Scots had decided that nothing would tempt them from their commanding position on the hilltop; now it seemed that a full-scale attack on to the wilting English army would rapidly bring immediate victory. James launched his own column, and the adjoining one (under Crawford and Montrose). They tore down the hill, crossed the stream at the bottom, and came up a slight slope to the English line.

But a charge up a slope of 200 yards can take the edge off the most enthusiastic warrior. Although Surrey's men were pushed back they were not scattered, and soon the Scottish drive forward had stopped. At that point the Borderers should have added their weight to the Scottish attack. Two factors prevented this: one was that the

Borderers had lost whatever cohesion they had had once they put their opposites to rout; the second was that Lord Dacre was waiting in reserve with 1,500 cavalry behind the English lines. On seeing the havoc created by the Borderers, but at the same time noting their vulnerability, he brought his men smartly forward into the Borderers' flank. On that wing, therefore, there was now a confused mass of struggling men. Whatever happened, that locked-up mass could hardly have any further effect on the battle. But there were plenty of others, on both sides, who could.

They were, of course, on the Scottish right wing and the English left. The division on the right of the Scottish centre was commanded by King James himself, the right wing by the Earls of Argyll and Lennox. There was also a reserve commanded by the Earl of Bothwell which contained some French men-at-arms. Opposite King James was the Earl of Surrey, so the two commanders-in-chief were directly opposed. Surrey's division contained at least 3,000 Yorkshiremen and numbered about 5,000 altogether. On his left was a division, also numbering 5,000, commanded by Sir Edward Stanley. It was composed of men from Lancashire and Cheshire.

King James's men charged vigorously into Surrey's division as the latter was ascending the Branxton slope. James had armed himself with a pike and was in the front rank, but before his division had covered the 300 yards to the English line it had lost a good number of men to accurate cannon-fire and archery. When the two forces closed, the English bills, which were shorter than the Scottish pikes, proved a good deal more manoeuvrable. Finding their long pikes – to which they were unaccustomed – far too cumbersome, the Scots abandoned them and resorted to lighter weapons. This was unwise, for their swords were considerably shorter than the English bills, and much less effective.

Meanwhile, the extreme right of the Scottish army had been held in reserve. Their inactivity had been noted by Stanley who decided to give them a surprise. Under cover of the rain and mist he was able to move around to his left unobtrusively, and then, taking advantage of a gulley, to come up the hill unobserved. When they appeared they were at close quarters to the Highlanders opposing them, and announced their presence with several well-directed flights of arrows. Surprise at their unexpected appearance, and inability to retaliate to the well-directed arrows, had a devastating effect on the Highlanders. Unable to get within range, they fell back. Inevitably they were soon colliding with the front ranks of Bothwell's reserve detachment, and the English following up were able to pick easy targets in the general confusion. Bothwell himself was killed. In this quarter at least, the battle bore a close resemblance to the Battle of the Standard. Perhaps the spirit of old Thurstan, as well as that of St Cuthbert, was presiding over the scene. The Scots in this division were so undisciplined that they busied themselves looting their own dead rather than setting about the English. It did them little good, for they were soon chopped down by Stanley's men.

As this part of the Scottish army gave little resistance, Stanley's men soon turned round and charged down the slope again into the other fighting. Here, around James IV, were the *élite* of the Scottish army, worthy of better support than their flanks had given them. The fighting in this sector was bitter and long. James IV was killed, but the fighting went on. Only as night fell did the task seem hopeless and the Scots respond to the call to abandon fighting. Many, of course, did not do so but took a chance on finding a way back to Scotland. Casualties had been high on both sides in this part of the field. The final casualty lists were said to include 12,000 Scots and 4,000 English.

Much discussion has gone on as to how the Scots, with an advantage of artillery, position, and numbers, could have lost this bloody battle. It is not difficult to find a reasonable explanation. The Scottish army, although large, consisted of largely untrained troops, who were therefore undisciplined. Although well armed, they did not know how to use their arms, let alone how to fight in formation with them. It is perhaps possible to exaggerate this point, for the Scots threw away their new acquisitions when they found they were unable to make good use of them, but the effect on morale of finding that an alleged winning weapon was merely a liability was undoubtedly enormous. The Scottish army was also badly handled; brave though James IV was, he had no business to be fighting in the front ranks of an army he was supposed to be commanding. His subordinate commanders appear to have been of inferior quality. One of them, the Earl of Home, who commanded the Borderers on the left wing, was subsequently executed for inactivity amounting to treachery during the battle. He had apparently agreed with Dacre that their men would no longer continue fighting each other, although it was obvious that there was much to be done both in this sector and elsewhere. Whether the charge was justified or not seems doubtful; there had to be a scapegoat and Home was the best one to hand.

Had James IV won the battle instead of losing it there would doubtless have been high praise for his tactical skill in choosing such an excellent position, his prudence in not abandoning it in the face of English provocation, and his inspired dash to attack the English just when they were at their most vulnerable.

The explanation of the result is always seen more easily from the victor's viewpoint. Surrey's army was lean, hungry, and fit. They had everything to fight for. By contrast the Scots had done little to make them battle-fit. In fact, their forages had probably contributed to the reverse effect. When the English finally entered their camp they found it full of comforts, including large quantities of mutton, beer, and wine. Good rations make a man fight well if he is well-exercised but can have a very bad effect if he is not.

Surrey and Howard were capable commanders; Dacre and Stanley were soldiers with a touch of enterprise which usually brings complete disaster or complete victory. At Flodden they brought victory.

Described as above, the Battle of Flodden probably seems a very clear-cut affair. Needless to say, it was undoubtedly the exact opposite on the field itself. As the English arrows sped home, horses panicked and companies of men surged to and fro. As the Scottish pike companies began to move, the rough ground caused them to lose their formation, and, when they closed, English and Scots became too closely mingled for anyone to know how the battle was going. Dacre's charge probably killed some of his own side who were unable to get out of the way; in the rain, the darkness, and the general confusion there must have been many a man who found he was fighting one of his own side, and found it out too late.

One view of the Scottish strategy which has never been put forward might tentatively be advanced here. When James realized that his left wing had run away with itself and was perhaps lost to the battle, and the right wing was of such doubtful quality that it was only worth committing as expendable or in the poised moment of victory, he might have decided that his only chance was to smash a way right through the centre of the English line. If he broke through at that point he could, if he wished, put himself on the way to Scotland, but even if that was not his intention he would have cut the English army in half; his wings could then roll down the slope and complete the victory.

If that was his intention, it did not work. The English centre was too solid, and his impetus was lost even before he reached it. Instead of leading an advance therefore, he was caught in a desperate mêlée and killed. All other theories of the battle imply that he was a stupid field commander, but it could have been otherwise; unfortunately for the Scots the English stood a little too firm and the Scottish king and commander was killed. Perhaps, like many a general before and after him he was a good tactician but an unlucky general.

On Pipers Hill there is a memorial which was erected in 1910. Pipers Hill is about 100 yards from base to summit and has a gradient of about one in five from every angle. It was the scene of heavy fighting during which the ground became so slippery with blood that the surviving soldiers took off their boots to get a better foothold (or so it was said).

It seems that James refused to let the commander of his artillery open fire on the English before they had assembled after crossing the River Till because of the challenge to meet Surrey 'on a fair field'. James had spent the previous night at Ford Castle where his personal effects remained untouched until 1940.

The Battle of Winceby

11 October 1643

O n the Ordnance Survey map of Lincolnshire will be found the hamlet of Winceby. It is marked on the signposts on each side but there is no name by the roadside to indicate the place itself. However, if the visitor takes the A158 from Horncastle and turns off to the B1195 for Spilsby he will come upon it 1¼ miles along the Spilsby road. If he reaches the turn to Old Bolingbroke, he has gone too far and must retrace his steps. There is a square-built Georgian house on the left of the road as he comes from Horncastle and that was doubtless the Roundhead headquarters. The Parliamentarian troops were drawn up in three divisions along the B1195 facing north, with Cromwell in the van, Fairfax in the centre, and Manchester in the rear. About half a mile further north another ridge crosses the road and on this the Royalists were drawn up in triangular formation, Savile on the right wing, Henderson on the left, and Widdrington to the centre. Why, in the autumn of 1643, some of the cream of English youth should be thus drawn up ready to slaughter each other requires some explanation.

The last battle described in this series – Flodden – had taken place a hundred and twenty years before. (There had, of course, been plenty of other battles involving English arms in the meantime, but not in the area concerned in this section.) Flodden was the last of the medieval-type battles to be fought in this country and, after it,

239

weapons and tactics changed completely. The bow disappeared from armies and was replaced by firearms. For many years firearms were less efficient than bows but they had the enormous advantage that they could be used by young and old with very little practice. The bow, on the other hand, needed incessant, lengthy practice and a good physique. A further point was that ammunition for firearms was much easier to transport. When bullets were effective they went right through armour so that even with erratic shooting it was inevitable that armour would now be discarded. And with the removal of heavy armour on both horse and man there was no longer need for the heavy draught-horse type of animal; instead, a lighter, faster mount took the field, and a whole complex of cavalry manoeuvres was evolved. However, after a time the popularity of the cavalry arm produced its own set of problems. Horses need forage, can go lame, fall ill, bolt, prove uncontrollable in battle. Born cavalrymen are not easily come by, and any sort of cavalrymen take some time to train.

All this had been taking place against a background of growing economic progress, and political development. When Henry viii had broken with the Church of Rome and appointed himself head of the English church, monasteries had disappeared, church lands had passed into private hands, and the enclosure acts had begun to alter the appearance of the countryside. The reigns of Edward vi, Mary, and Elizabeth had seen this economic change continue and develop; they had also seen plots, some of which had led to fullscale battles, but nothing to compare with the destructive, internal rivalries of the past.

But in the middle of the seventeenth century England was once more torn apart by Civil War. It was not, however, a recurrence of the situation which had caused the Wars of the Roses but something entirely different, although no less suicidal. It was an altogether more complex matter. The people who made up the armies of the Civil War were not, as is often thought, people of similar views and aspirations, any more than today all those who vote Conservative are rich and privileged and all those who vote Socialist are poor and deprived. Then, as now, there were a host of different reasons which caused a man to side with one party or the other. Conscience undoubtedly played a large part but so also did tradition, regional affiliations, and temperament.

The Civil War probably became inevitable when Elizabeth died unmarried; for the next heir was James VI of Scotland who became James I of England. His personal qualities – or lack of them – made him a useless king but that in itself would not have mattered greatly. Unfortunately he possessed obsolete ideas on the power of the monarch, and brought up his son to share them. James believed that kings held their position by divine right, according to a strict hereditary law of succession. This had never been an English custom and, indeed, if it had been strictly adhered to James I would never have sat on the English throne at all. However, this crackbrained idea went with one that the king had a 'royal prerogative' which entitled him to ignore, or set on one side, any Parliamentary law of which he did not approve. Needless to say, his ideas led to a series of plots, some of which had obscure aims and peculiar adherents. The best known is the Gunpowder Plot of 1605 for which Guy Fawkes, and his fellow conspirators, were killed outright, or executed in a slower and more spectacular way.

By the time James I died, relations between king and Parliament were extremely poor, and an open breach had been prevented only by James's idleness and personal cowardice. However, when (in 1625) his son Charles succeeded him, hopes ran high. Here was an intelligent, courageous, and virtuous young man. It seemed that England was now set fair for a Golden Age. Unfortunately, it was on a course for a disastrous Civil War.

The stages by which this became inevitable do not concern us here. The Royal Standard was set up at Nottingham on 22 August 1642, and Charles invited all his supporters to rally to him there. Meanwhile Parliament appointed the Earl of Essex as commander-in-chief. Then followed nine years of virtually continuous war, although there was a short pause between 1647 and 1648. Needless to say, throughout this long suicidal contest both parties believed they were protecting the Constitution. Even the Parliamentarians believed that they were fighting for the true rights of the Crown. This, of course, was slightly offset by the fact that the Royalists believed that the Parliamentarians were a host of fanatical bigots and the Parliamentarians considered that the Royalist supporters – and the king too – were not to be trusted. Broadly speaking, country districts supported Charles, and the towns, particularly on the eastern side of the country, supported Parliament. There were, of course, exceptions; it should be remembered that one third of the aristocracy supported Parliament. Unfortunately, close neighbours, friends, and even relations were divided in their sympathies.

The first battle, at Edgehill, was fought on 23 October 1642. It was inconclusive. Even so, Charles could have moved on to take London if he had been determined enough. Instead, he was deterred by the train-bands which opposed him at Turnham Green, and fell back to Reading. He offered peace to Parliament – on his terms – but when they rejected his offer, retired to Oxford. But while Charles was inactive there was plenty of fighting going on elsewhere. The result was that the Parliamentary forces gained control of the east and south, including most of the ports, while the north and west, including Wales but excepting the town (and port) of Pembroke, came under Royalist control. In the spring of 1643 local fighting was vigorous but not significant. The summer was more decisive and some important battles took place in the Midlands. Notable among them were Chalgrove Field (18 June 1643) in which Hampden was killed; Lansdown (5 July) when Waller's Parliamentary army was beaten by Hopton; and Roundway Down (13 July) when the Parliamentarians, now nicknamed 'Roundheads', were beaten again. The valuable port of Bristol was then captured by the Royalists. Now was the time for Charles to march on London, and take it, which he should have been able to do. Disastrously for his cause, he failed to make the move. It is said that he paid too much attention to local commanders who wished to consolidate the recent victories in their areas.

Instead, he suffered a setback which he could easily have avoided. It was caused by an attempt to be too clever strategically. Having taken Bristol, he decided it would be wise and timely to capture Gloucester, which was the only major port held by the Parliamentarians in the west. He began the siege on 10 August, but broke it off when Essex came from London with a powerful force, determined to relieve Gloucester at all costs. Charles, possibly over-influenced by cavalry opinion, decided not to fight in the siege-lines but to withdraw and manoeuvre to ambush Essex on the road back to London (after resupplying Gloucester). It was an interesting plan, but in the first Battle of Newbury, where the ambush took place, the execution went sadly wrong. The assumption that Essex's young, inexperienced train-bands would scatter and flee when subjected to a cavalry charge proved ill-founded, and at the end of the day it was the Royalist cavalry who had sustained most of the losses. Charles ordered his troops back to Oxford and the Roundheads were able to occupy Reading.

Meanwhile, a new figure had appeared on the scene in eastern England. This was Colonel Oliver Cromwell. Cromwell was not, as is often thought, a humble artisan who rose to high command for political reasons; on the contrary, he was a country gentleman with distinguished connections, and a thoroughly capable field commander who rose in rank through sheer merit. Not least of the reasons for his success was his insistence on the careful selection of all subordinate commanders. After Edgehill he criticized the Parliamentary army as consisting of 'old decayed serving-men and tapsters', but equally well he did not want people who thought that the accident of birth entitled them to command. What he wanted was the dash and courage of the young country gentleman combined with professional knowledge and enthusiasm, but with it a strong religious feeling which would temper a man in victory and sustain him in reverse.

By the autumn of 1643 Cromwell's views were beginning to show results. His cavalry had already proved itself in battle at Grantham and Gainsborough. Since June, Sir Thomas Fairfax and his son had been besieged by the Marquis of Newcastle in Hull. On 26 September Cromwell slipped across the Humber and took off Sir Thomas Fairfax. As Newcastle's army were so unvigilant as to let him do that he returned later and took off 500 cavalrymen as well.

Stung by this defiance, Newcastle took action to prove that he still held the initiative. An attempted Royalist coup in King's Lynn had been suppressed by the Earl of Manchester, and the latter moved towards the castle of Old Bolingbroke[1] – now in ruins, but then

1 The castle had belonged to the Dukes of Lancaster; it will be remembered that Henry IV was originally Henry of Bolingbroke before he took the crown from his cousin Richard II.

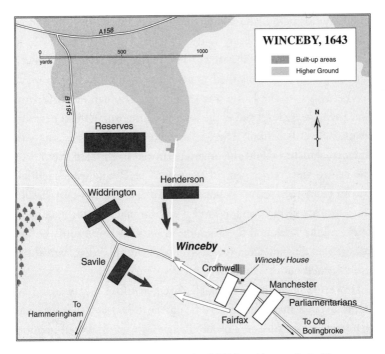

WINCEBY, 1643

Built-up areas
Higher Ground

0 500 1000
yards

A158

B1195

N

Reserves

Henderson

Widdrington

Winceby

Savile

Cromwell

Winceby House

Manchester

To
Hammeringham

Parliamentarians

Fairfax

To Old
Bolingbroke

This battlefield is difficult to find. Take the A158 from Horncastle to Skegness and turn off onto the B1195 for Spilsby. The site is 1¼ miles along this road. (Lincolnshire)

housing a substantial Royalist garrison. Bolingbroke was a Royalist outpost in a predominantly Parliamentarian area and it was as important to the prestige of the former to hold it as it was to the latter to reduce it. Manchester's peremptory order to the Royalists to surrender was defied with gusto, possibly because they knew that Newcastle had every intention of relieving them in the near future.

Newcastle moved south. The combined army which approached Bolingbroke was composed of three divisions: one under Savile, one under Widdrington, and one under Sir John Henderson. The force was only small, numbering under 3,000, but decisive battles have often been won by small armies. The Parliamentarian army was a little larger and probably totalled little over 4,000.

The course of the battle was surprising. The wings, Henderson and Savile, were level and to the fore, Widdrington in the centre was about 500 yards behind. The Parliamentarians were drawn up with one detachment behind the other, Cromwell in the lead, Fairfax in the centre and Manchester in the rear. The Roundhead intention was to block the road to Bolingbroke and cause heavy casualties to the Royalists if they tried to force a way through. As the country is open, rolling land, and the Roundhead position could easily be by-passed this did not seem the most intelligent approach, but in the event turned out to be the most effective.

However, once the first shot is fired, battle is likely to be an unpredictable matter. Henderson, on the Royalist left wing, sent his dragoons forward in a probe. Dragoons were mounted infantry whose horses had neither the physique nor the spirit for battle; thus dragoons usually dismounted and harassed the opposition with carbine and fowling-piece. If at close quarters they used swords or hand-guns – the 'dragons' (i.e. fire-breathers) from which they took their name.

As the dragoons approached Winceby farm (the Georgian house), Cromwell charged. A lucky shot found his horse and while he was obtaining another the initiative passed to Fairfax, who was doubtless only too glad to vent his frustrations and settle a few scores with the Royalists. He noted that Widdrington had hung too far back, that Henderson was too far to the left, and that Savile had pushed too far forward. In a cavalry battle this was, of course, only a matter of minutes but in a fast-changing situation there is always a vital moment in which the battle may be won or lost. Often in these pages we have seen the right wing push too far ahead and drift out of the battle. This did not quite happen at Winceby, for Savile's dash to the right was too well-controlled. It is not known whether Savile intended to bypass the Roundhead position and take Manchester's division in the rear or whether he planned to converge on Cromwell's sector as that came forward to engage the dragoons. Whatever he intended was not put into effect, for just as he was streaming past the Parliamentary army on their left Fairfax put in a sudden and tremendous charge. Hit sideways with great force at a moment when they themselves seemed to possess the initiative, Savile's troops reeled to the right and backwards. Cromwell's men soon turned to help, as did some of Manchester's although keeping a wary eye for moves from Henderson and Widdrington. But there was no trouble from them; having seen a third of the Royalist army tumbled out of their saddles, Widdrington and Henderson gave the order to retire. It was not a decision which reflected much credit on them but it may be that they saw the battle as no more than a skirmish and had no wish to sacrifice valuable men in what seemed a dubious tactic.

But it was serious enough for Savile and for Henderson's dragoons. If you turn off the B1195 towards Hammeringham you will note that the ground to the north falls away into a hollow. This is where Savile's disrupted wing soon found themselves – virtually helpless victims of the Parliamentary swordsmen, for they were trapped in a field with high hedges. To the Parliamentarians it was a lovely day, and the area is still known as 'Slash Hollow'.

Winceby was a small, strange, but important battle. It enhanced Cromwell's reputation, but Fairfax was really the architect of victory; it showed the Royalists that the opposition cavalry were as good, if not better, than their own, and should not be under-rated;

and it contributed in no small measure to the ultimate Parliamentary victory.

For the visitor it has certain advantages. Although not easy to find, it is easy to look over as a whole. And, with the benefit of time and hindsight, he will probably see half a dozen ways in which it could have been won – by either side.

The Battle of Newark

21 March 1644

In spite of the defeats at Newbury and Winceby, the Royalists had finished the year 1643 in a stronger position than they had started it. Charles held the West Country, west of a line running approximately through Manchester to Portsmouth; this included the great assets of Bristol and Oxford. He also held a substantial portion of the north, from Berwick to Hull and Carlisle to Preston in what was very roughly a square formation. He also held Newark, which was a strategic strongpoint. Parliament held the remainder, though, of course, in the areas controlled by each side there were still pockets of resistance here and there. But in effect it was a stalemate and to gain a clearcut victory each side hoped to enlist outside help. Naturally enough the Parliamentarians turned to the earnest Covenanters of the north and the Royalists to the Catholics of Ireland; not unexpectedly these new allies proved frequently to be intractable and often an embarrassment.

The Scots ultimately promised to produce an army of up to 15,000 men, but the price of it was that Parliament had to swear to reform the English Church which the Scots felt to be highly unsatisfactory. The Scottish view of a satisfactory church was an extreme form of Scottish Presbyterianism. The Irish arrangement looked like being even more difficult to accommodate, for the Irish contingents consisted of enthusiastic Romanists and rebels who had only

249

recently, and for this purpose, been pardoned for fighting against their English overlords.

Both sets of reinforcements started to arrive in England in late 1643 and early 1644. Brisk fighting began almost at once. The Hull Parliamentarians, who had been trapped in Hull for months, now emerged and cut across the country to engage the Irish army at Nantwich. By now the Marquis of Newcastle, far from putting pressure on the Parliamentarians in Hull, had himself had to fall back to York, where he was threatened by Scots from the north and Yorkshire Parliamentarians from the south.

These moves made Newark more important than ever. It had been in Royalist hands since July 1642 although in February 1643 the Roundheads had made a strong attack on it. By the spring of 1644 its strategic value was paramount. At Newark the Fosse Way (the A46) which links Leicester, Nottingham, and Lincoln, crosses the Great North road (A1), and all this at the point where the A1 crosses the Trent. No one who visits this delightful town – which has a number of relics of the Civil War – can fail to grasp its strategic importance. In the Civil War that importance was that it blocked the route between the Parliamentary forces at Lincoln and those at Nottingham, Derby, and Leicester, while at the same time keeping open communications between Newcastle, York, and Oxford. As the Royalist army depended heavily on arms bought in Holland and landed at Newcastle or in Yorkshire ports, the value of the through route to Oxford was more than important: it was vital.

This being so, the Parliamentarians were determined to take it. On 29 February 1644 Sir John Meldrum moved to Newark with 7,000 men. His army was composed of 2,000 horse and 5,000 foot. It had eleven guns and two mortars. 'Foot' were usually made up into regiments about 1,200 strong of which 400 would be pikemen and the rest musketeers. The latter had early flintlocks which had a range of up to 400 yards but were far from accurate. However, accuracy was of no great account if the opposition were good enough to remain in close formation. Muskets were heavy, and were usually propped upon forked sticks; they were also slow and a rate of five rounds in ten minutes would be the best which could be expected. Within half an hour a musketeer would have discharged all the shot he could carry and would have to return to get to work with the sword he carried. The idea of having a sword attached to the barrel – i.e. a bayonet – had not been invented at the time of the Civil War and if a man's sword was not in the way of his musket, his musket would hamper him from using his sword. When their ammunition was gone, musketeers usually retired rapidly inside the squares formed by pikemen. The forked stick, carried for propping up the musket when taking aim, was also useful for putting down in front of a defensive position to discourage charging horsemen.

The pikemen also carried swords, but with 16 and 18-foot pikes and some body armour were slow-moving. At Pinkie, dragoons had galloped up to pikemen, discharged their guns into their faces, and ridden away unhurt.[1] But if muskets were slow, cannon were even slower. Those at Newark seem to have had a calibre of 8 in. and would launch a shot of about 40 lb.

On 6 March Meldrum captured Muskham bridge, over the Trent, destroying Holles' regiment in the process. From there he gained control of 'The Island', that part of Newark which is enclosed by the waters of the Trent. When the reader visits Newark he will notice various earthworks and defences but most of these date from a later stage in the siege, and were not in existence at the time of the battle

1 Muskets are said to have derived their name from the word *moschetto*: a form of hawk.

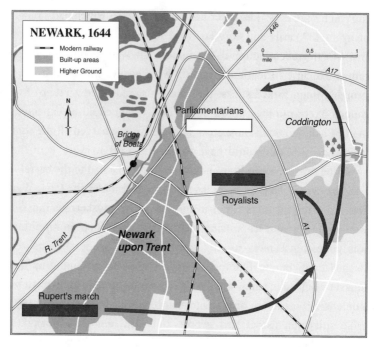

NEWARK, 1644

Modern railway
Built-up areas
Higher Ground

N

0   0,5   1
mile

A46
A17
A1

Parliamentarians

Coddington

Bridge
of Boats

Royalists

R. Trent

Newark
upon Trent

Rupert's march

Newark-upon-Trent on the A1 has a number of relics from the Civil War. The
visitor will notice various earthworks and defences but most of these date from a
later stage in the siege and were not in existence at the time of this battle.
(Nottinghamshire)

we are describing here. Meldrum was now able to surround Newark
completely.

It was obvious that the Royalists were in a critical position.
Colonel Lucas, the governor of Belvoir Castle, a few miles away,
came over with a force to try to break Meldrum's lines, but he
failed, and was driven off. Fortunately for the Royalists, Charles had
already realized the impending danger and had sent an urgent letter

to Prince Rupert to give the matter his attention. Rupert left Chester on the 12 March and marched southwards to Shrewsbury and Bridgnorth, collecting reinforcements and war material as he went, then came in to Lichfield. At Lichfield he linked up with Lord Loughborough who had assembled about 2,500 men at Ashby de la Zouch. Meldrum tried to intercept Loughborough's force but the men he sent to do this failed completely. By now Rupert had about 6,500 men, which included some very good and experienced troops.

Meldrum, somewhat disconcerted at the rapidity of Rupert's moves, concentrated his army at the Spittal. Rupert was not merely intent on trying to relieve Newark; he was also fully determined to kill or capture most of Meldrum's army. By marching up from the south-west, Rupert planned that the Roundheads should not slip away. He left Bingham at 2 a.m., on a moonlit night, and occupied Beacon Hill, from which Meldrum had recently retreated. But the Roundheads were not going to retreat without a battle. Most of their army was at the Spittal (now a victim of the railway age) and was in two foot divisions, with cavalry screening the front. Rupert kept a very small troop (Colonel Gerard's) in reserve and sent Colonel Tillier's foot (about 500 strong) to attack the bridge of boats which was Meldrum's means of reaching 'The Island'. He then led the left wing himself and, with the right commanded by Colonel Sir Richard Crane, charged into the Parliamentarians. As the Royalists broke through, the Roundhead foot fell back to the defences on the Spittal. It was a lucky occasion for Rupert, for his full force had not yet come up. A hint of what might have happened was given when Colonel Rossiter, leading a force of Roundhead cavalry, burst through the Royalist lines and captured Colonel Gerard who had expected no such thing. But soon the rest of the Royalists came up and fanned out to surround Meldrum's force, and a detachment set off to capture the bridge of boats and cut off Muskham. Events went a little differently from expectations, for the Roundheads at the bridge of boats broke them and the Royalists took to their heels.

Rupert then decided that to save casualties he would starve out Meldrum; it seems that he had heard by devious means that Meldrum was very short of food, and that two or three days should suffice. Much to Meldrum's chagrin, his regiment of Norfolk redcoats mutinied; he then asked for terms.

Meldrum was granted an honourable surrender and allowed to march out with the 'Honours of War'. This seventeenth and eighteenth-century convention allowed besieged garrisons, who had fought well but whose position was hopeless, to march out on reasonable terms. It suited both victor and vanquished as it saved money, time, lives, and material. If, however, terms were refused, the siege continued and no mercy at all would be shown to the garrison if the citadel eventually fell. Meldrum was allowed to march out with drums, swords, baggage, horses, personal belongings, and colours, but had to leave his firearms behind. The Royalists therefore acquired eleven cannon, two mortars, and 3,000 muskets. One of the cannon was named 'Sweet Lips'. It had been cast in Hull and was said to have derived its name from a woman of easy virtue who had flourished in the town in the previous century. It seems doubtful whether the Puritans would have cared greatly for the name.

The Battle of Marston Moor

2 July 1644

Newark, in spite of many pressures, held out till 1645, but on the 8 May in that year it surrendered by order of Charles. But, although the Battle of Newark had been a bright spot in Royalist fortunes in early 1643, events were not going so well for them elsewhere. The Scots were gradually moving southwards and in April linked up with Fairfax's army at Selby. The combined force was now so large and formidable that Newcastle sent an urgent message to Charles at Oxford saying that if he did not have immediate help he would soon lose the whole of the north. Charles was hard pressed to know what to do as he was short of troops himself but handed over a substantial cavalry force to Prince Rupert and told him to head north, collecting all the reinforcements he could *en route*.

Rupert left Shrewsbury on 16 May with 2,000 horse and 6,000 foot. He moved into Lancashire first. That county had sent so many soldiers to the Royalist armies in previous years that it had subsequently fallen to the Parliamentarians for little effort. Now, as Rupert showed the flag again, it came back to the Royalists with equal ease. He also made a few gains from elsewhere, such as Derbyshire, which supplied 500. Brig. Peter Young, who has made a lifelong study of the Civil War, considers that this probably brought Rupert's numbers up to 13,000. With this he hoped to link up with the 5,000 under Newcastle in York; but first he had to break through twice his own numbers of opposing Roundheads. There was little in his favour but he himself was a man of much enterprise and dash, whereas his opponents were commanded by elderly, though experienced, generals. Perhaps his greatest asset was that the Parliamentarian force had three commanders, each of whom had firm, though unenterprising views; they were Major-General Leslie, Lord Fairfax (father of Sir Thomas Fairfax), and the Earl of Manchester.

Rupert reached Skipton on 26 June 1644. He was then forty-three miles from York. He stayed at Skipton three days, preparing his army for the forthcoming battle.

His arrival at Skipton and his preparations were not unknown to the Roundheads. They were in somewhat of a quandary what to do. If they stayed besieging York they would be cut apart by Rupert's army. If, on the other hand, they maintained the siege of York but detached an army to deal with Rupert they would probably have been outflanked and defeated with ignominy. They therefore took the third course, which was to break off the siege and put their whole force against Rupert on his way to relieve the town. As Rupert advanced, and came to Knaresborough, a mere eighteen miles from York, they lifted the siege and deployed their combined forces, 27,000 strong. The site they chose was Marston Moor, six miles to the west of York.

This was a thoroughly sound move, and as they waited for the forthcoming battle with an army which would outnumber Rupert's by more than two to one they felt no slight confidence in the manoeuvre. But, as the hours slipped by, and nothing more than Rupert's vanguard was observed their confidence began to be displaced by irritation and finally by dismay.

Rupert, of course, was too old a hand at the game to fight where his opponents wanted him to fight, and on their terms. Furthermore he had made an accurate estimate of the strength and weaknesses of both sides. He himself had speed and manoeuvrability, enterprise, and a unified command. The Parliamentarians had superior numbers, little enterprise, and a triumvirate at their head. Doubtless he smiled grimly to himself as he left his advance party within sight of the Roundhead armies while he himself pressed north to Boroughbridge, where he crossed the Ure, followed it by crossing the Swale at Thornton Bridge, and came along the Ouse to York. There he relieved the town and joined up with Newcastle's men, thus gaining another 5,000 men. He made it all look very easy, though if the modern visitor follows his route today he may not think it too easy, and will be somewhat impressed by the audacity of the plan.

Unfortunately for the Royalist cause, Rupert had rather more courage and dash than common sense. If he had continued to manoeuvre as skilfully as before he could have led the Roundheads a merry dance and kept a grip upon the communications of the north. But, as had been seen as early as Edgehill, once Rupert started moving he could not easily stop. Some of his troops had different ideas, and settled down to a little drinking and looting. When therefore he decided to use his increased numbers for battle, still short by some 9,000 of the strength of the opposition, the Roundhead generals were astonished to hear of this turn of events. Their view, not surprisingly, had been that Rupert would now hold York and use it for a base to cut off their own communications. Strategically Rupert was now in an excellent position, as his opponents knew. In fact the only move available to them seemed to be to cut off Rupert from his sources of supply. They therefore set off south-west and were approaching Tadcaster before they heard the almost incredible news that Rupert was now coming out to fight

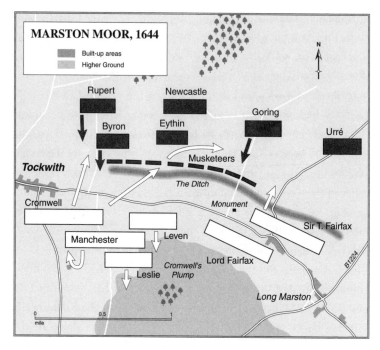

MARSTON MOOR, 1644

Built-up areas
Higher Ground

Rupert

Newcastle

Goring

Byron

Eythin

Urré

Tockwith

Musketeers

The Ditch

Cromwell

Monument

Sir T. Fairfax

Manchester

Leven

Lord Fairfax

Cromwell's

Leslie *Plump*

Long Marston

0   0.5   1
mile

Take the B1224 from York and turn right at Long Marston. The battlefield lies along the Long Marston to Tockwith road and is marked by a monument. (North Yorkshire)

against their superior numbers. They promptly made an 'about turn' and set off back to Marston Moor. The last time they had drawn themselves up on this battlefield they were expecting an attack from the south-west; now, however, they faced one from the north-east.

Marston Moor probably looks much the same today as it did in 1644. It is an open windy plain which extends between Tockwith to the west and Long Marston to the east. The distance between the two is 1½ miles, and as the two armies deployed they covered that area evenly. The visitor will probably approach it along the B1224 from York and turn along the Marston Lane which will take him to Tockwith. He will see a memorial on the right of this road and will note a ditch to the east of it. There is another ditch running parallel with the Marston Lane, but he may not notice this from the road. On such hazards battles are lost and won. As he moves along this road he will be passing behind the Roundhead position, with Fairfax on the right wing, Leven and Crawford in the centre, Manchester in the left centre, and Cromwell on the left wing. On the hill behind him is a knob of ground which was once covered with trees. It is known as Cromwell's Plump, and was Leven's headquarters. The ground slopes very gently towards the Royalists' position and thereafter is flat. Nobody recorded how wide the ditch was at the time of the battle nor how much water it contained. On the Royalist side, Byron commanded the right wing, facing Cromwell; Eythin and Newcastle were in the centre; and Goring commanded the left, opposite the elder Fairfax; Rupert commanded the reserve. It was an ideal area for a cavalry battle – or seemed to be. Both sides were anxious for a solution by battle and both equally unaware of the urgency felt by the other side. Yet in spite of it all, the early hours of 2 July were spent by both in trying to manoeuvre their forces into the most favourable position. Had Rupert launched an attack on the Roundheads as they were coming up to the battlefield, history might have been different. Equally, if the Roundheads had launched an attack before the Royalists expected them, the battle might have had a different ending. But both sets of commanders had troubles enough of their own at that stage without thinking of giving any to the enemy. The Scots' foot had made excellent headway on the march south-west the previous day and were approaching Tadcaster before the message to return reached them. When the armies formed up at Marston Moor therefore the Roundheads were still short of some of their best infantry. But, fortunately for them, Rupert had his own troubles. When the Roundheads had left their siege-lines and come out to deploy at Marston Moor on the earlier occasion, they had abandoned all sorts of equipment which the Royalists could not forbear to loot. Then, when the Royalists were assembled, they refused to march until they received their arrears of pay. Even with all these disadvantages, Rupert would probably have been wise to attack, as his opponents were in a worse state of confusion than his own side was.

Rupert placed a line of musketeers along the ditch dividing the two armies. His own area was open moorland, superb country for cavalry manoeuvre; the Parliamentarians on the other hand had some rye fields in their territory. The Royalist musketeers were doubtless positioned to disrupt the enemy formation rather than form part of a defensive line. If the Roundheads once got themselves into a tangle, Rupert would know very well how to exploit it.

The Royalist dispositions – as would be expected – consisted of horse on the wings and foot in the centre. The right wing had about 2,500 horse, the left about 2,000, and the centre consisted of 10,000 foot. There were a few hundred musketeers and sixteen guns. Rupert's reserve division consisted of 650 horse. The Roundheads had, of course, the advantage of superior numbers, and this apparently gave them approximately 7,000 cavalry and 20,000 foot. They had twenty-five guns.

Marston Moor was an extraordinary battle. As the day wore on, and both sides had placed their troops in what seemed to be reasonably satisfactory positions, the Roundheads waited for the inevitable Royalist attack. To their surprise it did not come. Hour succeeded hour. Apparently Rupert was having some acrimonious discussion with at least one of his subordinate commanders, but this was not the only reason for the delay. It is one thing to hurl yourself into a battle when and where you can see an obvious opportunity but an entirely different matter if the opposition outnumbers you and presents no obvious weakness. By four o'clock in the afternoon the Roundheads realized that by numbers alone the initiative probably lay with them. However, they did not act at once; instead they waited till evening when they could see from their slight eminence that the Royalists had dismounted, had lighted fires, and were taking an evening meal. It seemed too good an opportunity to miss. At a single cannon shot the whole Roundhead army moved forward. Darkness seemed to have fallen early for July and now the reason was seen. There was a clap of thunder and a scud of rain. Marston Moor had begun with a thunderstorm.

The Royalists were surprised, and the Roundheads were over the ditch before Rupert's force had alerted sufficiently to check them. On the right, Sir Thomas Fairfax pushed well ahead and roused the extreme left of Goring's wing. Making the perennial mistake he set off in pursuit but by the time he had broken off and rallied his troop he found that the rest of Goring's men had spotted the gap and with a desperate charge cut up the Roundheads very badly. Fairfax, seeing the hopeless disarray of his command, promptly retired from the field.

But it was harder going in the Roundhead centre. As the Royalists set to with their normal dash, the Scottish troops reeled and staggered under the blow. But they held. Then up came the Scottish second line, and it was the turn of the Royalists to fall back. So far, the Roundhead right had been beaten and the centre was just holding its own. On the left, however, it was a very different story.

Cromwell, who commanded the Roundhead left wing consisting

of 3,000 men, had hurtled into Byron's troops. Byron – his opposite – had apparently made a tactical mistake in that instead of letting his musketeers disrupt the Roundhead formation and then widen the gaps, he had charged himself and made it impossible to use his musketeers. As a result, although the Royalists checked the Roundhead charge with much difficulty, their losses were very heavy and the Roundheads were soon in control. The only bright spot for the Royalists was that Cromwell himself was wounded; unfortunately for the Royalists it was not serious and soon 'Old Noll' was back in command.

Rupert, seeing that disaster was opening up on this wing, now flung himself and his reserve into the fray. It was in vain. Although the vigour and desperation of his charge, combined with some very pretty swordwork, enabled him to break through the Roundhead lines, he was soon surrounded by Scottish foot. This is when he desperately needed more Royalist foot, or better still another wing of cavalry. But he had nothing to match the dour Scottish infantry, commanded by Leslie, and soon was in flight himself.

Yet, although the battle was now virtually won for the Parliamentarians, the confusion on the field was so great that few of the combatants had any idea of the position.

On both sides terrified men were fleeing from the field. Royalists on the right were rushing for safety over Tockwith Moor, while in the Roundhead centre many of the Scottish foot were wishing they had never left Scotland, which they certainly never expected to see again. Some of the commanders were in similar confusion.

At this delicate stage, with a Parliamentarian victory virtually won but with an excellent chance of its being frittered away in the general confusion, leaving a stalemate, Fairfax, who had lost his command, came over to the Roundhead left. There he met Cromwell, whose wound had been tended, and who was now looking for a decisive part to play. This was the 'luck of battle' – the opportunity which is presented to some commanders but never to others. Fairfax reported his own success which had turned to failure, and Cromwell was able to make an assessment of the general scene. The situation in the middle was stable enough and favouring the Roundheads; the Roundhead right wing was in confusion with the Royalists now plundering Fairfax's baggage-wagons; but the Roundhead left had complete victory and capacity to spare. It was the work of minutes for Cromwell to assemble a cavalry force and turn it on to the Royalist left wing. By moving forward and then wheeling sharply right Cromwell was able to come on to the rear of Goring's men. There are few situations more disconcerting than to be attacked in the rear at the time when you think you are consolidating an undisputed victory. Goring's division was no exception; surprise and confusion at this unexpected attack from an impossible source filled them with confusion and dismay; they put up little fight. The last to give up the struggle were Newcastle's Whitecoats. Here there was no dismay, no panic. Surrounded, and without hope of assistance they fought on, scorning surrender. The casualties in this battle were high, and particularly so in this quarter of the field. The Royalists were said to have lost over 4,000 killed; 1,500 were taken prisoner. The Roundheads got off much more lightly, losing a mere 300 killed, although many more had sword cuts to remember the battle by. But, as we have often seen in these pages, the heaviest casualties may occur when the battle is virtually over, sometimes completely over, and naturally enough, to the losing side. Nevertheless, the huge disparity between the casualty figures on each side requires some explanation. How did 4,000 men meet their deaths for a cost of only 300?

Clearly a good number, possibly a hundred or two, fell in the first charge made by Fairfax from the right wing of the Parliamentarian army. We recall Fairfax's cavalry doing terrible execution at Winceby in 'Slash Hollow' the previous October. Doubtless they were equally effective among the bushes and clumps running across the moor. There would have been other heavy casualties on this (the left of the Royalist army) when Cromwell put in that final charge into the rear of Goring's men who were caught plundering. Many had probably discarded their weapons and were staggering along with armsful of loot, under the impression that the battle was won and it was a Royalist victory.

Equally there would have been a number of casualties in the other wing. Many would have fallen on both sides – in Cromwell's first charge. It will be recalled that Cromwell launched 3,000 men, and 3,000 men can cause a lot of damage. After Cromwell had left the field, his men – now commanded by the dashing Major-General Lawrence Crawford – sustained a series of heavy charges by Rupert's force. Rupert, of course, was well aware that victory or defeat hung in the balance in this quarter, and spared no effort. Rupert, as we saw, cut and slashed his way through, but was then engulfed by the Scots foot under Leslie. It seems that Rupert was unhorsed, for it was reported that he had to hide himself in a beanfield. Presumably, darkness had now fallen.

The credit for final victory probably lay with Fairfax, who seems to have wandered about the field, even through the Royalist lines, unrecognized. When he met Cromwell that portion of the battlefield must have looked something like his own earlier, though doubtless more bloody. Experience told him that this was a point in which half the Roundhead army could easily disappear from the field in pursuit – or perhaps under the impression that they had lost the battle if they were near enough to see what was happening to the remnants of their right wing, now being plundered by the Royalists under Goring.

Even so, these desperate killing-grounds would only seem to account for about half the Royalist casualties. Where then did the others come from?

It is not possible to be sure but it would seem that they would mainly be musketeers, who were handled very ineptly in this battle. Apart from those lining the ditch, who were ridden over in the first charge, there were three regiments of musketeers, each numbering about 750, who were positioned ahead of the Royalist army, covering the centre. Doubtless they were meant to disrupt the Roundhead advance and perhaps fire into the flanks of the cavalry as they swept by. Possibly they were not meant to remain in that position at all, but the surprise of the Roundhead advance caught them unawares. They were – to use a military cynicism – candidates for 'six feet of earth or a decoration'. As it was, they undoubtedly got the six feet of earth. It seems likely that they would have been wiped out almost to a man, just like the Whitecoats (they were in fact drawn from Rupert's Bluecoats, and Byron's regiment). But had the battle gone the other way they would have been the heroes of a Royalist victory.

As we have seen, Marston Moor was a decisive battle, and went to the Roundheads partly because of their initiative and partly because of Royalist mistakes. It was, of course, somewhat foolhardy of Rupert to take on superior numbers when his own men were exhausted by the strenuous manoeuvres of the previous few days. But decisive or not, the Roundheads made singularly poor use of their victory. Not only had they destroyed an army; they had also badly damaged Prince Rupert's reputation. He was no longer the invincible cavalry commander. In that process Cromwell's own reputation had increased even further. Cromwell had the modern approach of careful and ruthless selection of his subordinate commanders. There was one criterion – and it was merit.

Rupert's reputation was not the only one to be damaged in this battle, and the criticism of him was as a battle commander rather than on personal grounds. The same cannot be said of some of the other commanders. Eythin had criticized Rupert's battle-plan and probably contributed to the delay which eventually induced the Roundheads to attack. Newcastle was over-cautious and Goring – thought he most successful Royalist commander – perhaps too reckless. On the Parliamentarian side Lord Fairfax, father of the dashing cavalry commander, Sir Thomas Fairfax, was so dispirited at seeing his infantry routed that he rode off the battlefield, went to his home ten miles away and straight to bed. Leven and Manchester both rode off the field but, whereas Manchester subsequently collected both his wits and some fugitives and returned, Leven was well up with the leaders in his panic flight and did not stop – it is said – till he reached Leeds. There must have been some ingenious explanations when some of these distinguished generals were subsequently required to comment on their actions. They had plenty of time to do so, for the Roundheads camped at Marston Moor for two days, trying to reorganize, and hardly aware that they had won a battle. Rupert was a little quicker to recover. He assembled the remnants of his cavalry in York and eventually collected some 10,000 men to march north-west, to meet Montrose. He was in no danger of pursuit. Having given thanks to God for their great and surprising victory, the Parliamentarians saw no further ahead than retaking York. Had they pressed on towards Oxford they might have defeated Charles's 'Oxford' army, and brought the war to an end that year. But their chances were frittered away.

This was the biggest battle of the Civil War and was second only to Towton as the biggest battle ever fought on English soil. It is interesting to move from one battlefield to the other and to sense the peculiar difference and atmosphere of each. Marston Moor, of course, had many less casualties, and was less horrific, but even the pious psalm-singing Roundheads showed little mercy once their blood was stirred. Doubtless they saw themselves as inflicting due punishment on the enemies of God. Although allegedly despising the lace, the rich clothing, and the elaborate swords of the Royalists, they stripped the corpses very thoroughly; within twenty-four hours every corpse on any battlefield was stark naked, divested by the victors or by the vulture-like ghouls who trailed behind the armies to rob the dead or the defenceless. The Royalists, for their part, would feel equal justification in their victories for withholding quarter; they saw the Parliamentarians not as pioneers of democratic government but as rebels against a king appointed by divine right, and as such deserving no mercy.

The Battle of Rowton Heath

24 September 1645

York surrendered to Parliament on 16 July 1644, two weeks exactly after Marston Moor. But, even with the north virtually gone, there was still some prospect of a Royalist victory. The Marquis of Newcastle, admittedly, could not see it, and sailed for Holland, taking no further part in the war, but Rupert, looking back, considered his men had acquitted themselves reasonably well against superior numbers. However, prospects looked bleak in the south midlands where Parliament had two considerable armies, commanded by the Earl of Essex and Sir William Waller. Fortunately for the Royalists both these commanders had a high opinion of their own abilities and a low opinion of the other's. That fact, often expressed, completely ruled out any co-operation between them. It was a godsend for the Royalists, for they were able to tackle each army in turn, and achieve victories. Had Essex and Waller combined nothing could have saved the king. Instead Charles was able to beat Waller at Cropredy Bridge in Oxfordshire, and then turn on Essex. Essex had noted that the export of Cornish tin paid for the import of Royalist ammunition and therefore decided to occupy Cornwall and stop this vital trade. He was already in Devon, where he was campaigning with moderate success. Yet although he did not realize it at the time, disaster was stalking him; for Charles had already decided to bring him to battle. Essex hoped that Waller would have interfered with the progress of the Royal army but this proved a false hope, and Charles was already in Launceston when Essex had only reached Bodmin. Essex's ineptitude as a strategist was soon fully revealed, and on 2 September 1644 his hungry and bewildered army was forced to capitulate at Lostwithiel, on the River Fowey. Six thousand surrendered, and handed over forty-two guns and a mortar, and 5,000 muskets. Had Charles then pursued a bold policy, he could have marched on London and probably taken it. But the general apathy which appeared to infect both sides in this war now seemed to influence him as well. Instead, he made a half-hearted attempt to capture Plymouth, which failed, and then decided to relieve besieged garrisons of Royalists in Basing House, near Basingstoke, at Donnington Castle, near Newbury, and at Banbury. Nevertheless, he dallied too long and when, in October, he decided to return to Oxford there were 18,000 Parliamentarians between him and his home base. His own force numbered approximately 9,000. Notwithstanding this disadvantage, he decided to give battle at Newbury on 28 October 1644. This time the chosen site was on the north of the town, around Donnington Castle. Cromwell was not his usual enterprising self in this battle and the result was a Roundhead failure more than a Royalist victory. Charles was able to push his army through to Oxford; and later both Donnington Castle and Basing House were relieved. The war then petered out for the year 1644, and the armies went into winter quarters. (Campaigning in the winter was regarded as futile by both sides; the obvious disadvantages outweighed any chance advantages.)

However, during the lull in hostilities, two events took place which eventually led to victory for the Parliamentarians. A new regular army of 20,000 men, the 'New Model' Army, was created. At the same time, by the 'Self-denying Ordinance', command of this army was left to professional soldiers, and such well-known, though inactive, figures as Manchester and Essex retired. Into their place went vigorous professionals with Sir Thomas Fairfax at the head and Cromwell as second in command. This was the army which won the Battle of Naseby in Northamptonshire on 14 June 1645, the battle which virtually clinched the war for the Parliamentarians. Charles was not captured, and he spent the following eight months trying to raise another army. His only hope lay in Scotland where the Marquis of Montrose had raised a considerable following. By 15 August Montrose had taken Glasgow and controlled all the vital ports of Scotland. Alas for hopes; many of Montrose's Highlanders slipped away to stow their plunder, and, while Montrose's force was thus depleted and small, Leslie defeated him at Philiphaugh, near Selkirk, with the army which had been serving in England (13 September 1645). After this victory the Covenanters took cold and savage revenge for the slaughter of Kilsythe, when Montrose's troops had ignored all pleas for restraint, even those issued by Montrose himself. Leslie's dragoons now shot down prisoners in cold blood, and are reported to have flung eighty men, women, and children off Linlithgow Bridge into the waters of the Avon some fifty feet below. In this time of blood and revenge Charles's hopes for help from Scotland now disappeared.

But the war was not quite over. Although Goring had been defeated at Langport on 10 July and Rupert had surrendered at Bristol on 11 September, all Charles could think of was the brilliant campaign of Montrose in Scotland. He could scarcely realize that all hope from that quarter would disappear for ever within a few days. Charles deserved both admiration and criticism at this stage. He refused to give up hope; but when Rupert surrendered Bristol, which he and others were confident he could hold for at least four

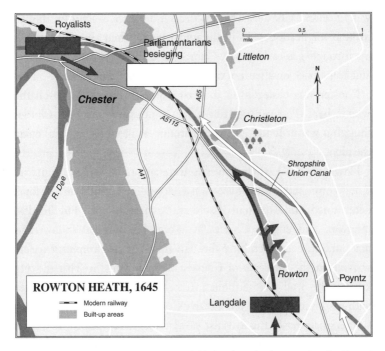

It is still possible to follow the course of this battle today by crossing the Dee at Holt Bridge and proceeding to Rowton Heath. It is also worth entering the city and looking over the battlefield from the walls. (Cheshire)

months, he turned against his nephew and forgot the long record of devoted service and brilliant victories Rupert had brought him. In that black autumn the Royalist cause was crumbling everywhere, but Charles, who had not heard the bleak news of Philiphaugh, was still optimistic in mid-September. Possibly he realized that his enemies were almost as bitter between themselves as they were against him. At all events he was holding grimly on to a small army consisting of some 3,000 cavalry and 1,000 infantry. He decided his best course was to relieve Chester, which had been besieged since July, and to make it his headquarters in the north-west. Then he would march up through Lancashire and Cumberland, link up with Montrose, and come back on a path of conquest, driving all before him.

Chester was besieged on the east side only; it was open on the west, where the river Dee flows. It was not therefore impossible – though it was arduous – to march around to the west side and enter the city.

However, the Parliamentarians were not to be caught napping. Their commander in that area was Colonel-General Poyntz, a dour, determined, and experienced soldier. Poyntz had tried and failed to intercept and engage Charles at Worcester but had followed in hot pursuit, even marching through the night. In consequence he arrived on the outskirts of Chester at 6 a.m. on the 24th. Poyntz knew very well that although Charles himself was in Chester with his infantry, and a few cavalry – a total of not more than 1,000 – the remainder of the Royalist cavalry under Langdale was on the outside. Poyntz was short of troops himself, having not more than 3,000. Langdale, with the Royalist cavalry, halted at Rowton Heath.

The situation was now nicely balanced. If Poyntz could get to the besiegers and reinforce them, there was little chance that they would be dispersed by the Royalist army. But he had no reason for great confidence, for when Langdale charged at 9 a.m. Poyntz's troops fell back in confusion. Well they might, perhaps, considering the arduous march they had just accomplished. Both sides were in desperate need of reinforcements, but Poyntz was the one lucky – or skilful – enough to get his message through. In consequence he received another 500 cavalry and 300 foot from the siege-lines. They could be of no value to the siege at this point but they could be invaluable in an open battle. There was slight risk that Langdale could turn and destroy the remainder of the besiegers, for their lines were totally unsuitable for any cavalry action.

By the time Charles realized the situation, and appreciated the need to send out help to Langdale, Poyntz had attacked. It was then 3 p.m. The Royalist reinforcements were too late to influence the battle but not too late to be killed in it. Langdale's men attacked by Poyntz in the front, and harassed by the foot soldiers under Colonel Jones, were driven right back to the walls of Chester. There they fell into an appalling tangle with the rest of the Roundhead besiegers, as well as the reinforcements recently sent out from the city of Chester. Those inside the city manned the walls (which the visitor will doubtless walk around) and fired into the struggling mass at what they hoped were the right targets. Gradually the Roundheads gained the upper hand and forced the Royalists away from the walls in the direction of Hoole Heath. The Royalist cavalry, who found themselves battling in narrow and congested streets, had already tasted defeat at Marston Moor and Naseby and their morale was brittle. Six hundred were killed and 800 taken prisoner. Thus ended Charles' hopes of linking up with Montrose, of whose defeat he was still ignorant.

It is still possible to follow the course of this battle today by crossing the Dee at Holt Bridge and proceeding, like Langdale's cavalry, to Rowton Heath. The visitor will find the site of the first attack at Hatton Moor, on the A41 to Whitchurch and should then go on to Rowton Heath. He will find an inn – of later date – called 'Ye Old Trooper', then perhaps enter the city and look over the battlefield from the walls. Standing up there he will not be surprised to think that Chester still held out till 3 February 1646.

The Battle of Preston

17 August 1648

The final stages of the first phase of the Civil War dragged on till 19 August 1646, although Charles himself had surrendered to the Scots on 5 May 1646. They were besieging Newark at the time and Charles felt he would fare better politically in their hands than with the English Parliamentarians. Oxford, however, was not surrendered till 24 June, and the Marquis of Worcester defied the Roundheads at Raglan Castle until 19 August.

The Scots were delighted to be host to Charles and promised to assist his restoration to the throne, provided he would make Presbyterianism the religion of England. Much as Charles wished for the throne this condition was too great a burden for his will and his conscience. It would, he felt, be selling his soul, for he was by conscience, a High Churchman. After a time, the Scots wearied of his apparent dallying and handed him over to the English Parliament. This is no place to describe the shades of religious opinion which functioned in the English Parliament, but it may be noted that the intensity with which beliefs were held made agreement or compromise almost impossible. Charles observed, and waited. The Presbyterians were in the majority in Parliament but a minority in the nation. Charles therefore appeared to give careful consideration to their views, which he discussed in infinite and totally unnecessary detail, but all the while was in correspondence with a variety of possible allies, in Scotland, in France, and even in England.

In March 1647, the Presbyterians caused a crisis by issuing an order for the disbandment of the New Model Army, ostensibly because of the expense of keeping it up, but actually because it included too many of their opponents, who tended to be more tolerant though not necessarily less devout. The New Model Army, however, refused to be disbanded and with the approval of Fairfax and Cromwell removed the king from Holmby House, North-amptonshire, where he was under house arrest, and bore him off to Newmarket, the army's headquarters. The army then marched on Parliament, and as many of the Presbyterians had hastily, though perhaps prudently, removed themselves, had no difficulty about obtaining a majority. With this they offered Charles favourable terms which he would have done very well to accept.

Charles, however, leapt to the mistaken conclusion that he could do better. Seeing the conflict between the Presbyterians and the army, he came to the opinion that he could now turn the tables militarily. On 11 November 1647 he slipped away from his loose guard and reached the Isle of Wight. There he was confined to Carisbrooke Castle but not otherwise impeded. He began rapidly to organize his military return.

The effects were not seen until 28 April 1648, but on that date some north-country Royalists seized Berwick and proclaimed for the King. Soon, there was support elsewhere. There was a rebellion in South Wales, where the army had so much resented the order to disband that it had joined with the local Royalists in Pembrokeshire. Cromwell was sent against them and was kept besieging Pembroke Castle until July. The Irish, under Lord Inchiquin, were also up in arms. The Scots voted to raise a new army, which they hoped would

number nearly 40,000. Even the south-east showed Royalist sympathies. The rising in Kent was quickly suppressed by Fairfax but
the trouble in the eastern counties took longer to crush. Even so, the
revolt was by no means over. There were plenty more Royalist
sympathizers there and elsewhere, as, for example, in the Midlands.

In Scotland the situation was not quite as promising as it looked.
The Duke of Hamilton and his supporters paid lip-service to the
Covenanter's ideals but their hearts were not in their cause in the
same way as the Earl of Argyll. Hamilton was not a very experienced
soldier and badly needed an efficient second-in-command. In the
event, he received the Earl of Callander, an ardent Royalist, and an
authoritarian of rigid political and military views.

Although by no means ready for a trial of strength, Hamilton
invaded England on 9 July with a mixed force, many of whom had
no proper training, let alone battle experience. His force was short of
every necessary supply, including ammunition. It had to try to live
on the country it passed through and, as the weather was unbelie-
vably adverse, with bitter winds and driving incessant rain, the
condition of this army may be imagined.

Hamilton rested for six days at Carlisle, where he was reinforced
by Langdale who brought 3,000 foot and some cavalry. Lambert, his
Parliamentarian opponent, had not the numbers to match him,
and fell back to Penrith. Hamilton followed up quickly, though
not perhaps quickly enough, but was unable to trap Lambert in
Appleby, where they had a brief clash. Lambert disengaged and
Hamilton paused in the area, waiting for reinforcements which
trickled in very slowly and inadequately. All this was taking far too
long, for in July Cromwell was free of Pembrokeshire and able to
head north. But even his army was in a poor state, ill-shod, and
much battered by the weather which made the going so bad. Every

serious trouble in the muddy lanes, lost their way, and failed to link up as planned. But they gave a good account of themselves when attacked. On the morning of the 18th they reached Wigan and would have made a stand, but the powder they were carrying was wet and there was no more to replace it. They pressed on to Warrington, but at Winwick, where a lane and a bank made the nucleus of a defensive position, they stood. For several hours the battle raged between the half-starved, weary Scots, and Cromwell's outnumbered but jubilant Roundheads. Some of the heaviest fighting took place on the green by Winwick Church, but eventually, after a thousand Scots had fallen, the rest retreated to Warrington, where they barricaded the bridge and prepared to fight again. But the Battle of Preston was over. Hamilton and Callander set off north, after telling the remaining 2,500 Scots to make the best terms they could. They did not see the campaign as lost, and were planning to link up with other Royalists elsewhere – in Wales or the Home Counties. Gradually, however, their remaining forces were thinned by desertion and sickness, and, finally, on 25 August Hamilton was taken prisoner at Stafford. Hamilton would have made an excellent company commander, brave, loyal, and persistent; but in any task requiring planning and staff work, assessment and administration, he was disastrous.

The second phase of the Civil War had ended in defeat and disgrace for the Royalists. Even worse, all trust had gone, and the Parliamentarians felt that they must punish, and take no further chances. Hamilton, Lucas, Lisle, and Holland, were all executed, and many of those who had served under them were transported to the Barbados plantations.

Nor was there any sympathy for Charles. He had twice tried to escape from Carisbrooke; now he was put under close guard at

Hurst. The army had now had enough of both the Presbyterians and Charles. The former were dealt with by a military *coup d'état*, when forty-one were imprisoned and ninety-six told never to come near the House of Commons again.

On 1 January 1649 the King was put on trial on grounds that 'to levy war against the Parliament and realm of England was treason'. Charles refused to plead in any way. On 30 January 1649 he was beheaded on a scaffold erected before the windows of Whitehall Palace (now demolished). He met his death with courage and dignity.

BOOK THREE

The Midlands

Introduction

For the man who is interested in warfare and who likes to walk the ground, deducing how battles were lost and won, there is no more fascinating study than the early battlefields. Here his theories will be as valid as those of any historian, military or otherwise, and he may well have a flash of insight that will solve a mystery which has lasted for a thousand years. The early battlefields are often set in open countryside which has changed much less than the landscape elsewhere; this makes his task easier. He will be advised to equip himself with an up-to-date large-scale map, a prismatic compass, and perhaps a pair of binoculars. The binoculars will save his legs, and perhaps more if he uses them to inspect herds of cows. I have encountered more than one farm where a bull was loose in a field with a footpath running through it!

Battles and battlefields throw much light on history at any period but the interest of the early battles is that small bodies of men fighting with primitive weapons often determined the shape and composition of future nations. At Hastings approximately 9,000 Normans changed the course of history; in earlier battles smaller numbers had accomplished nearly as much.

To understand the early battles it is necessary to see oneself as a member of one side or the other; it does not matter whether as victor or vanquished. Having taken sides you should approach the battlefield from the direction by which your own army approached. As you do so you should consider all alternative courses of action – apart from making a hasty retreat. Are you, as you move forward, sufficiently alert to the possibilities of surprise? As you ponder on your possible courses of action – and the enemy's – making, in fact, a military appreciation, that long-past situation will suddenly become almost embarrassingly real. You may perhaps experience that peculiar feeling, half apprehension, half excitement, that you are now on the most dangerous path you have ever trod. At the same time you may feel that this is destiny and that you would not wish it otherwise. You, for better or worse, are playing your part in great events. Once the battle has begun you will have no time for thoughts, speculative or otherwise. You will be driven by the needs of the moment, and whether you are alive at the end of the battle will depend on training, luck, and perhaps even your own skill at arms. Whatever happens, even if you come through without a scratch (which is unlikely), you will never be the same person again.

In considering battles, do not believe contemporary accounts without question. Some are entirely reliable but they are far outnumbered by those which are not. Few military dispatches avoid bias of one sort or another, and when one compares the accounts of opposing sides in any battle it is often difficult to realize they are describing the same events and place. Minor successes are magnified; major setbacks glossed over. Sycophants were just as plentiful in former times as they are today. Critics of a successful and powerful person were however much less plentiful. Nowadays it is commonplace for people whose naval experience is limited to a Channel crossing to criticize the tactics at Trafalgar or Jutland, and other people of no military experience at all are apt to be very severe indeed with the Montgomeries, Slims, MacArthurs and Pattons;

rather less was heard of such armchair strategists in medieval times. Not unwisely the valiant non-combatant preferred to wait till his subjects and their near relatives were dead before voicing his criticisms; he might otherwise have been offered practical opportunities to exercise his military knowledge.

It is widely known that once the first shot is fired, or the first blow struck there descends on any battlefield 'the fog of war'. Orders are given, misinterpreted, misunderstood, delayed, even disobeyed. Confused and conflicting reports are sent back to commanders who are hard put to distinguish which side is which in the confused struggling mass ahead of and around them. Almost every report is alarmist or exaggerated. A few lucky hits by arrows or gunshot could throw a whole line into confusion and the actual ground might display all sorts of unexpected qualities. The Battle of Agincourt was partly won by the English bowmen but was more a matter of a battle lost to the French by treacherous mud than won by any great skill from their opponents. Unfortunately in the very early battles there is no record of the exact date on which they were fought. Undoubtedly they would have been in the summer months but the result in many turned perhaps on whether there were leaves on the trees, and whether the ground was wet or dry. Walking on the steep side of a chalk down is entirely different in wet and dry weather, and as you walk it you will undoubtedly envisage fighting on it. Look for the local hazard: the clump of thorn bushes, the sharp little slope, the spongy patch near a spring or stream, and the ground which looks smooth from a short distance but which is very rough and disconcerting when you are on it.

You needed an iron nerve to fight in these early battles. As you moved up towards the enemy you were encouraged by the competent look of your fellow soldiers, and the exhortations of your leaders. This was easy enough. When the enemy came in sight there probably seemed to be rather more of them than you had expected. The front lines would meet. There would be noise, confusion and swaying of the first few ranks. For most of the army it would be a matter of watch and wait. Some would be pressing forward, eager to take their turn; others might not like what they saw, which was decidedly less pleasant and easy than they had been led to expect. These – not many perhaps – might perhaps decide to drop to the rear and slip away, but in most battles that would have been foreseen. There would be a ring of medieval 'military police' waiting at the rear to take care of just that contingency, and the less resolute would reluctantly realize that the only way out of the battle was through the front. Later when the battle was being decided and most men were fighting for their lives some might take that chance to disappear. Their subsequent account of the battle would doubtless explain both the significant part they had taken in it and the miracle by which they had survived. But there would be no one to contradict the details. If you really got into the thick of it in a medieval battle, you would be exceptionally lucky if you came out to tell the tale.

One very good way of understanding what went on in a battle is to play it out as a war-game. War-gamers set out their toy soldiers and weapons on a model of the battlefield. They then throw a dice in turn to decide what moves each can make. The rules are quite complicated and some battles go on for days.[1] The most interesting part of the game is the light it throws on the battle. You may have heard that in a certain battle the numbers were 50,000 and the area over which it was fought was two square miles. By the time the battle is fought as a war-game, the size, shape, and surface of the battle-

1 See *Charge* (a manual for War-gamers) by Brig. P. Young and Lt Col J. P. Lawford.

ground will probably be well known. Even if it is not the mere extent of the battlefield may throw some doubt on the original contemporary accounts. It will be clear that there is a limit to the number of troops who could have been engaged on any piece of ground. Perhaps you will make precisely the same calculations – and mistakes – as the original commanders. But you will not suffer for them as they did.

Were these ancient warriors so different from ourselves? Were they immune from fear, pain, discomfort? Not so very different and not immune from anything. The Saxon soldier, the Briton, the Norman, the Cavalier, the Roundhead: they were harder than untrained men today but not necessarily tougher than the *élite* of modern armies. Over and over again it is training and discipline which tells, and there are many men in today's regiments who would have given as good as they got in those long-past battles.

The Battle of Mount Badon

AD 516

The Battle of Mount Badon or Mons Badonicus has been somewhat of a mystery for over fifteen hundred years. Records are scanty and there has been much speculation over its exact site. It was an enormously important battle, and its result delayed the subjugation of Britain for fifty years. It was undoubtedly a masterpiece of strategic and tactical planning. Perhaps much of the mystery stems from the fact that Badon was chronicled by scholars and monks who were far away in time as well as place, and did not know the area in which it was reputedly fought. Looking at it today with no special prejudices to air, and being concerned only with what the late Col A. H. Burne so aptly called I.M.P. (Inherent Military Probability), the obscurity of Badon seems a little less impenetrable. Col Burne's contribution to the study of ancient battlefields was invaluable but this does not of course mean that one would always agree with his deductions. Here we agree on the site but differ on the disposition of the forces and the course of events. Col Burne accepts most of Geoffrey of Monmouth's account (written in the twelfth century) though he acknowledges that on other matters Geoffrey's versions were somewhat imaginative.

The visitor to any battlefield will first ask who fought it and why. Once this is established the course of the battle – even the choice of site – becomes much more obvious. To understand Badon we have to return in history nearly a hundred years before it occurred.

Badon was fought in 516 and was a battle between Saxons and Britons. The Britons were the inhabitants of these islands when the Romans landed in 55 BC. After the Romans had been in occupation for nearly five hundred years the Britons had become soft and unaccustomed to warfare. Long before the Roman legions finally left Britain in the first half of the fifth century a new force had appeared on the scene. This was the Saxons. They had first appeared in the Channel as early as the second century AD. They were great fighters and seafarers and, when they settled, skilful farmers. The Romans had a healthy respect for them and even admired them but had created a special command to deal with their marauding. It was under the 'Count of the Saxon Shore' and he had a fleet of warships and a chain of forts to help him in his task. The Romans are always thought of as a land-based people swinging along their magnificent roads to confront the enemy in set-piece battles. But the Romans were flexible and adaptable, and had mastered many sorts of fighting. They were not too proud to adopt the techniques and camouflage of their opponents if it seemed likely to bring success. And it usually did. They even painted themselves, partly for camouflage, partly to inspire fear.

But the Romans had too many troubles at home to be able to stay and protect Britain from the Saxons. The Roman empire was rotten within, and slowly but inexorably the outposts were withdrawn. As the legions left Britain other would-be conquerors were waiting to take their place. The Caledonians – the Picts – were ready to swarm over the walls which the Romans had built to keep them out – the Antonine Wall, and Hadrian's Wall. The future looked ominous for the Britons who had been protected so long.

There were other threats than these. Swarming in from the north and west was another intensely warlike people – the Scots. At first they raided the Midlands and the south but later they moved north-east, settled, and gave their name to Scotland.

The Romans had done almost everything for Britain except teach them to defend themselves. They had made roads and cities, built houses, developed agriculture and mining, and even imprinted their own civilization on their subject people.

It is not perhaps entirely fair to blame the subsequent defeat of the Britons on their lack of military experience during the Roman occupation. Many Britons had served in the Roman legions, and were as skilled and brave as their fellows in arms. But courage and skill are no substitute for numbers if the opponents are no less able, unless that courage and skill can be used behind adequate fortifications, or adapted to an entirely different mode of warfare. This the Britons did not appreciate early enough or widely enough. But on one occasion they did use exactly the right tactics against their opponents and that was at Mount Badon.

The last Roman legions were withdrawn from Britain in 410 AD. Soon the Jutes arrived and settled in Kent. The situation was not entirely clear-cut. The Jutes had arrived by invitation but had quarrelled with their hosts and driven them out. They demanded the south-east. There were still Romans in Britain but they had no military power. In the *Anglo-Saxon Chronicle*, our source for the sequence of the main events, we read:

443 In this year the Britons sent across the sea to Rome and begged for help against the Picts, but they got none there, for the Romans were engaged in a campaign against Attila, King of the Huns. And then they sent to the Angles, and made the same request of the chieftains of the English.

Unfortunately for the Britons the hoped-for saviours proved to be the next aggressors. At first their visits were no real threat but in 477 the formidable Aelle arrived with his three sons. 'They killed many Britons and drove some into flight.' Aelle was clearly a warrior king whose principal pastime was making himself an intolerable nuisance to his neighbours far and near. He found Britain a tempting target with people to be conquered and rich land to be plundered and occupied. One of his sons, Wlencing, gave his name to Lancing, near Shoreham, and another, Cissa, to Chichester. The Britons made the fatal mistake of trying to hold him off from fixed defences with no sally-ports. They allowed themselves to be besieged in the old Roman fort of Anderida, now called Pevensey. As a base for the Romans under the command of the Count of the Saxon Shore, Anderida had had many advantages when the Roman fleet patrolled the Channel and the walls of Anderida could hold a large mobile striking force. But Anderida was not a place in which to be trapped as the unfortunate Britons soon found. Aelle and Cissa besieged it, captured it, and killed every man, woman, and child within the walls.

Pevensey is a fortress which has seen plenty of action and much blood spilt. Those who visit it today will find the ruins of a Norman castle in a corner of the Roman walls, and that castle also saw some severe fighting during the Middle Ages. Nearly a thousand years later, Pevensey was cunningly adapted for anti-invasion warfare, for in 1940, when a German landing was expected, gun emplacements were built and blended deceptively into the old walls. They may be inspected today.

After the massacre at Pevensey, Aelle founded the Kingdom of the South Saxons, which became known as Sussex.

From then onwards, the Saxons arrived in increasing numbers.

Some landed further west, and founded the Kingdom of the West Saxons or Wessex; others founded Essex, the county of the East Saxons. Angles, Saxons, and Jutes all came from contiguous areas and it is surprising that the early chroniclers managed to distinguish them. All were formidable in war, but none more than the Saxons whose achievements were only too well known on the Continent. One of our sources is Gildas, a sixth-century monk. Describing their effect on Britain he wrote:

> famine dire and most famous sticks to the wandering and staggering people, priests and people swords on every side gleaming and flames crackling were together mown to the ground . . . fragments of bodies covered with clots as if congealing of purple-coloured blood, mixed in a sort of fearful winepress, and burial of any kind there was none except the ruins of houses, the bellies of beasts and birds, in the open . . .

At first the Britons could do little except flee or stand and be slaughtered. Many chose to take their chance in the woods, for there was no safety in the towns the Romans had left. The Saxons did not occupy the buildings they had not troubled to destroy; this concept of civilized life was beyond their grasp, but they used the Roman roads to penetrate deep and wide into Britain. Out of their misery the Britons had to evolve a new form of life and warfare. Like their ancestors of some five hundred years before they began to display the skills of guerrilla fighting which had impressed the first Roman invaders. We know from Roman accounts that the Britons were highly mobile, could race around in chariots, alight, fight, and leap back on to their horses and chariots. But these skills had long been forgotten, and were never completely revived. Instead the Britons developed a more cautious form of warfare, with a technique for ambushing the isolated or unwary. They were slow to learn the lesson of avoiding pitched battles and we read (in the *Anglo-Saxon Chronicle*) such laconic statements as:

495   In this year two chieftains, Cerdic and his son Cynric came with five ships to Britain at the place which is called Cerdicesora, and they fought against the Britons on the same day.

501   In this year Port and his two sons Bieda and Maegla came to Britain with two ships at the place which is called Portsmouth and there they killed a young British man of very high rank.

508   In this year Cerdic and Cynric killed a British king whose name was Natanleod and 5,000 men with him, and the land right up to Charford was called Netley after him.

514   In this year the West Saxons came with three ships at a place which is called Cerdicesora and Stuf and Wihtgah fought against the Britons and put them to flight.

These early battles were strenuous and bloody enough to impress the chroniclers but they were not decisive. The Saxon invaders would celebrate their victories with plunder and senseless destruction but at that stage had little in the way of constructive ideas for consolidating their gains. Had the Britons been well led they could have ambushed these marauders on their return to the coast, and recaptured most of the spoils. But, apart from certain isolated occasions, they seldom did so. The Saxons either set sail for their homeland or settled near the coast in this new country.

Many of the Britons had fled far beyond the furthest point of Saxon penetration, deep though that was in places. The Saxons referred to all the Britons as the '*Waelisch*', which meant foreigners, and this, in time, gave the name to the country where some Britons settled and survived – Wales. But before Wales became a country much more blood was spilt and it was by no means all British.

By this time the Britons had been driven to desperation. Gildas' account of their misfortunes is substantiated by Bede who wrote:

> Consequently some of the miserable remnants, being taken in the mountains were slain in heaps. Others, constrained by hunger coming forward, yielded hands to their foes to undergo for the sake of food perpetual slavery, if indeed they were not immediately killed. Others, sorrowing, sought countries over sea. Others, remaining in the fatherland, led a wretched life in mountains, woods, and steep crags, always with apprehensive mind.

But, it is a constant fact of military situations that matters are seldom as bad as they seem, or for that matter as good as they might be. It is obvious to us nowadays with our long experience of guerrilla warfare that, if a conquered people are determined, they can first of all make life very hazardous and unpleasant for their conquerors, and then, when enough time has passed, defeat them. But to do both they need leaders.

Guerrilla warfare, to us the modern term, can be waged from two very different bases. It can be mounted from a town where the resistance fighter is able to hide himself in a crowd, or it can be waged by ambush from retreats in the woods. The second form has usually been the most popular, though not necessarily the most productive of results. Living in the woods, surrounded by trusted companions, can rapidly develop into a complacent and inactive comradeship. Robin Hoods have existed in many countries, and in many centuries, and few of them have been more than a minor nuisance to the government in power. In sixth-century Britain it was easy to be an inactive Robin Hood. Apart from the trackways and uplands most of the country was wood and thicket; today it is not easily realized how dense uncleared thicket can become in a few years, or how dangerous marshy low-lying areas rapidly become when drainage is neglected. Little of the land had been cleared in Roman times, and by 516 over a hundred years had passed since those peaceful days. Even after centuries of intensive clearance and agriculture, a hundred years of neglect would make much of England unrecognizable, if not impassable. Anyone who has any doubts about this should go and look at a garden – there are plenty around – which has not been touched for a year pending speculative building, or 'development' as it is now flatteringly called. The Britons would have had no shortage of inaccessible hideouts; but their problem would have been to find the leaders to organize resistance, train their scattered bands, and mount an effective counter-attack. The weakness of guerrilla forces is that if they can be tempted to stand and fight on open ground they tend to disintegrate.

But the Britons had a leader – a man of genius. Some called him Arthur, others Ambrosius Aurelianus. There has been much learned debate as to who Arthur may have been, but for the purposes of this battle it does not greatly matter. Whether the Briton general was named Ambrosius Aurelianus, or Arthur, can never now be established. One theory is that 'Arthur' was the name by which Ambrosius Aurelianus was known. It is unlikely that the rank and file Briton referred to his leader as King Ambrosius Aurelianus. Ambrosius was a Roman aristocrat whose parents had settled in Britain and had been murdered by the Saxons. He had missed being killed himself and had built up a resistance force. Guerrrilla leaders seldom use their true names. Gildasa describes him thus:

Ambrosius Aurelianus being leader, a modest man, who alone by chance of the Roman nation had survived in the collision of so great a storm, his parents doubtless clad in the purple, having been killed in the same, whose progeny now in our times having greatly degenerated from their ancestral excellence, to whom, the Lord assenting, victory fell.

Bede put it rather more coherently:

But when the hostile army [the Saxons], having destroyed and dispersed the natives of the island had returned home, the Britons by degrees to resume strength and spirit, emerging from the hiding places, wherein they had concealed themselves, and with one accord imploring celestial help lest they should be destroyed even to extermination. They had at that time for their leader Ambrosius Aurelianus, a modest man, who alone by chance of the Roman nation had survived the aforesaid storm, his parents, bearing a royal and distinguished name, having been killed in the same. Under this leader therefore the Britons took heart, and challenging their victors to battle obtain the victory by the help of God.

'A modest man'. Great generals often are, though not, of course, invariably. There is, of course, no reason to believe that Arthur and Ambrosius were not different people, that the former had his headquarters at Glastonbury, and trained his forces in Cornwall, to which the Saxons had not penetrated, and that Ambrosius was based on North Wales, where he became an expert at hill-fighting. But it is just possible that they were the same man, and the scraps of folklore which have passed down, of the Round Table, of trusted counsellors, and a symbolic sword which only the born, bred, and educated leader could wield, all seem in keeping.

The Latin meaning of Ambrosius is 'immortal', and the name lingers on in the Welsh 'Emrys'. Aurelianus means 'golden'. Arthur is thought to derive from the Celtic word for 'the bear' – a not unsuitable name for a guerrilla leader.

We see from the *Anglo-Saxon Chronicle* that the main Saxon raids were separated by several years. There would be a raid, a battle or two, and the return to the homeland or the shoreline, as described above. The first Saxons had neither the administration nor logistical support to mount a long campaign into areas where the opposition was unknown and food supplies would be precarious to say the least. But in 516 – which is an approximate date, for Gildas says it was the year of his birth – a Saxon force of considerable strength was moving west along the Ermine Way (between Silchester and Swindon). It was reputed to have been led by one Aelle but this can hardly have been the Aelle who had first appeared in 477. But whether Aelle or one of his descendants, and whether 516 or twenty years earlier it makes no difference; it was a tough resourceful fighting force which was probing north-west along the Ermine Way. Perhaps they were a little nervous at being so far from their base: they should have been. But as mile succeeded mile along this Roman road, beautifully straight, and not a Briton in sight, it looked as if the Saxon reputation had cleared the way before them. They had no reason to use scouts or proceed cautiously. At the end of this stage of the road there was said to be another old Roman town, and beyond that the sea again. They were right. Swindon lay ahead and also what would become known as the Bristol Channel. But so, unknown to them, did Ambrosius and his Britons.

As they approached Badon it looked no different from anywhere else along the route. They were, as it happened, at a point which had seen other and bitter battles. They marched along the plateau, down

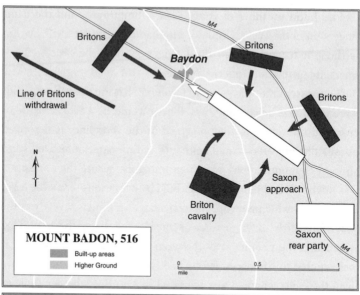

Britons

M4

Baydon

Britons

Britons

Line of Britons
withdrawal

N

Saxon
approach

Briton
cavalry

Saxon
rear party

M4

MOUNT BADON, 516

Built-up areas
Higher Ground

0   0.5   1
mile

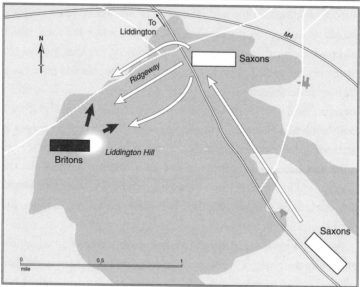

To
Liddington

M4

N

Saxons

Ridgeway

Britons

Liddington Hill

Saxons

0   0.5   1
mile

the dip, and up the slope into what is now Baydon village. When they were half-way up that slope, the trap was sprung. It is not difficult to reconstruct the probable sequence of events. Possibly two swift flank attacks from the cover close to the road, perhaps another force directly in front, possibly cavalry which would send the Saxons reeling back down the hill, and probably an attack around the rear over the route they had just covered; this would make sure that once tumbled to the bottom of the dip they would stay there. It would be a difficult position for the Saxons to fight their way out of.

Nennius, a ninth-century historian, whose accuracy is considered more doubtful than most of the early historians, stated that Arthur was the victor of Badon and that it was the last of twelve consecutive victories. He gives the Saxon casualties as 440. There is no reason to believe that this figure is anything but a wild guess, as indeed many battle casualty figures even of recent battles often are. But at least he does not number them in thousands as many early historians tend to do.

Possibly the total Saxon force was 3,000. This 'army' would be spread out along the road. The Britons would doubtless have liked to have caught them all in the trap but this, even with the advantage of greater numbers, would have been impossible. But once the initial ambush had succeeded, with devastating effect, the Britons would fade away into the undergrowth. The Saxon rear party would then come up, perhaps bury the dead but certainly halt and take stock in Badon itself. It would have been a severe and costly shock but doubtless they decided that the Britons had done their best but lost

Baydon is the highest village in Wiltshire. If you continue west up the road from Baydon village this will take you to the Ridgeway crossing, and on your left you will see Liddington Hill fort. (Wiltshire)

heart and given up. There was no reason why they should not press on, though perhaps cautiously.

The next day they did so. About five miles on from Baydon the Ermine Way is crossed by the Ridgeway, which will figure again in this book in subsequent battles. The Ridgeway was one of the great strategic roadways of Britain. It stretches through Wiltshire and Berkshire and then links up with the even older Icknield Way which goes right through to the Wash. Some parts of this ancient trackway are now modern roads, with tarmac, signs, and heavy traffic; other parts are almost as wild as they were a thousand and more years ago – it was an old road even in Roman times – and the rambler who tramps along the lonelier parts of it will feel that perhaps he is not so far removed from the feelings of earlier travellers.

But most of the users of the Ridgeway had considerably less romantic thoughts about it than the modern rambler. To the Roman legionary, to the Briton, and to many another it was as glamorous as Queen's Avenue, Aldershot is to a modern soldier. To the Saxons who suddenly came across this important trackway crossing their own it betokened much, and none of it romantic. This showed why they had been ambushed at Baydon; this was the highway on which the Britons linked up. And where there is a crossroads the chances are that there is a means of defending it.

They proceeded to look for this strongpoint. Less than a mile to the east they find it. It is Liddington Castle, an iron-age fort on a 900-foot hill. It has a useful high bank and ditch, and on the hill slopes are traces of other works which made the path of the attacker hazardous. Here, it seems, the Saxons located the rest of the force which had inflicted such damage on them the previous day. Perhaps there had been another brush at the crossroads and the Saxons had been led in pursuit to Liddington. Up till recent times Liddington was known as Badbury Castle, i.e. the burgh at Bade.

The second phase of the battle and indeed the first, is somewhat confused by the fact that some writers – notably Geoffrey of Monmouth – considered that the Saxons occupied the hill fort and the Britons were attacking them. This seems less than probable – to put it mildly. It seems more likely that the Saxons, thinking they had come to the last stronghold of the Britons in that area were determined to wipe them out and avenge the previous day's defeat. As they pressed to the assault they would find this 900-foot hill a tougher proposition than they had expected. But once committed there would be no thought of drawing back. And once more the cavalry for which both Ambrosius and Arthur were famous would come into action. Some think that much of the battle took place on the open ground between Liddington and Badbury. Perhaps the last stages did, when the Saxons had been flung back from the hill slopes, retired to the hollow field below it on the northside, and then, tired and dispirited, were cut to pieces by the British cavalry coming from either side of the Ridgeway.

Geoffrey of Monmouth (several hundred years later) describes the Saxon slain as being 'many thousands'. Whatever the number it was undoubtedly most of their force. Doubtless a few survived to tell the story of disaster – a few always do, and the tale loses nothing in the telling. But it would soon be obvious enough to the Saxons what had happened; their invasion army, which was the strongest which could be mustered, had been annihilated. It was clear that if that had been the fate of what had looked like an all-conquering army, central Britain was best left alone for the time being. It was forty years before the *Anglo-Saxon Chronicle* records Saxons in Wiltshire again. In 552 Cynric 'fought against the Britons at a place called Salisbury'.

It is not recorded as a Saxon victory but only as a fight. In all probability it was an attempt by the Saxons to capture the ancient earthwork fortress of Old Sarum, and anyone who looks at the banks and ditches of Old Sarum today will not envy them their task. Presumably they by-passed it because, in 556, they are recorded as fighting against the Britons at Barbury. This was Cynric and Ceawlin at the battle of Beranburgh just north of Barbury Castle (another Iron-Age fort). Beranburgh looks a slightly improbable site for a battlefield as the Saxons would have had to pass by the hill without attacking and being attacked, and then been caught on the flat plain in front. However, it is an important nodal point where six roads meet, and even if one doubts the actual site there can be no question that plenty of battles, large and small, must have been fought in the area.

But no other battle compares with the achievement of Badon. There the flower and pride of the Saxon army was outwitted, crushed, and finally destroyed by a conglomerate force which behaved with superb discipline, and was clearly expertly led. No wonder accounts of it survived in Welsh epic poetry. At every stage it was adroitly handled, – as the Saxons would ruefully have agreed had they survived to tell the tale.

The Battle of Dyrham (originally Deorham)

AD 577

In spite of the setbacks of Badon, in the year 516, the Saxons were making steady progress and consolidating their gains elsewhere in Britain. Now they were coming at settlers; now too they were beginning to have a better appreciation of the potential of the country they were conquering. By this time they had been in contact with Britain for three hundred years. Much can happen in that space of time; it is perhaps hardly credible that it is only just over three hundred years since Cavaliers and Roundheads were fighting a bitter civil war in this country. The progress of the Saxons can hardly be compared with that in Britain between the seventeenth and twentieth centuries but it would be equally wrong to imagine them as the same in the third century AD as in the sixth.

Some time in the sixth century – it is impossible to estimate when – Saxons occupied the deserted city of London, which became the country of the Middle Saxons, or Middlesex. So now we had Jutes in Kent, and Saxons in Essex, Sussex, Middlesex, and Wessex, and probably also in Surrey (which means 'southern people'). The Angles had given their name to East Anglia, where there were the North Folk and South Folk. Above the Humber they had created the Kingdom of Northumbria, the northern part being known as Bernicia and the southern part, which is now mainly Yorkshire, being given the name of Deira. Combined forces from these areas had forced their way into the Midlands to create Mercia. Mercia was a 'march', that is a border state, and it extended to what is now Staffordshire. Beyond that the Britons were in force and among their bases were Wroxeter and Chester. They were now calling themselves the *Cymru*, which means comrades.

In short the Anglo-Saxons now held the eastern half of the country and some of the Midlands, and the Britons held the western parts, including Cornwall, Devon and Somerset, Wales, Gloucestershire, Herefordshire, Shropshire, and the north-west. This stalemate could continue almost indefinitely unless the invaders could effect a strategic breakthrough. It was necessary to cut a line through the British areas to the sea, and then widen it. Clearly it would be extremely difficult to do this in the north-west, though it would have to be done eventually. The obvious point for a drive forward was where Aelle had failed some forty years before.

By now some new names had appeared on the military scene. Ceawlin has already been mentioned in the previous chapter as having been in action at Barbury, in combination with Cynric who had put the Britons to flight at Salisbury four years previously (552). In 560 we read that Ceawlin succeeded to the Kingdom of Wessex and Aelle to the Kingdom of the Northumbrians. Some of these warrior kings traced their descent back to Woden (the god whose name is commemorated in Wednesday); doubtless they seemed worthy of their lineage.

Ceawlin was clearly an outstanding warrior. He and his brother Cutha sometimes fought side by side, at other times went on separate campaigns. In 568, says the *Anglo-Saxon Chronicle*, 'Ceawlin and Cutha fought against Ethelbert and drove him in flight into Kent.' Ethelbert was a powerful king and this was no mean achievement. Doubtless the quarrel had sprung from a border incident. Three years later we hear of Cutha again.

> 571   In this year Cutha fought against the Britons at Biedcanford and captured four towns: Limbury, Aylesbury, Bensington and Eynsham, and in the same year he died.

This campaign of Cutha's is an interesting one. It looks as if he had gathered up a force in East Anglia and then driven south-west through Bedford and Aylesbury, reached the Thames at Benson just north of Wallingford, and then travelled along the river to Eynsham. Here he would be on the edge of Briton-held country, and the opposition would be too strong for him to continue. Perhaps he had been wounded, or the effects of the Thames Valley marshes proved more deadly than British swords, for he died at the end of this successful campaign.

But as one warrior fell and was laid ceremonially to rest there were a dozen others ready to take his place. Often they bore the same names or names remarkably like their predecessors. Four years after Cutha's great campaign, which nearly cut right across England from east to west, another great probe is on the way to an even more significant victory. The *Anglo-Saxon Chronicle* has the laconic entry:

> 577   In this year Cuthwine and Ceawlin fought against the Britons and killed three kings, Conmail, Condidan, and Farinmail, at the place which is called Dyrham; and they captured three of their cities, Gloucester, Cirencester, and Bath.

The statement is in the best tradition of cryptic war despatches, such as 'I came, I saw, I conquered.'

Doubtless the Anglo-Saxons had now got the measure of the situation. Possibly they had sailed around the coasts and formed a very fair idea of the strength and weakness of the British position. If Cutha's thrust could have been sustained it would have struck at almost precisely the same point as Ceawlin reached. But now it was Ceawlin's turn. We do not know anything about his preliminary moves but we do know that during the previous twenty years this king of Wessex had gradually been pushing towards the north-west of his kingdom. There must have been hundreds of skirmishes and ambushes and raids in those years and all the while Ceawlin was consolidating his position, building an army and getting ready for the drive forward. But, on the other side, the fighting men were no novices. They knew well enough what was in train, and what was in Ceawlin's mind. Under normal conditions the kings of Bath, Cirencester, and Gloucester would have been happily fighting each other, disputing some border territory or other. But misery makes strange bedfellows, and Conmail, Condidan, and Farinmail, had held their strategic and tactical conferences. By a stroke of good fortune Ceawlin's invasion route led right through the centre of their territories so there could be no question of one fighting for his life while another stood idly by pondering when or where to intervene – if at all. A look at the map shows that Ceawlin was planning to slip through the middle of their strongholds to break through on to the Severn estuary at Berkeley. But the movements of his large army would doubtless have been faithfully reported by scouts and spies, and even though he had slipped past Bath there must have been a huge force waiting to confront him somewhere. As it happened, it was at Dyrham, but it was in a badly-chosen position.

Nobody knows exactly how Ceawlin advanced to Dyrham but it is a fair assumption that he came from Melksham to Box and on to Marshfield. He could perhaps have gone via Chippenham but that would have made his approach too obvious. Approaching by

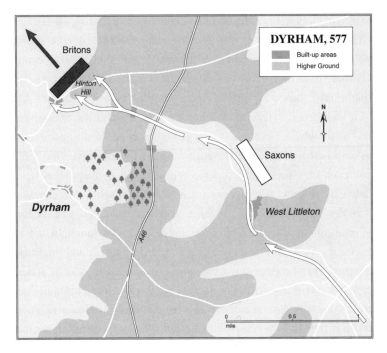

This battlefield is very close to where the M4 crosses the A46 east of Bristol. (South Gloucestershire)

Marshfield he still had the option of cutting back south and west and reaching the Severn near Weston. He would have had to fight sooner or later, and doubtless he wished for nothing better, but a good general calculates his chances and takes a risk well aware that his opponent is also calculating – and miscalculating – too. But even Ceawlin must have drawn in his breath when he came to Dyrham and wondered who would be standing victor on that battlefield by nightfall.

A look at the map suggests that Ceawlin had brought his army through West Littleton. He may have thought that his three principal opponents were mainly intent upon guarding their own cities but, as it proved, they had concentrated their forces at the point he was almost certain to try to pass – Hinton Hill. Needless to say there have been a host of other theories about approach routes he might have chosen but they all lead to Hinton Hill.

It was a good defensive position but like all defensive positions it had its drawbacks. It overlooked a key crossing on the approach road to both Bath and Bristol but was of value only as an untakeable base, and even then for a limited period only. When an army takes up a defensive position several consequences are immediately set in train. The first is that although the strongpoint gives a temporary feeling of immunity it also diminishes the sort of aggressive morale which is necessary for a field victory. The second effect is that one might be tempted out of a rugged position and then caught by a swift attack which sends one's army floundering among the very obstacles on which one was relying to upset the enemy. If the enemy decides to try to slip by, it is necessary to attack at some point before his army has crossed the line you are planning to hold. Furthermore, if the enemy decides to besiege you at this point he has the resources of the countryside to draw on while you have your stores only, and in sixth-century Britain these would not be very extensive. The last and greatest liability is that you may be surrounded and with morale at zero point have to fight to the end hoping to kill enough to destroy the attack or, alternatively, to break out.

It looks as if Ceawlin's warriors were first confronted about 300 yards ahead of the camp position. The technique of this type of fighting varies little from country to country and age to age. The attacking troops send their front line to crash forward as far as they can go, then stand aside – if still alive – to let the second rank stream through the gaps they have made. Defensive troops on the other hand try to check the onslaught a few hundred yards ahead of their lines, either by ditches or fortifications full of resolute men, and then, if and when the line wavers, put in a heavier attack if it seems appropriate. From that moment the course of the battle becomes highly unpredictable, depending on the skill of one commander and the rashness of another. A commander with a strong hold on his troops can afford to let them press on knowing he can withdraw them if needed; one with lesser discipline would be ill-advised to do so for he might not see them again, if ever, till the battle was over.

The joint command does not seem to have worked very success-fully once the first blows were struck. There is always a chance when keen rivals band together for mutual defence that one group will cheerfully let another take more than its share of the enemy without doing much to take off the pressure. The Britons would have had bows but these were not as formidable as they would become later. Their armour was light, and on the Roman model, but it is unlikely that many would have possessed it. The Saxon rank and file had no armour at all, but their leaders usually had a chain-mail shirt and an iron framework helmet. They had spears, bows, and shields. The spears – on both sides – were simple seven-foot shafts with iron heads, which could be used for thrusting or thrown like a javelin. Spears were handled with great dexterity for they were the principal weapon for hunting; an arrow was less reliable. Sometimes a man would loose off an arrow and if he missed be hard put to get in a spear-thrust. A spear was a more reliable weapon than a bow.

The sword was much beloved, and some swords were very richly ornamented. They were about thirty-three inches long, without much taper or point but with a keen edge on each side. The hand was partly protected by a cross-bar and the end of the hilt was a pommel, a rounded knob that helped to keep the hand from slipping off; it also gave balance to the blade. The balance of a weapon is a curious quality, but when it is right for the user he will twirl spear, javelin, or axe like a tennis-racquet. After the first exchange of spears and arrows at Dyrham it was undoubtedly close-quarter fighting. The Saxons, whose numbers were probably greater than had been anticipated, would soon be fanning out around the hill, perhaps climbing more swiftly than expected. Here the Britons were too much on the defensive, and they lacked a single general of genius. Ceawlin was the veteran of a hundred encounters. He loved fighting – as all his nation did – but he fought to win. Somewhere, once, there was a detailed account of this battle, but today we only have the place, the result, and the names of the three 'Kings' of whose existence we would not otherwise have known, for their names are in no other records. But even without that account, from what we know of what happened before and after and from an examination of the ground, it is not difficult to bring the vital battle of Deorham once again to life.

Ceawlin was through to the Severn. He captured Gloucester, Cirencester, and Bath with ease, for most of the usual defenders of these former Roman towns were lying dead on the slopes of Hinton Hill. But his fighting life was only half over. He had split the Waelisch (the Britons) and from now onwards some would be in Cornwall and the West, and even in Brittany, while the others would be in Wales and the north-west. But there were plenty of people left to fight. Seven years after Dyrham the *Anglo-Saxon Chronicle* reports him as being in north Oxfordshire.

584 In this year Ceawlin and Cutha fought against the Britons at the place which is called Fethanleag and Cutha was killed there, and Ceawlin captured many villages and countless spoils and in anger returned to his own land.

Fethanleag was probably Fringford, a village four and a half miles north of Bicester. Historians have avoided comment on the reason for the Saxons fighting a battle in this place or the possible course of it but as it is on the old Roman road it is fairly obvious that this is where they marched head-on into the East Anglians. Ceawlin continued to fight but his great triumphs were over. In 592, 'Gregory succeeded to the Papacy at Rome. And in this year there occurred a great slaughter at "Woden's barrow" and Ceawlin was driven out.' Woden's Barrow is now called Adam's Grave. It is at Alton Priors, Wiltshire. Finally comes the last significant entry.

593   In this year Ceawlin, Cwichelm and Crida perished. And Aethelfrith succeeded to the kingdom.

Ceawlin undoubtedly died with his sword in his hand but where, by whom he was slain, and how he died will never be known. There are plenty of possibilities. Four years later we hear that his successor 'continually fought and contended against the English or the Britons or the Picts or the Scots.' It must have been sad for Ceawlin to die at that moment with all those splendid enemies to fight.

The Battle of Ellandun

AD 825

L ike all early battles Ellandun is still somewhat of a mystery. The exact site was not recorded, nor the numbers involved, nor the casualties; we do, of course, know the result. Nevertheless, by the use of information about previous and later events it is possible to make very close deductions about Ellandun. But even if we had a full and detailed account of Ellandun – and other battles – it would not fully explain them in isolation any more than the Battle of Alamein in 1942 would be comprehensible if separated from the background of the Second World War. The only way to understand Ellandun is to take a brief look at the events of the 248 years since the vital strategic battle of Dyrham had been fought in 577.

Although the first stages of the Anglo-Saxon conquest of Britain had already taken over one hundred and fifty years of steady fighting the Britons were still strongly entrenched in Wales, in the area west of the Pennines, and also in Cornwall. Ceawlin's breakthrough to the Severn estuary in 577 had been a major strategic gain but even with this setback the Britons were still a formidable force. This did not worry the Saxons, who had their hands full with using the lands they already occupied. The Saxons regarded fighting as a natural and desirable part of life, so the presence of hostile Britons on their borders seemed by no means unusual or unwelcome. The pace of conquest was partly dictated by logistical problems and partly by the need to keep a watchful eye on the activities of one's comrades in arms and fellow-countrymen; there was not much point in occupying fresh territory if a neighbour took advantage of your absence to raid your homelands.

The next stride forward for the Saxon conquest came in AD 604 (or perhaps 605 or 606). This was the great battle of Chester. (The Romans had called the town Deva, but after they had left many Roman cities came to be known as 'ceasters' and later as 'chesters' or 'casters'. Thus we find Winchester, Worcester, Colchester, Doncaster, etc although these were not the names by which the Romans knew them.)

The battle of Chester became possible because Aethelfrith of Bernicia (northern Northumbria) had crushed his neighbour the King of Deira (southern Northumbria – approximately the area of modern Yorkshire). Aethelfrith was a formidable, utterly ruthless warrior. Two years before his Chester campaign he had had a devastating victory over the Scots at what is thought to have been Dawston in Liddesdale. His own Saxon army sustained heavy losses but the Scots were annihilated; the *Anglo-Saxon Chronicle* bluntly states that no king of the Scots ever afterwards dared to lead an army against Northumbria. Events subsequently proved it wrong but the chronicler was a historian not a prophet. The exact site of the battle is not known but this does not mean that it is undiscoverable. All over England there are many areas which are known to have been battlefields; one day perhaps a combination of military historians, archaeologists, and local folklorists may produce interesting theories about some of these sites.

The King of all Northumbria, and conqueror of the Scots then took his army to the west:

Aethelfrith led his army to Chester and there killed a countless number of Britons and thus was fulfilled Augustine's prophecy by which he said 'If the Britons do not wish to have peace with us, they shall perish at the hands of the Saxons.' There were also killed 200 priests who had come there to pray for the army of the Britons. Their leader was called Brocmail and he escaped with fifty men.

Although we can only estimate the numbers involved this must have been a tremendous battle. The Britons, well aware of the threat to their position, had put a combined force from Wales and Cumbria into the field. Undoubtedly there was a split in the command and direction of the battle but even with this the Britons must have put up a desperate fight. The presence of the priests on the battlefield shows the determination with which the Britons approached the contest; it was not the first nor the last time that clerics would appear on battlefields and be massacred for their trouble, but it is not a pleasant thought. Aethelfrith had no doubt assumed that their presence in the fighting area had invalidated their status as non-combatants, if indeed he thought so deeply of it at all. More probably he saw them as the evil exponents of a spurious religion which should be eradicated. The Saxons had recently been converted to Christianity, and doubtless regarded themselves as the defenders of their new faith. The *Chronicle* states:

601 In this year Gregory sent the pallium[1] to Britain to Archbishop Augustine, and many religious teachers to his assistance; and Bishop Paulinus who converted Edwin, King of the Northumbrians to baptism.

Perhaps Aethelfrith, who was Edwin's son, thought he was

1 Archbishop's cloak, denoting episcopal authority.

fighting a Holy War. Like many converts to a religion he would be more zealous for his religion than those who had been born in it. Furthermore Aethelfrith's view of his Christian duty was unlikely to have included a merciful attitude to the spiritual comforters of his opponents, particularly as the Augustinians would have stressed their iniquities.

The Saxons were by no means a homogeneous people. In 607 the King of Wessex is reported as fighting against the South Saxons and, as it was significant enough to be recorded in the *Anglo-Saxon Chronicle*, this was clearly no border skirmish. The next King of Wessex remained on the throne for thirty-one years. In 614 he was involved in a major battle at Beandun, and killed 2,045 Britons. Times were turbulent and unsettled; heathenism returned in Kent and Middlesex. The power struggle went on. Aethelfrith, the victor of Dawston and Chester at last met his match – or perhaps merely bad luck – in 617. He was killed by Raedwald, King of the East Angles. His successor, Edwin, banished all of Aethelfrith's sons before going on to conquer the rest of Saxon England, except Kent.

Christianity did not appear to have a markedly restraining influence on the Saxon rulers in their petty kingdoms. The conquest of the remainder of Britain became secondary to establishing who was paramount chief among the settled portions. Apart from the need to keep a watchful eye on any upstarts in one's own domains the Saxon king had to be ever vigilant against being swallowed up by his neighbour, and preferably to avoid it by himself making an aggressive move. These moves took many forms and at times displayed a subtlety which is not uncharacteristic of the twentieth century. In the year 626 the King of Wessex sent an assassin to kill King Edwin of Northumbria. The plot miscarried, for he killed two of the bodyguards but only wounded the King. The Saxons were by no means averse to a little treachery if it suited their purpose, but Edwin's reaction to the attempt to kill him was to boil with moral indignation. By a happy coincidence his wife had borne him a daughter on the night of the attempted assassination, and Edwin promised Paulinus, the new Bishop of Northumbria that if Paulinus would pray to God for a victory over the King of Wessex he (Edwin) would give this same daughter to God's service. Paulinus prayed fervently and Edwin took a large army into Wessex. The result was all that could be desired. Edwin won a devastating victory in Wessex and killed five minor kings; in return for this divine favour he built first a wooden and then a stone church at York. He had not however killed the right man, one Cwichelm, for we find the Wessex king fighting a drawn battle with the King of Mercia two years later. Otherwise Edwin thrived on his new religion; he acquired East Anglia and Essex from the dominion of Kent, he drove the Picts back beyond the Forth and he even built a fleet on the west coast which enabled him to conquer the Isle of Man and Anglesey.

The title at which all these war lords were aiming was that of Bretwalda. By this time the Saxon conquests had developed into seven separate kingdoms, known collectively at the Heptarchy. They were Wessex, Mercia, Northumbria, East Anglia, Essex, Sussex, and Kent. Wessex, including what is roughly known as south and south-western England, was the most powerful, and the other gradually fell into that order of importance though the lesser ones occasionally had their moments of glory. The title of Bretwalda passed from Northumbria to Kent, thence to Mercia, and thence to Wessex. The details of this struggle for power do not concern us here but it is necessary to know the trend of events if we are to understand the battle which it brought about.

Edwin's growing power alarmed his rivals, but their reaction was not to accept it as inevitable; instead they adopted determined counter-measures. The next two probable victims on Edwin's march of conquest were Penda of Mercia and Cadwallon of Gwynedd (N. Wales). The former, who was a relentless heathen, and the latter, who was allegedly a Christian, found no problem over allying for their common safety. Their combined force met and defeated Edwin's in the Battle of Hatfield in 633. If this was Hatfield (Herts) it was a curious place for him to be brought to battle by a Midlander and a Welshman but perhaps they had noted his exposed flank as he ventured so far from his base, perhaps to conquer Middlesex and Kent, and they caught him at a vital tactical point. But 'Hatfield' – which means an open heath – might have been anywhere, and more probably was somewhere between the Midlands and Yorkshire. After their victory Cadwallon and Penda lost no time in invading Northumbria where the former – and probably the latter – were responsible for a series of cruelties which caused comment even in those hardened times. Edwin's name is commemorated by the town he founded, 'Edwin's burgh', now Edinburgh.

But, of course, fortune ebbed and flowed. Cadwallon's ebbed right out when he was killed by Oswald who had raised a combined force of Northumbrians and Scots and marched south bearing the Cross as a standard. Readers of *British Battlefields: the North* will recall that in 1138 the Cross, travelling in the opposite direction, won the Battle of the Standard for the English. Without his formidable Welsh ally, Penda was not strong enough to hold the northern areas but this did not mean that he was by any means a spent force. Penda seems to have been a remarkable person. According to the *Anglo-Saxon Chronicle* he did not succeed to his throne till he was fifty but he seems to have held it till he was eighty, when he was killed in battle. These figures have been disputed as being improbable but as everything about Penda was improbable – his intelligence, ingenuity, endurance, and persistence – it does not seem entirely fair to dispute his age in that context. Penda seemed to believe that it is better to wear out than to rust out for when not fighting the Northumbrians he was busy killing off the kings of East Anglia on one side of his kingdom and wresting the lands of the Hwicce from Wessex on the other. The Hwicce were once a very powerful tribe whose territories formerly occupied the area of Worcestershire and Gloucestershire; now all they are remembered by is the Wychwood forest which preserves their name. Penda, although unable to reconquer Northumbria still maintained a series of border wars with Oswald. In one of these, in 643 Oswald was killed at Oswestry (Oswald's tree). Possibly the tree was subsequently believed to have magical powers. Oswald had a reputation for holiness which extended well beyond Northumbria. His hands were buried at Bamburgh, where they did not decay, and many miracles were attributed to his relics. He was succeeded by his brother, Oswin, who ruled for twenty-eight years. He too was said to be a devout Christian but as he had his neighbour, Oswin of Deira, murdered after a disagreement it seems that he took his Christian obligations fairly lightly. Meanwhile Penda rampaged on elsewhere. In 645 he was reported as having put Cenwedh, King of Wessex, to flight, but did not succeed in killing him. The *casus belli* was that Cenwedh had deserted his sister; presumably the sister was Penda's not Cenwedh's and the latter had jilted her. The indefatigable Penda eventually met his match at Winwaedfeld, an unidentified battlefield thought to have been in Yorkshire. Oswin was his conqueror. Penda himself was killed, and with him thirty princes. If the dates are correct, Penda would then have been eighty – as mentioned earlier. It is by no means impossible. No ageing warrior would ever wish to die in bed and we have similar examples of ancient men on battle-fields in Thurston of York at the Battle of the Standard, and the Earl of Northumberland at Bramham Moor though both were a few years younger than Penda was reputed to have been. Penda's 'elimination' removed the final obstacle to the religious conversion of Mercia. Thenceforth England was a Christian country. It also seemed as if Northumbria would now be the dominant kingdom, and the title of Bretwalda become theirs by hereditary right. Before Oswin died in 670 he had driven the Picts back to the Tay, extracted tribute from the Cumbrians and Welsh, and established a strong though decen-tralized grip on his Saxon sub-units. He was an early exploiter of the 'scorched earth' policy in that he kept the lands between North-umbria and Scotland so barren that not even a Pictish army could find sustenance on them.

His son was equally able. He captured Cumberland and West-morland from the Britons and even invaded Ireland. Unluckily for him, for Northumbria, and for England generally, he was killed fighting the Picts in 685. His successors were of a different stamp. Their weaknesses were quickly recognized within and without Northumbria. The Picts were soon back and harrying the north – scorched earth or not – and the Mercians not only broke away but proceeded to establish a dominant kingdom themselves. They made East Anglia, Kent, and Essex dependent states, took the territory north of the Thames from Wessex, and even annexed Northumbrian lands south of the Trent.

As the years go by we receive fuller though still fragmentary entries in the *Anglo-Saxon Chronicle*. Readers will appreciate that though the *Chronicle* was begun in the ninth century, under orders from Alfred, there were several differing versions. In later years, after Alfred's death, this history of England became much more continuous. However, even in the early stages it gives us much useful information on which we may build up a picture of the composition, morale, and motivation of Saxon armies. There is an illuminating account of local rivalries just before the great Offa of Mercia came to power. They concern Cynewulf, King of Wessex. Cynewulf and his counsellors of the West Saxons deprived his kinsman, Sigebehrt, of his kingdom (except for Hampshire) because of his unjust acts; he retained Hampshire until he killed the ealdorman who had stood by him the longest. At that point Cynewulf drove him out completely and he lived in the Weald until a swineherd stabbed him to death. The swineherd, it is recorded, was avenging the death of the ealdorman. This tribal, perhaps even domestic, loyalty explains how the Saxons kept their armies together. Presumably there was no lack of leadership nor discipline either.

Thirty-one years later Cynewulf was having trouble with one Cyneheard, who was the late Sigebehrt's younger brother. Cyneheard was the first to move. Learning that Cynewulf was at Merton visiting a mistress, he surrounded the house. Cynewulf heard the approach of unwelcome strangers and rushed to the door. Realizing that this was a plot to murder him, and that his thegns, his personal bodyguard, whom he had sent to a discreet distance, would not be able to help he resolved to kill Cyneheard before he himself went under. He managed to wound the assassin but was himself struck down by many blows. The women screamed and the bodyguard heard. They rushed up but they too were outnumbered. Nevertheless, they died to a man, fighting like demons. The next day the rest of Cynewulf's thegns heard the news and came to the spot. There they found Cyneheard barricaded in, but very ready with rewards and promises if they would transfer their allegiance and support him as the new king. The thegns laughed the offer to scorn and set to[1]. At the end of a desperate fight Cyneheard and his supporters were all dead except for one – and he was badly wounded.

Such loyalties and long memories are found in other primitive societies, but not all. Where they exist they account for much inter-tribal tension, even inter-family tension, but they ensure that when battles are fought they continue till one side has gained victory – probably at great cost – by annihilating the other. This then was the new phase of the Saxon wars, not as campaigns of adventure and conquest, but hard, relentless struggles against a competing unit, which might be another kingdom or merely a rival power faction.

In spite of the hazards of life in these early centuries, kings managed to have long reigns. Cynewulf, as we saw above, reigned for thirty-one years, and was somewhat unlucky to have his life ended then. Offa, the great king of Mercia, held his kingdom for thirty-nine years.

Offa might with justice be called the first King of England. He was more than the successful leader of a regional faction. All that we know of him shows the statesman, the strategist, and the man who was rightly respected in other countries. He corresponded with the great Charlemagne. He defeated and drove back the Welsh, as the Britons were now called, and he built a dyke from Chepstow in the south to a point two miles south of Prestatyn in the north. (Why he did not take it all the way to the sea is still not understood.) Offa's Dyke is still impressive and it needs little imagination to visualize what it must have symbolized twelve hundred years ago. But, of course, any ideas that these dykes were more than token defences, is

---

1 Compare Harold's shield wall at Hastings.

probably erroneous. They marked boundaries and they marked them in a convincing way. Nobody crossing Offa's Dyke could be under any illusion that he was in his own territory.

Precisely the same consideration applied by Wansdyke. The Wansdyke is an impressive fortification which extends from Portishead in the Bristol Channel to the Inkpen Beacon in Berkshire – a distance of sixty miles. It consists of a bank with a ditch to the north side. The bank is high enough and the ditch deep enough to be a considerable obstacle to an attacking army, though its delaying effect would be only temporary. The Wansdyke runs through farms and private property. The author found no difficulty inspecting it but was informed by landowners that car-drivers are regarded with some suspicion unless they have asked and been granted permission to cross land. This attitude does not stem from unfriendliness but has a more serious cause. A growing menace is cattle- and sheep-stealing from large farms. The procedure is that a car-driver makes a reconnaissance by day – but takes good care not to approach anyone who might note the car number. At night a lorry will follow the car-driver's directions and steal – perhaps slaughtering on the spot – valuable livestock. The innocent battlefield visitor may thus be regarded with suspicion unless he declares his identity and intent. In most places it is not necessary, but where roads are marked 'private' it is. It is very rare indeed for a farmer to object to a visit by a genuine archaeologist or student of military history.

The visitor will notice that dykes are often broken, and the height of the rampart also varies from place to place. In the eastern section of the Wansdyke the bank is approximately fifteen feet high; in the western sector it is approximately four feet. Broken sections, i.e. places where the dyke has not been built, are accounted for by the former presence of other long-vanished defences – a densely-tangled thicket perhaps, or a marsh. It is necessary to look for possible traces of such features in sectors where battles took place, for such obstacles would have determined the path of armies. Nowadays most roads have been straightened, but over the country there are still places where a road wanders back and forth in a zigzag across apparently flat, featureless country. Perhaps in former times it was the track over a marsh, with fallen trees, standing trees, or a pool diverting it first one way and then another.

We know very little about Wansdyke, which may or may not have once been called Wodensdyke. The man responsible for its construction was probably Ecgbert who became King of Wessex in the year 800, but it may have been started by his predecessor Kenulf. Some writers have contended that it was built by the Mercians but this theory is, to put it mildly, unlikely, as the ditch faces the wrong way for their purposes. The great Offa had died in 794 and his successors were less statesmen than warlike predators. Two years after Offa's death the new King of Mercia raided Kent, captured its king, cut off his hands and blinded him. The Wansdyke might not stop an army but it would stop lightning raids of this type if properly patrolled. Ecgbert was no mean warrior himself. In 815 he was reported as ravaging Cornwall from east to west; if he went this distance from his base he would need some sort of defensive line between his own kingdom and the turbulent Mercians.

Beornwulf, who was defeated at the Battle of Ellandun in 825 seems to have become King of Mercia by a *coup d'état* the previous year. Like all usurpers who obtained the throne by an adroit move he needed to give his army something to do and something to think about, as well as some rewards, lest they should look upon their new ruler with too critical an eye. There was, of course, every chance of being toppled off his throne by an incursion from Wessex.

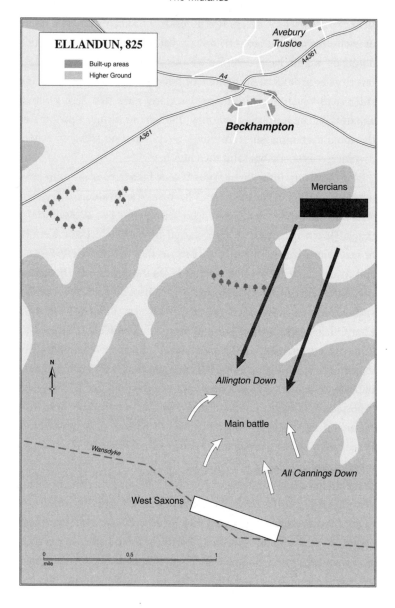

ELLANDUN, 825

Built-up areas
Higher Ground

Avebury
Trusloe

A4361

A4

Beckhampton

A361

Mercians

N

Allington Down

Main battle

Wansdyke

All Cannings Down

West Saxons

0   0.5   1
mile

Beornwulf therefore decided on a pre-emptive strike. He probably moved east as if to attack a target in south-eastern England and then doubled back and came racing down the Berkshire Ridgeway. At Overton he would twist again, leaving the Ridgeway, and having made a survey from the superb observation point at Silbury Hill would then come up the track by All Cannings Down. On the way he would encounter other defensive earthworks, for this was clearly considered to be a vulnerable spot. It is a confusing area to identify, but an up-to-date large-scale map will help the visitor. Allington itself is on the other side of the Wansdyke and thus far removed from the battlefield; he must also ignore All Cannings, interesting though this is. The best route to the battlefield is from Beckhampton north of the Wansdyke, which will bring him between Allington Down and All Cannings Down. Here on the forward slopes we believe that the Battle of Ellandun was fought.

This opinion is based less on the similarity between the names of Ellandun and Allington than on the probable strategy of Beornwulf. Beornwulf was no novice at the art of war; whatever qualities he might have lacked, tactical appreciation would not be among them. He would know very well that if he made his approach tot he Wansdyke obvious a suitable reception would be there to greet him. He would therefore wish to achieve one of the first principles of war – deception of the enemy – and having come down the Ridgeway rapidly, possibly with the advantage of surprise, he would then send a small party ahead to suggest that he was marching by the quickest possible route to Salisbury. At that point Ecgbert would throw everything in his way, he hoped, but Beornwulf by a swift change of

Take the A4 from Marlborough to West Kennett and walk up to the Wansdyke. This will take you through the battlefield. (Wiltshire)

direction would be over the Wansdyke and on Ecgbert's flank, if not actually behind him.

What went wrong? Why did Ecgbert gain victory and why was it, as the *Anglo-Saxon Chronicle* puts it, 'a great slaughter was made there'?

Undoubtedly Ecgbert was the more experienced general. He had been on the throne for many years and had fought a number of successful campaigns against the Britons. It is unlikely that he would not have had spies and scouts in Mercia, and even some perhaps in circles very close to Beornwulf's councils. And, as a good soldier, he would believe in winning his battles before he fought them. Winning this battle would mean preparing all possible approach routes so that an invading army would have already encountered much resistance before it reached the Wansdyke. The ground at Allington looks highly dangerous, with forward earthworks, flanking slopes, deceptive hollows, and an enclosed arena. Once among those slopes Beornwulf's army would have little room for manoeuvre in any sense of the word. One visualizes his army trapped between the two sets of earthworks, desperately trying to force its way up to the Wansdyke and break through, harassed by flank attacks, and unable to retreat and regroup without being disrupted. It was, it must be remembered, Saxon against Saxon, the same weapons, the same techniques, the same dogged courage. Both armies would have learnt something from their forays against the Britons, and both probably had Cornish or Welsh in their ranks as bowmen or spearmen. The West Saxons would have some advantage from the fact that they were uphill to the Mercians; in all battles where hand-thrown missiles – spears, axes, or darts, or even arrows – were used the men on the upper slope had a slight but vital margin of range. Missiles could be flighted to carry further from a height. The reader may test this by taking a javelin and throwing it first uphill and then down. The difference in range may be a surprise, as perhaps it was to the Mercians in 825. An oncoming spear (or javelin) is difficult to judge and always pitches closer to you than you anticipated, as many an unwary spectator of a javelin-throwing event has experienced. Spear-throwers who charge downhill have the advantage of range, and impetus, and if their spears fail to find targets they may be recovered. The spearman charging uphill is in a vastly inferior position. Beornwulf having put his men into that disadvantageous attack would not be able to recover them and prevent their slaughter. Like many brilliant tactical moves his rapid feint and change of direction deserved success. Unfortunately for his army he met an even shrewder tactician and 'there was a great slaughter'. It was not the end of Beornwulf, for he escaped from the field and turned his attention to East Anglia, where he was killed later in the year. It was, however, the end of Mecian paramountcy. Four years later Ecgbert took a great army into Mercia and carried all before him as far as the Humber. The Northumbrians fought back but were decisively defeated at Dore, and acknowledged Ecgbert as Bretwalda. The following year he was conducting a successful campaign against the Welsh.

He was not always successful. There was a new and formidable threat on the English throne. In 787 three Viking ships had arrived in Dorset, landed their crews, and ravaged the country. By the time of Ecgbert's reign the Vikings were a continuous threat. In 836 he lost a battle to them, although two years later he won an even larger one against a combined force of Vikings and Welsh at Hingston Down near Plymouth. By that time something was known of these relentless northern warriors. They were called Danes but many of them came from other countries. At this stage Ecgbert was the only

English king to put up much of a defence against them, and after his death in 839 England sank steadily into decline.

Ecgbert was a remarkable king. He reigned for thirty-seven years and was the ancestor of all subsequent monarchs of England, save four. His early life had been spent in exile, some of it at the court of Charlemagne, and he would never have obtained the throne at all if a cousin had not died prematurely.

By the time of Ecgbert's reign the Saxons were a very different people from those we described earlier in the book. They were Christian and in many ways cultured and civilized. They had established settlements by clearing forests, and often named them after the local chief, as in Wolverton (Wulfhere's tun – 'tun' meaning a village). 'Ham' meant home, and Birmingham was the home of Beormund's people. Many English place-names have English origins, but this is a large and complicated subject which concerns us here only in that it occasionally gives some guidance to the sites and approach roads of battlefields.

Before leaving Ellandun we might look at sites which other writers have suggested. Wroughton, immediately south of Swindon, has been suggested, and so has Lydiard Tregoze, just to the west. Amesbury has also had its supporters. However, at none of these places is there any reason why they should have been chosen for a major battle in contrast to Allington which is in exactly the right place for the strategic and tactical situation of the time.

The Battle of Ashdown

AD 871

The early years of the ninth century saw a bloody and disastrous succession of battles against the new invaders. Apart from bare dates we have no details of these encounters, for the Vikings usually won and there were seldom survivors. The Vikings were terrible adversaries. Opinion is divided whether the word 'Viking' comes from 'Wicing', meaning warrior, or from 'Wic', the creek by which they penetrated far inland in their shallow-draught boats. They were hated by the Saxons, who had now settled into being a Christian, agricultural community, and their cruelty, destruction, and heathenism caused them to be branded as uncivilized barbarians; however, in recent years, archaeological discoveries have established that the Vikings had a well-developed culture of their own.

But to the Saxons they were an appalling problem. In their long graceful boats they could range far and wide, for if the wind failed all would take a turn on the oars, and it was not unusual for them to cover 200 miles in twenty-four hours. On land they would often appropriate horses, of which there were many in East Anglia, and thus widen the range of their raiding. When they were victorious they sacked and burned towns and churches, monasteries, and villages; if by any chance they encountered strong resistance they would move on and carry their brand of destruction elsewhere where they were not expected. Capturing their leaders availed nothing for these were merely local chiefs who were useless as hostages. And the complete disregard they had for the lives of their opponents was matched by their attitude to their own. In a storm they would drive their boats at top speed, glorying in the savagery and danger of it all, often letting them smash on the rocks because they would not trouble to shorten sail. Small wonder that the Saxons soon included in the Christian services the words 'From the fury of the Norsemen, good Lord deliver us' (*A furore Normanorum libera nos*). Curiously enough some of these Norsemen were to settle in France, become known as the Normans (in English as well as Latin), and develop the motte and bailey castle which was the military answer to their own type of raiding.

As the news of the vulnerability of England travelled back to Scandinavia and the adjoining countries, raids became more continuous and were made by larger bodies of men. Soon too the Vikings, who were short of land in their own country, began to settle. This new and ominous trend drew Saxon attention away from their own fratricidal squabbles. In 841 we read that:

> In this year Ealdorman Hercbehrt was killed by heathen men and many men with him in the marsh and later in the same year many were killed in Lindsay, East Anglia, and Kent.
>
> In 842 many were killed in London and Rochester.
>
> In 843 King Aethulwulf fought against the crews of 35 ships at Carhampton, and the Danes had possession of the battlefield.

Whether called Danes, Vikings, or Norsemen made no difference, but usually they were known as Danes, as we will call them from now on.

In 845 the people of Somerset and the people of Dorset fought against the Danish army at the mouth of the Parret and there made a great slaughter and had the victory.

The only salvation apparently was in unity, difficult though it might be for the Saxons to achieve.

In 851, we read:

In this year the men of Devon fought against the heathen army at Wicgeanburg and the English made great slaughter there and had the victory. And the same year 350 ships came into the mouth of the Thames and stormed Canterbury and London and put to flight Brihtwulf, King of the Mercians, with his army, and went south across the Thames into Surrey. And King Aethelwulf and his son Aethelbald fought against them at Aclea with the army of the West Saxons and there inflicted the greatest slaughter that we ever heard of until this present day, and had the victory there.

Aethelwulf had presumably learnt something from his previous defeat, and now had won a victory. Unfortunately it was not enough. The Danes were filtering through in all directions. Some had fortified themselves in Thanet and Sheppey and could not be driven out. In desperation the West Saxons deposed Aethelwulf and elected his son in his place. But events became no better. The Danes even burnt Winchester, the capital of Wessex, and sacked York. Northumbria was occupied by them and reverted to barbarism; those inhabitants of Yorkshire who were not killed were made serfs. The northern thrust had been made by the 'Great Army', under two Kings, Guthrum and Bagsaeg, but even after its northern conquest it was still land-hungry. One section went off to East Anglia where it fought King Edmund. Edmund was a rare combination, efficient, saintly, and a good military leader but these qualities did not bring him victory against the Danes. He was taken prisoner, and tortured to make him worship Danish gods. He refused and was used as target practice for bowmen. His body was recovered and buried in what became the Abbey of Bury St Edmunds. The Danes then proceeded to divide East Anglia among themselves.

It was now the turn of Wessex. After Aethelwulf's deposition his three elder sons, Aethelbald, Aethelbert, and Aethelred ruled in succession, In 870 when the 'Great Army' sailed up the Thames and launched itself into Wessex Aethelred came out to meet them, aided by his eighteen-year-old brother, Alfred. Aethelred's contribution tends to be overlooked in comparison with that of his younger brother but this is neither accurate nor just. Brilliant though Alfred was, he would have had no chance to display his abilities had not Aethelred been almost equally capable.

Alfred would, of course, have been exceptional in any age and was a giant in his time. As a child he had been sent to Rome to be baptized by Pope Leo. From early youth he had shown great promise as a scholar, and had been given that special type of leadership which brings out the best in men whatever their abilities and interests. Vitally important at that time was his military ability. He was an inspiring figure on the battlefield but he knew – as all good generals do – that there is a lot more to winning a war than a single victory. In those days – and perhaps up to the present century – boys took to war as naturally as they do to football or boxing today. And just as many a modern lad practises football in every spare moment he has, dreaming of a great opportunity against another country, so did Saxon lads, particularly those of royal blood, practise for war. Thus when the Danes moved into Mercia and took up winter quarters at Nottingham, Burgred, King of Mercia, appealed to Aethelred and Alfred to help him. Alfred was sixteen at the time but a veteran of many battles and skirmishes.

By this time the Danes were a large organized force. This conferred disadvantages as well as advantages. The old style small raiding forces could live off the country, had no disciplinary problems, needed few orders, and did not need to hold ground. This new army had a logistical problem; it needed to be near food supplies, it needed space to deploy, and it needed a unified command. Furthermore it was not operating against unprepared and helpless monks or villages; it was confronted with an armed countryside, full of look-outs, a place where food would be difficult to obtain and where stragglers or small foraging parties would be cut off and exterminated. It had lost surprise and it had lost much of its mobility. It could indeed send raiders on horseback for isolated forays but the mass of the army was bound to be slow-moving and cumbersome. Alfred would have noted that. Like the Saxons, the Danes fought with swords sometimes, but their favourite weapon was the battle-axe. It was a two-handed weapon and in the hands of the right man it could be used adroitly for thrusting and parrying. Nevertheless, although the axe was a far more versatile weapon than is usually believed, it carried one considerable disadvantage. It needed space. It could not be brought into action rapidly in a surprise attack unless the attacked men were in open order (widely separated) and, if they were in open order, it would be that little easier to split a way through them, whirling axes notwithstanding. There is, of course, a peculiar fascination about a weapon which is swung, whether it is axe, sword, or rifle butt, but there is often an excellent chance that it may do more damage to your friends than your foes, as your own side are likely to be closer to you. And although it could be used as a spear it was a poor substitute. All this Alfred would have noted when he went to help the Mercians at Nottingham, and fought a drawn battle with the Danes. It was a man's weapon, the axe, and the Danes loved it; they could slice an enemy in half with an axe, and literally carve a path to victory. Soldiers are very conservative about weapons, and sentiment about them often blinds them to the need for change. 'I would like to see the machine-gun that could stop one of my cavalry charges' a pre-1914 officer once said – and a year later he did. The battle-axe even after it had failed to save the Saxons at Hastings, and was discredited as a weapon, still managed to worm its way back into favour with the Normans, and in the twelfth century was Richard the Lion Heart's favourite weapon.

The Danes, flushed with their East Anglian and other successes, set up headquarters at Reading. They realized that they had not yet met the full power of Saxon resistance and that it would be concentrated somewhere in this area. Apart from anything else, they would be outnumbered, and they were experienced enough to know that a disparity in numbers can be nullified if the lesser force fights behind defences – or at least from prepared positions. There are, of course, other factors which can equalize numbers: weapons, experience, training, and tactical handling, but the most consistent is fortifications. Surprisingly perhaps, they made a rampart between the rivers Thames and Kennet on the right side of the royal city. We have two different accounts of the subsequent events, one from the *Anglo-Saxon Chronicle*, the other from Asser, Bishop of Sherborne and a contemporary of Alfred.

While some of the Danes were making the defences others 'scoured the country for plunder'. They were soon proved right in their expectations of resistance for:

They were encountered by Ethelwulf, the ealdorman of Berkshire, at a place called Englefield, both sides fought bravely and made long resistance. At length one of the pagan jarls was slain, and the greater part of the army destroyed; upon which the rest saved themselves by flight, and the Christians gained the victory.

Four days afterwards, Aethelred, King of the West Saxons, and his brother, Alfred, united their forces and marched to Reading, where, on their arrival, they cut to pieces the pagans whom they found outside the fortifications. But the pagans, nevertheless, sallied out from the gates, and a long and fierce engagement ensued. At last, grief to say, the Christians fled, the pagans obtained the victory, and the aforesaid ealdorman Ethelwulf, [victor of Englefield] was among the slain. (*Asser*)

It was a disaster for the West Saxons and the Danes realized it. They themselves had sent out strong reconnaissance parties which had been beaten. The Saxons, overconfident perhaps, had thereupon attacked the Danes in their new stronghold and after bitter fighting had been cut to pieces. The Danes had not planned such a clever strategy in that they had drawn the Saxons to fight in a disadvantageous position but once it had happened they had taken full advantage of it. Now was the time to follow up the victory and carve Wessex in half. Four days later – a day to rest and to bury the dead, a day to regroup, a day to confer and get ready, and on the march on the fourth, if not earlier – they would have covered the ten miles from Reading to Streatley and come up the long slope to the Ridgeway. No doubt they kept a wary eye to the right as they went diagonally up the track, and perhaps had a few look-outs along the skyline. But nothing happened and they would have concluded that the Saxon morale had been destroyed at the barricades and there

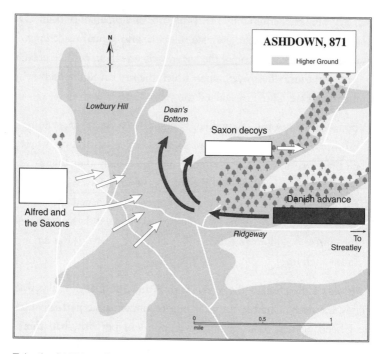

Take the A417 from Streatley and turn left just as it leaves the village at the sign for the Golf Club. The road goes past the club and becomes the track leading to the Ridgeway. (Berkshire)

would be no more resistance in that part of the country. Once on top of the Ridge they were safe from surprise attack; doubtless the Saxons would now keep well out of their way.

But the Saxons were there, hundreds of them. Chroniclers have a loose way of describing an army or the dead after a battle as 'thousands'. It is doubtful if either side numbered more than a thousand on this occasion, for the Danes would have left some men to protect their base and the Saxons would have found it difficult to concentrate their forces until they knew exactly when and where the Danes would move. And even today you could conceal a thousand men along the Ridgeway, all ready to spring out and ambush the unwary. In those days they could have laid up within weapon reach. Some undoubtedly did but the main force was held in reserve for the shock attack.

Alfred's problem was to manoeuvre this invasion column into a trap. It was no good fighting in a head-on clash along the Ridgeway. The Danes were hard men to beat at the best of times and in a straightforward fight were as likely as not to come out the winners as they had, he knew only too well, at Reading. The need was to lure them to a position where they would be too cramped to make full use of their weapons. It would not be easy. His army was there along the Ridgeway by Roden Downs. Just north of the Ridgeway and south of Lowbury Hill, site of the old Romano-British temple, was a superb battlefield, like a parade ground, if that was what you wanted. It is an open piece of slightly hollow ground, and it still has a thorn tree in the middle of it. The Danes would like that: it would give them room to swing their axes.

Alfred drew them towards it by a decoy party. This, the Danes thought, when they caught sight of them, was the rest of the Saxon army. They moved forward to cut them to pieces, but the Saxons fell back. The Danes were in two divisions, and it was very necessary for the Saxons to decoy them all into the right position before they launched their attack. If the Saxons went in too soon the Danish rear party would come in behind and they too would be trapped. And that was not Alfred's plan at all.

As they deployed on the battlefield which had been chosen for them, the Danes suddenly noticed that the main Saxon force was not in front of them but had suddenly appeared from behind them, cutting off their retreat. They suspected that they were the object of a tactical plan and they hastily re-formed, putting their two Kings in the middle, and positioning the jarls and lesser chiefs on the front and flanks. They put stakes in the ground, as this was the tried way of holding up an enemy charge; then they waited for the next Saxon move. The Saxons came forward and also put down stakes against a possible Danish charge. They too divided their army into two groups, but this was because Aethelred was not yet at the field. He was busy praying in his tent, and would not leave it. He took so long over his devotions that the Danes had begun the battle before he arrived. Alfred was in a desperate position, for without Aethelred's division he had not enough men for the tactical thrust he had planned. Asser put it:

> The Alfred, though possessing a subordinate authority, could no longer support the troops of the enemy unless he retreated or charged upon them without waiting for his brother. At length he bravely led his troops against the hostile army, as they had before arranged, but without waiting for his brother's arrival; for he relied on the divine counsels, and forming his men into a dense phalanx, marched on at once to meet the foe.

What Alfred knew, and the Danes as yet did not, was that to the east of Lowbury Hill, and behind the Danish position was a precipice falling to what is now known (and marked on the map) as Dean's Bottom. 'Denu' is the old English word for a dene or valley, but 'dene' can also derive from Dane. As Danish weapons have been found at the bottom of this valley it seems as if at least a part of Alfred's plan worked. Driving with tremendous force on to the Danish lines he made them fall back to give themselves more room. The Saxon casualties would have been very high as they charged up the slopes on to an army which was prepared to receive them. Only superb leadership could have taken that Saxon force to the point at which the retreating Danes, unfamiliar with the countryside, would find a precipice behind them, if they were not already over it. The visitor will do well to be careful or he might share their experience. And as the rear line steadied and came forward involuntarily the swinging axes would do as much harm to their own side as to the Saxons. Something like panic would infect the Danes for there are few more unnerving experiences than trying to confront an enemy who is trying to push you over a precipice which lies just behind you and which you dare not turn round to look for. At that point, Aethelred's men, heartened by the successful conclusion of his prayers, hurled themselves into the battle. To the Danes it looked as if fresh tides of reinforcements were on the way. Some tried to fight their way out sideways but Alfred's flankers took care of that and shepherded them on to the deadly slopes.

And when both armies had fought long and bravely, at last the pagans, by the divine judgement, were no longer able to bear the attacks of the Christians, and having lost the greater part of their army, took to disgraceful flight. One of their two kings, and five jarls, were there slain, together with many thousand pagans, who fell on all sides, covering with their bodies the whole plain of Ashdune.

There fell in that battle King Bagsac, jarl Sidrac the elder, and jarl Sidrac the younger, jarl Osbern, jarl Frene, and jarl Harald, and the whole pagan army pursued its flight, not only until evening but until the next day, until they reached the stronghold from which they had sallied. The Christians followed, slaying all they could reach, until it became dark.

The *Anglo-Saxon Chronicle* records the death of two kings not one, and the same number of earls. It says 'many thousands were killed and they continued fighting until night.'

And, as on many battlefields, you may still perhaps hear and even see the fighting, in the morning mists at certain times of the year. Imagination, no doubt, and self-deception, but real enough to those who claim to have seen it re-enacted in ghostly but frightening reincarnation.

The Battle of Ethandun

AD 878

Ashdown, although a great victory, had merely checked the Danes, not ended their campaign. Alfred's efforts to follow it up, and drive the Danes out of Wessex, met with very moderate success. Two weeks after Ashdown, he fought another Danish army at Basing, near Basingstoke, and there – the *Chronicle* bluntly and briefly reports – 'the Danes had the victory.'

And two months later, King Aethelred and his brother Alfred fought against the army at Merton, and they were in two divisions; and they put both to flight, and were victorious far on into the day, and there was great slaughter on both sides, and the Danes had possession of the battlefield. And after this battle a great summer army came to Reading.

Clearly there is some characteristic in these Danish armies which the chronicler omits, perhaps because he does not know it or perhaps because he does not understand it. Why did the Danes win these battles? Presumably it was not merely a matter of numbers. Both sides had enormous casualties. Why at Merton did they put the Danes to flight and yet lose? Were the Danes experts at luring their opponents on to destruction, perhaps in a series of enveloping moves? All in all it suggests that there was much more subtlety in these battles than a mere rabble of spear-throwers meeting a collection of battle-axe swingers in a head-on clash. It looks as if the Danes were capable of fighting delaying actions and then committing reserves at the critical moment.

There is of course another explanation, and that is that Alfred knew when to break off his engagements. Alfred was a highly intelligent general who underrated neither his enemies nor his task. The war was one of constant mobility. Alfred was, doubtless, constantly harassing and diverting the Danish invaders. Occasionally his strategy brought him to a pitched battle. The time and place were probably of his choosing, although there were doubtless occasions when he made a mistake and the Danes held the initiative. The Danes should not have had superiority of numbers, for the population of England was probably 900,000 at that time; but Alfred may have known only too well that in a pitched battle the Danes were, man for man, better than the Saxons. It seems that Alfred used small groups to inflict hammer blows in hit-and-run tactics. Aethelred had died after the Battle of Merton, and Alfred, still very young, had to fight a war in which he did not dare commit all his forces. One great defeat and his kingdom was lost. At Wilton (near Salisbury), still in 871 – a year of battle if ever there was one – the Saxons took on a huge Danish army and put it to flight, but had to retreat hastily when the Danes rallied. The cost to both sides was punitive. The Saxons were fighting for their kingdom so, even though outnumbered and often outfought, they made the Danes respect them. Eventually, after heavy losses on both sides, a truce was signed at the end of the year 871.

The year 872 seems to have been a comparatively uneventful period though there can be no doubt that it must have been full of minor clashes and skirmishes. By this time both armies had acquired a healthy respect for each other. The Danes knew that, until the

Saxons were finally conquered and crushed, their own gains could not be regarded as secure. The Saxons – or at least Alfred – realized that the Danes might come up the Thames via Reading, might drive up from Portsmouth and Southampton by Winchester, or might even swoop down from Northumbria through Mercia. Faced with this triple-pronged threat he had to evolve a strategy which would defeat these relentless heathen savages. In 873 the Danes busied themselves in Northumbria, but they also established a strong base in Lindsay. In 874 they moved across to Repton in Derbyshire, conquered the Mercian kingdom, and installed a puppet king there.

In 875 they were up in the north again, based on the Tyne and ranging far and wide and into Scotland. Guthrum, and two lesser chieftains moved to Cambridge. For the time being the Danes seemed to have abandoned their efforts to split Wessex in two by advancing from Reading. Doubtless they knew that preparations had been made for them along the Ridgeway and other trackways. By this time Alfred had Wessex very well organized militarily and was an expert at lightning commando-type raids. It was the Danes' own technique, but they themselves were particularly vulnerable to it. Alfred carried the war to them by sea. In 875 he engaged seven Danish ships, captured one, and put the rest to flight. He was, very rightly, determined not to let his enemies settle down. This phase of the war became a vicious deadlock with plenty of activity but no thrustful moves.

Suddenly the Danes broke it. The Cambridge army slipped away south and west, and next appeared at Wareham in Dorset. One large contingent had marched to the coast, embarked, and come round by sea: the ultimate effect was that a huge Danish force had outflanked the Wessex army and was now posing a threat from the rear. Many in this force seem to have been mounted, although they would not have contemplated fighting from horseback, horses being regarded merely as personnel carriers.

Alfred seems to have moved almost as swiftly and he had the advantage that he was operating from interior lines. He swept down to Dorset and had the Danes boxed in before they realized what had happened. Instead of being able to forage and settle in, they were trapped. Possibly Alfred had his navy behind them at sea. At all events they decided to ask for terms and even gave him hostages of high rank. Furthermore they swore on the 'holy ring', a most sacred Icelandic symbol, that they would promptly leave England. Their humiliation was complete. Their great strategic enveloping move had trapped no one but themselves. Alfred trusted them; they could not possibly break so important an oath. But they did. Under cover of darkness they mounted their horses and slipped away to Exeter. Some had embarked and were making the dash by sea but these ran into a storm and it is reported in the *Anglo-Saxon Chronicle* that 120 ships were lost at Swanage. When he heard the news of the Danes' treachery, Alfred cursed himself for trusting them but wasted no time in setting off in rapid pursuit. Unfortunately for him, his enemies had had too much start and were safely in the fortress before he could intercept them. There again they asked for terms.

The battle of wits had lost none of its sharpness. As Alfred knew, and the Danes also knew, he could not afford to keep his army besieging them in Exeter. If the Danes' supplies began to run low they could be revictualled from ships. They would not, in any event have to hold out for long. Armies at this period, and for a thousand years later, had a limited campaigning season because every able-bodied man was needed for the spring sowing and again the autumn reaping. During the bad weather all armies stayed in winter quarters; campaigning in wet, snow, mud, and short days was too hazardous to be embarked on voluntarily. At Exeter the Danes knew that if Alfred did not break in immediately his men must withdraw to get in the harvest which was now due. If they did not, his army and kingdom would probably starve, and their fighting qualities next summer after a winter of exceptional and unnecessary deprivation would be negligible. To help Alfred make up his mind, the Danes offered even more hostages, so many in fact that he could not fail to accept their offer. And this time they kept to the terms he gave them, more or less. Some returned to Mercia and others went to Gloucester but they did no more fighting. It is unlikely that Alfred trusted them but he felt that for the time being they were under control. He was wrong.

This campaign of Saxons against Danes, or more particularly of Alfred against an unknown Danish strategist is one of which we have tantalizingly few details. This winter (877–8) the Danes broke all the military rules. Instead of lying up for the winter months, preparing their weapons, quarrelling and drinking, they began a new campaign. On the 6 January 878 or thereabouts, they slipped quietly up to Chippenham, set up a battle headquarters, and launched a series of lightning attacks far and wide on the astonished Saxons. Where they had come from no one precisely knew, probably from Bristol, with reinforcements which had slipped down from Mercia. Surprise, speed, and ruthlessness drove all before them and soon Alfred, with his command scattered and disintegrated, was a homeless fugitive. The best he could do was to take a small band of loyal adherents into the fens of Somerset. There they dispersed for secrecy and safety. But the Danes were not having matters all their own way for it was reported that an attempt to invade Devon, with twenty-three ships was decisively defeated. Whether this Saxon army was led by Alfred or not is not known.

Possibly 878 was a mild and dry winter. Whatever the weather and conditions, neither side allowed them to affect plans. From his secret retreat Alfred issued instructions for the mobilizing of his army. It took weeks. The Danes found out where he was and tried to attack him but attacking an enemy who is hiding in the fens and has local guides is a frustrating task. As often as not your own army will be decoyed into treacherous bogs or ambushed where it is unable to escape. Alfred was fighting for survival. Whether the legends of the burnt cakes, or his creeping into the Danish camp disguised as a minstrel to hear their plans are true or not is immaterial. They could well have been. He was desperate, and he needed to know something of the Danish dispositions. When he eventually moved out in May 878 he was joined by a host of men who had all been summoned to meet him. This was a carefully planned and timed operation. Then he set out to meet the Danes.

The place where he met them and won a decisive battle has been a matter of some controversy. The name Ethandun has been taken to mean Heddington in Wiltshire, which is not improbable, Eddington and Yattendon in Berkshire which are highly unlikely, Edington in Somerset, and Edington in Wiltshire. The last is the one we favour.

If opinions on the whereabouts of the battle-site vary so, no less do views of how the battle was fought even among those who prefer the Edington (Wilts) site. Some of these views appear to us to be unnecessarily complicated. The obvious inference is that the Danes, having heard that Alfred had broken out of Somerset, and somehow assembled an army, would immediately set out to crush this possible danger before it could rally too many forces and perhaps capture various strategic points. Their main headquarters was still at Chippenham and they would head south-west rapidly towards Somerset. Fourteen miles south of Chippenham they would

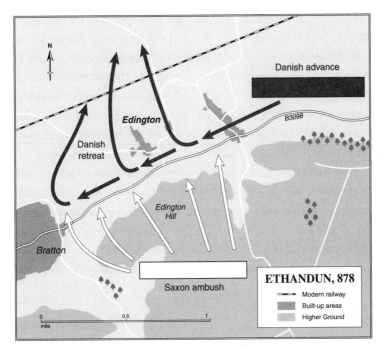

ETHANDUN, 878
- - - Modern railway
Built-up areas
Higher Ground

Take the B3098 from Westbury to Edington. The ambush position is along the side of the hill. (Wiltshire)

come on to the B3098 and turn towards Westbury. They would not at this stage expect to be anywhere near the Saxons. Alfred already knew that surprise is a war-winning factor, and in the last round of battles had been surprised himself – with disastrous results. Doubtless he sent some misinformation to the Danes, and made sure they had no idea of the trap he was laying for them. Where the B3098 runs along the side of Edington Hill the visitor will note that some of the slopes are covered with woods and bracken. In 878 all the slopes would have been covered. They would be leafy and opaque. It was a perfect ambush position. If matters went badly, and the Danes had too many troops the Saxons could retreat up the hill and perhaps occupy the hill fort known as Bratton Castle or even go right back to Battlesbury Camp. But they were not there to fight a defensive battle. Their total aim was to catch the whole Danish force unawares. Their numbers were obviously much greater than the Danes would expect, if the latter expected anything at all.

And the Danes, who would have been watched all the way till they reached the road, obligingly walked right into the trap. When their whole line of march was strung along that dangerous piece of road the Saxon attack would hurl itself on to them with all the pent-up rage and hate of men who have been living on the run in the woods for months. The *Chronicle* puts it briefly but clearly:

And there fought against the whole army and put it to flight, and pursued it as far as the fortress, and stayed there a fortnight.

Now indeed it was the Britons' turn. The Danes were so shocked, cut up and demoralized by this sudden and overwhelming defeat that they lost heart. It was, of course, a crushing blow to morale to have your great and victorious army destroyed by an enemy whom you thought you had yourself destroyed. The extraordinary aftermath of this battle was that Guthrum, the great Danish war leader now decided that he had been following false gods and they had betrayed him. After the peace treaty, which this time was honoured, he was formally baptized. It was not, of course, the end of the Danish threat, for there were many different contingents, but the main force had been defeated and from then onwards Alfred saw his strength and authority increase. There was of course endless intermittent fighting, and some compromise, but the Anglo-Saxon kingdom had been saved, and the first steps to converting the Danes from paganism had already been taken.

Some writers have suggested that the main fighting took place south of Combe Hill. This implies that the Saxons would have fought uphill on to Danish prepared positions. Alfred would never have done anything so foolish, nor for that matter would the Danes, setting out to deal with what they thought to be an insurgent rabble fifty miles away, take up a defensive position on top of a barren ridge.

The visitor will have no difficulty in visualizing the ambush, the desperate fight, the Danes being tumbled down the slopes, and then the bitter pursuit to Chippenham.

The Battle of Blore Heath

23 September 1459

The five hundred and eighty-one years which elapsed between the Battle of Ethandun and the Battle of Blore Heath were, of course, as eventful as any of those in our early history. However, many of the battles which occurred in them took place in areas covered by other books in this volume, and certain of them, such as Evesham and Northampton, though geographically in the Midlands were so closely linked with other battles, and so vital to the chain of events, that they were discussed in *British Battlefields: the South*. As far as possible an attempt has been made to preserve historical as well as geographical unity in this volume. Nothing is more frustrating than to be standing on a battlefield well aware of what happened but completely baffled as to why it happened. Thus Lewes is so closely linked with Evesham that the latter is meaningless without the former. The events of the Wars of the Roses are extremely complex and the main sequence of battles falls outside this section; however the two Midlands battles recorded here were apart from the main stream and are not closely linked with events before and after. When we reach the Civil War the converse applies and the main sequence appears in this section.

The period between Ethandun and Blore Heath saw many developments, both in weapons and methods of warfare, but the main principles remained unchanged, as they still do. Thus numerical superiority may be offset by adequate defences, better tactics, or more efficient weapons; surprise confers great advantages, but if the initial advantage is not consolidated the success of the opening moves may have created dangerous liabilities which a cool and astute opponent may soon begin to exploit. The political pattern seemed to confirm the somewhat doubtful claim that history repeats itself. The Danes settled down just as their ferocious predecessors, the Anglo-Saxons, had done before them, and soon the blend of German and Scandinavian tribes became the loyal Englishmen who fought successfully at Stamford Bridge but unsuccessfully at Hastings.

The years immediately after the Normal Conquest did not see any major battles on English soil. Not until 1138 do we find what might be described as a representative army taking the field in this country. There were of course endless sieges, skirmishes, and minor clashes before and after, but it is not until 1264 that we see the second great battle. (We might perhaps have to include Fornham in 1174 if we knew enough about it to determine its scale.) The year 1265 saw the decisive battle of Evesham, but then nearly a century elapsed before Boroughbridge in 1322. Neville's Cross took place in 1346, and Otterburn, over forty years later, in 1388. The early fifteenth century saw decisive and bloody battles at Homildon Hill in 1402 and Shrewsbury in 1403. There were, of course, numerous battles overseas in this long period. From Gerberoi[1] in 1079, through Crécy, Poitiers, Agincourt, Beaugé, Formigny, and many others all over Europe, Englishmen were almost continuously in arms, sometimes for English causes, sometimes not, sometimes in victory, sometimes in defeat.

---

1 The occasion when William the Conqueror, fighting rebels led by Robert, his son, was wounded and unhorsed. Tokig of Wallingford, an English thegn, whose sister had married Robert d'Oilly, the builder of Oxford Castle, gave his own horse to William to make his escape, but was himself killed.

In 1455 at St Albans there began a long series of battles which only ended at Stoke Field, near Newark in 1487. These were the infamous Wars of the Roses. Some hold that these wars ended with the Tewkesbury blood bath of 1471, but there were other battles still to come, not least that at Bosworth in 1485, before succession to the English throne was settled.

A very brief explanation of the Wars of the Roses is necessary here to give the background to the savage battle of Blore Heath which we examine next.

The baronial war to which has been given the name 'Wars of the Roses' was not known by that name at the time, nor for many years afterwards. It was however fairly well represented by the White Rose of York against the Red Rose of Lancaster, in that a Lancastrian held the throne until he was driven from it by Yorkist supporters.

The root cause of the wars is held to be 'the will of Edward III who had distributed his realm so evenly that his descendants were equally and immensely powerful. Then, when his grandson, Richard II, ruled somewhat unwisely, he was toppled off his throne and undoubtedly murdered by his very rich cousin, Henry of Bolingbroke. Thus when the descendants of the Duke of Lancaster seized power from the holder of the throne there was certain to be a conflict with the descendants of the Duke of York who had, as it happened, married the female heir of the line immediately senior to the Duke of Lancaster. Henry of Bolingbroke and Lancaster retained the throne he had seized from Richard II, but had to suppress various revolts. His son, Henry V, as a popular and successful warrior, had no problems over his title to the crown but when he died at the age of thirty-three he left a son and heir less than a year old. This infant was destined to have the most disastrous reign in English history.

But the succession of a minor would not have mattered greatly, had he been reasonably capable later, for the Lancastrian line was now well-established; unfortunately this infant, Henry VI, was intermittently mad and never very competent when sane. Furthermore he married a French wife of great courage, skill, and determination who was subject to vindictive and rancorous hatreds.

The Wars of the Roses were not a civil war in the sense that the term is usually understood. There was no ideology involved; it was a power struggle between two groups of over-powerful families. It did not involve the majority of the country, and the contestants, very wisely, took care that it should not disrupt production and commerce. Thus the Battle of Northampton was fought outside that city, whose inhabitants remained undisturbed, though doubtless alarmed. Periodically, noblemen changed sides; in the later stages the war was fought in bitterness and revenge for real or supposed wrongs, and any trace of higher motives disappeared. There was a regional aspect to the war in that London, the Midlands, and the south-east were Yorkist and the west, north, and Wales were Lancastrian. There were of course discrepancies in this regional pattern, and we find Lancastrian supporters in the south and Yorkist supporters in the north.

The early years of Henry VI were years of almost unbroken misfortune. The conquests of his father, Henry V, were gradually lost, and as disaster succeeded disaster overseas they were matched by mounting turbulence and disorder at home. Soldiers who had spent all their previous lives in France came home ready to sell themselves to the most affluent trouble-maker they could attach themselves to. A considerable part of the recent French disasters could be attributed to the stupidity of Somerset, Henry VI's chief minister. Somerset's deficiencies and high-handedness were obvious to everyone except Henry and it therefore seemed like divine intervention when Henry went mad, and the Duke of York, the next in line for the throne, was appointed Protector. York put Somerset in prison and replaced Henry's incompetent ministers by able and responsible men. Unfortunately this happy state of affairs did not continue long; for Henry vi's wife, Queen Margaret, produced a son after nine years of barren marriage, thereby ensuring the continuance of the Lancastrian line, and Henry vi recovered his wits sufficiently to mount the throne again. Henry's first act on re-assuming power was to release Somerset and reappoint him chief minister.

It was the last straw. York, normally a mild and patient man, was stirred to action. He called out his retainers and friends and marched towards London. Henry vi met him at St Albans. The ensuing battle was far different from the later embittered blood bath but it was vigorous enough, and in the course of it Somerset was killed. York asked for forgiveness from the king, who was his prisoner, but also resumed his own position of supreme authority (1455).

But blood had been shed and Margaret was not likely to rest till York's had joined it. The pity of it all was that Henry himself, though not an able king, had a character which could fairly be described as being saintly; York, although not of quite such high standards, certainly had no wish to do more than use his abilities in the best interests of the country. Many of the other personalities whose fortunes – and heads – rose and fell were less villainous than mistaken. It has been aptly said that an imagined wrong is much more deadly than a real one. The Wars of the Roses were overfull of both.

In 1465 Henry, by merely exercising his constitutional rights as the monarch, was able to dismiss York's supporters from office. Nobody, not even York himself, was unduly disturbed. The hated

Somerset was dead, and nobody wished to see a fratricidal war. But, with turbulent and over-powerful families, some of whom were richer than the king himself, with suspicion and bitterness on all sides, and large numbers of trained but not well-disciplined soldiers everywhere, there was clearly more trouble looming. Where would the next clash come?

Margaret, believing that York and his supporter, the young Earl of Warwick, would effectively prevent her son's ever attaining the throne, spent the next two years swearing in adherents to her son's cause: she distributed silver swan badges as symbols of allegiance to him. Some of her supporters were even more active than she was. They provoked a riot in London when the Earl of Warwick, captain of the Calais garrison, was on a visit to Westminster. Warwick was lucky to escape with his life; it was now clear that if he set foot again in England he might be assassinated or put to death on a trumped-up charge. His father, the Earl of Salisbury, who had vast estates in Yorkshire, decided that matters had now gone far enough and that the Yorkists should reassume power. He began assembling his retainers in Middleham castle, ten miles south-west of York, possibly with the intention of marching on London. The Duke of York was at Ludlow Castle (or perhaps close by at Wigmore) from which area he was able to rally supporters from Wales. Margaret, not unmindful of the dangerous concentration of force which would occur if Salisbury joined York, now intensified her recruiting in Lancashire and Cheshire. The outcome of this was that the Lancastrians soon mustered a very considerable force which was put under the command of Lord Audley; it was said to number nearly 15,000.

At the beginning of September 1459 Salisbury made his move. His force numbered about 4,000. This was clearly not enough to capture London even if Warwick came over from Calais with a substantial force to attack from the other side. Henry VI had moved to Worcester where he had a useful force though not an army, and Queen Margaret was at Eccleshall where she was able to continue recruiting yet keep a wary eye open for any Yorkist moves. The whole atmosphere was very brittle. War was inevitable but neither faction knew when or where to strike the first blow. A wrong move could easily lead to bloody and humiliating defeat.

Salisbury's move towards Ludlow caught the Lancastrians by surprise, but Margaret, who was a strategist of no mean order, rapidly grasped the fact that she could catch him in a trap. Margaret had reasoned that Salisbury's army was bound to march somewhere through the Stafford – Stoke line and assumed that Eccleshall, lying fourteen miles south of Stoke, would be as good a place as any to intercept it. However, Salisbury's intelligence service was clearly as good as Margaret's, so he took the road through Newcastle-under-Lyme and marched swiftly towards Market Drayton. This out-flanked Margaret but would not put Salisbury out of reach of Henry VI's troops later if the latter moved quickly enough, which was unlikely. Salisbury went through Market Drayton and camped just south of the town on the hill which to this day is known as Salisbury Hill. So far so good, and everything going to a neat though delicate plan.

But now Salisbury was due for a shock. His scouts came up with the highly unwelcome news that a large force of Lancastrians, estimated at about 15,000 but probably exaggerated, was a few miles to the north-west, under the command of Lord Audley. Their camp may be seen today on the map, marked as Audley Brow. Salisbury, although he had a good position and was protected by the River Tern, decided that it was not in his best interests to give

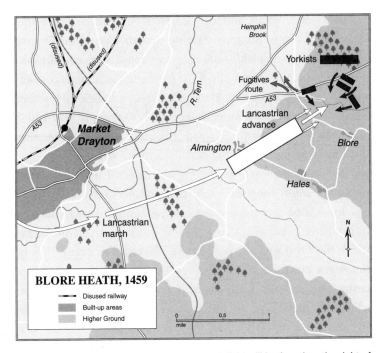

Take the A53 out of Market Drayton; the battlefield will be found on the right of this road after three miles. (Shropshire)

battle then and there. In consequence, he struck camp while it was still dark and moved north-east with the intention of slipping up to Nantwich; from there he might still outflank the Lancastrians. However, on this occasion Audley was not caught unawares, and was soon on Salisbury's heels. Salisbury gave up the attempt to reach Nantwich and instead withdrew in an easterly direction. Audley, knowing that he had superior numbers did not hurry overmuch, and keeping Salisbury's rearguard in sight made a leisurely pace which enabled the rest of his army to catch up with the vanguard.

There was, however, nothing leisurely about Salisbury's activities in the remainder of his army. Having reached what seemed to him an almost ideal ambush position he proceeded to exploit its possibilities to the full. Just south of the present A53 the land falls away sharply into the bed of the Hempnill Brook, a fast-flowing stream which doubtless carried more water in 1459 than today. The bed of the brook is about twenty feet wide; the sides rise steeply and then slope more gradually. On the north side there was plenty of cover and Salisbury deployed his troops in concealed positions with a centre line confronting the Lancastrian advance, and the remainder equally divided between two diagonally-stationed wing formations. Immediately ahead of the front line he ordered a trench to be dug which was filled with sharpened stakes. His archers were mainly on the wings but there was a reserve force immediately behind the centre line. In case Audley should try to outflank this position, which was presumably at that time the most fordable part of the stream, he had stacked up his baggage-carts on the exterior lines. These, if nothing else, would give protection from the cross-fire of those rightly famed Cheshire bowmen.

Salisbury's tactics were ingenious and daring but, of course, he had no option but to make a bold move if he were to survive at all. His aim was to draw the maximum number of Lancastrians into a position from which they could neither extricate themselves nor use their weapons to good advantage, and at the same time to encourage them to pursue their disastrous tactics until they were hopelessly defeated.

The first Lancastrian wave rushed down the slope, crossed the brook and mounted the other bank. By now all formation had been lost but, no matter, the Yorkists were retreating. Excitedly the Lancastrians waved on their followers who, seeing that success was imminent, also poured down the southern slopes into the river bed. As they did so the first line came up the bank and obligingly fell into the trench full of sharpened stakes. The knights were in the most trouble but the general confusion here looked no different from any other battle of the time, and the rest of the Lancastrians were only too glad to push on to join in and share the victory. Soon the whole river bed was full of Lancastrians trying to cross. At that point Salisbury threw in his reserve line and opened up with his wing archers.

The scene in that hollow must have been appalling. As the first wave of Lancastrians and some wounded decided they had had enough and began to retreat, they were carried forward by the centre of the Lancastrian army struggling up from the hollow. By now the Yorkist bowmen were pouring arrows on to the closely-packed men and horses, as they floundered on the river bed. This, as it became churned up and blocked with the bodies of fallen men and horses, became a trap from which there was little hope of escape. Some in desperation tried to move downstream but the Yorkists were mindful of that and had blocked the way. Others realizing there was no retreat, but no way forward either, tried to creep along the north side of the brook and reach safety that way. The Cheshire archers, from which so much had been expected were forced down the slope into the confused and closely-packed ranks below. Their little silver swans made them perfect targets. Horses were useless, for the far bank was too steep for them to mount. Only when a macabre stepping-stone of fallen bodies had piled up was it possible to get a few horses over. By that time some of the bowmen were said to have changed sides and were fighting their way out through Audley's rearguard rather than face the death-pit in the valley below. Others had no choice. The slope toward the brook is steep and once the army was set in motion there was no way of stopping the onrush except by falling. And falling meant being trampled to death. The first clash had occurred at 1 p.m. and all through that bright September afternoon desperate men were trying to fight their way out of the death-trap; others no less determined were resolved they should not. The hours went by, the brook filled up with corpses – it was said to have run red with blood for three days afterwards – and still the Lancastrians could neither mount the slope nor redeploy on the far side where they were also exposed to Yorkist arrows. Knight after knight tried to lead a breakthrough but was brought down well short of success. Among them were Venables, Dutton, Troutbeck, Leigh, Done, Egerton, and Molyneux. Some rallied around Audley when in a last final effort he forced his way over the stream, up the bank, and on to the northern slope. Here, half-way up the ridge, where his monument stands today, he too fell. It was the end of the Lancastrian effort, and pretty nearly the end of the Yorkist effort too, for by now their arrows had gone and their losses had been by no means light. Some Lancastrians were now able to move down the river bank towards Market Drayton but it only delayed the inevitable, for they were caught in the meadow where the Hempnill joins the Tern, and were slaughtered where they stood. But, of course, there were also a few Yorkists too who became over-confident in the wake of the battle. They were killed or captured when they pursued too recklessly and ran into larger forces of Lancastrians.

It was without a shadow of doubt a brilliant and unexpected Yorkist victory. The Lancastrian losses were given as 2,400, and their humiliation was greater. But it was not decisive, as Salisbury knew. If Margaret, five miles away, and Henry ten miles away, brought up their combined army, his own mauled forces would be quickly battered into defeat. Clearly he could not stay at Blore Heath; he must press on with all speed and join the Duke of York at Ludlow. But once he set out for Ludlow his army on the march would be an easier prey than if it stayed.

Once more he used deception. Realizing that Margaret would think he would rest and celebrate his victory he set off again as soon as darkness fell. His men did not grumble; they knew their lives depended on this stratagem. But he left his guns behind with an Austin friar to fire them during the night.[1] Queen Margaret's army, approaching the wood, and hearing the guns going all night long considered that Salisbury was celebrating his victory with drunken revelry. But the next morning when they advanced for the kill they found the woods empty except for the friar. Asked with some irritation what he thought he was doing he replied that the army had gone and left him behind and that he had stayed where he was firing the guns because he had been afraid to leave in the dark.

Salisbury reached Ludlow, but his brilliant victory was wasted in the fiasco of Ludford which took place less than a month later, on 12 October just outside Ludlow. There, realizing they were once more heavily outnumbered – perhaps 6–1 – the Yorkist army left the field during the night, and the Lancastrians were the victors in a bloodless battle.

Ironically Salisbury was killed a year later, after the Battle of Wakefield. Wakefield, which took place on 30 December 1460, was another tactically brilliant battle, almost modern in its concept, but this time the losers were the Yorkists. Salisbury escaped from the field, but was captured and, in the rancorous atmosphere then prevailing, was put to death. His head was displayed on the gates of

1 'Save only a Fryer Austyn schot gonnes alle that nyght in a parke that was at the back syde of the fylde.' (*Gregory – 15th century*).

York. Next to his was the Duke of York's head, crowned by Margaret with a paper crown. On the other side was the head of Rutland, York's second son; he was seventeen.

The Battle of Edgcote

26 July 1469

The ten years between Blore Heath and Edgcote were filled with a succession of battles, each bloodier than the last. One of the most extraordinary features of this war was the way fortune ebbed and flowed. As we saw, the Yorkists won brilliantly at Blore Heath but gave up without a fight at Ludford. The following July, Warwick, now at the peak of his military and political ability, won a crushing victory at Northampton. The Duke of York then took control of London and it seemed obvious to everyone that the Yorkists were now in an unchallengeable position. However, it did not appear that way at all to Queen Margaret who was busy rallying a formidable army upon the Scottish border. York set off north to settle matters once and for all. He took young Rutland, his second son, to give the youngster some more battle experience. With him also was Salisbury, the victor of Blore Heath; he was sixty. In medieval warfare boys went on campaigns as soon as they were strong enough to hold a sword. When very young they were kept at a safe distance from the fighting, after having helped arm their knights; thus they could quickly flee from a lost battle or, if their side won, they could join in the pursuit of the fugitives and emulate the callous ferocity of their elders. Occasionally plans went wrong. Rutland, although neither novice nor child in medieval warfare, had not yet received the command to which his rank entitled him.

However, he failed to get away quickly when the Yorkists were defeated at Wakefield and was mercilessly killed by a Lancastrian paying off a grudge. Nor was Salisbury's age any safeguard. He was beheaded the day after the battle.

Wakefield was a tremendous shock for the Yorkists. Tactically it was remarkable close to their own unexpected victory at Blore Heath the previous year, but at Wakefield it was the Yorkists who fell into the trap. And now it seemed as if nothing could stop the Lancastrians. They pushed on to St Albans and this time decisively reversed the defeat they had sustained in the first battle of the war. Fittingly, Warwick, the architect of the earlier Yorkists' victory at St Albans, was now in command of the defeated army.

But there was a cloud on the Lancastrian horizon. It was Edward, Earl of March, eldest son of that Duke of York whose head was now stuck on a spike at the gates of York, wearing its paper crown. Edward, only nineteen, but over six feet tall and a leader of outstanding ability had already shown the military genius which would bring him the crown within weeks. Just before the Yorkist defeat at St Albans, Edward had won a brilliant victory at Mortimer's Cross in Herefordshire. Now he was hotfoot for London, where there was plenty of Yorkist support.

Margaret wavered. After letting her seven-year-old son decide what form of execution her prisoners should suffer after the victory of St Albans, she fell back towards the north where she knew she was safe. If Edward wanted to fight her, let him find her there. There she would give him a suitable welcome.

The outcome was Towton in 1461, the greatest, bloodiest, and most bizarre battle ever fought on English soil. At the end of it there was no one to prevent Edward, Earl of March, taking the crown as Edward iv.

There were of course other battles after Towton, devastating though that had been. Other Lancastrians fought back at Hedgeley Moor and Hexham, and held out for a while in a few castles. But these were not serious opposition. Queen Margaret and Henry VI were fugitives; and the country was solidly Yorkist.

It is all the more extraordinary to find that in 1469, after eight years of consolidating his power, the brilliant Edward IV should be captured after the Yorkist defeat at Edgcote. Edward, however, had two dangerous enemies – the Lancastrians and himself. The Lancastrians he could usually overcome, but his own personal weaknesses were another matter.

Although brave as a lion, a military genius, and as enduring as a marathon runner, Edward had two fatal deficiencies. When not in danger he became a self-indulgent idler, and when the fighting was over could never remember the reasons which had caused it.

After Towton he left the 'mopping up' operations to his cousin, Warwick. Warwick was a first-class soldier in spite of his defeat at the second St Albans; he was not however the equal of Edward IV. Politically, Warwick was far superior to his cousin and if Edward had treated him with reasonable common sense the two would never have clashed. But common sense seems to have been notably absent from Edward. When Warwick had not merely crushed the last of the Lancastrian resistance in the north but also made an agreement with the Scots that they would no longer support Queen Margaret, he felt, rightly, that he was a soldier and statesman whose advice should be respected.

Edward thought otherwise. He considered that Warwick needed cutting down to size. When Warwick suggested that Edward should take a French wife, the king announced that he had just married a Lancastrian widow secretly. When this shocked Warwick, Edward flaunted his defiance by giving his new wife's family and friends various important appointments. Warwick's annoyance and discomfiture merely amused him and he decided to increase it by humiliating him still further.

But Warwick 'the Kingmaker' was also a proud man. He knew, better than most, that the Yorkist cause might have failed at St Albans in 1455 if his enterprise had not won the day, and he was not likely to forget the fact. He had, of course, served the Yorkist cause with unswerving loyalty. He was older than the King, and more experienced in war. In some ways he was as powerful.

At this stage the position was complicated by events abroad. Warwick had felt that an alliance with France would remove support from Queen Margaret and strengthen Edward's position. Edward decided otherwise. To humiliate Warwick he made an alliance with the Duke of Burgundy – who hated the King of France – and married his sister to the Duke. Warwick was given the humiliating task of escorting her to this marriage. Edward had now pushed the 'Kingmaker' too far.

Lancastrian resistance, although suppressed, had not been extinguished completely. For one thing there was the gallant resistance of Harlech Castle, which was now in its seventh year of siege. It was not, admittedly, a very intensive siege for the castle had access to the sea but it was a long gruelling process none the less. One of the besieged was the future Henry vii and it has been suggested that his experiences during the siege of Harlech contributed to his subsequent grudging outlook. The annoyance which the continued Lancastrian resistance caused to Edward was noted with approval by the King of France, and he helped to keep it going with cash payments. In June 1468 he had attempted to launch a vigorous attack on the Yorkists from near Harlech and thus relieve the castle.

However, the scheme went awry. He had financed and transported Jasper Tudor with an army to north Wales in French ships, but, after the initial success of plundering and burning Denbigh, Tudor's army was soundly defeated by Lord Herbert, the besieger of Harlech. Soon afterwards Harlech itself fell. These events convinced Warwick that if his humiliating position were to be relieved he must take the initiative himself.

Warwick's subsequent actions did him little credit, but it should be borne in mind that Edward's ingratitude had placed him in an intolerable position. He chose to ally himself with the Duke of Clarence, Edward's younger brother, 'the false, fleeting perjured Clarence', who was subsequently murdered by being drowned in a butt of Malmsey in the Tower of London. Clarence was considered too unreliable to hold any position of state authority but was heir to the throne, as Edward at that time had no sons. (When he did they became the unfortunate Princes who were murdered in the Tower in the reign of Richard III.)

In the Spring of 1469 there was a Lancastrian rising in the north. It was led by a mysterious figure known as 'Robin of Redesdale', a person who has never been properly identified and now, of course, never will be. Many believed that he was Sir John Conyers, one of Warwick's relations, though his aims, which included a better standard of living for the poor, hardly seem to put him in that environment. The first phase of the rebellion was defeated but then a second stage began, commanded by one Robert Hillyard, called 'Robin of Holderness'. This was even less successful than the other, and was defeated at York, after which Robin of Holderness was executed. But Robin of Redesdale was now active in Lancashire, with a larger army than ever.

Warwick at this time was in Calais where, unknown to Edward, he had married his daughter to Clarence. This daughter, Isabella Neville, was immensely rich and the marriage therefore made Clarence potentially richer than the King.

Edward, as usual, was slow to take action. Throughout his career he had often been dilatory to the point of disaster, though once roused he proved unstoppable. On this occasion he delayed a little too long.

In June 1469 he decided to move north and deal with Robin of Redesdale. He probably knew that Warwick was backing the rising but gave no special attention to the fact. He made a leisurely progress through East Anglia, assembling an army as he went. At Nottingham he learnt that Robin of Redesdale's army was no rabble but a well-organized and disciplined force. He decided to wait for reinforcements from Wales, which would be available now that Harlech had fallen. They were commanded by Lord Herbert, who had now been awarded the title of Earl of Pembroke. Edward then heard the unwelcome news that Warwick had come from Calais with a substantial force and was now moving north. Edward was now in a trap. He was about to be caught between Redesdale's army marching south and Warwick's army marching north. Owing to his own dilatoriness he had so far assembled only a small force, assuming that Pembroke would be able to deal with Redesdale, and he himself would then arrest Warwick, whose army would not be large. His assumptions were all incorrect. Redesdale had come down from Lancashire much more rapidly than had been anticipated. Edward did not know exactly where this northern rebel had got to, but he moved back south-east so as not to be caught by the closing of the trap. Edward was right in thinking that Pembroke's force was on its way from the west but he could not know that Pembroke and his co-commander the Earl of Devon had quarrelled over billeting arrangements – always a delicate matter when accommodation is limited. In some fury, Devon had taken his substantial army to Deddington, a few miles further south on the road to Oxford. There was a substantial castle there with a huge bailey and it was a reasonable place for a camp. Apparently this army had most of the bowmen. Pembroke, with a smaller force but by no means a bad one, decided to block the routes from Daventry and Northampton to Banbury. This could be done by siting his camp midway between the two roads, and midway also between Wardington and Thorpe Mandeville. Redesdale was in fact farther west but the position was strategically sound – provided Redesdale's army was not too formidable. Four miles north-east of Banbury, in exactly the place Pembroke wanted it, was a flat piece of valley known as Danesmoor. It was sheltered and it had water; it was concealed by three low hills. With luck he could stay quietly there while the full weight of the attack went down the Banbury–Oxford road and fell on Devon. If Devon won he would be so mauled as to be glad of assistance; if he lost he would have done so much damage to Redesdale that the latter's battered army would be no problem.

It seems almost inconceivable that Pembroke posted no sentries on those hills, but military history abounds with examples of commanders thinking that the enemy was so far away that the most elementary drills were neglected. But perhaps he did post look-outs and they fell asleep, or were quietly killed. Whatever the reason, he woke up on 26 July to find the hills occupied by Redesdale's men.

Pembroke was in a difficult position. Common sense told him that his forces were to small and too short of archers to do anything but retreat and try to re-form in a better position. But first he had to extricate himself, secondly he had to hold his army together; if not winning, they were quite likely to desert, or even join his opponents.

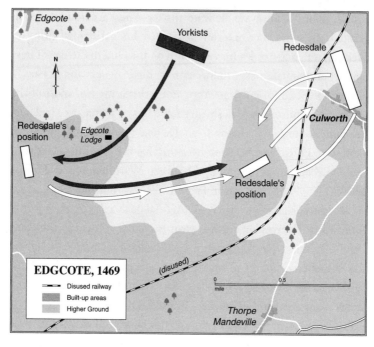

EDGCOTE, 1469

Disused railway
Built-up areas
Higher Ground

Take the A361 out of Banbury and turn right at Wardington to reach Edgcote Lodge and Culworth. (Northamptonshire)

He decided that boldness was the best and only possibility. He attacked.

The first objective was the hill to the north (near Edgcote Lodge). Without adequate cover from archers this was an expensive way of fighting, but his determined Welshmen clawed their way up the hill and took it. Half-way up this hill, and over to the left is a grove of trees. As readers will have noticed on other battlefields it was the custom to plant trees on grave pits as some sort of memorial, and it seems most probable that this is all that remains of the former grove.

And doubtless there were other grave pits of which no surface trace remains.

So far so good for Pembroke, but the cost had been enormous. He turned now to the second hill. Fighting his way along the crest of the slope, and using a pole-axe with deadly effect he led his men to their second victory. He now had easy access to the road by Thorpe Mandeville and he would have been wise to have settled for limited success and broken off the engagement. But with complete victory in his grasp such an action would have been unthinkable.

He pressed on to the third hill – the one by Culworth. At this point matters began to go seriously wrong. Now more than ever he needed numbers. Redesdale's army, while holding him on the crest, was now fanning out and around him on to both sides of the hill. Pembroke had no one to stop them and soon had the humiliation of seeing the territory he had so painfully captured once more in Redesdale's hands. To his credit his showed neither fear nor dismay but concentrated on Culworth in the knowledge that once the last central point was captured the other area could be retaken. And it would have been so but for an accident of war.

On to the scene came a mob of irregulars from Northampton, not trained soldiers at all, but a motley collection of plunder-seekers who had been assembled by Sir John Clapham, a Lancastrian. As this force came into sight they shouted 'A Warwick, a Warwick' – a battle-cry which had been heard on many a field in the past fifteen years. Pembroke's men promptly assumed that this was the vanguard of the Earl of Warwick's army and that further resistance was hopeless. They fled. As they broke in disorder, Devon who had now come up from Deddington saw the scene, with Warwick's banner of a bear and ragged staff waving over the hilltop. It was clear to him that the battle was over and he did a very fast 'about turn'. Victory was thus thrown away.

Losses had been high on both sides, and remarkably even; 2,000 Welsh and 1,500 English. The inevitable executions followed. Many knights and esquires had died in the battle or there would have been more scenes of vengeance afterwards. Pembroke and his son were stoned and then executed; Devon was beheaded in Somerset, and Rivers at Kenilworth.

Edward heard the news of Edgcote at Olney, Buckinghamshire. He was not dismayed; he had fought back from worse positions. But his confidence was not shared by his followers; they deserted wholesale. Finally he was taken into custody himself and kept under guard at Warwick Castle.

But Warwick was fighting a losing battle. He did not wish – yet – to throw in his lot with the Lancastrians, and he dared not aspire to the throne – although it could easily come to his descendants. Having extracted a promise from Edward that he would behave in a more responsible manner, he freed him. Once more Edward became king in fact as well as name.

The sequel will surprise nobody. Once more Warwick and Edward quarrelled. In March 1470 Edward raised an army to defeat a rebellion in Lincolnshire. He did this with such swift efficiency, at Empingham in Rutlandshire, that it became known as Lose-coat field; it was said that the rebels threw off their coats to run away the faster. Warwick and Clarence, realizing that this was an event full of foreboding for them too, wasted no time in leaving the country. They would return – but each to his individual disasters.

The Battle of Edgehill

23 October 1642

Edgcote, which we described in the last chapter, was one of the last battles in the Wars of the Roses. Edgehill, which we examine next, was the first battle in the Civil War, and occurred nearly two hundred years later. During the interval the country had been mercifully free from civil war, although English soldiers – and sailors – had often been engaged in warfare overseas. There had, of course, been many military developments since Edgcote had been fought out with pole-axe, spear, and bow. Of these more later.

The Civil War was entirely different from any earlier wars in England. All its predecessors had been inter-baronial struggles in which one large faction had fought with another. Although such conflicts as John against the barons in 1215, Simon de Montfort against Henry iii in 1265, Edward ii against the barons in 1322, and the Wars of the Roses during the mid-fifteenth century had all ostensibly been wars fought for the oppressed against the oppressor, they bore no relationship to democratic struggles as we understand them today. But during the reigns of the Tudors – Henry vii, Henry viii, Edward vi, Mary, and Elizabeth i – the monarchy had become less absolute, power had shifted to the emergent middle classes, and the old aristocracy had declined in strength and influence. Admittedly most of the more turbulent and powerful families had been killed off before Henry vii came to the throne, but this did not mean that others could not have risen to take their place if there had been a power vacuum. By the time Elizabeth was on the throne the pattern of English politics had been established, although she herself was fighting a rearguard action for the maintenance of royal power. However Elizabeth was a realist and, being a woman as well, she was able to make the best of what seemed to her a not entirely satisfactory situation.

Her successor, James I, was aptly nicknamed 'the wisest fool in Christendom'. He had plenty of learning but no wisdom. He suffered from two delusions: one, that he was king by divine right, and two, that he could ignore the nation's laws and customs if it suited him. When he died in 1625 the country welcomed with relief his son, Charles I, who seemed in every way a much more attractive and balanced personality. Alas for hopes. Charles held many of his father's beliefs and had the courage and conviction to maintain them even if the face of the most obdurate resistance. There were, of course, plenty of faults on both sides. To Parliament, Charles appeared a dangerous fanatic who was trying to put back the governmental clock some two hundred years; to Charles, Parliament seemed to be full of misguided and obstinate men who would unheedingly destroy the kingdom, the Established Church, and the dignity of the throne. An added complication was that there were sharp divisions of opinion among the supporters of both sides. Charles undoubtedly acted very foolishly at times, but his mistakes were matched by those of his opponents. Unfortunately most people are brought up to see Charles as an obstinate tyrant whose people rebelled and, after a suicidal war, beheaded him. In fact some of Charles's actions, although arbitrary, ultimately benefited the nation: 'Ship Money' is an example. War became inevitable when Charles went to the House of Commons, with 300 men, to arrest his five chief opponents. They were in fact in touch with a Scottish army which had crossed the border, with the intention of coercing him into establishing a Presbyterian Church, so he had some justification in suspecting them of treason. However, the Five Members had received advanced warning of his intention and disappeared. Charles then left London and never returned until he was brought back by his Parliamentarian opponents.

It was obvious from the beginning of 1642 that civil war was inevitable and both sides began making preparations for it.

Once war was certain, and during the course of it, the dilemmas which had confronted Members of Parliament were presented to ordinary families. Just as today a family will often vote Conservative or Labour without having much sympathy for personalities or programmes but supports it as the better of two bad alternatives, so feelings were mixed in the Civil War. It was certainly not a class war, for plenty of the nobility fought against the King; conversely it had certain feudal aspects, for some of the landowners were able to take their tenantry to battle without any more opposition than barons had experienced in the Wars of the Roses. Allegiances were partly regional, for Parliament had the enormous asset of London, Bristol, Hull, and Plymouth (the main ports), and many other large towns. However, Oxford, Newark, Worcester and Chester remained firmly royalist.

With London went much of the south-east and Home Counties, though of course these areas also had pockets of royalist sympathizers. Certain areas changed hands during the war. Bristol fell to the Royalists in 1643 but could never rival London as a strategic asset. Wales was almost completely Royalist, and remained so. The navy with the exception of a few officers, was strongly Parliamentarian; this did not mean that Charles was entirely without shipping, for his supporters managed to produce a small navy by sheer ingenuity, but the defection of the navy was a great blow to the Cavalier cause. The war produced great flexibility in improvisation. Oxford became a capital city with its own Parliament and administrative offices. Uniforms, swords, pikes, armour, and gunpowder were manufactured, training was organized, resources were co-ordinated. As in other wars, even as late as the Second World War, people donated their personal possessions without demur. Superb family and college plate was melted down for the intrinsic value of the metal. This was bad enough, but it was matched by the destruction later of other beautiful objects – such as stained class – by over-zealous Puritans who thought that plainness and ugliness denoted sincerity and progress.

Both armies were composed of cavalry in regiments of approximately 500; dragoons – who were mounted infantry – armed with carbines and swords, infantry who carried pikes, muskets, and swords; and artillery who had a variety of pieces ranging from 64-pounders to 5-pounders.

Numbers tended to fluctuate. An infantry regiment nominally had a strength of 1,200 but was seldom up to this figure. The infantry, which consisted mainly of conscripts, was divided into pikemen, who were placed in the middle, and musketeers on the flanks. Most of their muskets were matchlocks with a range of 400 yards, but these could fire on an average only once every three minutes. The front rank would fire, step to the rear, and the next rank took their places. This provided a steady fire provided the wind did not blow away the powder from the pan nor rain extinguish the match. Wheel-locks – with a flint and a process like a cigarette-lighter – were less vulnerable to weather but too easily damaged and thus made unworkable. However, musketry fire did substantial damage. When a musketeer had fired his twelve rounds – and sometimes before – he closed up to the pikemen where they both withstood the enemy charge, whether by cavalry or infantry. The pikeman had an eighteen-foot pike, and needed to be well disciplined and drilled if he was to do more damage to his opponents than to his own side. When pikemen met pikemen this became known as 'at the push of pike'.

Pike drill may be seen sometimes performed by units of 'The Sealed Knot', the society, some 3,000 strong, which re-enacts battles of the Civil War in costume. It was founded by Brigadier Peter Young, who is a great authority on the Civil War – and on many other wars too – and now has branches all over England where its men and women (and even junior) members disport themselves at weekends[1].

The armies in the Civil War were tiny by modern standards, varying in size from 5,000 to 12,000. In some ways this was an advantage, for communications were poor, maps were so inaccurate as to be almost a liability, and telescopes (known as 'perspective glasses') and watches were very rare indeed. The lack of watches made any concerted, timed attack impossible.

One feature of the Civil War which is often overlooked is its length. The first phase lasted from 1642 till 1646 – four long bitter years. To many, it then seemed all over, but in fact five more years would pass before the last shots were fired. King Charles I was executed two years before the last phase of the war finally ended. In that war, as in many since, it was not the shock of battle or the list of casualties which produced the strain but the long, apparently unending struggle in which ordinary life was totally dislocated. At

1 The only qualification for entry is an interest in practical military history.

such times it seems as if the world will never be the same again. And indeed, often it is not.

Although war was inevitable during 1642, neither side was ready to fight for most of that year. Charles raised the standard at Nottingham on 22 August but was not by any means ready at that date; he was short of both men and guns, and, if the Roundheads had tried to capture him, it is unlikely that his army could have stopped them. Parliament already had 15,000 men commanded by the Earl of Essex. Essex was an experienced soldier but was lethargic. He had no cause to love the Stuarts, for, some thirty years before, one of James I's favourites had seduced his wife, contrived a humiliating divorce, and then married her with James's approval. However, James's upstart favourite – who had now been made an earl – had not stopped at murder to help his plans along, and this fact now came out. Even James could not wink at this, and the two were put on trial and subsequently convicted. Essex was doubtless well rid of his former countess but the circumstances of the divorce soured him for life. The commander-in-chief of the Royalist army was Lord Lindsey, but the outstanding leader was Charles' nephew, Prince Rupert of the Palatinate, who was General of the Horse. Rupert was a brilliant all-round soldier (and subsequently a most capable Admiral). He was twenty-three at the start of the war but had already commanded a cavalry regiment at the age of sixteen, when he had been taken prisoner; he had spent the subsequent three years' internment studying his profession.

After raising the standard, Charles would have liked to have marched straight to London, but with Essex in his path, with twice his numbers, this was not practical. Instead, he moved towards Shrewsbury, planning to pick up reinforcements on the way. He arrived there on 20 September.

Essex moved towards the west also, but without any very clear idea of where he should be going. Somewhere, for all he knew, Charles might slip past him and head for London. As a middle course, he moved towards Worcester. After a brisk skirmish, his forces occupied the town. He then stayed there though he should have merely used it as a base while he headed off Charles from London. But while Essex was still pondering on the advantages which the possession of Worcester gave him Charles slipped by him and reached Edgcote, four miles south-east of Warwick. When Essex realized what had happened he set off in pursuit and came to Kineton.

Now Charles was in a quandary. Should he press on and hope to capture London, with Essex crowding hard to his rear, or should he turn and give Essex a bloody nose? Encouraged by Rupert he decided on the latter course. Essex's lethargy once more betrayed him, for if he had pressed on while Charles was still collecting up his detachments he could have outmanoeuvred the King and linked up with his own base in London. Instead he allowed Charles to make his dispositions along the Edgehill ridge.

Edgehill – which was once called Ratcliffe or Redcliff – is a three-mile sandstone ridge which rises sharply out of the plain – at times almost sheer but with some very steep paths; it faces north-west. At the time it was almost entirely open. There was some scrub on the fields at the base.

Both armies at this stage had a strength of 13,000 men, but the Roundheads were superior in infantry, the Royalists in cavalry. This being the first major battle of the war it had, inevitably, an indecisive beginning. Neither army wished to take the initiative and lay itself open to a brisk counter-attack. The cavaliers might have remained on the ridge for days, blocking Essex's path to London, yet been

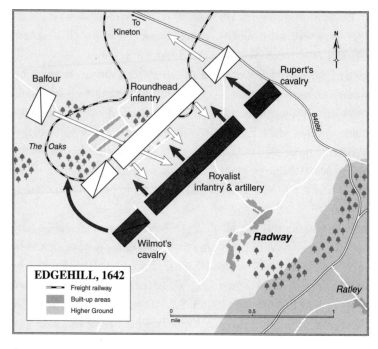

Take the B4100 from Banbury and turn onto the B4086 for Edgehill. This battlefield is more easily circuited than inspected closely. (Warwickshire)

unable to go ahead themselves, had the deadlock not been broken by a Roundhead gunner who sighted Charles and fired at him. Charles was on Knowle Hill. The shot fell short, landing on Bullet Hill, but it was enough to decide the King that it was time to teach the Roundheads their lesson. Abandoning his strong position he moved carefully down the steep slope and deployed the plain below. At 1 p.m. the two armies faced each other midway between Kineton and Radway. Formation was as described above: infantry in the centre, cavalry and dragoons on the flank. But within that bare description of disposition there was much that could be said. Both armies were amateurs; neither had had anything but the most rudimentary training; and the Cavalier foot were deployed in the Swedish manner which none of them properly understood, and they were also very shallow. The Roundheads were a little deeper but still in two lines, each probably six deep. This would have given them a front of ten miles with the centre on the Kineton-Radway road. The right was probably resting on the Oaks plantation. The Cavaliers apparently made no attempt to outflank them although they scattered the dragoons on both of the Roundhead flanks.

The centre of the battle may be identified by the monuments at Battleton Holt. After the initial tentative moves to close there began a not very effective artillery duel. Rupert, fretting to take the initiative, then charged straight at the Roundhead cavalry who were stationed on the left. The effect of the arrival of this brilliant and aggressive force was too much for the earnest but untrained Roundheads. Between King's Ley Barn and Kineton they broke ranks and tried to flee. Even the neighbouring infantry decided that the Royalist cavalry was too much for them. But it was also too much for Rupert's cavaliers. They decided that the battle, – and perhaps the war – was now won, and swept on towards Warwick. However, after two miles, they ran into some Roundhead reserves. They were commanded by a Captain Cromwell and, ominously, this hastily-assembled force checked the brilliant Cavalier attack.

Quite unknown to Rupert, an almost equally brilliant Cavalier cavalry success was occurring simultaneously on the left flank; this was commanded by Lord Wilmot but, whereas Rupert had gone too far, Wilmot's action went too wide.

Equally unknown to both of them was that the infantry had met in the centre. The Cavaliers had apparently gained a psychological advantage by firing their muskets as they advanced, and in the opening stages pushed back the Roundhead infantry. But their triumph was short-lived. Soon they settled down to some indecisive slogging 'at push of pike'. After an interval they broke off this close-quarter fighting and fired their muskets desultorily at each other.

But matters were not static elsewhere. Rupert's cavalry were somewhat disorganized, some having decided, now the war was apparently won, to plunder the Roundhead baggage in Kineton. After a two-mile charge they were of course so dispersed that Rupert could scarcely hope to re-form them. Wilmot's contingent, not having gone so far, were in slightly better case, and some of them turned and came back towards the centre.

At this point, Balfour, commanding the Roundhead cavalry, decided to take a turn in the game. Advancing from a point just behind Battle Farm, parallel with the Radway-Kineton road he came forward in two separate charges, driving for the Royalist centre and left. The Royalist left consisted of untrained Welsh infantry who – good though they could be on other occasions – were right out of their element here. According to Roundhead sources, they disappeared from the field forthwith. Balfour's cavalry was now up at the centre, right up by Battleton Holt. Here they captured Feilding, commanding of the centre brigade, and some other senior officers. They were now also among the Royalist guns, which they wished to spike but could not through lack of nails. However they immobilized them so that the Royalists would not be able to salvage them; they also killed the gunners. Balfour then retired. The problem with cavalry successes was to consolidate them. Unless there was infantry in close support, cavalry gains could not be held. (This fact made the Charge of the Light Brigade in the Crimean War as wasteful as it was spectacular.)

However, frustrating though Balfour found it to have to retire, he did not waste time nor emotion but now applied himself to where he might be most effective. As the Roundhead infantry advanced to the Royalist centre, Balfour wheeled his cavalry and came in on the Royalist flank. The shock sent the whole Royalist line reeling back. The Royalist standard was captured and the Royal standard-bearer, Sir Edmund Verney, killed. The Royalists fell back to a new line behind the brook.

And then at this critical stage, the battle petered out. Fighting still went on, and men were killed, but drive and concerted purpose had left the field. Both sides were exhausted, and both undoubtedly confused. It is one thing to fight a battle, another to win it, and yet another to be able to profit by your victory. This is where the much-maligned staff is at its most useful. But neither side had a proper staff.

When Rupert at last appeared back on the field, dusk was falling. He has of course been much criticized for allowing his cavalry to ride right off the field in an impetuous charge, but restraining a successful cavalry charge requires superhuman powers. Prince Edward (later Edward I) was criticized for a similar action at the Battle of Lewes in 1264, when he returned to find his side had lost the battle. Rupert did not have the embarrassment of finding a lost cause but, even if he had, it would not have been possible for him to do anything about it. His men, and still more their horses were completely blown, and to attempt to mount another attack was clearly impossible. Nor were the Roundheads in any better shape.

The verdict of history was that Edgehill was a drawn battle; but there are some who argue that, because Charles finished the battle nearer London than the Roundheads did, and was able to make Oxford his headquarters, then this must be accepted as a Royalist victory. Certainly Charles held the ridge while Essex retired to Warwick leaving many of his guns on the field. Essex may be said to have lost the battle but it is difficult to claim that the Royalists had had the better of the fighting.

Described like this it might appear that Edgehill was a fairly gentle conflict. It was by no means so. Casualties were high on both sides. Cromwell was disgusted with the quality of some of the Roundheads whom he described as 'old decayed tapsters and serving-men', but they stood and fought, apart from the wings who were simply brushed away by the cavalry charges. There was heavy fighting around Battleton Holt, which did not exist in 1642 ('holt' means a wood) and trees may well have been planted to mark grave-pits. Little Graveground contained 500 bodies; Great Graveground close on a thousand. There were other pits also, and there are parts of the field where the number of bullets and cannon-balls indicate the intensity of the fighting – and thus casualties. One of these areas is Lower Westcote Farm.

The visitor can look over the field from the top of Edgehill, particularly from the Edgehill tower, and can also drive around it. To walk the centre of the battlefield requires permission from the commanding officer of the Ordnance Depot which occupies most of the site; it is not wise to venture on Ministry of Defence land in these security-conscious days without preliminary written clearance. But, as a view of the field and the whole feel of the battle can be obtained from the perimeter, many visitors will be content with that.

Charles stayed on the field the night after the battle, making himself as comfortable as possible in King's Ley Barn. He thought the Roundheads might renew the struggle as they had received substantial reinforcements by then but they did not and he moved on to Oxford. In spite of having lost his standard in the middle of the battle, he was fortunate in having it back, for it had been recaptured by one Captain Smith, who was knighted for his courage and enterprise.

But advantage – or victory – was frittered away. Charles's only hope of winning the war was to capture London at the earliest opportunity and hold it. Without it he was certain to be defeated, through lack of money and materials if nothing else. Instead, he lingered in Oxford. Essex was scarcely more enterprising but he did make an effort to outflank Charles by marching, though sluggishly, in a south-easterly movement. On 4 November 1642 Charles reached Reading, being then slightly ahead of Essex who was still only at Woburn. Even then Charles did not press on, and it was nine days later before he confronted the City Trained Bands, 24,000 strong, at Turnham Green. Meanwhile Prince Rupert had won yet another of his swift victories at Brentford but there were another 3,000 Roundheads guarding the Thames bridge at Kingston. The Royalists were in fact outnumbered by some 1,000 men. Turnham was a critical point in the war, and it was a battle which was not a battle. Charles, seeing the strength of the opposition, paused and redeployed at Hounslow. Essex advanced and retook Brentford. The conflict was still wide open. A swift drive by Charles, headed perhaps by Rupert, might have punched a way through the enthusiastic but battle-inexperienced trained bands. But Charles hesitated. After a few days at Oatlands Palace, Weybridge he retired to Reading. Both armies then went into winter quarters.

The Battle of Chalgrove Field

18 June 1643

Edgehill was not by any means the only scene of conflict in 1642. Battles, small or large, were taking place all over the country as Cavaliers and Roundheads struggled for control of their own districts. In the eastern part of the country, it seemed as if the Roundheads were invincible, for they captured the whole coastline and hinterland from Hull to Portsmouth. In the west, it was a very different story, for Hopton decisively thrashed whatever opposition the Roundheads could mount in Cornwall and Devon. In Wales, everywhere but Pembroke fell to the Royalists. In the north, there was a bitter struggle between Lord Fairfax, an ardent Parliamentarian, and the Marquis of Newcastle, an equally convinced but more energetic Royalist. At the end of it Newcastle controlled the north from Newark to Scotland, with the important exception of Hull, which he could not take. By the end of 1642, both sides believed that they had only some unimportant clearing operations to finish in the areas they had overrun before engaging in a final decisive battle with the main opposition elsewhere. Both were of course completely wrong. But they went into winter quarters reasonably well satisfied with themselves. Winter campaigning was considered impossible for reasons explained earlier in this book, but that did not inhibit skirmishes and sieges.

During the winter there were renewed attempts at negotiations which proved quite fruitless because neither side would compromise. Yet both realized that the struggle was costly and suicidal. The strain of providing food, clothing, and especially pay was an almost insurmountable burden, particularly for the Royalists. Nor were all parts of the armies in complete sympathy with each other, and it was by no means unknown for one regiment to loose off a few shots in the direction of another of their own side. Other armies have occasionally smiled frostily when one of their more exuberantly conceited regiments is having a bad time from the enemy, but it is highly undesirable that they should assist the process in any way.

The year 1643 was destined to be a year of battles, but this was not particularly apparent at the outset. During the early months, Charles was trying to improve his position in the Midlands and Prince Rupert took Cirencester on 2 February. Essex remained dormant apart from authorizing an attack on Brill (north-east of Oxford), led by John Hampden, which was repulsed. Sir William Waller was more effective. He cut two Royalist regiments to pieces at Winchester, and followed it up by capturing Farnham Castle, Arundel Castle, and Chichester. He then set up his headquarters in Bristol and thus effectively barred the Royalists from contact with their supporters in the far west and South Wales.

Confined in the west and with Essex in force on the south-east, Charles drove hard at the northern midlands. Royalists captured Ashby-de-la-Zouch, Tamworth, Stafford, and Lichfield. The Roundheads countered this by sending Lord Brooke to rally the opposition. Lichfield came under siege twice, and there was hard fighting around Birmingham. Success in this area would effectively cut off the northern Parliamentary forces from the south, but equally Waller's masterly campaigning in the west meant that Charles in Oxford was cut off from his western supporters and threatened by

Essex in the south. Nevertheless, Charles had evolved a strategy which might perhaps win him the war. It was to hold Essex's army while the Marquis of Newcastle brought down his great army from the north, and the Welsh and western armies forced a way past Waller. Then, with the whole Parliamentary army in confusion, Charles planned to push right through Essex's army and all three Royalist contingents would then link in the capture of London.

For a time it seemed as if this plan might succeed. April was not perhaps a very happy augury, for Essex moved up and besieged Reading on 16 April and Charles, with Prince Rupert and Prince Maurice failed to relieve it; they were defeated at Caversham Bridge on 25 April, and Reading fell to the Roundheads on the 27th. Soon after this Essex's army was gravely weakened by disease. Slowly and indecisively he moved up towards Oxford but by mid-May the position was changing rapidly in the Royalists' favour. A huge convoy of arms and ammunition reached Oxford on 15 May and from then onwards the Royalists were the equals of the Roundheads in numbers of properly armed men. The day after the arrival of this vital convoy, the Royalists received equally welcome news from Stratton, in Cornwall, that Hopton had achieved a decisive victory over the Roundheads. This latter event meant that Waller was no longer able to bar Charles from his west country supporters though he could still do so from his Welsh ones.

On 10 June Essex was at Thame. He was still very hesitant but he had sent a detachment to occupy Islip as a preliminary to a further advance on Oxford. Perhaps he felt that to ask for more from his disease-battered army before he paid them would be asking too much. He knew that a convoy bringing £21,000 was on its way to him, and he felt that the arrival of this would put his men in a good mood for further activity. However, he was not the only one who knew about the convoy, for one of his mercenaries had deserted to the Royalists a few days before, and given the news about the convoy to very interested ears.

On 17 June Prince Rupert set out from Oxford with a force of just over 2,000. It comprised three regiments of horse, one of dragoons, a mixed group of horse and dragoons numbering 150, and 500 foot.

The speed and unexpectedness of this move took the Roundhead outposts by surprise. Rupert overwhelmed Tetsworth, Postcombe, and Chinnor in quick succession. Chinnor put up more of a fight than the others and there were a number of casualties but Rupert did not linger there; he set the town alight and rode on.

But the convoy which should be lumbering somewhere towards Thame, and should undoubtedly be in this region was nowhere to be found. If news had got to the Royalists about the convoy, other news had also certainly got back to the Roundheads about Rupert's raiding party, and the convoy had briskly dispersed. Where it had concealed itself in that tangle of woods and thickets could not easily be discovered – certainly not by a small detachment venturing into enemy-held territory where the whole countryside would now be alerted. Furthermore Essex's army at Thame would wish for nothing more than to cut Rupert off before he could get back to Oxford. It would be madness to try to go back the way he had come, so he moved off in a southerly sweep, planning to cross the river at Chislehampton Bridge. What he did not know immediately was that John Hampden, one of the original 'Five Members' and a great fighter in every sense of the word, was at Watlington. When the news was brought to him he realized that although Hampden's force was small, perhaps not much over a few hundred, it could delay him long enough to allow other Roundhead reinforcements to catch up. Then indeed he might be in trouble, and, if he reached the bridge, be unable to cross it. His own men and horses were by now long past their best; they had been on the move for twenty-four hours. As they slowed down, Hampden's men began to be visible to the rear.

Rupert had to act quickly, which was no novelty to him. He sent a detachment of food ahead to secure Chislehampton Bridge – for there was an excellent chance that the Roundheads would try to get there first. He then halted at Chalgrove Field, an open space one and a half miles east of Chislehampton. As usual he stationed the foot in the centre, placed the cavalry on the wings, and lined the hedges with dragoons. To his slightly irritated amusement the Roundheads adopted a similar formation, and advanced very slowly. On both sides the dragoons started picking off their opponents but the Roundheads made no attempt to bring the Royalists to battle. It was obvious that they wished to delay hostilities as long as possible and allow the reinforcements, which could not be far away, to catch up with them. And while they were in contact, the Royalists could not resume their journey.

Rupert, of course, would have none of this. He sat for a few moments watching these leisurely manoeuvres, then behaved like a man annoyed by a few wasps. First he leapt straight into the Round-head dragoons, who promptly fled, then he formed up his cavalry and gave the order to charge the Roundhead horse. Suddenly the entire picture changed; cavalry, foot, and dragoons were all locked in desperate and bloody fight, pistols firing, swords flashing, men, horses, bodies, everywhere. In the middle of this essentially cavalry battle, John Hampden received two bullets in the shoulder. He knew that the wounds were serious and in great pain he rode back to Thame. Six days later he died, and even his opponents who had little cause to love him, acknowledged that it was an appropriate end for a brave and resolute man. He did not see the end

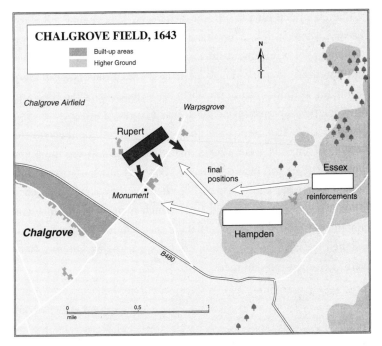

Chalgrove is on the B480. Take the Warpsgrove road out of Chalgrove; this will lead you past the Hampden monument which marks the battlefield. (Oxfordshire)

of the battle when a final Cavalier charge scattered the Roundheads in all directions. His plan had almost worked, for by that stage some of Essex's men had come up, but it had of course been frustrated by Rupert's initiative at the beginning. By the end of the battle the Royalists were nearly dropping with fatigue, but they had taken 100 prisoners and killed forty-five of their opponents. As a mission the enterprise had failed in its main objective but had inflicted the greatest possible blow on enemy morale by killing Hampden.

The Hampden monument, on the corner, may or may not show the spot where he fell. Monuments are often – though not always – placed at spots convenient for them rather than on the exact place they are meant to mark. The battlefield is one of the easiest of all to visit, lying as it does just to the north of the junction of the B480 and the Chalgrove-Warpsgrove road. It was a cornfield in June 1643 and it was in 1972. It is impossible to predict what will be there in the future but there is a fair chance that the visitor will see the scene much as Rupert and Hampden saw it. Both were men of foresight. If perhaps someone had whispered to them as they confronted each other that one day an airfield from which men could fly in metal containers would skirt their battlefield they would have nodded and weighed the information without undue surprise or comment. Both were very open-minded men.

The Battle of Lansdown

5 July 1643

The next significant battle in the eventful year of 1643 was in the west country. Waller, some of whose successes were mentioned in the previous chapter, now controlled Bristol and Gloucester and had most of his army deployed in the vicinity of Bath. He was a highly professional soldier who had learnt his trade in southern Europe. Now, in his mid-forties, he was one of the most respected of the Parliamentary generals. Nevertheless, the Royalists decided that, reputation or not, Waller could be and must be beaten.

To do so required a combined operation employing the victors of Stratton, from Cornwall, and an army from Oxford commanded by Prince Maurice. Hopton, the architect of the Stratton victory had no small difficulty in persuading his officers to march their men from Devonshire when Plymouth and Exeter, Bideford and Barnstaple, were all in Roundhead hands and presumably ripe for the taking. The combined army added up to 7,000, of which just over half were infantry. Waller was believed to have approximately equal numbers.

The delicate question as to which of these senior generals should have supreme command was settled by Hopton being given the main command, Maurice, however, being given a free hand with the use of the cavalry. The Roundhead cavalry was the equal of the Royalist and more numerous, but its infantry was of lesser quality.

With Waller in such a strong position the Royalist strategy was to split his armies and roll them up in two phases. This would be easier to plan than to execute. During the month of June they were tidying up the position in Somerset by occupying such towns as Wells, Taunton, and Bridgwater and at the end of the month they occupied Bradford-on-Avon, Wiltshire, which is nine miles south-east of Bath. Bath was the first objective, but to attack it from the south meant negotiating the Avon under Roundhead fire and it was therefore considered more expedient to approach from the east. To do so the Royalists moved in a north-westerly direction but when they reached Monkton Farleigh and Waller had given no sign of coming up on their flank they decided to push on to a better attacking position north of the city. There were indeed a few skirmishes in the area east of Bath, but they were in the nature of light harassing brushes and not to be taken seriously. A further five miles took the Royalists to Marshfield where they camped on the night of 4 July. By this time Waller was alert to the Royalist intentions. He realized that if they marched south-east from Marshfield they would soon occupy Lansdown Hill which was a valuable strategic point; in order to prevent this, he marched out of Bath himself and occupied the hill.

The armies were now five miles apart, and inevitably there was some skirmishing in between. Very early on 5 July Waller despatched a medium-sized force up to the Marshfield outposts to upset the Royalists as they were making their march dispositions. It created considerable alarm and disorder. However, Hopton soon had his men *en route* for Bath, by the tracks which would take them past Lansdown. As they approached the hill, they observed that the Roundheads were so strongly entrenched, with earthworks and wooden defences protecting their position, the whole area being screened by flanking woods. Hopton and his officers decided this

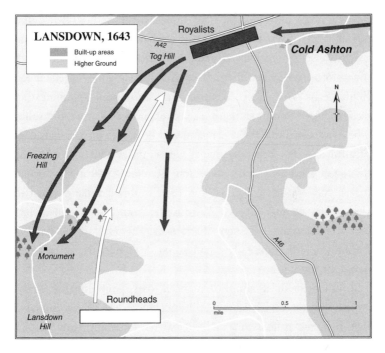

The A46 Bath–Stroud road runs through the middle of the battlefield area but take the A420 to Tog Hill. Turn left to Freezing Hill and continue to the Granville Memorial on the edge of Lansdown Hill. (Gloucestershire)

was neither the place nor the time to attack. They halted and skirmished but were not going to commit military suicide. Pending a new strategy, the Royalists began to march back to Marshfield.

It was an awkward moment, and the Roundheads of course recognized it. The morale of a retreating army, even if it has not been defeated is not high, and it seemed very right to Waller to lower it further by launching a heavy attack of 1,000 cavalry and dragoons on to the retiring Royalists. And at first it went remarkably well. The dragoon were able to move up under cover of hedgerows and devastate the Royalist flanks; the Roundhead cavalry charged into the Royalist rear and drove them so hard that they tangled with the unfortunate foot soldiers. It could not have gone better for the Roundheads. But Prince Maurice had introduced an interesting tactical disposition by stationing a section of foot among the cavalry. These were mainly the Cornishmen who had won the battle of Stratton and they began to give Waller's cavalry a lot of trouble. As this great harassing sweep – which included 1,000 men – began to lose momentum and peter out, the Royalist cavalry put in two very sharp counter-attacks. Within the hour the Royalists had driven their opponents right back over Tog Hill to the base of Lansdown Hill, where they had stood despondently not so long before. It was 2 p.m.

Royalist morale was now at its peak, perhaps unduly so. Those strong positions on Lansdown Hill somehow seemed less formidable than before – at least to the Cornishmen who had already killed a substantial number of Roundheads. They also had tremendous faith in the leader, Sir Eric Hopton, who, ironically perhaps, was an old friend of Waller's from former campaigns when they had fought side by side. The fact that they were now opposing each other did not really disturb this long-standing friendship, but, of course, neither did their friendship diminish their military efforts.

The hill confronting the Cornish infantry is four miles long, and well wooded. The visitor will find the centre of the Roundhead position marked by an obelisk, commemorating Sir Bevill Grenvill,[1] who was in command of the Cornish infantry, and was killed at that point. The battle which took place that afternoon was a tribute to the

[1] Spelled Granville on the monument. Contemporary accounts often show considerable variation in name-spelling.

amazing fortitude and resolve of the Cornishmen. Whatever else happened, they ploughed on. Others supported them, fought alongside, and even forged ahead, but the steady rolling unrelaxed pressure which carried the day undoubtedly came from the tough and wiry Cornishmen.

They needed all the drive and resolve they could muster. As they came up through the woods, meeting frontal fire, cross-fire, and some heavy artillery which the Roundheads had placed on top of the hill they paid dearly for their success. But they made their enemy pay too. Some regiments – which shall be nameless – found the pace and the fire too hot, and slipped away through the concealing woods. Some cavalry who were caught in plunging fire rode back to Oxford and gave an account of the battle which indicated how lucky and how wise they were to be there at all. They had of course been badly handled and misused but it was not an excuse the Cornishmen would have paid much heed to. For the cavalry – if they had been handled right and stuck it out – could have completed the victory when at last the foot and the musketeers reached the last barricade. For the sad part of it was that though they had reached the top of the hill there were still Roundheads in force behind a stone wall, and with guns too, and neither side had the strength for the last clinching effort.

Like Edgehill, the battle was ultimately indecisive, but like Edgehill it eventually became a Royalist victory. As darkness fell and neither side had the strength, ammunition, or even the will to renew the struggle, both commanders debated what to do. If the Roundheads attacked, the exhausted Royalists might be tumbled down the hill and utterly routed; equally, if the Royalists put in a final successful attack at dawn, the way to Bath would be open.

As it was, Waller, with the view of a campaigner rather than a battlefield commander, gave the order to return to Bath.

It should have been a moment of tremendous triumph for the Royalists. Although Grenvill had been killed, they had won the hill against impossible odds. And then, in the moment of elation came an appalling setback. An ammunition cart suddenly blew up close to Hopton, wounded him, and blinded him. For a while he could neither speak, nor see. Apparently dying, he was carried off the battlefield past his dismayed army. First Grenvill, now Hopton. It would be limitless folly to try to press home the attack against Bath at this stage. Reluctantly, but not by any means slowly, the Royalists abandoned their hard-won position and set off back in the direction of Oxford. But, of course, on Cold Ashton, Tog Hill, Freezing Hill, and the slopes of Lansdown there were several thousand men who would never fight on that or any other field again.

The Battle of Roundway Down

13 July 1643

As they moved back toward Oxford from Lansdown, the Royalists felt frustrated and dejected. Apart from the blow of losing such inspiring leaders as Grenvill and Hopton they had other troubles; they were short of ammunition, they were short of food, and the countryside seemed to be turning against them. They rested at Chippenham for two days and then moved on to Devizes; by this time Waller's cavalry were harassing the rearguard and the Royalists were glad to get into the town where they could collect their thoughts and decide on their next action. Waller had already invited them to fight it out by deploying his own army on Roundway Down, three miles north of Devizes, but they had not accepted the challenge. Hopton, who was now able to speak but not to walk, approved a plan by which his infantry and artillery would defend Devizes while the cavalry broke out and made for Oxford.

The Royalists were now in a sad case. They were short of ammunition, and one of the most vital deficiencies was match to take the light to the powder. Hopton ordered that all the bedcords in Devizes should be collected and boiled in resin; this ingenious expedient solved the match problem but there was still a grave shortage of powder and ball.

However, as Devizes held its hastily contrived outer defences, Prince Maurice succeeded in slipping round Waller and reaching

Oxford – a night ride of forty-four miles. Time was no longer on Waller's side, as he doubtless realized, for the Royalists would soon be rushing reinforcements to help their comrades who were besieged in Devizes. Waller's forces, however, still outnumbered the Royalists and, as he redoubled his efforts to capture Devizes, he also sent in surrender terms. Hopton appeared to be considering them but in fact was waiting for the relief he felt could not be far away.

The relief force was at Marlborough, fourteen miles off. It was commanded by Wilmot whom we last spoke of at Edgehill. It was a wholly cavalry force but it had two light guns; its total numbers did not exceed 1,800. On the morning of 13 July it was approaching Devizes which had been under heavy artillery fire for the previous twenty-four hours.

Waller, however, still had the initiative. He could turn on Wilmot's cavalry and deal with them in pitched battle, in which he outnumbered them, or he could draw them off with a portion of his army while he used the remainder to complete the capture of Devizes. He must not, of course, allow himself to be trapped between Wilmot's 1,800 horse and Hopton's 3,000 infantry from Devizes, even though he still outnumbered the combined Royalist force by over a thousand. What he could not have expected was that the Devizes army would stand idly by, in spite of Hopton's urgings, and let him annihilate Wilmot's relief force. Wilmot, unaware of the fate in store for him, continued along the old road from Marlborough to Devizes, which runs north of the present road and is in fact the track which skirts just south of Heddington. This road was (and is) crossed by another which runs south-west to Devizes, and the crossroads are right in the middle of Roundway Down where Waller had tried to tempt the entire Royalist army to battle just before they entered Devizes. It was, of course, a perfect place for a cavalry battle.

To the north were Morgan's Hill and King's Play Hill, and to the south was Roundway Hill, then known as Bagdon Hill.

As Wilmot crossed the Wansdyke (a few miles from where the decisive battle of Ellandun had been fought eight hundred years earlier), Waller's army came into view over Roundway Hill. Wilmot had no doubt that Hopton's army from Devizes would be coming up fast to catch Waller in the rearguard and calmly made his battle dispositions. He might have been less sanguine if he had known the true state of affairs. Facing his left flank he could see a very formidable force, Sir Arthur Hazelrigg's 'lobsters'. They were, in fact, cuirassiers with close-fitting armour which was very difficult to penetrate.

Wilmot, being a cavalryman, turned his attention to the wings and hit both simultaneously with vigorous charges. This left the Round-head infantry in the middle standing by inactive and unharmed apart from the occasional stray musket-ball which found a target in their ranks. They could not take part in the battle themselves for the wings were an indistinguishable fighting mêlée.

The scene at this point is best described in the words of Richard Atkyns, a cavalier who took part in the battle.

Twas my fortune in a direct line to charge their general of horse [Sir Arthur Hazelrigg]; he discharged his carbine first, and afterwards one of his pistols, before I came up to him; and missed with both; I then immediately struck into him and touched him before I discharged mine, and I am sure I hit him for he staggered and presently wheeled off from his party. Follow him I did and discharged the other pistol at him; and I'm sure I hit his head for I touched it before I gave fire and it amazed him at that present but he was too well armed all over for a pistol bullet to do him any hurt, having a coat of mail over his arms and a headpiece musket proof.

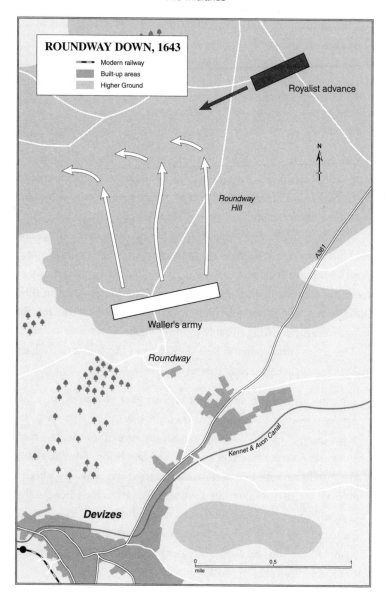

ROUNDWAY DOWN, 1643

Modern railway
Built-up areas
Higher Ground

Royalist advance

Roundway
Hill

Waller's army

Roundway

A361

Kennet & Avon Canal

Devizes

0   0.5   1
mile

Atkyns was not to be put off:

> I came up to him again and having a very swift horse stuck by him for a good while and tried him from the head to the saddle and could not penetrate him or do him any hurt; but in this attempt he cut my horse's nose that you might put your finger in the wound and gave me such a blow on the inside of my arms amongst the veins that I could hardly hold my sword; he went on as before.

And so the running fight continued. Eventually Atkyns was shot in the shoulder but not seriously.

There must have been a hundred or so fights like it. In the course of the battle, Waller's cavalry had been swung around so that the only way they could escape was to the west. As they spurred their horses off the battlefield, hoping to find a point to regroup they suddenly realized that the gentle plain over which they were galloping was a mere plateau. They were now at its edge – a drop of 300 feet. There was no stopping. Down that deathtrap hill they rode, slithered, and fell, and many of their pursuers with them. This indeed was a bloody ditch. Not since Ashdown had there been a scene like it, and even then it was less dramatic. The unbelievable had happened. Waller's invincible cavalry had been put to flight by a force of half their number, and at the end of it had not merely been beaten but had been literally smashed to pieces. Even the Roundhead infantry, standing neglected in the middle of the field had no conception of the disaster which had overtaken their army.

But their turn too was coming. Hopton's army, waiting in Devizes,

This battlefield is only a few miles from where the battle of Ellandun was fought eight hundred years earlier. Take the A361 from Beckhampton to Devizes. (Wiltshire)

had not taken long to make up their minds – particularly with him urging them on. Out they came, hoping to save Wilmot's cavalry from too severe a defeat, or perhaps to change probable defeat into narrow victory. As they breasted the hill all they could see was the Roundhead infantry, still uncommitted. On the flanks Wilmot's cavalry were re-grouped to deal with this last target. The isolated Roundheads had no hope at all. On the one side, they took the shock of the Cornish infantry; on the other, Wilmot's triumphant cavalry. Six hundred were killed, the rest captured. It was a fitting end to a most extraordinary day. Never before had the Royalists had such a victory, and never would they do so again.

The First Battle of Newbury

20 September 1643

The unexpected but extremely important victory at Roundway Down swung the war once again in the Royalists' favour. Prince Rupert lost no time in consolidating these gains. With a balanced force of cavalry, dragoons, infantry, and artillery he moved promptly to Bristol and laid siege to the town. The ensuing battle lasted a day only but included more vigorous and continuous fighting than many a campaign on other occasions. Rupert himself turned the scales in one quarter, for he collected up retreating men and led them back into the fight although his horse was shot under him in the process. This siege, incidentally, was the last occasion when bows and arrows were employed by English armies. They were used by the Cavaliers in conjunction with fire-pikes to set the defences on fire. Stones were thrown and boulders rolled and in many ways this battle of Bristol bore close resemblance to the great medieval sieges.

Dorset and Devonshire soon fell to the Royalists although a few points still managed to hold out. Charles now decided to open up the road to South Wales, and promptly called on Gloucester to surrender. He was firmly but courteously refused. Prince Rupert would have liked to attack Gloucester forthwith and batter his way in, but Charles thought that the cost in casualties at Bristol had been so high that a second assault of that nature was not justified, however valuable the prize. Charles's action in deciding on a set-piece siege at Gloucester has been heavily criticized but there is as much to be said for it as against it. Elsewhere the war seemed to be going so well in the King's favour that his supporters might well have assumed that he would be back in London by Christmas. In the north, in June, Newcastle had beaten the Fairfaxes at Adwalton Moor, and at one moment it seemed as if a Royalist rising in Kent might march on London and seize power.

In this hour of need Parliament rose to the occasion with remarkable vigour. Six regiments of London Trained Bands were added to Essex's army, and supplies were found for the entire force on an adequate scale. This gave Essex a total army of 15,000, with which he marched to the relief of Gloucester. Rupert had insufficient men to stop this huge force and so had to keep out of its way as it pressed on westwards; it relieved Gloucester on 8 September, arriving in the nick of time, for Massey, the Governor, was down to his last three barrels of powder.

However, Essex's move had put his army in a vulnerable position. He was now between a hostile Wales, a hostile west country, and Charles's Oxford army. Charles, in fact, had moved quietly to Sudeley Castle, Gloucestershire, on 7 September. There he watched to see what Essex would do to extricate himself from the middle of a triangle with three hostile sides.

Essex moved up the Severn to Tewkesbury, trying to give the impression he was going to attack Worcester instead of slipping back to London. Charles promptly moved up to Pershore so as to stay between Essex's army and the capital. Essex then doubled back on the Cirencester-Swindon line, reaching the latter on 17 September. Charles came back too, marching parallel to but fifteen to twenty miles north of Essex's army. Everything depended on who could

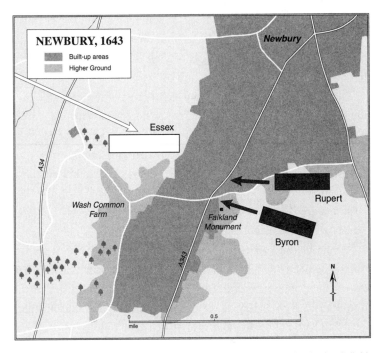

NEWBURY, 1643

Built-up areas
Higher Ground

Newbury

Essex

A34

Wash Common
Farm

Rupert

Falkland
Monument

Byron

N

0   0.5   1
mile

Take the A343 out of Newbury and turn right at Essex Street for the battlefield.
(West Berkshire)

reach Newbury first; if it were Essex, he would be within reach of
safety; if it were Charles, he could cut off Essex and probably
destroy his army, which by this time must be low on supplies, and
perhaps on morale too as any army must be if hunted on a series of
forced marches. Essex looked well set to reach Newbury first, but
Rupert put in a superbly-timed attack at Aldbourne Chase, causing
considerable confusion though little real harm, and delayed the
Roundheads so much that they had to camp at Hungerford.
Fortunately for them, the Royalists made hard weather of this stage

too and spent the night at Wantage. When, on the 19th the Royalists reached Newbury they found the Roundhead advance party allotting billets for the expected units of their own army. Essex by that time had reached Enborne, two miles west.

The First Battle of Newbury, which occurred the next day, was fought south of the town on the fields sloping down to the river Kennet. The Second Battle of Newbury, which we describe later, was fought north of the town, close to the River Lambourn.

The battlefield of First Newbury is now, inevitably perhaps, encroached on by new building. Fortunately some of the key positions are commemorated in the names of the streets. The area was, however, well enclosed in 1643 though by hedges not houses.

Morale in the two armies was in sharp contrast. The Royalists were in comfortable billets, had the satisfaction of knowing they had cut off their opponents from their base, and could surmise that the Roundheads were weary, short of food and supplies, and inexperienced in battle. This Royalist army had a good opinion of itself and its social importance, and doubtless looked forward to the thought of riding over and cutting up a few upstart churls the next day in the course of a brilliant victory.

The Roundheads were indeed in a poor way. They had marched for miles but apparently to no avail (if one excepted the relief of Gloucester). They had also lain up overnight in the wet and the cold; however – as we saw at Towton[1] in 1461 – men can be nearly frozen to death overnight but fight like demons the next day if they are sustained by bitter-enough hatred. It was so at Newbury.

The only course open to the Roundheads was to force a way through on the meadows by the Kennet. It would not be easy

1 *British Battlefields: the North.*

because the Royalist cavalry would be expecting just such a move. Fortunately for the Roundheads, it seemed to be the only tactics the Royalists envisaged, for they had made no attempt to occupy Wash Common Farm or the patch of higher ground slightly north of it. This area is directly west of the Falkland Monument which is easily found on the A343 just south of Newbury. The high points could have been secured effortlessly without weakening the disposition nearer Newbury, for the front there was narrow anyway. The armies were equally matched in numbers, having about 12,000 each, but the Roundheads had nothing to match the quality of the Royalist cavalry.

The battle began soon after first light. The Roundheads probed their way along the meadows and appeared to be offering themselves as lambs for slaughter by the Royalist cavalry. But, just as the battle settled to a grinding slog, Royalist morale took a decided toss. Guns opened up from the Roundhead right flank, from that very point on the 400-foot contour line which the Royalists had failed to occupy the night before. It was humiliating, and irritating, but not disastrous. There were in fact only two light guns involved, which the Roundheads had pulled into position during the night, but two guns can do a lot of damage and the Roundheads having got them there with difficulty would not have neglected to organize their defence.

Sir John Byron was now given the task of ejecting the Roundheads and their two guns from this eminence, which is known as Round Hill. It was captured, but the cost was very high. Among the many who fell at that point was Lord Falkland. Taking the Round Hill was a formidable achievement, for the Roundheads had a brigade on it by the time the heavy fighting began; but taken it was.

Elsewhere, Prince Rupert's cavalry had charged the Roundhead infantry vigorously but without much effect. In the meadows it looked as if a stalemate was developing. Artillery on both sides was pounding away steadily. Both armies were determined to cling to the part of the ridge they held and if possible to extend their position, but each side was equally determined the other should not. There was heavy fighting along Skinner's Green Lane. Eventually it seemed to the Royalists that their best chance was to knock a hole in the Roundhead infantry, much of which consisted of inexperienced Trained Bands. To their astonishment and annoyance, these city regiments stood up to repeated charges and some remarkably accurate artillery fire. It was said that they far surpassed the Royalist infantry. Their desperate dogged resistance was a foretaste of the qualities of the great British regiments which would fight on less unhappy occasions than a murderous Civil War. Civil wars, when people of common heritage, kinship, and interests fight each other, have rightly been described as 'unholy wars', but a redeeming feature of this one was that both sides showed the same tenacity and enthusiasm.

By nightfall both sides were thoroughly exhausted, but the Royalists had the more serious problems. The cavalry on which they depended so much had taken heavy casualties, and powder was so short that they were unable to keep up artillery counterfire; in fact the Roundheads were firing three shots to the Royalist one.

An urgent Council of War took place in Newbury that evening. Should Charles wait for the ammunition which was hourly expected, or should he withdraw to Oxford? If the ammunition did not arrive, he might be in a parlous state the next day, with his cavalry badly mauled, and nothing to fire from his twenty guns. Prince Rupert would have preferred to have stayed, but it was a bluff which might have been called. Essex might have renewed the fight the following morning and, with conditions as they were, could have inflicted a severe defeat on the Royalists. Equally he might have decided it was impossible to break through, and set off back for Gloucester. But when he sent out patrols on the morning of the 21st he found that the Royalists had gone. His weary but elated army plodded on towards Reading. They were harassed by a few cavalry charges from Rupert on the way but there was no more real fighting. The First Battle of Newbury had been drawn, but there was no doubt in anyone's mind that it was a strategic victory for the Roundheads. Gloucester was still in their hands. The Royalist road to Wales was blocked, and Essex's new army had proved that it could stand up to the worst the Royalist cavalry could do to it. Altogether, at the end of a triumphant summer, matters began to look ominous for the Royalists.

The Battle of Cropredy Bridge

29 June 1644

Even though Newbury had been a strategic reverse, the Royalists were still in a very strong position in the autumn of 1643. After their successes in the north and west it seemed obvious common sense that Charles should now attempt what he had thought about earlier in the year – a triple drive on London. But, unfortunately for his cause, neither his northern nor his western supporters wished to move far from their home areas. Then followed the disaster of Winceby in October and it suddenly became clear that the Roundheads had good cavalry as well as good foot.

Even so, the future did not look too good to the Roundheads either. All their three main armies had taken hard knocks and there was the problem of keeping pay going and preventing desertion. Pym died in December, and he was a more serious loss even than Hampden had been. Strenuous attempts had been made to raise an army from Scotland, but the price demanded by the Covenanters was thought to be almost too high. There would be morning and evening prayers, two sermons on Sundays, fearful penalties for loose women and loose-livers who consorted with them; drunkenness and irreverent speech were virtually capital offences. But 21,000 men are 21,000 men, and Parliament was prepared to pay almost any price in this hour of need. Up on the border there were people who were a little sceptical about how disciplined this host might prove to be, but for the most part they were wrong. Charles meanwhile had arranged for help from Ireland; the fact that his new allies were as fanatically Roman Catholic as the Scots were Low Church spread a feeling of gloom on both sides during the winter of 1643.

With the spring the war quickly warmed up again. Waller won a dramatic and unexpected victory at Cheriton (Hampshire) on 29 March 1644 and the Roundheads were equally active in the north. On 20 April York was besieged. Strategically this was very dangerous, for any attempts to relieve it would make the Royalist lines extremely vulnerable and perhaps lead to even more serious setbacks elsewhere. The Irish army, from which much had been expected, had been caught unawares and routed at Nantwich in January. Everything depended on what Rupert could do with a hastily assembled army from the north-west.

At that moment Charles turned to close friends and received extremely bad counsel. It was suggested that if he withdrew from Reading and Abingdon his army would be more compact and mobile. The first result was that Essex and Waller promptly reoccupied the two towns, thereby boxing him in more closely. Oxford, at any moment, might come under siege, and Charles's army become useless in the war. Hastily but without clear plans he moved out to Worcester. Massey was coming in from Tewkesbury; Charles's only hope was to make a swift drive and link up with Rupert in the north-west.

Astonishingly, Essex, renowned for his lethargy, now showed speed and resolution, but in the wrong direction. Without caring for protests, he set off to recover the West Country. This took the immediate pressure off the King who now fell back to Woodstock. At that point his position changed dramatically. He regrouped his army, fitting it out with reinforcements from Oxford, and appeared about to launch an army of 10,000 into the thinly defended eastern counties. For a few days he had total victory within his grasp. He could have swung east and south and gone on to a virtually defenceless capital. But, instead, he hesitated.

Of all the unexpected twists in this remarkable war this was probably the strangest. At the beginning of June Charles had been in a trap. Then, owing to an inexplicable decision by Essex, the trap had been opened and Essex had departed to the west. That still left Waller with a large army at Kineton, but a few rapid moves could dispose of that danger.

But, instead of moving east, Charles marched his army toward Banbury. On 28 June his scouts sighted Waller's army near Hanwell Castle, some 2½ miles north-west of Banbury. The Royalists therefore took up position at Grimsbury and both sides looked at each other's strong hill positions and pondered how to tempt the other into a more vulnerable area. There was considerable skirmishing between the cavalry of both armies, but it was obvious to Charles that this could go on indefinitely without drawing such a seasoned old warrior as Waller.

Charles then decided to move off. (Readers will note that the armies were now within a few miles of the site of the Battle of Edgcote (1469). Charles set off in the direction of Daventry – the A361; Waller took note of what was happening and began marching in parallel, a mile away, up the A423. This was not a very happy position for the Royalists, whose manoeuvres were in full view. Marching with another army on one's flank is a somewhat unnerving procedure; it is vastly better to be followed by an enemy, for then you can provide all sorts of little surprises for him in the form of ambushes or deceptive moves.

At this point news came in that there were Roundheads on the

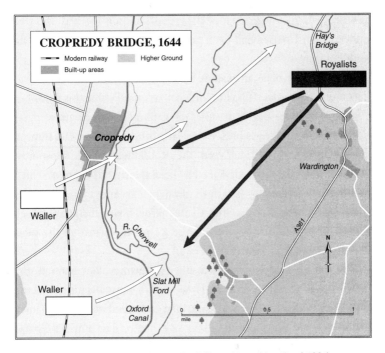

CROPREDY BRIDGE, 1644

- Modern railway
- Built-up areas
- Higher Ground

Hay's Bridge

Royalists

Cropredy

Wardington

Waller

R. Cherwell

A361

N

Waller

Slat Mill Ford

Oxford Canal

0   0.5   1
mile

The approach march and battle may be followed by taking the A423 from Banbury and turning off by Great Bourton. (Oxfordshire)

road ahead. Undoubtedly these would be planning to join Waller, so Charles sent his advance guard ahead to cut them up before they could do so. It obeyed its instructions so quickly that in no time there was a gap in the middle of Charles's column. Waller was not the man to miss such an opportunity and slammed in a two-pronged attack. The rear party was fortunate in finding a ford over the Cherwell at this point at Slat Mill and came right in behind Charles's rear-guard. The forward prong bore straight on to Cropredy Bridge which it captured without trouble. Roundheads then poured across

417

and drove hard towards Hays Bridge, passing on the way the tree under which Charles had been taking an early dinner[1] only half an hour before.

It could have been an instant Roundhead victory, but the Cavaliers saw it otherwise. The Earl of Northampton, still in his teens but a veteran in war, put in a series of vigorous counter-attacks and hurled the Roundheads back over Slat Mill ford. Cleveland showed similar initiative, and battered the Roundheads who were now heading towards Hays Bridge. He held them at the point which might be described at Charles's dinner-table and then, aided by some useful attacks from Stuart Lifeguards, drove them right back across the bridge. In the process, the Roundheads lost all the guns they had just taken over the Cherwell.

But the river still separated the two armies, hot though the fighting was at the bridge and the ford. Eventually, after taking some heavy losses, the Royalists gained command of Slat Mill ford, but they could not force their way over the bridge. For a long hot summer afternoon Cropredy Bridge was the scene of brave and bitter fighting. As evening approached, Waller's army came under Royalist cannon-fire; it was said that target-spotting was done by the King through his 'perspective glasses' and that he also fired some of the cannon himself. By now Waller was withdrawing. Unfortunately for the Royalists they could not follow up their brilliant victory for the Roundheads were just about to be reinforced with another 4,000 men. Nevertheless, Charles's Oxford army was safe from threat, Waller's army mutinied soon afterwards, and the King felt free to drive down to the west country and complete his unfinished business with the Earl of Essex.

1 'Lunch' was just coming into use to describe what nowadays might be known as a 'snack'. 'Dinner' denoted the main meal of the day, usually taken around 11.30 a.m.

The Second Battle of Newbury

27 October 1644

While the Royalists were feeling reasonably pleased with themselves over the Battle of Cropredy Bridge, another and much greater conflict was looming. This was the huge, confused, but decisive Battle of Marston Moor, of 2 July 1644. Its result was that the Royalists were destroyed in the north, and one of its most disastrous effects was that the Marquis of Newcastle became so angry with Rupert that he refused to continue fighting for the Royalist cause.

But matters looked better in the south and west. After Cropredy, Charles had moved to Weymouth, then Tavistock, then Exeter. At this stage Essex was about to invade Cornwall, where he hoped to prohibit the export of tin on which Charles depended to pay for munitions.

As soon as Essex reached Launceston he realized the appalling mistake he had made. Charles was close by with a larger army. The outcome was the dramatic Royalist victory at Lostwithiel on 2 September 1644. Although this was a triumph for the Royalists in every way it did not take them much further towards winning the war. And it did little to offset the tremendous losses entailed by Marston Moor. And, dotted here and there over southern and western England, there were still formidable points of Roundhead resistance, as for example at Plymouth, Weymouth, and Poole.

Some Royalist strongholds like Banbury Castle (now completely destroyed), Basing House, and Donnington Castle (Newbury) were still under siege, and it did not occur to Charles to leave these places to their own devices while he made a decisive move to end the war by advancing on London. While he pondered on what to do next, vital time slipped away, and the Roundheads recovered from their reverses and rebuilt their armies. When, six weeks later, Charles came back to Salisbury he could muster only 10,000 men, whereas his opponents had close on 17,000.

Nevertheless, the Roundheads retired gently in the face of the Royalist advance. On 18 October the Roundheads who had been besieging Donnington Castle fell back to Basingstoke. This meant that much of the Parliamentary army was now in north Hampshire but, in spite of his numerical disadvantage, Charles seemed intent on relieving Basing House. By 21 October he was at Kingsclere, ten miles away.

At this point Charles was prevailed upon to take advice. It would, of course, have been tantamount to suicide to press on to Basing, and instead he moved to Newbury, which was eight miles north-west. He then despatched a brigade to relieve Northampton Castle and waited to see what his opponents would now do. With luck they might draw away from Basing and give him a chance to relieve it. They did, but only to come to Newbury where Charles, having hived off the brigade, was now only 9,000 strong. Against this the Roundheads brought 17,000 men.

This battle could have seen the end of the war. At the outset it seemed as if there was no hope at all for the Royalists. But Charles, who had a fine eye for a tactical site, had chosen wisely. The centre of his position was Shaw House, a formidable structure surrounded by earthworks constructed for some ancient but unknown battle. His

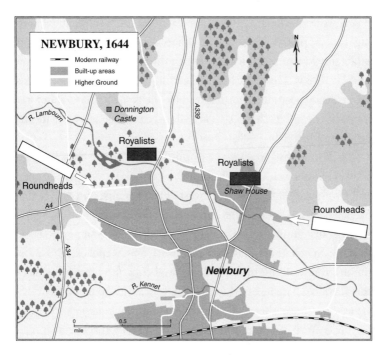

NEWBURY, 1644

- ▪▪▪ Modern railway
- ▨ Built-up areas
- ▨ Higher Ground

R. Lambourn

■ Donnington Castle

A339

Royalists

Royalists

Roundheads

Shaw House

A4

Roundheads

A34

Newbury

R. Kennet

0   0.5   1
mile

N

This battlefield is easily found by taking the A34 out of Newbury and turning off for Donnington Castle. The obelisk just outside Naseby village on the B4036 is unfortunately misleading as it is well away from the battlefield. (Berkshire)

right was covered by the Kennet and Newbury itself, his left by the Lambourn, and behind was the formidable Donnington Castle, with its massive drum towers, giving him perfect observation of his enemies. The position was undoubtedly a good one but not perhaps as good as it seemed to the Roundheads. To them it looked almost impregnable. In consequence they decided a single attack was impossible and resolved instead on the somewhat complicated device of an attack from front and rear simultaneously.

The rear attacking party was then allotted the somewhat exhausting task of marching an extra thirteen miles so as to approach undetected from the Wickham Heath direction. Much of the value of this move was lost by Charles's learning what was happening, and he made disposition accordingly. Had he known more about the numbers he might have attacked the frontal party which in fact numbered less than 5,000.

The Roundhead attack was co-ordinated by cannon-fire. The Earl of Manchester was to attack from the east while Skippon, Waller, and Cromwell came in from the west. The plan miscarried. Whether Manchester did not hear the appropriate signal, or merely thought it was Royalist gunfire is not known. However, when Skippon attacked west of Speen there was no response from Manchester. Nevertheless, the Roundheads were doing well enough. They rolled back the Royalists, some of whom began to flee in spite of Charles's efforts to check them. The situation was looking grim for the Royalists until Cleveland and Cansfield put in three tremendous charges which pushed the Roundheads right back to Speen. By now, dusk was gathering but at long last Manchester put in his attack. He was met by Lisle and temporarily pushed back, but numbers soon began to tell. After an hour's dogged fighting it was so dark on the battlefield that both sides hesitated to continue lest they should attack their own men. The Roundheads, having failed to co-ordinate in daylight, were apprehensive about what might happen if they continued their efforts in the dark. The gunners, not knowing what targets to choose, stopped firing, and the foot and cavalry disengaged.

Second Newbury had been as indecisive as First Newbury and once more Charles slipped away under cover of darkness. He rode to Bath where he joined Prince Rupert. His army withdrew north and were in Oxford by nightfall of the 28th. The Roundheads had had the best of the fighting but nobody enjoyed the fruits of victory. Even Donnington Castle was in Royalist hands and still holding out.

The Battle of Naseby

14 June 1645

The year 1644 came to an end with no sign of a breakthrough in the war for either side. Charles seemed the more active, and probably felt, with some justice, that if he had taken complete command from the beginning he might have won the war. His attitude in the continued negotiations with Parliament was noticeably harder.

At this stage Parliament took the steps which ultimately decided the result of the war. By the 'Self-Denying Ordinance' senior and less experienced officers were encouraged to retire voluntarily. That took Essex, Manchester, Waller, and other commanders of unhappy record out of the firing-line altogether. Cromwell stayed, but, as he was the foremost cavalry commander of the day, that was no handicap.

Simultaneously the Roundheads overhauled the rank and file of the army. The 'New Model' was formed consisting of eleven regiments of horse – a total of 6,600 – 1,000 dragoons, and twelve foot regiments each numbering 1,200. These were a combination of the best of the old armies plus a good number of pressed men. They were well-armed, well-clothed, well-trained, and well-disciplined. They were also properly paid. Sir Thomas Fairfax was commander-in-chief with Cromwell as his deputy. Soon it seemed more appropriate to call these men Ironsides rather than Roundheads.

The Royalist strategy in the spring of 1645 was to thrust north through Worcester to Chester and then pick up reinforcements in the north, where there would still be plenty of sympathizers in spite of the disaster of Marston Moor the previous year. Rupert and Maurice cleared the way by victories at Ledbury and Chester, but Charles was slow to move.

Meanwhile, Cromwell, who was enjoying his first independent command, was sent to the Midlands to upset any Royalist plans. He lost no time in showing his ability and determination. He defeated the Earl of Northampton near Islip, compelled the surrender of Bletchington House, took 200 prisoners in a battle at Bampton, and made a vigorous though unsuccessful attack on Faringdon Castle. However, he could not prevent Charles leaving Oxford with an army numbering 11,000.

Both armies now began manoeuvring for advantage. Fairfax came up from the west and threatened Oxford; Rupert countered the move by capturing and sacking Leicester. Charles, although aware that his army was large and well balanced, was not prepared to risk it in the open against vastly superior numbers. He therefore moved to Daventry and deliberated how he could relieve Oxford.

Fairfax, however, was aware that he had the initiative. On 12 June he broke off the investment of Oxford and moved swiftly to Kislingbury, eight miles east of Daventry. This was close enough to Charles to clash with the outposts. Charles had no intention of being forced to fight at a disadvantage on ground not of his own choosing and he retreated that night to Market Harborough. This move put him within reasonable reach of his base at Newark.

But Fairfax was hot on his heels. He reached Guilsborough, four miles south of Naseby, the next day. The news surprised the king and he saw that it was necessary to give battle. The position was by

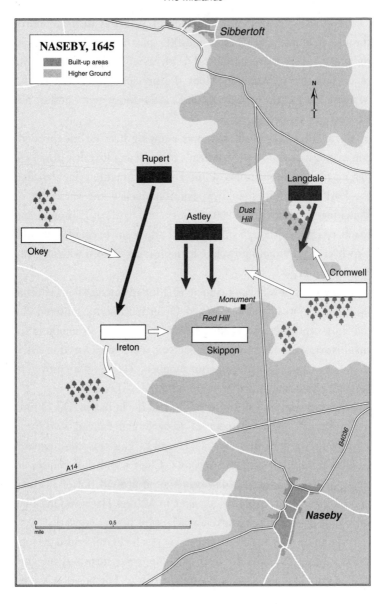

NASEBY, 1645

Built-up areas
Higher Ground

Sibbertoft

N

Rupert

Okey

Langdale

Astley

Dust
Hill

Cromwell

Monument

Red Hill

Ireton

Skippon

A14

B4036

Naseby

0   0,5   1
mile

no means unsuitable. Two miles south of Market Harborough was a ridge of high ground covering the two miles from East Farndon to Great Oxendon, from the B4036 to the A508. Charles deployed his army along this position by 8 a.m. on 14 June.

Fairfax, following, breasted the Naseby ridge four miles south, and realized that this was going to be a major battle. He noted that the ground between Naseby and Clipston was marshy. If he could persuade Rupert to charge over it and up the ridge, this would be a good start for the day. Rupert, of course, had his eyes just as wide open as Fairfax and instead veered right on to the line of the Sibbertoft–Naseby road.

Fairfax saw Rupert's counter-move and promptly began to close left to meet it. This peculiar manoeuvre shifted the battlefront one mile west of the original line. The area between them was now bounded by Dust Hill to the north, Red Hill to the south, and Sulby to the west. The centre was Broadmoor. The battlefield monument (*not* the Naseby obelisk) is just below Red Hill to the left of the road.

By 10 a.m. the armies were in their new position. On the Royalist side, Rupert commanded the cavalry on the right wing, Lord Astley had the foot in the centre, and Langdale took the cavalry on the left. The front was approximately a mile long. There was very little artillery on the Royalist side, as most had been left in the previous position. Opposite, Cromwell commanded the cavalry on the right, Skippon the centre foot, and Ireton the cavalry on the left. Cromwell also stationed 1,000 dragoons on the left behind Sulby hedges under the command of Okey; these were in advance of the main Ironside

The Naseby–Sibbertoft road runs right through the battlefield. The monument is on the west of this road. (Northamptonshire)

line. (This was a similar disposition to Edward IV at the battle of Tewkesbury.) The Ironsides had all their guns.

Rupert began the battle with a typical charge, and Astley's foot were closing rapidly at the same time. Rupert aimed at the centre of Ireton's position but Ireton's men veered somewhat to the right. A flank attack by Okey's dragoons did nothing to stop him; he charged right into Ireton's left, and then settled down to cut and thrust with the sword. This was a tough bloody period, but the Royalists got the better of it and forced a way through. Rupert was then able to regroup. Looking for another target, he decided to press on, but this move achieved little, for there were only the baggage-wagons to attack and what happened there could not affect the present battle. However, Rupert was careful not to waste too much time – not wanting to be accused of another Edghill – but his absence from the field at this time was disastrous for his side.

In the centre, the Royalist infantry had begun well and were forcing the Ironsides back. In attacking Ireton, Rupert, though pushing back the left wing, had left the right half and its commander intact. Ireton now used this part to attack Astley on the flank, as the latter's magnificent foot stormed up the hill. This was not intolerable for the Royalist foot but it was unwelcome. Even less welcome was the arrival of Okey's dragoons, who now advanced in a cavalry charge. Meanwhile, Cromwell had launched a tremendous cavalry charge on to Langdale's cavalry who were finding their way over the broken ground at the foot of the hill. It was full of rabbit-holes and bushes, and anyone caught there would be at a disadvantage. Cromwell needed only to use his leading regiments to wreak havoc in this area, but even these he was able to recall when their work was done. In the rear, he still had uncommitted troops.

This became the turning point of the battle. As Astley's infantry fought their way up Red Hill Ridge encountering no mean resistance from Skippon's foot, they received not only the shock of Ireton and Okey but now a tremendous blow on the other flank from Cromwell's cavalry. Even the forward units, who had ridden down Langdale, were turned back into the fight, and the second and third lines went in completely fresh.

At this point Rupert came back to the field, but with his horses blown could do no more than be a spectator. The sight he saw was enough to sicken anyone, heroic though it was. Astley's infantry having fought their way up the ridge, having been attacked on three sides, were now being forced down again. They fought to the last, and were wiped out almost to a man – 4,000 of them. Many of the cavalry fought it out to the end too, although it could not affect the result. But finally, with the King and Rupert gone, those who could tried to leave the field.

As on all battlefields the scenes of the heaviest fighting may be traced by names or grave-pits. Red Hill Ridge and Red Hill Farm need no explanation.

This was probably the most decisive battle of the war and Charles should never have fought it. He was outnumbered by two to one, 14,000 to 7,000, and he was short of cavalry. Added to that, Rupert once again moved off the field in the wrong direction after an initial success. And the hard fact is that the Royalists probably underrated their opponents and paid dearly for it.

The Battle of Worcester

3 September 1651

Cromwell called the Battle of Worcester the 'crowning mercy'; other might have had a different name for it.

It occurred six years after Naseby, that great, decisive but badly-managed battle which had sealed the fate of the Royalist cause. After it, Charles was little more than a fugitive, though for a time it seemed as if he might once again turn the tables with the help of Montrose. But in September 1645 Montrose was defeated at Philiphaugh. There was still an army in the west of England but this too was beaten by Fairfax at Langport in September 1645, and from then onwards the Royalists were forced westward until they surrendered in the spring of 1646. In April 1646, after watching his enemies gather round Oxford for what would surely be the last and most fateful siege of the war, Charles slipped away and surrendered to the Scottish Covenanters who were then in camp at Newark. He felt that it might be easier to make a deal with the Scots than the English Parliament, but he was mistaken. The Scots were adamant that he must make Presbyterianism the religion of England – a stipulation which was quite unacceptable to Charles. The Scots would have none of his temporizing and abruptly handed him over to his English opponents.

Still Charles felt he could save something from all the wreckage. There was an apparently irreconcilable conflict between the

Presbyterians, who held the majority in Parliament, and the Independents, who drew the line at a state-imposed religion. Cromwell and Fairfax supported the Independents, as did the New Model Army as a whole. When the Presbyterians tried to dismiss the New Model, which it saw as the mainstay of the opposition, it refused to disperse. Instead it marched to London and seized power.

The Independents then offered Charles moderate terms but unwisely he refused them. He escaped to the Isle of Wight where he was kept under surveillance at Carisbrooke. He had long been negotiating – some would say intriguing – for a last uprising, and now it came. But it failed. In three months Cromwell and Fairfax had suppressed it. The last decisive battle was at Preston in 1648.

Charles was now sent to Hurst Castle, from which he could not escape. In January 1649, a packed High Court tried the King and condemned him to death; Charles refused to try to defend himself.

He was executed in Whitehall on 16 January 1649, meeting his death with exemplary courage and dignity.

A republic was now proclaimed but peace was still far away. First there was a mutiny amongst the army Cromwell was about to take to Ireland; then followed his relentless campaign against Irish resistance which is still a vivid and bitter memory in parts of Ireland to this day.

But the Scots had not struck their final blow. A new army was raised to fight for the cause of Prince Charles, later to be Charles II. Cromwell defeated it at Dunbar in September 1650 and went on to overrun the Lowlands and much of central Scotland.

It seemed all over, but it was not. In 1651 when Cromwell was at Perth, he learnt that Prince Charles had slipped past him and was marching rapidly down through England, picking up reinforcements on the way. It was a critical moment. There was no army between the Prince[1] and London. However, he gained few recruits on his southerly march and lost many Scots from desertion. He decided therefore to pause at Worcester and let supporters come in from Wales and other areas which had for so long stood firmly by his father. Ironically, he set up his standard in Worcester nine years exactly after his father had set up his standard at Nottingham – on 22 August. Coincidentally, Cromwell marched into Nottingham on the very same day.

With 15,000 men only, in the heart of a hostile country, the future did not look very promising to Prince Charles. Cromwell, by forced marching south, was now closing in on him. By the time Cromwell reached Evesham, sixteen miles from Worcester, he had 30,000 men, and his army was still growing. He had quite clear in his mind what he had to do, and was quite ruthless. The Royalist army must not merely be beaten but completely and finally destroyed. To accomplish this he must surround it and block every avenue of escape. This he now proceeded to do.

The subsequent battle took place in the fields north of Powick bridge. The Severn runs north-south through Worcester, but to the south of the city it is joined by the Teme. Charles stationed his army on the north bank of the Teme and destroyed all near-by bridges on the Teme and Severn. This put him in the apex of a triangle and presumably he expected to inflict very heavy casualties on the Cromwellians who tried to cross the river to get at him. The Severn being swift, deep, and forty yards across was likely to be of great assistance in this. The Teme, although only ten feet wide, was also ten feet deep and fast-flowing. It looked like being a difficult time for the Cromwellians.

1 He had in fact been crowned as Charles II at Scone.

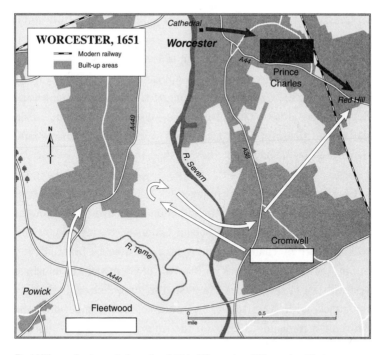

Red Hill may be traced along the A44 in Worcester. (Worcestershire)

Cromwell decided on a triple attack. He spent several days collecting boats from up and down the river, and, of course, they were there to be had in abundance. Several of the largest of these were towed upstream to a point where they could be made into bridging pontoons. One of these was to be used to cross the Teme with 11,000 men, the other to bridge the Severn. There was one further target to be attacked. This was Fort Royal outside the east wall of the town. It formed the rear headquarters of the Royalist position.

The southern party (under Fleetwood) approached the Teme

with difficulty. Charles had left a rearguard on the south bank and it fought a strong delaying action around Powick Church.

Miraculously both 'bridges' seem to have been a success, though perhaps some of Fleetwood's men appear to have swum across or forded higher up. Cromwell's contingent is said to have crossed the Severn first, although in planning it was meant to come in on the second phase of the attack. Both reached the meadows, and there, step by bloody step, they pushed the Royalists back to St John's.

Charles seems to have encouraged his troops in the early phase of the battle and then ascended the cathedral tower to direct operations from that observation point. Seeing Cromwell's army now in two sections, with no chance of joining up again quickly, he decided to put in a swift counter-attack on that part of Cromwell's army which was still east of the Severn. He wasted no time. Personally leading the attack, with every soldier he could collect at short notice, he delivered a tremendous blow on the troops Cromwell had not yet committed to battle. He swept all before him and reached the eminence known as Red Hill.

With a less able opponent than Cromwell this counter-attack might have turned the battle. Cromwell, however, was not the man to relinquish a gain. Coming back across the bridge he hurled his troops into what he sensed was the key area of the conflict. Three hours bitter fighting followed. Only when Charles could no longer rally the Scottish cavalry to keep up their attack was the battle decided. Then, as darkness fell, panic raced through the Royalist ranks. The cavalry – or what was left of them – galloped off and left the infantry to their fate. The unfortunate foot had no chance at all; many were taken prisoner but most were killed. But they did not stop fighting; in some parts the struggle went on well into the night.

Few of those who managed to escape from the battlefield were able to reach safety. It was a complete, devastating and final Roundhead victory. And it was, at last, the end of the Civil War.

Appendices

1 Asser's Account of the Battle of Ashdown

Asser's account seems to be a combination of rhetoric, fact, and surmise. This is hardly surprising, for it was one of many battles, and even if Alfred discussed it personally it is probable that he had some difficulty in recalling exactly what occurred.

. . . In the next year (869) was there a mighty famine, and death among men, and plague among beasts. And the aforesaid Heathen host rode back to the Northumbrians and came to the city of York, and there abode one whole year. And in the next year (870) they made their way through Mercia to East Anglia, and in a place called Theodford [Thetford] they wintered. In this same year Edmund, King of the East Angles, fought against that same host a desperate fight. But, alas, the Heathen won all too gloriously; and there was he slain, and the most of his men with him; and they held the death-stead, and brought beneath their sway all that land.

And in the same year did Archbishop Ceolnoth, the Bishop of Dorobernia [Canterbury], go the way of all flesh, and in that city was he buried in peace.

But in the year of our Lord's Incarnation 871, and the 22nd of the age of King Alfred, did that Heathen host, hateful to tell, leave the East Angles, and hied them to the realm of the West Saxons, and came unto a town royal, called Rædig [Reading], which lieth on the bank of Thames-stream River [*Tamesis flumensis fluminis*] to the south, in that part which is called Bearrocscire. And on the third day of their coming thither, then rode forth their chiefs, and many with them, to harry the land; and the rest were after making them a dyke between the two rivers, Thames and Cynetan [Kennet], on the right hand[1] of that town royal.

Then did Ethelwulf, Alderman of the land of Berkshire, with his comrades, cross their path at the place called Englefield; and there fought both sides full valiantly, and long did either stand their ground. Of the two Heathen captains the one was slain, and the most part of that host laid low. Then fled away the rest, and the Christians gat them the victory, and held the death-stead. Yet four days more, after this hap, and there came Ethelred, King of the West Saxons, and Alfred his brother, and joined forces, and gathered them a host, and drew nigh unto Reading, cutting down and overthrowing whomsoever of the Heathen they found without the stronghold, and made their way even unto the gates. No less keen in fight were the Heathen. Out they burst from every gate like wolves; and then waxed long the fight, and ever more deadly. But, alas, alas, in the end did the Christians turn their backs, and the Heathen gat them the victory and held the death-stead. And there, amongst the rest, fell the above-named Alderman, Ethelwulf.

Stirred by this woe and shame, the Christians, after yet another four days, went forth to battle against the aforesaid host, at a place called Æscesdun [Ashdown] (which in Latin is by interpretation Ash Mount), with their whole strength, and with a good will. But the Heathen formed in two divisions, of like size, made ready their shield-wall [*testudo*]. For they had, as at that time, two Kings and many

---

1 *i.e.*, to the south. Until the sixteenth century the East, not the North, was the top of the map.

Chieftains; and the one half of their army gave they unto the two Kings, and the rest unto all the Chieftains together. And when the Christians saw this, they too, in like manner, parted their host in twain, and as keenly formed their shield-wall.

But Alfred, with his men, as we have heard from truthful eye-witnesses, came the quicker to the field and more readily. Nor wonder was it; for his brother King Ethelred was still in his tent, fixed in prayer, hearing Mass. For ever would he say that never while he lived would he leave his Mass before the Priest had ended it, nor, for any man on earth, turn his back on Divine Service. And even so he did. And much availed with the Lord the faith of that Christian King, as in what followeth will appear most plainly.

The Christians, then, had thought best that Ethelred the King, with his force, should take battle against the two Kings of the Heathen; while Alfred his brother, with his band, should be told, as was meet, to chance the fight [*belli sumere sortem*] against all the Heathen Chieftains. And when thus on either side they were in good order, and the King tarried long in prayer, Alfred, then second in command, could stand the advance of the foe no longer. Needs must be either draw him back from the battle, or charge the enemy ere yet his brother came into the fray. And, at the last, in manly wise, charged he, with the rush of a wild boar, leading his Christian forces against the foemen's hosts, even as had been fore-planned (save only that the King was not yet come), for he trusted in God's counsel and leant upon His aid. So drew he together his shield-wall in good order, and advanced his banner straight against the foe.

But here those who know not the place must be told that it was no fair field of battle, for the Heathen had seized the higher ground, and the Christian battle-line was charging uphill. There was also in that same place a lone thorn-tree and a low, which we ourselves have

438

beheld. Around this, then, came the lines together, with a mighty shouting, in warrior wise, the one side bent upon all mischief [*perperam agentes*], the other to fight for life and land and dear ones. This way and that swayed the battle for a while, valiant was it and all too deadly, till so God ordered it that the Heathen could stand against the Christian charge no longer. Most part of their force were slain, and with all shame they betook them to flight.

And in that place fell there by the sword one of the two Heathen Kings, and of their Chieftains five, and many a thousand of their men beside them. Yea, and, moreover, thousands more, scattered over the whole breadth of the field of Ashdown, were cut to pieces far and wide. And there then fell there Bægsceg their King, and Sidroc the Elder, their Chieftain, and Sidroc the Younger, their Chieftain, and Osbern the Chieftain, and Frena the Chieftain, and Harold the Chieftain. And the whole Heathen host fled them away all that day and all that night, even unto the next day; till they that escaped got back into their stronghold. And even until nightfall held the Christians the chase, and smote them down on every side.

And after this, again fourteen days, Ethelred the King and Alfred his brother, with their united force, hied them to Basing to fight against the Heathen. There joined they battle, and stood to it long. But the Heathen gained the day and held the field. And when this fray was lost and won, came there from over sea yet another Heathen host and joined the horde. And in the same year, after Easter, Ethelred, the aforesaid King, after ruling his realm well and worshipfully amid many a trouble, went the way of all flesh, and is buried in the monastery at Wimborne, where he awaiteth the Coming of the Lord and the First Resurrection with the just.

In the same year did our Alfred (who until then, while his brothers lived, had been in the second place) take upon him, so soon as ever his brother was dead, the sway of the whole kingdom, by the grant of God, and with all goodwill of the land-folk, one and all. For even while this brother was yet alive might he eftsoon have won it, would he have taken it, and that with the assent of all men: seeing that both in wisdom and eke in all good ways was he better than all his brethren put together – yea, and, in especial, a surpassing warrior, and, in war, had ever almost the best of it. Then began he to reign, as it were unwillingly. For it seemed unto him that never might he, all alone, with but God for aid, endure so grievous a stress and strain of heathendom; whenas, even along with his brothers, while they lived, full hardly and with great loss might he abide it.

So reigned he one full month, and thereafter, on the hill called Wilton, on the southern bank of the river Guilou [Willy] (from which river the whole of that shire is named), fought he, with but few behind him, against the whole Heathen host, a fight all too unequal. Up and down most part of the day raged the fight full stoutly. Then were the eyes of the Heathen opened, and they saw to the full their peril. And therewith bore they up no longer against their unremitting foe, but turned their backs and fled away. But, alas, through the rashness of the pursuit they tricked us. On they came again to battle, and win the victory, and were masters of the death-stead.

2 Ludlow's Account of the Battle of Edgehill

Edmund Ludlow's account of Edgehill is noteworthy, for the majority of descriptions of the battle are from the Royalist viewpoint. This one comes from the opposite side.

. . . The night following [Powick Bridge] the enemy left Worcester, and retreated to Shrewsbury, where the King was; upon which the Earl of Essex advanced to Worcester, where he continued with the army for some time, expecting an answer to a message sent by him to the King from the Parliament, inviting him to return to London. This time the King improved to compleat and arm his men; which then he had effected, he began his march, the Earl of Essex attending him to observe his motions; and after a day or two, on Sunday morning, the 23rd of October, 1642, our scouts brought advice that the enemy appeared, and about nine o'clock some of their troops were discovered upon Edge-hill in Warwickshire. Upon this our forces, who had been order'd that morning to their quarteres to refresh themselves, having had but little rest for eight and forty hours, were immediately counter-manded. The enemy drew down the hill, and we went into the field near Keinton. The best of our field-pieces were planted upon our right wing, guarded by two regiments of foot, and some horse. Our general having commanded to fire upon the enemy, it was done twice upon that part of the army wherein, as it was reported, the King was. The great shot was exchanged on both sides for the space of an hour or thereabouts. By this time the foot began to engage, and a party of the enemy being sent to line some hedges on our right wing, thereby to beat us from our ground, were repulsed by our dragoons without any loss on our side. The enemy's body of foot, wherein the King's standard was, came on within musquet-shot of us; upon which we observing no horse to encounter withal, charged then with some loss from their pikes, tho very little from their shot; but not being able to break them, we retreated to our former station, whither we were no sooner come, but we perceived that those who were appointed to guard the artillery were marched off; and Sir Philip Stapylton, our captain, wishing for a regiment of foot to secure the cannon, we promised to stand by him in defence of them, causing one of our servants to load and level one of them, which he had scarce done, when a body of horse appeared advancing towards us from that side where the enemy was. We fired at them with case-shot, but did no other mischief save only wounding one man through the hand, our gun being overloaded, and planted on high ground; which fell out very happily, this body of horse being of our own army, and commanded by Sir William Balfour, who with great resolution had charged into the enemy's quarters, where he had nailed several pieces of their cannon, and was then retreating to his own party, of which the man who was shot in the hand was giving us notice by holding it up; but we did not discern it. The Earl of Essex order'd two regiments of foot to attack that body which we had charged before, where the King's standard was, which they did, but could not break them till Sir William Balfour at the head of a party of horse charging them in the rear, and we marching down to take them in the flank, they brake and ran away towards the hill. Many of them were killed upon the place, amongst whom was Sir Edward Varney the King's standard-bearer, who, as I have heard from a person of honour, engaged on that side, not out of any good opinion of the cause, but from the sense of duty which he thought lay upon him, in respect of his relation to the King. Mr [William] Herbert of Glamorganshire, Lieutenant Colonel to Sir Edward Stradling's regiment, was also killed, with many others that fell in the pursuit. Many colours were taken, and I saw Lieutenant Colonel Middleton, then a reformado in our army, displaying the King's standard which he had taken; but a party of horse coming upon us, we were obliged to retire with our standard; and having brought it to the Earl of Essex, he delivered it to the custody of one Mr [Robert] Chambers, his secretary, from whom it was taken by one Captain

[John] Smith, who, with two more, disguising themselves with orange-colour'd scarfs (the Earl of Essex's colours), and pretending it unfit that a penman should have the honour to carry the standard, took it from him, and rode with it to the King, for which action he was knighted. Retreating towards our army, I fell in with a body of the King's foot, as I soon perceived; but having passed by them undiscovered, I met with Sir William Balfour's troop, some of whom who knew me not would have fired upon me, supposing me to be an enemy, had they not been prevented, and assured of the contrary by Mr Francis Russell, who with ten men well mounted and armed, which he maintained, rode in the lifeguard, and in the heat of the pursuit had lost sight of them, as I myself had also done.

I now perceived no other engagement on either side, only a few great guns continued to fire upon us from the enemy: but towards the close of the day we discovered a body of horse marching from our rear on the left of us under the hedges, which the life-guard (whom I had then found) having discovered to be the enemy, and resolving to charge them, sent to some of our troops that stood within musquet-shot of us to second them; which though they refused to do, and we had no way to come at them but through a gap in the hedge, we advanced towards them, and falling upon their rear, killed divers of them, and brought off some arms. In which attempt being dismounted I could not without great difficulty recover on horse-back again, being loaded with cuirassier's arms, as the rest of the guard also were. This was the right wing of the King's horse commanded by Prince Rupert, who, taking advantage of the disorder that our own horse had put our foot into, who had opened their ranks to secure them in their retreat, pressed upon them with such fury, that he put them to flight. And if the time which he spent in pursueing them too far, and in plundering the wagons, had been employed in taking such advantages as offered themselves in the place where the fight was, it might have proved more serviceable to the carrying on of the enemy's designs. The night after the battle our army quartered upon the same ground that the enemy fought on the day before. No man nor horse got any meat that night, and I had touched none since the Saturday before, neither could I find my servant who had my cloak, so that having nothing to keep me warm but a suite of iron, I was obliged to walk about all night, which proved very cold by reason of a sharp frost.

3 Relics of the Battle of Edgehill

Brigadier Peter Young, DSO, MC, who is the most authoritative writer on Edgehill, has kindly allowed me to quote the following notes on relics of the battle.

In July 1967 Miss M. Fell of 58 Keswick Walk, Wyken, Coventry, presented three lead musket balls to the author. These were picked up on the battlefield some 80 years ago by her grandfather, a Mr Hemming, a native of Kineton – of the family of John Hemming or Hemminge (d. 1630), actor and co-editor of the first folio of Shakespeare. Two of the bullets weigh 1¼ oz. and the other 1⅛ oz. The line round the circumference caused by the bullet mould can be clearly seen on the two heavier bullets. The author has a bullet from Marston Moor which weighs just over an ounce, and five from Naseby, one of which weighs fractionally more than an oz., and the others just under. During a search of the Gravesend Copse area, using mine detectors, a leaden musket ball, weighing approximately 1¼ oz. was found (1967).

Another bullet, given to a Mr Prickett, and now in the possession of David Fisher, was weighed in the author's presence (6 August 1967) and found to be 2lb. 14¾ oz. In theory a minion was a 4-pounder and a falcon a 2¼-pounder. This bullet would be too large for the latter, and would have made a very inaccurate projectile for the former; fitting the barrel very badly and therefore having altogether too much 'windage' it would wander in its flight. It was picked up at Moorlands Farm and must, therefore, have been discharged by the Parliamentarian artillery. A similar ball was found at Hornton by a Mr Yates.

On 5 August Mr T. Jeffes of Radway showed the author two cannon-balls given to him by a Mr Griffin in 1964. These came from the Thisleton Farm area and had been taken thence in about 1941, when the War Department took over. They weigh approximately 23½ lbs. and 12lbs. respectively, from which one would conclude that they were fired by a demi-cannon and a culverin respectively. One would expect that balls found in the Thistleton Farm area would be from the Royalist guns. Certainly they had two demi-cannon – theoretically 27-pounders – and two culverins – theoretically 15-pounders. The Parliamentarians lost two 12-pounders in the battle, and it is not impossible that the second bullet was ammunition for one of them.

Mr Martin Jeffes showed the author a musket bullet similar to those sent him by Miss Fell. He had discovered this (c. 1963) while ditching about a quarter of a mile NW of the present Radway Church. This could be a Parliamentarian bullet fired during the last phase of the battle.

A ball weighing 19 pounds and two others weighing only half a pound each, are in the possession of Lord Leycester Hospital, Warwick. They were found near Thistleton Farm and should therefore be Royalist missiles. The three small balls may be caseshot, but they could have been fired from a robinet, which was a ¾-pounder.

During the construction of the Central Ammunition Depot, Kineton (1942), six or more cannon balls were found in the vicinity of the Graveyard. Their weight is said to have varied from 6 to 22 pounds, but it seems that their exact weight and precise location were not properly recorded and so this proves very little.

In 1922, during the construction of the Ironstone Railway from Edgehill to Kineton, some cannon-balls were found in a disused brick-kiln at a point described as 300 yards east along the Arlescote Road from the foot of Bullet Hill. These must have been some of the shots from Ramsey's wing which, as Bulstrode tells us, 'mounted over our Troops, without doing any Hurt . . .'

Other relics of the battle include hand made nails, a seventeenth century horseshoe and part of the rim tyre of a heavy vehicle found during the mine detector search of Great Grounds (1967), a spear (pike?) head found by Mr Yates of Hornton, and a pikehead found at Upland Farm in 1950, and now in the Banbury Museum. The same Museum possesses a sword found in Broughton Churchyard, while Mr L. Todd of Manor Farm, Ratley, found another sword in 1950. Grimmer remains were found in about 1880 near the ford on the Little Kineton to Kineton road; the skeletons of several men, perhaps Parliamentarian runaways, or men detailed to escort the baggage train.

One is struck by the fact that a number of these cannon balls do not fit neatly into the various types of artillery used in 1642. One would expect to find 27 or 15 pound balls for demi-cannon and culverin, yet we find balls of 23½, 22 and 19 pounds. It is evident that theory and practice did not go hand in hand. Yet this is not so surprising when we recall the charges of inefficiency levelled against the

446

Parliamentarian artillery, and the difficulties of the Royalists in providing a train at all. Their troubles are illustrated by a petition recently found in the Public Record Office by Dr Ian Roy:

> When his late Matie: was to take the feilde, the firste Councell of war appointed Sr John Heydon Sr John Pennington Sr Bryan Palmes Sr George Strode and John Wandesforde to forme and conduct the traine of Artillery att Edge hill, Sr George received woundes which were helde mortall, and John Wandesforde alone brought of the trayne to Oxforde and his Highenesse Prince Ruperte did Commaunde dragoones to dismounte and Imployed those in that Saruice.
>
> SP.29.66. No. 46)

One can only admire the Prince's talent for improvisation. The comments of the dragoons are best left to the readers' imagination.

4 Accounts of the Sieges of Hereford and Colchester

Mention has been made in the text of various sieges. Many of these were battles in miniature and even more demanding. Here we reproduce two examples: an account of Hereford, as described in a letter to the Lord Digby from the Governor (reproduced by kind permission of Mrs C. M. F. Parsons); and of Colchester, in the second phase of the battle, from the Beaufort manuscripts.

My Lord,

A Numerous and Active Army closely besieging us hath rendred me, and those engaged with me, (in regard of perpetuall duty, without reliefe of Guards for five weeks together) incapable of presenting your Lordship with an exact Relation thereof: I can therefore hint it only for a better Mercury. The Officers, Gentry, (whereof I shall send a list) Clergy, Citizens, and Common Souldiers, behaved themselves all gallantly upon their duty, many eminently; to particularise each, would be too great a trespasse on your Lordships more weighty affaires. Briefly beleeve me (my Lord) the walls of their valiant breasts were all strongly lined with Courage and Loyalty.

On the 30th of July, I sent out a party of 20 Horse over Wyebridge, who discovering their Forlorne-hope of horse, charged them into their maine Body; and retreated in very little disorder, and with losse only of one Trooper, (taken prisoner) some of the Scots falling. Immediately after this, their whole Body of Horse faced us, about ten of the Clock in the morning within the reach of our Cannon, and were welcomed with our mettall; good execution being done upon them, their Foot as yet undiscovered. About halfe an houre after, I caused a strong Party of Foot (seconded with Horse) to line the hedges, who galled them in their passage to the Fords, after whose handsome retreat, I began to ensafe the Ports, which I did that night. In the morning, appeared their Body of Foot, and we found our selves surrounded. I injoyned the Bells silence, least their ringing, which was an Alarme to awaken our devotion, might Chime them together to the execution of their malice. For the same reason, I stopt our Clocks, and hereby though I prevented their telling tales, to the advantage of the Enemy, I myselfe lost the punctuall observation of many particulars, which therefore I must more confusedly represent unto your Lordship.

Before they attempted any thing against the Towne, they invited us to a Surrendry, and this they did by a double Summons, one from

Leven, directed to me; the other from the Committee of both Kingdomes (attending on the affaires of the Army) sent to the Major and Corporation: but we complyed so well in our Resolutions, that our positive answer served for both Parties, which was returned by me to their Generall.

This not giving that satisfaction they desired, they began to approach upon the first of August, but very slowly and modestly; as yet intending more the security of their owne persons, then the ruine of ours: but all their Art could not protect them from our small and great shot which fell upon them. Besides this, our men galled them handsomly at their severall Sallies, over Wyebridge, once beat them up to their maine guard, and at another demolisht one side of St Martin's Steeple: which would have much annoyed us at the Bridge and Pallace; this was performed with the hurt only of two men, but with losse of great store of the Enemies men.

When they saw how difficult the Service would prove, before they could compasse their designes by force, they made use of another Engine which was flattery. The Major and Aldermen are courted to yeeld the Towne by an Epistle, subscribed by six of the Country Gentlemen, very compassionate and suasory: but upon our refusall to stoup to this lure, they were much incensed that they had been so long disappointed, and having all this while continued their line of Communication, they raised their Batteries, commencing at Wye-bridge, from whence they received the greatest dammage, but instead of revenging that losse upon us, they multiplied their owne, by the death of their much lamented Major Generall Crafford, and some others that fell with him. This provoked them to play hot upon the Gate for two days together, and battered it so much, (being the weakest) that it was rendered uselesse, yet our men stopt it up with Wooll-sacks and Timber, and for our greater assurance of eluding their attempt, we brake in Arch, and raised a very strong Worke behind it.

The Enemy frustrate of his hopes here, raiseth two severall Batteries, one at the Fryers, the other on the other side of Wye River, and from both these, playes his Ordinance against the corner of the wall by Wye side, but we repaire and line our walls faster then they can batter them, whereupon they desist.

About the 11th of August, we discover a Mine at Frein-gate, and imploy workmen to countermine them. When we had stopt the progresse of that Mine on one side of the Gate, they carried it on the other; which we also defeated by making a Sally-Port: and issuing forth did break it open and fire it.

About the 13th, they raise Batteries round about the Town, and make a Bridge over Wye River.

The 14th, Doctor Scudamore is sent by them to desire admittance for three Country Gentlemen, who pretended in their Letters to import something of consequence to the good of the City and County, free leave of ingresse and egresse was allowed them, but being admitted, their suggestions were found to us so frivolous and impertinent, that they were dismisd not without some disrelish and neglect: and the said Doctor, after they were past the Port, coming back from his company, was unfortunately slaine by a shot from the Enemy.

About the 16th, they discover the face of their Battery against Frein-gate, with five severall gun-ports, from hence they played foure Cannon joyntly at our walls, and made a breach, which was instantly made up; they doe the like on the other side with the like successe.

The 17th, a notable Sally was made at St Owens Church with great execution, and divers Prisoners taken with the losse only of one man, at which time little boyes strived, which should first carry Torches and Faggots to fire their works, which was performed to some purpose, and so it was at the same Sally-port once before, though with a fewer number, and therefore with lesse execution.

And I may not forget to acquaint your Lordship with those other foure Sallies, made by us at the Castle to good effect, and what emulation there was between the Souldier and Citizens, which should be most ingaged in them: Now their losse of Prisoners, slaughter of men, and dishonour of being beaten out of their works, which they found ready to flame about their eares if they returned presently into them, had so kindled their indignation, that presently they raysed Batteries against Saint Owens Church, and plaid fiercely at it, but to little purpose, which they so easily perceived, that from the 20, unto the 27, there was a great calme on all sides, we as willing to provide ourselves, and preserve our ammunition for a storme, as they could be industrious or malitious to bring it upon us: yet I cannot say either side was Idle; for they ply'd their Mine at Saint Owens, and prepared for Scaling, we countermined, imploy'd our boyes by day and night to steale out and fire their Works, securing their retreat under the protection of our Musquetiers upon the wall, and what our fire could not perfect, though it burnt farre, and suffocated some of their Miners, our water did, breaking in upon them and drowning that which the fire had not consumed, and this saved us the pains of pursuing a mine, which we had sunk on purpose to render theirs in that place ineffectuall.

The 29th, Leven (a merciful Generall) assayes the Towne againe by his last offer of honourable conditions to surrender, but he found us still unrelenting, the terror of his Cannon, making no impression at all upon our Spirits, though the bullets discharged from them, had done so much against our walls: this (though some of their chiefe Commanders were remisse and coole at the debate and some

451

contradictory) drives their greatest spirits into a passionate resolution of storming.

And to that purpose August 31th, and September 1, they prepare Ladders, hurdles, and other accommodations for the advancing their designe, and secuting their persons in the attempt, and played very hot with their Cannon upon Bysters gate, and the halfe moon next Saint Owens gate, intending the morrow after to fall on, presuming as they boasted, that after they had rung us this passing peale, they should presently force the Garrison to give up her Loyall Ghost, but the same night His Majesty advancing from Worcester, gave them a very hot alarum, and drawing a little neerer to us, like the Sunne to the Meridian, this Scottish mist beganne to disperse, and the next morning vanished out of sight. My Lord, I should give your Lordship an accompt of the valor of our common Souldiers and Townesmen, that would hazard themselves at the making up of breaches (to the astonishment of the Enemy, till their Cannon played between their leggs, and even the Women (such was their gallantry) ventred where the Musquet bullets did so, and I should acquaint your Honour, what frequent alarums we gave them by fire-balls, lights upon our Steeple, by Dogs, Cats, and outworne Horses, having light Matches tyed about them; and turned out upon their works, whereby we put the enemy in such distraction, that sometimes they charged one another; this recreation we had in the middest of our besiedging: and one morning, instead of beating Reveillie, we had a crye of Hounds, in pursuit after the traine of a Fox about the Walls of the Citty, so little were we dismaied at the threats or attempts of them. I may not forget one remarkable peece of Divine providence, that God sent us singular men of all professions, very usefull, and necessary for us in this distresse, and so accidentally to us, as if they had on purpose been let downe from Heaven, to serve our present and emergent occasions; as skilfull Miners, excellent Cannoneers, (one whereof spent but one shot in vaine throughout the whole Siedge) an expert Carpenter, the only man in all the Country to make Mills, without whom we had been much disfurnisht of a meanes to make Powder (after our Powder-mill was burnt) or grind Corne; that providence that brought these to us, at last drove our Enemies from us, after the destruction of four or five Mines, which since appears to be their number, the expence of 300 Cannon shot, besides other Ammunition spent with Muskets, the losse by their owne confession of 1200, and as the Country sayes 2000 men, we in all not loosing about 21 by all Casualties whatsoever. Thus craving your Lordships pardon for my prolixity, I take leave and rest

Your Lordship's most humble servant

BER. SCUDAMORE.

Being cut off from our forage, and having no provision of hay and oats in the town, on Satuday the fifteenth of July, about ten at night, we attempted to break away with part of our horse, ordering them to march northward, and join with the Scotch Armie, who, as we were informed by private letters, were upon their march to our relief . . . But the enemy having blocked up all the passes, we failed in our attempt, which upon second thoughts we thankfully acknowledged to Providence preserving us against our design. For had the horse passed we had wanted their flesh, upon which we fed six weeks; and their riders whom as we ordered, made the strongest part of our defence; for as their horses were slaughtered for our provision, they were armed with halberds, brown bills, and scythes, straightened and fastened to handles, about six foot long, weapons which the enemy strongly apprehended, but rather of terror than use, for they required such distances to manage them, that they could not be brought to fight in a gross. These were divided into three companies and commanded by my Lord of Norwich, the Lord Capell, and Sir Charles Lucas, who took their posts and hutted themselves upon the line, where they fed and lodged with their souldiers, a wise and worthy undertaking to revive the antient discipline; for though we humbly confess our sins, the primary cause which hath pulled down these judgments upon us, yet we look upon our luxuries and remissness in discipline as the proximate causes of our ruin. For many of our general officers in the former wars had such indulgence for their debaucheries that they adopted none to preferments but the companions of their pleasures.

The enemy began their approaches on the east part of the town, called Berrie fields, which we suffered with great silence from our cannon, for besides our want of ammunition we desired an assault, as the likeliest means of our relief; only to free us from surprise we were forced to fire some of the neighbouring houses of the suburbs, where the enemy might have lodged their whole army within pistol shot of our walls . . .

The last month passed quietly, for the enemy knew that we must be reduced by our wants, and we allowed them to make their approaches unchecked for lack of ammunition.

The besieged were at last compelled to reduce the allowance of bread to seven ounces a day. 'It was received without murmuring by the souldiers, though being made of mault, oats, and rye which had taken salt water, it was not only distasteful, but such unwholesome food, that many chose to eat their horse and dog's flesh without it. But the greater suffering was of the poor inhabitants, who were reduced to that extremity that they ate soape and candle, which they endured with notable resolution . . . But upon review of our magazine and the provisions of private families, we found our store so little, that it was thought fit time to send a letter to Fairfax, wherein we proposed that if he would grant a truce for twenty days, and a pass for a messenger to find out Sir Marmaduke Langdale, if we were informed that in that interim he were not in a condition to relieve us, then we would treat with him upon a surrender. But the insolent enemy refused it, whereupon we resolved to continue our defence, hoping that the justice of our cause and the temper of our proceedings might in some degree make us worthy of the protection of Providence and our friends.

5 Accounts of Lansdown and Second Newbury from Clarendon's 'History'

From Clarendon's *History of the Rebellion* I have taken accounts of the Battle of Lansdown and the Second Battle of Newbury. The book was begun in 1646 but not published until 1702; his battle descriptions are extremely vivid.

These extracts appear by courtesy of the Oxford University Press, who hold perpetual copyright on Clarendon's work.

After this disposition, and eight or ten days' rest at Wells, the army generally expressing a cheerful impatience to meet with the enemy, of which, at that time, they had a greater contempt, than in reason they should have; the prince and marquis advanced to Frome, and thence to Bradford, within four miles of Bath. And now no day passed without action, and very sharp skirmishes; sir William Waller having received from London a fresh regiment of five hundred horse, under the command of sir Arthur Haslerig: which were so completely armed, that they were called by the other side the regiment of

lobsters, because of their bright iron shells, with which they were
covered, being perfect cuirassiers; and were the first seen so armed on
either side, and the first that made any impression upon the king's
horse; who, being unarmed, were not able to bear a shock with them;
besides that they were secure from hurts of the sword, which were
almost the only weapons the other were furnished with.

The contention was hitherto with parties; in which the successes
were various, and almost with equal losses: for as sir William Waller,
upon the first advance from Wells, beat up a regiment of horse and
dragoons of sir James Hamilton's, and dispersed them; so, within two
days, the king's forces beat a party of his from a pass near Bath, where
the enemy lost two field-pieces, and near an hundred men. But sir
William Waller had the advantage in his ground, having a good city,
well furnished with provisions, to quarter his army together in; and
so in his choice not to fight, but upon extraordinary advantage.
Whereas the king's forces must either disperse themselves, and so
give the enemy advantage upon their quarters, or, keeping near
together, lodge in the field, and endure great distress of provision; the
country being so disaffected, that only force could bring in any
supply or relief. Hereupon, after several attempts to engage the
enemy to a battle upon equal terms, which, having the advantage, he
wisely avoided; the marquis and prince Maurice advanced with their
whole body to Marsfield, five miles beyond Bath towards Oxford;
presuming, that, by this means, they should draw the enemy from
their place of advantage, his chief business being to hinder them from
joining with the king. And if they had been able to preserve that
temper, and had neglected the enemy, till he had quitted his
advantages, it is probable they might have fought upon as good terms
as they desired. But the unreasonable contempt they had of the
enemy, and confidence they should prevail in any ground, together

456

with the straits they endured for want of provisions, and their want of ammunition, which was spent as much in the daily hedge skirmishes, and upon their guards, being so near as could have been in battle, would not admit that patience; for sir William Waller, who was not to suffer that body to join with the king, no sooner drew out his whole army to Lansdown, which looked towards Marsfield, but they suffered themselves to be engaged upon great disadvantage.

It was upon the fifth of July when sir William Waller, as soon as it was light, possessed himself of that hill; and after he had, upon the brow of the hill over the high way, raised breast-works with fagots and earth, and planted cannon there, he sent a strong party of horse towards Marsfield, which quickly alarmed the other army, and was shortly driven back to their body. As great a mind as the king's forces had to cope with the enemy, when they had drawn into battalia, and found the enemy fixed on the top of the hill, they resolved not to attack them upon so great disadvantage; and so retired again towards their old quarters: which sir William Waller perceiving, sent his whole body of horse and dragoons down the hill, to charge the rear and flank of the king's forces; which they did throughly, the regiment of cuirassiers so amazing the horse they charged, that they totally routed them; and, standing firm and unshaken themselves, gave so great terror to the king's horse, who had never before turned from an enemy, that no example of their officers, who did their parts with invincible courage, could make them charge with the same confidence, and in the same manner they had usually done. However, in the end, after sir Nicholas Slanning, with three hundred musketeers, had fallen upon and beaten their reserve of dragooners, prince Maurice and the earl of Carnarvon, rallying their horse, and winging them with the Cornish musketeers, charged the enemy's horse again, and totally routed them; and in the same manner received two bodies more, and roused and chased them to the hill; where they stood in a place almost inaccessible. On the brow of the hill there were breast-works, on which were pretty bodies of small shot, and some cannon; on either flank grew a pretty thick wood towards the declining of the hill, in which strong parties of musketeers were placed; at the rear was a very fair plain, where the reserves of horse and foot stood ranged; yet the Cornish foot were so far from being appalled at this disadvantage, that they desired to fall on, and cried out, 'that they might have leave to fetch off those cannon'. In the end, order was given to attempt the hill with horse and foot. Two strong parties of musketeers were sent into the woods, which flanked the enemy; and the horse and other musketeers up the road way, which were charged by the enemy's horse, and routed; then sir Bevil Greenvil advanced with a party of horse, on his right hand, that ground being best for them; and his musketeers on the left; himself leading up his pikes in the middle; and in the face of their cannon, and small-shot from the breast-works, gained the brow of the hill. having sustained two full charges of the enemy's horse; but in the third charge his horse failing, and giving ground, he received, after other wounds, a blow on the head with a pole-axe, with which he fell, and many of his officers about him; yet the musketeers fired so fast upon the enemy's horse, that they quitted their ground, and the two wings, who were sent to clear the woods, having done their work, and gained those parts of the hill, at the same time beat off their enemy's foot, and became possessed of the breast-works; and so made way for their whole body of horse, foot, and cannon, to ascend the hill; which they quickly did, and planted themselves on the ground they had won; the enemy retiring about demi-culverin shot behind a stone wall upon the same level, and standing in reasonable good order.

Either party was sufficiently tired, and battered, to be contented to stand still. The king's horse were so shaken, that of two thousand which were upon the field in the morning, there were not above six hundred on the top of the hill. The enemy was exceedingly scattered too, and had no mind to venture on plain ground with those who had beaten them from the hill; so that, exchanging only some shot from their ordnance, they looked one upon another till the night interposed. About twelve of the lock, it being very dark, the enemy made a show of moving towards the ground they had lost; but giving a smart volley of small-shot, and finding themselves answered with the like, they made no more noise: which the prince observing, he sent a common soldier to hearken as near the place, where they were, as he could; who brought word, 'that the enemy had left lighted matches in the wall behind which they had lain, and were drawn off the field;' which was true; so that, as soon as it was day, the king's army found themselves possessed entirely of the field, and the dead, and all other ensigns of victory: sir William Waller being marched to Bath, in so much disorder and apprehension, that he left great store of arms, and ten barrels of powder, behind him; which was a very seasonable supply to the other side, who had spent in that days service no less than fourscore barrels, and had not a safe proportion left.

In this battle, on the king's part, there were more officers and gentlemen of quality slain, than common men; and more hurt than slain. That which would have clouded any victory, and made the loss of others less spoken of, was the death of sir Bevil Greenvil. He was indeed an excellent person, whose activity, interest, and reputation, was the foundation of what had been done in Cornwall; and his temper and affections so public, that no accident which happened could make any impressions in him; and his example kept other from taking any thing ill, or at least seeming to do so. In a word, a brighter courage, and a gentler disposition, were never married together to make the most cheerful and innocent conversation.

Very many officers and persons of quality were hurt; as the lord Arundel of Wardour, shot in the thigh with a brace of pistol bullets; sir Ralph Hopton, shot through the arm with a musket; sir George Vaughan, and many others, hurt in the head of their troops with swords and pole-axes; of which none of name died. But the morning added much to the melancholy of their victory, when the field was entirely their own. For sir Ralph Hopton riding up and down the field to visit the hurt men, and to put the soldiers in order, and readiness for motion, sitting on his horse, with other officers and soldiers about him, near a waggon of ammunition, in which were eight barrels of powder; whether by treachery, or mere accident, is uncertain, the powder was blown up; and many, who stood nearest, killed; and many more maimed; among whom sir Ralph Hopton and sergent major Sheldon were miserably hurt.

Second Newbury

With his own, and the forces which had been under Essex, Major-general Philip Skippon fell upon the quarter at Speen, and passed the river; which was not well defended by the officer who was appointed to guard it with horse and foot, very many of them being gone off from their guards, as never imagining that they would, at that time of day, have attempted a quarter that was thought the strongest of all. But having thus got the river, they marched in good order, with very great bodies of foot, winged with horse, towards the heath; from whence the horse which were left there, with too little resistance, retired; being in truth much overpowered, by reason the major part of them, upon confidence of security of the pass, were gone to provide forage for their horse.

By this means the enemy possessed themselves of the ordnance which had been planted there, and of the village of Speen; the foot which were there retired to the hedge next the large field between Speen and Newbury; which they made good: at the same time, the right wing of the enemy's horse advanced under the hill of Speen, with one hundred musketeers in the van, and came into the open field, where a good body of the king's horse stood, which at first received them in some disorder; but the queen's regiment of horse, commanded by sir John Cansfield, charged them with so much gallantry, that he routed that great body; which then fled; and he had the execution of them near half a mile; wherein most of the musketeers were slain, and very many of the horse; insomuch that the whole wing rallied not again that night. The king was at that time with the prince, and many of the lords, and other his servants, in the middle of that field; and would not, by his own presence, restrain those horse, which at the first approach of the enemy were in that disorder, from shamefully giving ground. So that if sir John Cansfield had not, in that article of time, given them that brisk charge, by which other troops were ready to charge them in the flank, the king himself had been in very great danger.

At the same time, the left wing of the enemy's horse advanced towards the north side of the great field; but, before they got thither, Goring, with the earl of Cleveland's brigade, charged them so vigorously, that he forced them back in great confusion over a hedge; and following them, was charged by another fresh body, which he defeated likewise, and slew very many of the enemy upon the place; having not only routed and beaten them off their ground, but endured the shot of three bodies of their foot in their pursuit, and in their retreat, with no considerable damage, save that the earl of Cleveland's horse falling under him, he was taken prisoner; which was an extraordinary loss. Whilst this was doing on that side, twelve hundred horse, and three thousand foot, of those under the earl of Manchester, advanced with great resolution upon Shawhouse, and the field adjacent; which quarter was defended by sir Jacob Astley and colonel George Lisle; and the house, by lieutenant colonel Page. They came singing of psalms; and, at first, drove forty musketeers from a hedge, who were placed there to stop them; but they were presently charged by sir John Brown, with the prince's regiment of horse; who did good execution upon them, till he saw another body of their horse ready to charge him, which made him retire to the foot in Mr Doleman's garden, which flanked that field, and gave fire upon those horse, whereof very many fell; and the horse thereupon wheeling about, sir John Brown fell upon their rear, killed many, and kept that ground all the day; when the reserve of foot, commanded by colonel Thelwell, galled their foot with several vollies, and then fell on them with the but-ends of their muskets, till they had not only beaten them from the hedges, but quite out of the field; leaving two drakes, some colours, and many dead bodies behind them. At this time, a great body of their foot attempted Mr Doleman's house, but were so well entertained by lieutenant colonel Page, that, after they had made their first effort, they were forced to retire in such confusion, that he pursued them from the house with a notable execution, insomuch that they left five hundred dead upon a little spot of ground; and they drew off the two drakes out of the field to the house, the enemy being beaten off, and retired from all that quarter.

It was now night; for which neither party was sorry; and the king, who had been on that side where the enemy only had prevailed, thought that his army had suffered alike in all other places. He saw they were entirely possessed of Speen, and had taken all the ordnance which had been left there; whereby it would be easy for them, before the next morning, to have compassed him round; towards which they might have gone far, if they had found themselves in a condition to have pursued their fortune.

Hereupon, as soon as it was night, his majesty, with the prince, and those lords who had been about him all the day, and his regiment of guards, retired into the fields under Donnington-castle, and resolved to prosecute the resolution that was taken in the morning, when they saw the great advantage the enemy had in numbers, with which he was like to be encompassed, if his forces were beaten from either of the posts. That resolution was, 'to march away in the night towards Wallingford;' and to that purpose, all the carriages and great ordnance had been that morning drawn under Donnington-castle; so he sent orders to all the officers to draw off their men to the same place; and receiving intelligence at that time that prince Rupert was come, or would be that night at Bath, that he might make no stay there, but presently be able to join with his army, his majesty himself, with the prince, and about three hundred horse, made haste thither, and found prince Rupert there, and thence made what haste they could back towards Oxford. The truth is, the king's army was not in so ill a condition, as the king conceived it to have been: that party which were in the field near Speen, kept their ground very resolutely; and although it was a fair moonshine night, the enemy, that was very near them, and much superior in number, thought not fit to assault or disturb them. That part of the enemy that had been so roughly treated at Shaw, having received succour of a strong body of horse, resolved once more to make an attempt upon the foot there; but they were beaten off as before.

BOOK FOUR

Scotland and the Border

Introduction

There is a widespread belief that England and Scotland fought ferociously in time of war but that otherwise there was peace in the north. This is far from the truth. For centuries, families from either country would make forays across the border. When such raids became too continuous, too destructive, and too successful, a whole district would rise in arms and make a punitive reprisal. Nobody expected – or would have wished – otherwise. These activities stemmed not so much from greed, aggression, or patriotism, as from boredom and lack of leisure-time pursuits. There was seldom peace in the north and the result of this was that, when full-scale war came, there were abundant supplies of hardened fighting men to draw on. They did not, in those early days, care to travel too far from home and there was a tendency to leave early in a campaign with a good share of plunder. But, while they were fighting, they were not usually stopped while there was life in their bodies.

Nor was fighting always across the border. The 'other country' was always there but in one's own – on either side of the border – there were plenty of old and new scores to settle. Every family, every tribe, and every clan had a hated rival and opponent. In fact it was easier to fight one's neighbour than a foreigner; one had no particular grudge against the men one had never seen, but a neighbour or a kinsman – that was a different story.

In consequence, the borderers, whether English or Scottish, acquired over the centuries a formidable fighting reputation.

They were not, it will be freely acknowledged, necessarily better than men from other parts of the British Isles but they were certainly as good. Furthermore, they were remarkably consistent. Nowadays, in their wisdom, the politicians who so rarely seem to understand the implications of their reorganizations and economies, their rationalizations and modernizing, have abolished all the English border regiments. The Durhams are now part of the Light Infantry, an anonymous term which includes such regiments as the Shropshires, the Somersets, and the Duke of Cornwall's. The Northumberland Fusiliers are but another battalion of the Fusiliers, and the Border Regiment has been included in a Lancastrian unit. All these new companions in arms have a mutual respect, and accepted the amalgamations gracefully, if not entirely happily, but whether this is the best possible use of resources is another matter. It may be argued that regiments have never fought better than when they were the 24th or 42nd or 88th, but conditions were very different then and there have been few parts of the army more impressive than the County regiments in two world wars and innumerable other missions.

This book is not, of course, about the border regiments but it naturally makes many references to them, and in some ways explains their fine military records.

Scottish regiments are, very properly, famed throughout the world and have many would-be imitators. Regiments such as the Black Watch, the Greys, the Seaforths, the Gordons, and the Argylls, to name but a few, have fought with a distinction which has almost romanticized the bloody and ugly business of war.

In order to understand the battles which are described in detail later in this book, it is necessary to have a grasp of the main stages in the evolution of Scotland. It will be noted, perhaps with surprise, that Northumberland and Cumberland were once considered part of Scotland. Scottish history is only explicable by reference to earlier history and to geography. It is, unfortunately, not possible to identify many of the very early battlefields precisely, but the visitor who studies the campaigns and the country carefully will probably not be far wrong in his guess. Scotland is very much aware of her past, and rightly proud of the men who made it. We begin therefore by summarizing the main events and drawing attention to matters we feel were of lasting significance.

The fighting qualities of the Scots were noted even in Roman times. Then they wre known as Caledonians or Picts and they fought lightly armed and half-naked. Nevertheless they were a formidable threat to the well-equipped, trained, and disciplined Roman legions. Whether they acquired their name because they were *picti* (painted) or whether they were recognized as a branch of the Pictones, a tribe which the Romans had encountered in what is now Portugal, is not known, and never will be. Like many primitive warriors they painted themselves, partly to inspire fear and partly for camouflage; the Romans themselves sometimes did the same. When the Roman general, Agricola, pushed into Scotland in the year 80 he lost many men. But his campaign was meant to intimidate, so he devastated the country up to the Tweed. The next year he pushed further ahead and secured his victories by building a chain of forts between the Forth and the Clyde. Difficult though his progress had been before, it was now noticeably harder. In the year 83 he was campaigning up the east coast. Here he was coming to the heartland of the Caledonians. It would be pleasurable to walk over the battlefield where he fought with them at 'Mons Graupius' but our knowledge of that battle is so limited that we do not even know precisely where it was fought. It is generally believed that it was in the region just to the south-west of Aberdeen. However we do at least possess Tacitus's book, *Agricola*. Agricola was Tacitus's father-in-law and was at the time Governor of Britain, which was classed as a Roman province. Tacitus describes the campaign as follows:

> Sending on his fleet therefore to excite a wide and indefinite alarm by devastating several places, and with a light-armed force in which he had incorporated the most valiant of the Britons, and such as were tested by long fidelity he arrived at the Grampian hills, which the enemy had already invested. For the Britons [by which he means the Caledonians] never dispirited by the result of the late engagement, and anticipating vengeance or slavery, and taught at length that their common danger could be fended off by unanimity alone, had called into action the powers of all the states by embassies and confederacies. More than thirty thousand armed men were now available, and still all the youths were pouring in, and even those whose age was fresh and vigorous, distinguished in the field, and bearing their several trophies. On this occasion a chieftain, named Galgacus, eminent among the rest in valour and rank, is said to have addressed the assembled throng, clamouring for battle, to the following effect:

> We have no territory behind us, nor is even the sea secure while the Roman fleet hovers round us so that resistance and war, creditable to the brave, are also safest. The late engagements in which we strove with alternating success against the Romans depended for hopes and means upon our hands, because we, the noblest nation of all Britain, and therefore dwelling in its deepest recesses, and not even beholding the shores of bondsmen, have kept our eyes untainted by the infection of tyranny. Dwelling upon the utmost limits of the earth

and freedom, our very remoteness, the last retreat of heroism, has hitherto defended us. Now the extremity of Britain is exposed and the unknown is ever indefinitely grand. There is now no nation beyond us, nothing save the billows and the rocks and the Romans, still more savage, whose tyranny you will in vain appease by submission and concession. Alone of all men they covet with equal rapacity the rich and the needy. Plunder, murder and robbery, under false pretences, they call "Empire" and when they make a wilderness they call it 'Peace'.

This dramatic speech is highly revealing. Not only does it give numbers – and here we may trust them – but it also throws considerable light on the mental attitude of the ancient inhabitants of Scotland. The same attitude persisted in many later centuries. It showed an intense passion for freedom and independence, and an equally strong desire not to be conquered by the Romans whom they considered to be less civilized than themselves. Galgacus is apparently well informed about what went on in areas the Romans had already subdued:

Our wives and sisters, though they escape forcible violation, are insulted under pretexts of friendship and hospitality. Our possessions and properties they consume in taxes, our crops in subsidies. They wear out our bodies and strength in stripes and degradation, in clearing roads through fens and forests . . . Abandoning all help of indulgence therefore take courage at last, as well those who value their safety as they to whom glory is most dear. Do you believe that the same value is present in the Romans on the battlefield as is proportionate to their insolence in peace . . . they have nothing formidable to fall back on – empty fortresses, colonies of old men, borough-towns disaffected between refractory subjects and tyrannical governors. On the one side you have a general and an army; on the other the taxes, the mines and all the penalties of slavery; and to perpetuate these for ever, or to avenge them, now awaits decision on this plain. Therefore as you march to action, remember your ancestors – think of posterity.

This speech, somewhat abbreviated here, was received with great enthusiasm. Agricola therefore decided to add a few words to his own troops whose morale was high but perhaps not quite high enough. Tacitus mentions that they were with difficulty restrained within the trenches or fortifications. This suggests that when they observed the size of the opposing force they had hastily dug themselves in. Agricola's message does not really concern us for we are not commenting on the Roman martial spirit. His speech was steadier than that of Galgacus but not less inflammatory.

While Agricola yet spoke, [continues Tacitus] the enthusiasm of the soldiers began to show itself, and a strong excitement followed the conclusion of his address, and they flew at once to arms. In this ardour and impetuosity he so arranged them that the infantry auxiliaries, amounting to eight thousand, formed a strong centre and three thousand cavalry were dispersed on the wings. The legions took their position outside the entrenchments – an arrangement which would be a remarkable distinction to the victory if they succeeded without loss to the Romans – and a resource if they retreated. The lines of the Britons had so taken their stand upon the rising ground – for show and intimidation – that the van formed upon the plain, and the rest, in close array, rose in a manner line above line on the acclivity and the charioteers and cavalry, with cries and evolutions, occupied the intervening space.

It must have been a considerable strain to the nerves to wait through the preliminaries of a battle in those times. Having seen the opposing force and noticed that they outnumbered yours, or were better armed, you then had to listen to a long harangue designed to make you fight to the death and neither give nor ask quarter. It was a foretaste of the atrocity stories of which we should hear so much in later wars, and which would all usually be true in spite of efforts to discredit them.

The Scots (Britons or Caledonians) occupied the period before battle in the most extraordinary evolutions and manoeuvres. The Romans had already noted that they were able to run along their long chariot-poles while their horses were at full gallop and also to leap on and off the chariots while they were hurtling along at speed. Doubt-less they dismissed these antics as mere conjuring tricks designed to impress one's own side as much as to intimidate the enemy.

Then Agricola, as the enemy were superior in numbers, apprehend-ing a charge in front and on the flanks, expanded his ranks and, though his lines would apparently be too far extended and many recommended that the legions should be brought up, feeling more sanguine in hope and undismayed by difficulties, he sent back his horse and placed himself on foot before the standards.

At the commencement of the action the contest was maintained from a distance. The Britons, with long swords and narrow shields, firmly and dexterously parried and repelled the missiles of our troops, while they showered upon them a dense volley of their own; until Agricola called upon three cohorts of Batavians and two of the Tungri, to bring the encounter to the sword and closing fight, which was familiar to them from their experience of the service and inconvenient to the enemy, who carried small shields and unwieldy

473

swords. For the swords of the Britons, being unpointed, admitted of no collision or hand-to-hand encounter. Then the Batavians began to repeat their blows, to wound them with the bosses of their shields, to cut their faces, and drive back up the hill those who had opposed them on level ground. The other cohorts, joining in the attack through rivalry or enthusiasm, cut down all who met them, and through their anxiety for victory many were left fainting and unharmed. The troops of enemy cavalry now took to flight and the charioteers entangled themselves among the fighting infantry; though they had spread alarm not yet abated they were impeded by the close ranks of the enemy and the unevenness of the ground. Thus this part of the battle bore no resemblance to a cavalry engagement: after a long and inconvenient wait they were carried along with their horses, and frequently with unmanned chariots and riderless horses, and ran down all who stood in their panic-stricken path.

This account, which is translated fairly literally from the original Latin, at times seems stilted. Nevertheless, it gives a vivid picture of the chaos, confusion, and variety of the battle between Roman legions and Scots. Even a partisan Roman writer cannot obscure the fact that the wild tribesmen of the north had a steadiness and cohesion which more civilized nation might have envied. This becomes increasingly clear as the description continues.

And now the Britons, who had yet taken no part in the action and were posted on the hilltops looking with disdain at our unequal numbers, began to descend and enclose the rear of the Romans, and would have succeeded had not Agricola, apprehending this man-oeuvre, opposed their progress with four battalions of cavalry, reserved for emergencies; the more spiritedly they came on the more actively did he disperse them and put them to rout.

What now began to happen was that as the Scots folded themselves around the Roman rear so they themselves were encircled by
the Roman reserve cavalry.

Then, [says Tacitus], a strange and awful scene presented itself on
the plain. They pursued, they wounded, made prisoners and these,
when others came, they put to death. In one place companies of
armed men would flee before smaller numbers while others, unarmed, would voluntarily charge forward and rush to their deaths.
Arms, bodies and mangled limbs lay everywhere and the ground ran
blood. Sometimes, too, fury and courage inspired even the vanquished and when they approached the woods they rallied and cut off
the nearest of their pursuers, who were unprepared and did not know
the ground.

This was where Agricola's experience and generalship were of
paramount importance. He moved rapidly from one part of the field
to another and quickly sized up the dangers of the situation.
Realizing that he could lose many men in the pursuit, and might
even be counterattacked, he hastily posted cohorts along the
perimeter of the battlefield. Where there were undergrowth and
thickets he strengthened the line with dismounted cavalry. At the
same time he despatched other, still mounted, cavalry, to scour the
open parts of the woods and to harry the retreating Scots without
themselves being ambushed. The organized and methodical pursuit
upset the orderly Scottish retreat and men now broke away from
their companies and took to flight. Only darkness put an end to the
pursuit. Tacitus claims that ten thousand Scots were killed for the
loss of only three hundred and sixty Romans but he mentions that
among them was a senior commander, high in rank though young in
years. The figure of ten thousand for the Scots seems suspiciously

high. However, when we consider that the Scots were surrounded on one part of the battlefield, where they were presumably methodically slaughtered, and also put in a fighting withdrawal, their losses were probably in thousands. The Romans had won a day's battle but not a campaign, and for all they knew further resistance might already be assembling. They did not seem to be in entire control of the battlefield, for it is related that the Scots were collecting their wounded, and even trying to release prisoners. Agricola sent out reconnaissance parties the next day but they encountered no further resistance; 'the silence of desolation' was all around.

However, there was no chance of consolidating this victory, for winter was fast approaching. Winter meant withdrawal to 'winter quarters'. No one but a madman would try to campaign during the season of bad weather, particularly in Scotland.

It is a pity that the exact site of Mons Graupius is not known – although some say it is the Hill of Moncrieff. Much may be learned from a battlefield. If we knew the exact site we could work out the tactical plan: where Agricola stationed his reserve, how far away were the hills from which the Scots reserve watched the battle. There is mention of thickets and, to judge by the way the Romans encircled the Scots, thereby turning the tables and effecting a complete tactical surprise, it seems highly likely that the Scots used them for concealment. It should not be impossible to locate sites on which the battle as described by Tacitus could have been fought; and one might be so obvious that it would make the course of the battle perfectly understandable.

Mons Graupius, although the largest, was only one of a series of desperate battles the Scots fought with the Romans. Tactically, Mons Graupius was a mistake and the Scots did not repeat it. In future they did not oppose the Romans in solid formations which the

Romans could attack in their own way and in their own time; instead they resorted to raids and to luring the Romans into ambushes whenever possible. The Romans had had too much experience of this type of warfare to be caught often, and, instead of being drawn into wasteful fights in the heart of rugged Scotland, they decided to bar the Scots out of territories they themselves controlled. There were no more combined operations of the kind favoured by Agricola with the fleet sailing round the coast while the army probed inland. Instead, the Emperor Hadrian visited Britain in the year 120 and ordered that a wall should be built from the Tyne to the Solway. In its declining years the Roman Empire resorted to this expedient for keeping out what they called 'the barbarians'. Vast walls were built around whole countries, even though history had already proved the futility of such enterprise. 'If you wish for peace, prepare for war', and 'attack is the best form of defence' were well-known Roman slogans, but they did not always put them into practice. Hadrian's Wall, which took eighteen years to build and was strengthened by forts and towers at intervals, extended over seventy miles. It is an impressive monument today but was apparently less so to the Picts and Scots, for they attacked it incessantly and climbed over it apparently at will. As soon as two years after it had been built, the policy on which it was planned was abandoned and the Romans decided that it was necessary to push farther north. This brought to fame a Roman general named Lollius Urbicus, of whom little is known; but his achievements are a memorial of no mean kind. He drove the marauding Scots back to the line between the Forth and Clyde and then carried out the command of the Emperor Antoninus Pius to build yet another wall to hold them there. Unfortunately for Rome, the Antonine line proved to be no more impassable than Hadrian's Wall. Both are, however, a tribute to the Roman skill in military engineering, and are a joy to twentieth-century visitors; neither achieved its original purpose which was to keep out the northern raiders.

Our only source of information for the events of what might be called the early Dark Ages is Roman. In the year 200, the walls were clearly failing to control the border, for we have ominous reports of two tribes known respectively as the Caledonians and the Maeatae. So great was their menace that the Emperor Severus himself decided to deal with it, and in 208 he set off at the head of a punitive expedition. Like many a great general after him, he had to travel in a litter (he was elderly and much troubled by gout) and, like some of his successors, he was remarkably unsuccessful. But the Scots were not forgetful of the lesson they had learnt nearly 150 years before; instead of giving battle where it would have suited the Romans they led them on and on, frequently ambushing them but often merely melting away and letting climate and terrain do the rest. It is said, though doubtless with exaggeration, that Severus lost 50,000 men in this so-called punitive expedition. He was said to have reached 'the extremity of the island' whatever that may have meant. However, he seems to have had some success, for he extracted a treaty from the Caledonians by which they renounced their claim to some disputed territory. He is also credited with having built the 'Severus' wall but no one knows where it was meant to be, for no trace of it can be found.

Severus was, however, a fighter, pressing on, undeterred by losses and respected by his adversaries. His death in 211, when he was apparently planning another expedition, marks the end of formal Roman attempts to subdue Scotland. One hundred years later a brave attempt was made to intimidate the Scots when Theodosius was despatched to the border by the Roman Emperor, Valentinian.

Valentinian was a soldier of no mean order and, although the Empire he represented was crumbling, the Picts and Scots could not have been aware of it. Instead he drove them back with a series of vigorous attacks, isolating and cutting them off with a tactical skill which earned more than one victory. In respect for his achievement they ceded an unknown area which was called Valentia.

But it could not last; Rome was in decline. To their credit the Romans still tried to hold the boundaries of their Empire, but soon Rome itself was threatened and they had to withdraw. Perhaps their most durable monument, apart from Hadrian's Wall and the Antonine Wall, was Ptolemy's Geography. Although Ptolemy lived in Alexandria, Scotland appears in his atlas which lists seventeen tribes and nineteen towns. Some of this may be intelligent guess-work, or even mere hearsay, but much of it is probably well founded. You cannot fight a people for hundreds of years and sign treaties with them without acquiring some knowledge of their territories and resources. And if the Romans learnt something from the Scots, the Scots too must have learnt something from the invaders; not least was the need to combine, and yet, while combining, to fulfil a guerrilla role. It would not be an exaggeration to say that the Romans gave the first impetus to the unity of Scotland. Indirectly they initiated the tremendous religious fervour which has often spurred on Scottish armies. St Ninian, of whom very little is known, appears to have been the first missionary who tried to convert the Scots to Christianity. This was in the late fourth century and we do not know how much success he had in his lifetime, although he is said to have founded a church in Galloway. Even if the Romans had been able to stay in Britain and support him his task would have been formidable enough but as the Roman legions were all withdrawn during the early years of the next century it is hardly surprising that his achievements lacked permanence.

Saints in those days were not to be trifled with. A king who opposed St Ninian went blind. St Ninian restored his sight and enlisted him as a supporter. After St Ninian's death his relics cured the sick and terrified the wicked. Sixty churches were dedicated to him. However, his earthly achievements were as nothing to those of St Mungo of Strathclyde. When a hostile king mocked him for his poverty, a timely storm flooded the Clyde and swept away the royal granaries; fortuitously they were stranded just by the saint's house. Much displeased, the king and his chief minister rode off to punish St Mungo, and kicked him. The chief minister was then thrown from his horse and broke his neck; the king's foot swelled and caused his death; all his family then died one by one of the same affliction of the feet!

In the sixth century we find four different groups struggling for the mastery of Scotland. These were the Picts, the Britons, the Angles, and the Scots.

The Picts commanded the largest stretch of territory, for they were supreme in the whole area north of the Forth. At certain periods they divided into two groups, the northern and the southern, but most of the time were under one king who had minor kings under him. The Picts were Celts.

In the south-west, in the Strathclyde area, were Britons. These were the same stock as the inhabitants of Britain who had first opposed the Romans in 55 B.C. Four hundred years of Roman occupation had softened them, and after the Romans withdrew they were unable to defend themselves against the Saxons. Some settled in Cornwall, some in Wales, and some reached southern Scotland. Once in Scotland they had no choice but to recover some of their former warrior spirit. For centuries they were constantly under attack from north, east, and south. Not surprisingly, the inhabitants of that area in later years acquired a reputation for dour, tenacious military stamina.

On the west, in what is now Argyllshire (then called the Kingdom of Dalriada), was a colony of Celts who had come from Ireland. These, curiously enough, were known as the Scots. They contrived to maintain links with Ireland and also to avoid being absorbed by the northern Picts.

In addition there were the Angles. Some time during the sixth century, the Angles, who eventually gave their name to England, settled in the area just south of the Firth of Forth. This was called Bernicia and soon included the place which is now Edinburgh, as well as the fortress of Bamburgh in Northumbria.

Further to these there were three minor groupings which, though small, would play an important part in the future. These were Calatria, Mannan (note Clackmannan), and Galloway. The former two were eventually absorbed, but the inhabitants of Galloway were more enduring. Domiciled in the area now covered by Wigton and Kirkcudbright, it seemed at one stage that they, not the Picts, might dominate Scotland.

At the end of the sixth century, two hundred years after St Ninian had made his missionary attempt, the Picts were converted to Christianity by St Columba. Some part of Columba's success was due to the fact that he was a Christian soldier; when he laid aside the Bible for the broadsword, he earned respect from all sides. Among his other martial feats are said to be the slaying of a Loch Ness monster! Christianity, even if somewhat militant, caused national unity to become one step nearer, but it did not, of course, signify the end of battles, for war was a recreation and a way of life. During different periods, power ebbed and flowed from one area to another, but in the seventh and eighth centuries it is clear that a main area of hostility was building up along what we now describe as the border country. The activities of minor kings and chiefs on unknown battlefields are of significance to us only so far as they helped form a military pattern. Scotland was being born with all its remarkable regional characteristics. In the ninth century, Kenneth MacAlpin did much for the future kingdom of Scotland by transferring the seat of government from Iona to Dunkeld. Here the bones of St Columba were reinterred, making it a religious shrine as well as a political and military headquarters. But now, Scotland, like England, was attacked by more and more formidable foes. With Danes on one side and Norwegians on the other, it seemed that all that precarious Scottish unity and identity might be swept away. The Norwegians occupied the Orkneys and most of Caithness and Sutherland. The chronicle of battle, murder, and sudden death does not concern us here; suffice it to say that only at the beginning of the eleventh century did Scotland begin to assume her final form. Even so it would be the thirteenth century before the Scottish crown symbolized a physical Kingdom rather than a concept. Curiously enough, in the early part of this period, Scotland had to absorb refugees from Norman England; for, after the Battle of Hastings and the 'harrying of the north', many English wished for nothing better than to put themselves well out of reach of Norman law, taxation and tyranny.

Early in the eleventh century Scotland as we now know it began to take shape. Malcolm II , who reigned from 1005 to 1034, was largely responsible.[1] Malcolm gained Lothian and soon added Strathclyde to it. When Malcolm died he was succeeded by his grandson,

1 Scotland at this time was known as Alba.

Duncan. Duncan, who reigned for six years, has acquired an impressive reputation through being favourably represented in Shakespeare's *Macbeth*:

> *this Duncan*
> *Hath born his faculties so meek, hath been*
> *So clear in his great office.*

In fact, his six-year reign was one of almost unbroken disaster. His courage was not in question but his military skill did not match it. Every army he contrived to raise was scattered by his opponents and his fleet was no luckier. Macbeth, whose own claim to the throne was as good as Duncan's, eventually led a rebellion against this unhappy king and killed him at Bothgouanan, near Elgin. Macbeth's own reign between 1040 and 1057 was militarily successful. Furthermore he was an enthusiastic supporter of the church and distributed alms liberally. He was even said to have made a pilgrimage to Rome and distributed alms to the poor there. He was eventually killed in battle at Lumphanan in Aberdeenshire, not at Dunsinane where he fought an inconclusive battle. In view of this it might be wondered why Shakespeare depicted him as a treacherous villain and an unsuccessful one as well. The answer is that Shakespeare took his character from Holinshed, who in turn took his Macbeth from Wyntoun. Wyntoun was anxious to prove that the Scottish royal line stretched unbroken back to the dawn of history. As Macbeth was not of the direct line he had to be classed as a villainous usurper who had temporarily and illegally worn the crown.

Macbeth's successor was Malcolm iii also known as Malcolm Canmore. The distinguished name, 'Canmore' literally means 'big head' and is typical of the day when a man's name came from a physical deformity, his habits, or his job. Thus the Stuart was a sty-ward or pig-keeper; Ponsford meant 'fat guts'; Befin meant 'drinker'; and Cruikshanks described almost anyone with a limp. However, big head or not, Malcolm had a successful thirty-six year reign. Not only did he maintain a stable régime in Scotland; he also pushed his area of influence down to the Tyne. After one of his raids it was said that every cottage in Scotland had an English slave working in it. However, when William the Conqueror took an army and a fleet to Scotland Malcolm signed a treaty without fighting. It was, nevertheless, improbable that peace between Scotland and England could last, and we find that, when William went to France in 1079, the opportunity his absence presented to Malcolm was irresistible. Once again the Tweed-Tyne area was devastated. Once again, when the English took a great army to Scotland, it found no army to fight, nor supplies to live on, and eventually withdrew hoping that the threat had been enough; needless to say it had not. A somewhat better anti-invasion precaution was to build castles along the border route. One of them was New Castle on the Tyne.

In 1091 in the reign of William II (Rufus) Malcolm decided that the English would be fair game again, especially since Rufus was in Normandy, having considerable trouble with his brother Robert. On this occasion Malcolm miscalculated, for his forces were held and then forced to withdraw. Subsequently, Rufus came north with a large army and fleet. The fleet was wrecked in a storm, but the army invaded Lothian. Yet again there was no pitched battle, but Rufus annexed Carlisle and what is now Cumberland. This at the time was southern Strathclyde, the refuge of the Britons from Wales; it has been an English county ever since. Malcolm was prepared to give feudal homage to the English crown, but the annexation of part of Strathclyde was more than he could stomach. He travelled to Gloucester to protest in person to Rufus, but the English King refused even to see him. Once again Malcolm set out to harry the English border. Although his wife Margaret begged him not to go, he insisted on leading the expedition and ran into an ambush at Alnwick. It seems that some of his chiefs were not entirely reliable. Malcolm was killed, and, without his controlling hand, the army fell apart. Retreating hastily into Scotland, the Scots lost many men in trying to cross rivers which were swollen by rains; it was an unrelieved disaster. Malcolm's body was taken to Tynemouth in a peasant's cart. It was 1093. Seven years later William Rufus would be killed by an arrow while hunting in the New Forest and he too would make his last journey in a peasant's cart.

'Behind every great man stands a great woman.' In this case it was Queen Margaret. She was English by birth, being a granddaughter of Edward the Confessor, and did something to alleviate the miseries of those taken prisoner by her husband. She also established some refinements in the Scottish court and apparently took a leading part in administration when her husband was away. Her most noticeable characteristic was her piety, which went as far as self-mortification. As well as practising ascetic self-denial, she completed a routine of unattractive tasks, such as washing the feet of the poor and dressing offensive sores. She even made Malcolm take part in some of these ceremonies. When she died, four days after her husband, it was indeed a moment of truth; there was widespread reaction against the power she had wielded. Malcolm's brother tried to seize the throne in place of her sons and, to destroy a legend, to capture her body from Edinburgh Castle where it was still lying. Margaret's sons carried it away in secret but then had to flee themselves. The next few years saw brief reigns and intermittent bloodshed; then Scotland became more settled. In the twelfth century we find the notorious Alexander I, 'the Fierce', who married Sibylla, one of the illegitimate daughters

of Henry I of England.[1] Henry I, incidentally, founded Norham
Castle on the Tweed to help 'keep the border'; few castles have seen
as much fighting as Norham. Alexander established the monastery of
Scone, which he peopled with Augustinian monks from Yorkshire.
On the charters from his reign appear names – among them were
Bruce, Lindsay, Umphraville and FitzAlan – which were to recur
over and over again in Scottish history. In spite of his nickname,
acquired when suppressing some of his dissident subjects, Alexander
was genuinely religious. When he died in 1124, his brother David,
who succeeded him, was no less competent though less independent.
David had the backing of those Norman knights who had settled in
Scotland. He was therefore able to consolidate his kingdom and even
to extend it slightly. However, co-operation with the English throne
led him into considerable difficulties when the English crown was
disputed between Matilda, daughter of Henry I, and Stephen, his
nephew. As Matilda was David's niece he was bound to support her.
His support took a very practical turn in 1136 when he took an army
across the border and captured every castle in Cumberland and
Northumberland with the exception of Bamburgh. Stephen, always
ready for another long gruelling campaign, however strategically
unwise, set off north to teach him a lesson. The lesson, in the event,
was not needed, for David, recognizing a fellow warrior, promptly
signed a treaty by which he agreed to give no further trouble.

Treaties, of course, are only durable if they are made in good faith
and are enforceable. This one was neither. On the strength of an
insult to his son, David decided that England must be taught a
lesson once more; he therefore set off southwards, destroying and

1 Henry I's wife was even more devout and ascetic than Queen Margaret of Scotland had been but
Henry, the man who was said never to have smiled for fifteen years, had a distinct proclivity for
begetting 'natural' offspring.

burning. It was said that he tried to restrain the wilder atrocities but was apparently largely unsuccessful. Stephen came up to met him, and David then retreated skilfully. Near Roxburgh, the Scottish king laid a most ingenious ambush. Whether Stephen learnt of this through spies, or whether he had a nose for a dangerous situation, is not on record, but the result was that he slipped by, devastated the surrounding countryside, and returned south without loss. This manoeuvre was not entirely to Stephen's liking, for he enjoyed a battle as a modern man enjoys a football match, but the news from England was so ominous that he dared not stay away longer.

It now seemed to David that the north of England was his for the taking, and that afterwards he need only march to join up with his niece, Matilda. With suitable piety he waited till the end of Lent before beginning his invasion and then drove south like a Scottish Jenghiz Khan. He captured Norham castle and besieged Wark: the former strength of Wark is unfortunately not easily observable today but the fact that he made it impotent was in itself a terrifying threat. At the same time another Scottish army, under William Fitz-Duncan, was driving down to Clitheroe, where it swept away a hastily-assembled English force. This was a useful diversion and good for morale but not really relevant to the main push. David therefore called Fitz-Duncan's men back, and united them with his own force. His scouts informed him that a considerable English army was mustering on his route to York. But, if and when he captured York, the way to the south would be open. His army was now said to number as many as 26,000 – unlikely but just possible.

The situation was a little more complicated than it appears on the surface. Seemingly, David of Scotland was marching south to overwhelm the forces of the English king. Faced with this challenge, all the knights of the north would rally to repel the invader who had come to ravage their lands and enslave them. To some extent this is what happened, for Thurstan, Archbishop of York, a man of great age and venerability, mustered a large army whose members were encouraged to believe they were fighting a holy war. As a symbol of their divine commission they carried a ship's mast draped with four cathedral banners; at the top was a pyx enclosing a sacred wafer. But as a result of the Normanization of Scotland some of the English barons held nearly as much land over the border as they held in England and through this they owed allegiance to David because he was King of Scotland. Two of them, whose names are more renowned in Scottish than in English history, were Robert de Bruce and Bernard de Balliol. The pair galloped forward to David's camp and pledged that if he now retired his son would be made Earl of Northumberland. David rejected the offer. But, if the English army contained men with dual allegiance, the Scottish included even more divisive elements. Some were Norwegians from the Orkneys, others were Angles who had settled in Lothian; yet others were Normans, and with them were apparently German mercenaries. But the most separated of all were the men of Galloway, whose appearance well displayed their savage ferocity. They were poorly armed and almost naked, circumstances which did not prevent their insisting on their traditional right to be the van of the Scottish army. In that position they received the full shock of the English archers. These, though not possessing the length and accuracy of the longbowmen who would create such devastation in later battles, were more than a match for the unarmoured Galwegians, who were cut down at thirty yards' range. David himself was stationed behind them and, without being able to affect the issue, saw the Galwegian leader killed and the whole contingent plunged into confusion. On the right, Prince

Henry of Scotland, the aspirant to the Earldom of Northumberland, commanded a wing of Norman knights and Norwegian auxiliaries, which proved all too effective. Having borne away the English left, it pursued it into wet and soggy ground, but there they were caught by the English centre which had regrouped after its easy victory over the Galwegians. Prince Henry escaped from the trap he had created for his force but only at the expense of one hundred and eighty knights of his two-hundred-strong bodyguard.

This bloody clash, at Northallerton, went into history as 'The Battle of the Standard'. It could have been decisive had the disorganized Scottish army been harried and pursued back into its own lands. But Stephen was too preoccupied with his own civil war to be able to consolidate this unexpected victory. Instead, David was able to besiege and capture Wark castle, which had previously defied all his efforts to take it. A year later a truce was signed between David and Stephen in which David's son was granted the Earldom of Northumberland on condition that he assisted Stephen against Matilda (who was his cousin). To make good the promise, Henry now took up residence in England and Stephen was confirmed in his possession of the castles of Bamburgh and Newcastle. David was in no way inhibited by his solemn undertaking and two years later was fighting for Matilda at Winchester; he was lucky not to be taken prisoner in the dramatic siege of the castle. The situation then, and during the next eight years is bizarre in the extreme. Treachery seems to have been the rule rather than the exception. Contestants changed sides with almost frivolous alacrity, and Henry's allegiance to Stephen proved to be of short duration.

At this time David and his Scottish followers were firmly convinced that Carlisle and Newcastle were the true frontier towns of Scotland. This belief long persisted.

David, however, had his own internal troubles which throw some light on the uncertainties of kingship at this time. A renegade monk – from Lancashire – named Wimund, suddenly claimed to be Earl of Moray and raised a considerable and formidable force from the Western Isles. He proved to be unbeatable in that he could never be cornered in a battle; the only solution was to buy him off. Even that proved unsatisfactory, and Wimund ceased to trouble David only when a number of his own men, tired of his greed and irascibility, blinded him and confined him in a Yorkshire monastery. After all these troubles David might have looked forward with some confidence to a peaceful old age. But it was not to be. His son and heir, Henry, died young, and David had to go to enormous trouble to enforce the claims of his grandchildren. However, on balance, the verdict of history is that David exerted a positive influence for good. Church and state power both increased during his reign, although the method by which this was effected was not to everyone's liking. Normans, Saxons and Danes were encouraged to settle in Scotland. Fitzalans and Morevilles now begin to appear as Scottish landowners. Even more significant was the introduction of Norman law, Norman custom, and even Norman trade. The Normans were already in the Mediterranean and their discoveries such as rice, figs, almonds, pepper, and ginger were articles of commerce wherever the Norman tentacles penetrated, and Scotland was no exception. Whatever David's faults and mistakes, his contribution to Scotland's unity was considerable. The need for a strong king was all too apparent when his twelve-year-old grandson, Malcolm IV, succeeded him. Much of the ensuing trouble came from the house of Moray, and, when this was settled, Malcolm found himself getting the worst of hard bargaining over the border counties with Henry II of England. At the age of sixteen Malcolm was deeply affronted by Henry II's refusal to dub him a knight. However, even a king had to 'win his spurs', and it took a year's service in France in the English army before Malcolm gained that coveted honour. In view of the disturbed state of Scotland in his absence the knighthood was hard won; when Malcolm died at the early age of twenty-four the crown went to his brother William.

William, known as 'the Lion', reigned a surprisingly long time – forty-nine years – but his reign was not without its setbacks. He had the optimistic ambition of extending Scottish territory by adding in Northumberland and Cumberland; it was not an aspiration likely to find favour with a king like Henry II of England. But in 1173 he set off to translate ambition into fact. Aided by the men of Galloway, whose purposeless savagery was enough to drive the most passive opposition to heights of frenzied resistance, he invaded Northumberland. Then, somewhat erratically, he veered west and besieged Carlisle. By 1174 he was back at Alnwick where, injudiciously, he allowed himself to be separated from the main part of his army. In the morning mist, he was surprised by a party of English knights who promptly took him prisoner. He was sent south to Northampton castle and from there transferred to even safer custody at Falaise, the birthplace of William the Conqueror. The price of his freedom was the acknowledgement of Henry II as his feudal superior, the installation of English garrisons at Berwick, Edinburgh, Jedburgh, Roxburgh, and Stirling castles, and the acceptance of English jurisdiction over the Scottish church. This, the Treaty of Falaise of 1176, was a bitter pill to swallow but it remained in force for fifteen years.

William's absence and subsequent subjection to a humiliating treaty led to predictable disturbances in his own kingdom. Galloway became virtually independent and the north was no better. Not least of William's troubles was that he had to request permission from Henry II to take up arms against rebels in his own territories.

On Henry's II's death in 1189 the situation brightened notably for William. Richard I, Coeur de Lion, showed little interest in his English throne and during his ten-year reign spent only eight months in England. His ambition was to capture Jerusalem and his main interests were fighting in France or other overseas territories. He accomplished a neat stroke of business by selling back to the Scots their independence for 10,000 marks, thereby financing his next expedition and also gaining Scottish goodwill and friendship in the process. However, he did not relinquish Northumberland and Cumberland, which at that time were still thought to be Scottish by right if not by law.

In 1199 Richard I was dead and his place had been taken by his evasive brother, John, who, although a capable warrior when he bestirred himself, was not a man anyone could respect or trust. William's efforts to strike a bargain over the disputed counties led to nothing but frustration, and soon it seemed as though the two countries would be at war again. In 1204 John was trying to build a fortress at the mouth of the Tweed to dominate the town of Berwick, but every move he made to do so was frustrated by the Scots. Eventually, in 1209, John decided that the Scots must be taught a lesson and the fortress must be built. He assembled a huge army and marched north. William took up station at Roxburgh and it seemed as if a massive blood-bath was now inevitable. But, curiously enough, this was merely a show of force and neither king really wanted a fight to the death. In consequence, emissaries from either side negotiated a treaty. It was a simple enough arrangement: John agreed not to build his proposed castle at Tweedmouth and William agreed to pay 15,000 marks for any injuries John had suffered. The gainer was probably William who had everything to lose from an exhausting battle in the border country; even if he won it his army would be so weakened that the rebels in his kingdom would become uncontrollable. As it was, Caithness was within a hair's breadth of becoming an independent kingdom. It had produced intractable warriors with names like Sigurd the Stout and Thorfin the Ugly, and now had Guthred, who in 1211 looked like being the greatest menace of all. More by luck than skill William precariously hung on.

Limited though his achievements were, William probably deserved the title 'the Lion'. His setbacks might have ruined a lesser man. Kings have reigned for longer but few have seen such incessant action. When he died in 1214 Scotland was in no worse state than when he had inherited. This might seem a slight achievement for a fifty-year reign but it must not be forgotten that few kings have had to contend so long against so many discordant elements in his kingdom. And a man's work may often be judged by its aftermath; in this case the aftermath was Scotland's 'golden age'.

Like William, his successor, Alexander II, came to the throne young, indeed, he was only sixteen. Within a year he – or rather, his lieutenant, the Earl of Ross – had crushed the inevitable rebellion in Moray. Unwisely – perhaps because he listened to bad advice – Alexander allied himself to the English barons who were banding together against King John. His next move was to take an army over the border to besiege Norham Castle. He and his advisers had underrated the military ability of John, which, though it functioned only spasmodically, was in no way inferior to that of his father, Henry II or his brother, the more renowned Richard I. John's army came storming north; the bulk of it composed of mercenaries whom he could trust as long as his purse lasted – which was longer than some of his feudal subjects. Alexander withdrew to the Esk and then waited, prepared to give battle for Edinburgh. But it began to look as if by mutual consent a boundary between England and Scotland would eventually be agreed. It would become a 'march' – a frontier area where lands would be held by powerful barons, later to be known as 'marcher lords', who would be equally ready for an aggressive or a defensive battle, and to relish one as much as the other. They built and held great castles and feared no one; the only admiration they coveted was that of their traditional foes. Such men might not contribute much to the social life of the country in which they lived but they had a stabilizing effect on frontiers.

In 1216 King John of England died and was succeeded by Henry III, then a boy of only nine. His throne, in a country seething with turbulent barons, looked anything but secure, but eventually he had one of the longest reigns in English history – fifty-six years. Even more surprising is the fact that he retained it – except for one year – in spite of crass stupidity and exasperating folly. Equally, the first five years of Alexander's reign gave little promise of a bright future; but in 1221 he married Henry's sister. At the same time he married off his own sister to Hubert de Burgh, the Great Justiciar, who was the wisest and most powerful man in England at the time. Stability and peace were thus assured and Alexander's hands were freed to deal with internal problems. The first of these was Argyll, the old Dalriada, which had never been properly subject to the Scottish crown; it had come to the fore only when it had fostered rebellions or supported Scotland's enemies. Strangely enough, when Alexander led an expedition composed of men from Lothian and Galloway into Argyll there was no opposition. He therefore confiscated territory from potential troublemakers and distributed it to those whom he hoped would be his friends. It was a notable step forward but not the end of rebellion and disorder, which were inevitable; but they were no longer inevitably disastrous. An even more significant step was taken in 1237 when, at a conference in York, the frontier between England and Scotland was legally agreed. In return for abandoning his claim to Northumberland and Cumberland Alexander received lands in those counties to the value of £200 a year.

The year 1237 was therefore a vital one in the history of Anglo-Scottish relations. Before that date there had been endless wars and expeditions over a disputed unmarked frontier. After 1237 there were still centuries of battle and bloodshed to come; but it would be warfare of a different kind, in which a man's country would as often as not be more important than his clan or his family.

Five years after the Treaty of York, however, it seemed that the new stability would be shattered suddenly, the cause of which seems trivial to us today. In 1242 a tournament was held at Haddington. Now, tournaments, like football matches today, were meant to act as a safety-valve for violent feelings, to encourage knightly skills, and to provide spectacular entertainment. They seldom failed in the last capacity but, again not unlike the modern football match, were notable more for engendering ill-feeling than for dispelling it. A tournament was a miniature battle between troops of knights using lances; the only unwarlike concession was to point one's lance at an opponent's body and not his head. In between the tournaments there would be jousts, single-handed combats in which the jousters began with lances and continued with axes and swords. Two years before the Haddington incident there had been a tournament at Cologne in which sixty combatants had been killed.

At Haddington, Patrick of Galloway, Earl of Atholl, unhorsed Walter Bisset, a Norman baron from Moray. The same night Atholl's lodging was burnt to the ground and he himself died in the flames. The Atholls and the Bissets already hated each other, and this was clearly a matter which could only be avenged by blood-letting. To avert an internecine fracas which might lead to wide-spread trouble and disruption, Alexander – under pressure from his barons – agreed that the Bissets should be put on trial. Needless to say they proclaimed their innocence, and were probably telling the truth, but this availed them nothing. Too many people testified against them and as a result Bisset was banished and his estates forfeited.

Bisset promptly went to the English court where he did his utmost to poison relations between England and Scotland. His task was not difficult, for Henry was already suspicious of the close relationship Alexander was establishing with the French. As news of war preparations flew from one side to the other, so the armies grew. Eventually, Alexander took a great army to the frontier of North-umberland. Meanwhile, Henry took as big an army to Newcastle. A clash appeared imminent but, as on former occasions, there were too many people on each side who thought that a major battle would be damaging to their own interests. Messages were exchanged and, as a result, the two kings agreed not to fight. It was dangerous brinkman-ship, but the final calamity was averted.

Seven years later Alexander died, succumbing to a mysterious illness while on an expedition to conquer the Sudreys, in the Western Isles, which still belonged to Norway. He was succeeded by his son, a boy of eight, who became Alexander III. The year was 1249.

Quite unpredictably the new king reigned thirty-seven years during which there was very little formal fighting. Yet, all through his reign, there was a conflict between the pro-English faction, led by Durward, and the Scottish independence group, led by Comyn, Earl of Menteith, whose family included two earls and thirty knights. Initially the Comyn faction was in the ascendant. Then, with English help, the Durwards displaced it. The Comyns, however, were not to be brushed on one side lightly, as will be appreciated from their subsequent history. In 1257 they kidnapped Alexander himself and made him their prisoner in Stirling Castle. Durward fled to England. Henry III of England was furious at this treatment of one whom he had hoped would be his vassal king, but in that year he had too many subversive elements in his own kingdom to risk sending an army into Scotland. Applying what he thought was remarkable subtlety to the solution of the problem, he sent the Earls of Hereford and Albemarle, with John de Balliol (originally Bailleul) to a conference at Jedburgh. The English had a substantial force at Norham, with which it was hoped to achieve a counter-revolution in Scotland; the Comyns, however, had an equally large force hidden in the woods around Jedburgh. As the conference got under way, Scots spearmen appeared silently and surrounded the meeting-place. The result was a compromise in which Scotland became a regency with four Englishmen among the ten members of the Regency Council. The Comyns had triumphed.

Relations between the two countries were not unduly strained despite the wariness of all the principals. While never entirely sure of his position in regard to England, Alexander nevertheless managed to make a substantial and enduring contribution to Scottish unity. In 1262 he sent a message to King Haco of Norway suggesting that the Hebrides might now become part of Scotland by negotiation, but Haco treated the invitation with scorn and, in 1263, set out with a large fleet to reassert his claims and demand fealty in the islands. Initially he was successful, and received widespread homage, but an untimely storm decimated his shipping. After being driven on to the Scottish mainland, he was ferociously attacked by

Alexander's supporters. He escaped, but on the way home died from an undefined sickness.

Alexander was quick to take advantage of this military vacuum. First he reassembled an army which he proposed to launch against the King of Man who had given fealty to Haco. It was not necessary. Magnus, King of Man, presented himself to Alexander at Dumfries and swore homage. The Hebrides soon followed suit.

Towards the end of his long reign which had begun so inauspiciously but developed so well, there were ominous signs of trouble ahead. Alexander's children all predeceased him. He was only forty-four and had married again in 1285, but the best hope for Scotland's future lay in the infant daughter of his sister, Margaret, who had married King Eric of Norway after Haco's death. Margaret had died in 1283, and the infant 'Maid of Norway' was the only direct heir to the ancient line of Scotland. When her mother died, she had been acknowledged at the age of one by thirteen earls, eleven bishops, and twenty-five barons as heiress of Scotland, the Hebrides, the Isle of Man, Tynedale, and Penrith.

Two years later, as we saw above, Alexander married again, and the marriage-feast was held in Jedburgh Abbey. As part of the entertainment a pageant was held and included a popular medieval masque known as the Dance of Death, a sombre entertainment which included amongst its *dramatis personae* a rather realistic skeleton. The spectators were uncertain whether this was part of the entertainment or whether a ghostly demoniac figure had intruded; in consequence many predicted that the outlook for the king was baleful indeed. Nor were they to be disappointed; that winter had more than its share of ominous thunderstorms. On 19 March 1286 Alexander held a council in Edinburgh castle. It took all day but, although darkness had fallen on a particularly stormy night,

Alexander insisted that he must ride home to the queen at King-horn. He crossed the ferry and reached Inverkeithing. It was now so dark that no one could see beyond his horse's head, and, just outside Kinghorn itself, Alexander's horse suddenly stumbled over the cliff, killing its rider.

It was a shock for Scotland but not a calamity. A regency was proclaimed to reign for the young queen, who was still in Norway, and her succession was accepted.

Edward I of England, who had just completed the conquest of Wales in 1286 now saw a golden opportunity to unite England and Scotland. There was, at this time, no real enmity between the two countries; in fact they had much in common and considerable empathy. The battles and border skirmishes of the past were either forgotten or recognized as minor stages in the development of a rational frontier. There was no hint of the bitterness to come, neither in the relationship between England and Scotland nor in the internal politics of Scotland itself.

Edward's idea, eminently sensible, was that the unity of Britain might well be furthered by the marriage of his son, Edward, the new Prince of Wales, to little Margaret, the new queen of Scotland. Edward was careful not to propose to interfere with Scottish law or liberty and made this clear in the agreement he put to the Scottish regents. The regents accepted his good faith, although within months he was suggesting that, to guard against a rumoured rebellion, certain Scottish castles should be put in his hands, a proposal that was firmly refused.

In September 1290 a ship was sent to Norway to bring the seven-year-old queen to her kingdom of Scotland, a country she had never seen.

The details of that appalling journey are not known but it seems that, after an unduly long voyage in which the ship was tossed around by gales, she was landed at Kirkwall, only to die. The story, not surprisingly, passed into Scottish legend as the ballad of Sir Patrick Spens. It begins impressively, even if inaccurately,

> *The King sits in Dumfermline town,*
> *Drinking the blood-red wine;*
> *'O where shall I get a skeely skipper*
> *To sail this ship of mine.'*

Sir Patrick Spens is nominated and:

> *To Noroway, to Noroway,*
> *To Noroway, o'er the foam;*
> *The King's daughter of Noroway*
> *'Tis thou must fetch her home.*

Sir Patrick was not pleased:

> *O who is this has done this deed,*
> *Has told the King of me*
> *To send us out at this time of the year,*
> *To sail upon the sea?*
>
> *Be it wind, be it wet, be it hail, be it sleet,*
> *Our ship must sail the foam*
> *The King's daughter of Noroway*
> *'Tis we must fetch her home.*

The outward journey was bad enough, but the return was blighted by ill-omen before it even started. And

> *They had not sailed a league, a league,*
> *A league but barely three,*

When the lift grew dark and the wind blew loud
And gurly grew the sea.[1]

The ankers brake and the topmasts lap,
It was such a deadly storm;
And the waves came o'er the broken ship
Till all her sides were torn.

In the ballad, the ship, the crew, and Sir Patrick Spens all finished their voyage 'fifty fathoms deep'. The chronicler records with juicy relish:

'O loth, loth were our good Scots Lords
To wet their cork-heel'd shoon,
But long ere all the play was play'd
They wet their hats aboon

And many was the feather-bed
That fluttered on the foam;
And many was the good lord's son
That never more came home.

The fate of the unfortunate Maid of Norway is overlooked, or perhaps thought a price worth paying, if a fashion-crazy nobility – cork-heeled shoes, indeed – should receive their just deserts. Feather beds as well! What was Scotland coming to?

And long, long may the ladies sit
With their long combs in their hair,
All waiting for their own dear loves
For them they'll see no more.

1 The 'lift' was the sky or air, as in 'aloft'; 'gurly' is untranslatable but perhaps needs no translation.

It is, of course, a sad enough story, of this frail child, motherless and alone, flung around in unprecedented storms on her way to an unknown land, dying perhaps of fear and misery. For Scotland it was even worse, for now there was a disputed succession, carefully watched by an ambitious and dynamic King of England who did not question his right to intervene but was not yet clear about the timing.

In Scotland it appeared as though Bruce of Annandale was the only valid claimant, but this opinion did not commend itself to Edward. He held a conviction, not shared by the Scots, that he was 'Superior and Lord Paramount of Scotland' and should settle the affairs of that country. He announced this at Norham in May 1291 and again in June in an unknown field north of the Tweed. At the second meeting were eight claimants to the Scottish throne; in August the number had increased to twelve, but only three could be seriously considered: John Balliol, Robert Bruce, and Henry Hastings. Hastings was soon eliminated, and on 17 November at Berwick Castle Balliol was proclaimed by Edward the lawful heir to the throne of Scotland. Of the once mighty Berwick castle only earthworks remain and, as with many other castles, railway building has destroyed much of the former precincts. However, Berwick is still a fascinating town, and it may interest the reader to know that, when he stands on the platform of the railway station, he is on the site of the hall where Edward proclaimed Balliol King of Scotland. Technically, Edward's decision was undoubtedly correct, but he must have been as aware as anyone else that the result of appointing a weak character like Balliol could result in nothing but disaster for Scotland, however satisfactory it might be for English suzerainty.

Balliol reigned for four years but ran into trouble in the first month. The Scots nicknamed him 'Toom Tabard', a tabard being an outer garment worn to protect armour and often, when worn by heralds, emblazoned with someone else's coat-of-arms. 'Toom' means 'empty'. His first folly was to alienate the Macduffs, and it was soon followed by a revolt by his subjects against having to pay for one of Edward's expeditions against Galloway. The revolt never became a military rebellion, but in 1295, when Edward I was at war with France, and had an insurrection in Wales to contend with, Balliol signed a defensive alliance with France. A Franco-Scottish understanding had been in force in the past but had never been formal; this one in 1295 was the precursor of many a military alliance. In 1296 there were two Scottish invasions of Northumberland and Cumberland; they were ineffective, but Balliol, hoping to marry his son to the daughter of the King of France, and knowing that Llewellyn of Wales was also staging a rising with every hope of French aid, looked on the future with confidence. Therefore, when summoned to Newcastle to explain himself to his feudal overlord, he light-heartedly ignored the request, but he underestimated his overlord. Edward was in no hurry. He dealt with his Welsh problems, but deferred his campaign in Gascony to a later date. In 1296 he was ready for Balliol.

Berwick, now such a peaceful town, has seen many horrifying scenes, but few can have equalled that in 1296. Edward descended on it with devastating speed both by land and sea. His Welsh campaign had made him a master of this sort of combined operation. Berwick was the chief port and most prestigious border fortress of Scotland; Edward was therefore prepared to make an example of it and eliminate any further rebellious thoughts in the area. It may be argued that a swift bloody massacre at a key point ultimately saves lives because it prevents the endless dribble of casualties that occurs with a protracted resistance; but the sacking of Berwick cannot be excused even on that score. Not only the garrison but also the population of Berwick was put to the sword, a total said to be near eight thousand. Rather than eliminating long-term resistance elsewhere, it probably stimulated it. Medieval warriors often made this mistake. Brutality in one area often caused the inhabitants of another to fight with what has aptly been called 'the desperation of the doomed'. The response might be delayed for a year or more but ultimately it came – with greater emphasis.

Balliol, having refused to meet Edward before the capture of Berwick now sent him a message in which he renounced all allegiance. As Balliol had just alienated Bruce by depriving him of the lands at Annandale, his position was even weaker than it need have been. Edward moved on to Dunbar where, on 27 April 1296, the Scottish army was so disorganized that resistance was negligible. The occasion was called the Battle of Dunbar, and took place at Spott burn, two miles south of the town, but never in fact became a full-stage encounter. As Edward's vanguard approached, under the command of John de Warenne, the Scots engaged it half-heartedly. Before the main body of Edward's army had arrived they decided to break off the fight and leave the field. It was a classic example of a potentially strong army being humiliated because it lacked leadership and proper motivation. But what could be expected when a puppet king, already discredited, put a disorganized army into the field to challenge one of the most experienced and battle-hardened forces in Europe? Inevitably the surrender of the castles at Edinburgh, Roxburgh, Stirling, and Perth soon followed. Finally, Balliol himself submitted by presenting himself in simple clothing and carrying a white rod. Edward pressed on to Elgin but was magnanimous in his easy victory. He issued a general amnesty and affirmed that none of Scotland's laws should be changed. Nevertheless, he carried off the 'Stone of Destiny' from Scone, and installed it in Westminster Abbey under the Coronation Chair. At Edinburgh he was said to have picked up the famous Holy Rood, a crucifix brought there by St Margaret, and judged to be the most holy relic in Scotland. This latter act seems highly improbable for Edward was neither impious nor a fool but the story, impossible to disprove, would be excellent for rousing Scottish religious indignation.

There was, however, no need of additional refinement to stir Scottish feelings against Edward and his army. Before setting off for the postponed expedition in Gascony, taking the bulk of his army with him, he had appointed three Englishmen to administer Scotland: John de Warenne, victor of Dunbar, as Governor, Hugh de Cressingham as Treasurer, and William Ormsby as Chief Justice. The stage was now set for a series of battles which would continue intermittently for the next five hundred years.

The Battle of Stirling Bridge

11 September 1297

The situation in Scotland in 1297 is easy to analyse in the perspective of history; it was probably incomprehensible at the time. Edward had appointed three high-handed officials to administer the country in his absence. John de Warenne was a good soldier, as had been shown at Dunbar, but was inclined to be impetuous and to underrate the enemy; Cressingham was an obstinate man who saw his task as simply to extract the maximum possible quantity of taxes from the defeated Scots; Ormsby had no doubt that the best future for Scotland was to place it under an English system of justice. Of these the last was perhaps the worst, for, although men do not like being tyrannized or over-taxed, they will bear up if they feel there might ultimately be some redress in law. But the introduction of a foreign, and therefore imperfectly understood, legal system will rapidly drive them to desperation.

The Scots, of course, were a recently united nation. It was inevitable that once their accepted king proved incapable of preserving their welfare – as Balliol had so clearly failed – they would once more begin to revive their regional feelings and hostilities. Many Scots, of whom Bruce was one, felt that they had been betrayed because some of those who should have been their leaders had in fact fought for the English.

It is impossible to escape the conclusion that Edward I, so far-seeing elsewhere, was obstinate and short-sighted in his Scottish policy. His unfortunate choice of administrators has been mentioned already; it seems extraordinary that he should feel that he could erect a puppet king, destroy him, and still be accepted.

Warenne was a sick man in the winter of 1296. Had he been in normal health he would have been so active, and perhaps so royal, that the Scots would have accepted English suzerainty. The Warennes, whose legitimate line would die out in 1347, were a remarkable baronial family even by medieval standards. The first of them had come over with William the Conqueror and they were closely related to the royal family. At times they opposed the king; at others they served him with a casual haughtiness. Warenne had already defied a royal inquiry (held throughout the realm) to discover by what (*Quo Warranto*) barons held certain lands. When the Sheriff appeared, Warenne snatched down a rusty sword from the wall and said 'By this were my lands won by my ancestors, and by this will I hold them. This is my title deed.' His act of defiance was copied by others and the inquiry was abandoned. Warenne was accustomed to getting his own way by dash and fearlessness, which had already served him well at Dunbar. These qualities would doubtless have served him and his sovereign well in governing Scotland in the winter of 1296-7 if he had been able to display them. But, as we have noted, illness prevented his displaying them at that time, and when the next opportunity arrived he was at Stirling Bridge. Meanwhile, Cressingham and Ormsby had been exercising their talents to the full. The result of this combination of negative apathy and positive ineptitude was that the stage was set for the emergence of a leader of Scottish resistance – 'The hour calls forth the man.' A Strathclyde knight, one who had been thought too unimportant to be summoned to swear allegiance to Edward I, now came to the front, his name

William Wallace. He was one of the Britons from Wales who had settled in Strathclyde, indeed his name Wallace, or Waleys, means 'the Welshman', but he was a true Scot for all that, perhaps a better representative of Scottish nationhood than many better-known names. In May 1297 he became involved in a brawl in Lanark, the details of which are obscure. It seems to have been a quarrel with some English soldiers over a girl; some say she was his wife. An attempt was made to arrest him, and as a result Wallace killed the Sheriff of Lanark, one Hazelrigg. This made Wallace an outlaw – and more. A man who has defied the occupying army, is a fine guerrilla fighter, and has taken to the hills in a country where there is widespread discontent, can scarcely fail to become a national hero.

Initially the rising was not a success but that was no fault of Wallace. Stirred by his defiance, and perhaps feeling their own authority would be undermined unless they took action, the Scottish barons made an attempt to reassert their independence. The effort was a dismal failure; there was no unified command and, when they met an English force at Irvine in Ayrshire, they came to terms with more speed than dignity. This was 9 July 1297. Wallace, however, was not affected; he was organizing his own army, ably assisted by Andrew Moray of Bothwell. As soon as Wallace was able, he began besieging castles and acquiring bases. Meanwhile, the English army which had been so successful at Irvine had now decided to march forward to Stirling. It was rumoured to be 40,000 strong. Wallace was besieging Dundee castle when messengers brought him notice of this move. He promptly broke off the siege and hurried off to protect Stirling, which so aptly has been called 'the key to Scotland'. There he took up position where the ground rises up to the west of the Forth. By Cambuskenneth Abbey was a narrow wooden bridge, the only entry to Stirling. It was about a hundred yards upstream from the present footbridge and should not be confused with it, although the latter gives one a good idea of what it might have been like. Its exact position may be found from the base of stone pillars on each side of the river. It was a typical medieval bridge, only wide enough for two people to walk abreast. Doubtless it closely resembled the one over the Spott burn near Dunbar where Warenne had been so successful the previous year. There, in the face of a demoralized Scots army relying on making a defence along the steep banks of the burn, he had burst across, partly using the bridge and partly fording. Doubtless he hoped to do the same at Stirling Bridge. But the Forth is not the Spott; it is a fast-flowing river 250 feet across. And behind it was Wallace with 10,000 men who cared not in the least that they were outnumbered four to one. They were lean, hardy and alert, and, under a leader whom they respected, they were tolerably disciplined. They would obey orders and do nothing rash before the battle; during it and after it matters might be different. With some interest they watched the English army begin to cross the bridge and deploy on the bank in front of their own position. The figure of 40,000 seems unduly large for the size of a medieval army but, even with a quarter of this amount, the passage of the bridge would be slow. This was where all Wallace's prestige as a leader was needed to hold his men in check. It must have seemed incomprehensible to them that Wallace should allow the invader to pass such a formidable obstacle as the Forth unmolested. On the bridge they could have been held; it was a time-honoured method. Any guerrilla watching an enemy file into an ambush must wonder whether the ambush will be strong enough to hold them, and Wallace's men, as they watched large numbers of English cross the bridge, probably felt sick and disappointed at the sight. Still there was no order from Wallace. Among the English were a number of Scottish barons who

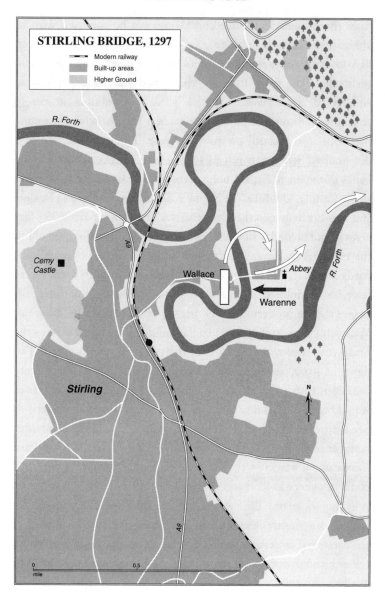

STIRLING BRIDGE, 1297

- ▭ Modern railway
- ▮ Built-up areas
- ▮ Higher Ground

R. Forth

Cemy Castle

Wallace

Abbey

R. Forth

Warenne

Stirling

N

0   0.5   1
mile

had entered English service when Balliol was king. They were better horsed and equipped than any of Wallace's upstart army.

Among Warenne's army was a Scot named Sir Richard Lunday. Just before the English army began to file across the bridge, Lunday had pointed out with some vehemence that a short distance downstream was a ford where sixty men abreast could cross. Wallace knew of the ford too and had posted a detachment there as a precaution. But wading a river in the face of the enemy is not to everyone's taste; it is exhausting and uncertain, damages weapons and equipment, and gives an army a highly vulnerable feeling. Warenne, with his triumph at Dunbar fresh in mind, decided he could risk the bridge.

By 11 a.m. half the English army was over and forming up on the other side. At its head was Cressingham, as brave as he was stupid, and a knight called Sir Marmaduke Twenge. Suddenly the Scots army rose up out of the cover and began to move down the slope. Twenge promptly gave the order to sound the charge and the English cavalry launched itself up the hill. In a moment, all was clatter and confusion. As the knights lumbered up the slope on to the points of Scottish pikes, so Wallace's archers teased and confused the rear with a shower of arrows. The archers were not a very formidable force, but they had plenty of arrows and were shooting downhill on to a clearly visible target; doubtless they were enjoying themselves greatly. An archer's life was a fine one if he had a clear target and enough ammunition, but if he ran out of arrows and was charged by enemy cavalry his chances did not amount to

The original bridge has now disappeared but the later footbridge gives a very good idea of its predecessor. Note the width and speed of the river here. A good appreciation of the tactical situation may be made by looking over the site from the castle ramparts. Do not be misled by the road bridge. (Stirling) much. Wallace's centre, with himself, Grahame of Dundaff, and Ramsay of Dalhousie, hurled themselves straight through the middle of the English army towards the bridge. Simultaneously he launched a flanking movement which swept along the north bank and looked like cutting off the English army from reinforcements. The Scottish attack had all the advantages which come from surprise and speed and they took good care not to lose them. Much of the English trouble stemmed from the fact that they had been forming up for an offensive and not a defensive action, and now it was too late to change. Soon, instead of charging, they themselves were being charged by the long Scottish pikes. So well was this part of the battle going that Wallace sent his reserve to cross the ford – of which the exact position is not now known, for it has been eroded away – and to fall on the English flank on the other side. Warenne was not unduly dismayed or upset; he was too good a soldier for that. Sizing up the situation on the opposite bank, he cleared his infantry from the bridge and in its place launched a stream of well-armoured knights who galloped over the planks and hurled themselves into the mêlée on the other side. It was a fine dashing piece of opportunism and, if it could have been continued, might have turned the battle. But, alas for hopes; the weight of the mailed knights and their chargers at this speed was too much for the bridge. Some say Wallace had previously sawn through some of its supports, for suddenly it began to crack and fall. For those English on the far side it was now kill or be killed; there was no way out of that iron ring. Gradually they were driven back to the banks of the river. Those who plunged in were nearly all drowned but a few scrambled out on the south bank only to be slaughtered by the Scots who had forded lower down. The rest of the English army was in retreat, hastily trying to avoid being cut off, but not often succeeding. Warenne rallied them at Torwood and inflicted heavy casualties on the advancing Scots, who had now grown careless. It was, however, of no avail, and reluctantly he abandoned the fight and spurred on to Berwick. His foot soldiers were not so lucky. Most of them were baffled by the loops in the river and were easily caught; the fate of a defeated army in a hostile countryside is not a pleasant one, and it is said that thousands of unburied corpses took their revenge in pestilence on the people who had shown them no mercy. Cressingham's body received special treatment: the skin was torn off it and made into purses and belts.

Wallace was now supreme. He was elected Protector of the Kingdom and was supported by the aristocracy, particularly those who had fought for Warenne and changed sides in the hour of victory. But the English still held Roxburgh and Berwick castles and Warenne had sworn he would be back.

The Battle of Falkirk

22 July 1298

Edward returned to England from France in March 1298. He summoned his English and Scottish barons to a Parliament at York but, not surprisingly, the Scots did not appear. Wallace was now supported by all the leading dignitaries in Scotland and, to show his strength, had led a savage raid into Northumberland. The bitter feelings aroused by this raid would persist for many years, but the Scots would be the chief sufferers.

Edward's task was not as easy as he would have wished. His northern barons were not entirely convinced that, having been enlisted, they would not find their sovereign had once again departed to his French wars, leaving them to subdue Wallace on their own. And subduing Wallace did not look like being easy. Edward, however, reassured them. By a pilgrimage to the shrine of St John of Beverley he convinced them that he was sincere; and by assessing his followers accurately he gave military and administrative confidence. If you had lands to the value of £15, you were required to present yourself for service, equipped with a hauberk, an iron cap, a knife, and a horse; if you had only 40 shillings or less, you only needed a sword and a knife and a bow and arrows. These you would have anyway; how could a man hunt for his food otherwise?

With this all-embracing system of enlistment Edward I had a considerable army by June 1298. Some chroniclers gave the number as 80,000, some as 90,000. Half that number would have been difficult enough to feed and manoeuvre; there is no means of checking the size of medieval armies or of casualties except on the basis of probability. Nevertheless, Edward's army included many men experienced in the French wars. Some of them were cavalry but there were also substantial contingents of Welsh and Irish infantry; the latter were scarcely likely to endear themselves to the Scots. Among the leaders were Antony de Beck, the warlike Bishop of Durham; Humphrey de Bohun, Earl of Hereford; Bigod of Norfolk; and Lord Basset of Drayton.

Whatever the true numerical size of this army, it was too large for Wallace to oppose in the field. Like a good guerrilla leader he fell back. Progress was not entirely easy for Edward as he advanced up the east coast; Wallace had destroyed everything of use to an invading army and Edward's seaborne supply system was noticeably erratic. At Dirleton castle, held by the De Vaux family of Norman extraction, Bishop Beck's army was nearly starving and had to raid the crops growing locally. Dirleton is a castle well worth a visit, although in 1298 it was undoubtedly less formidable than the present ruins suggest. At Kirkliston Edward halted and waited for his seaborne supplies; he was not in such a hurry as to risk his great host in a country of which it might be said (as it was said later of Spain) 'where small armies are beaten and where large armies starve'.

Wallace had his problems too. Guerrilla leaders who have become national heroes may not revert to the methods which brought them to power. There is no looking back. A king, however unregal, must fight like a king. Reluctantly Wallace mustered all his strength – an army said to number 30,000 – and with this he marched to Falkirk. If he was to check Edward, this was the place to do it. Once past

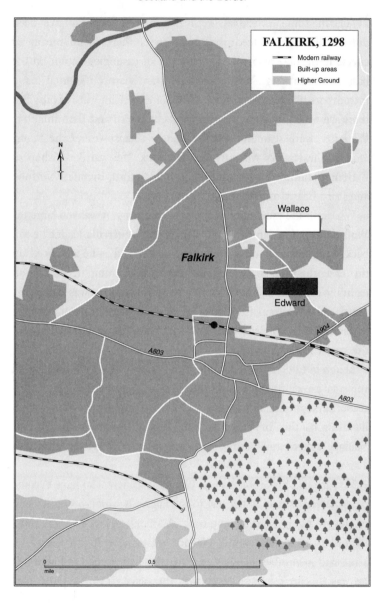

FALKIRK, 1298

Modern railway
Built-up areas
Higher Ground

Wallace

Falkirk

Edward

A904

A803

A803

0   0.5   1
mile

Falkirk the English were on their way to Stirling, and with that great army fanning out what could stop the conquest of Scotland? He is said to have chosen what was tactically a very strong position, with a morass in front and his flanks covered with rope-covered palisades. It is impossible to judge the strength of that position today, although it is easily identified, for a town has been built around and over it. What is described as 'the battlefield' is too small for the deployment of a mere fraction of the numbers said to be involved.

Both armies were in trouble before the battle started. Some of the Welsh had been fighting against the English in Wales a short time before and, now that they were in English service, were the first to complain of short rations. To cheer them up Edward had sent extra wine – an unfortunate move, for it resulted in a drunken brawl involving the near-by English. By the time order had been restored eighty Welshmen had been killed, and the remainder were threatening to join Wallace. Edward's reaction to what he felt was predictable Welsh disloyalty was so violent that the Welsh leaders were deterred from putting their threats into effect.

Much to the disgust of subsequent Scottish chroniclers, Edward was now assisted by a remarkable act of treachery. Patriotism was in those days often less powerful than self-interest or even dignity. Two barons, the Earl of Angus and the Earl of Dunbar, irritated at Wallace's rapid rise and pretensions, decided to betray him, and

This site is often confused with that of the 1746 battle (a Jacobite victory) which took place two miles south-east of the town, where there is a monument near Greenbank. The 1298 battle took place in the middle of the town on land which has now been built over. In spite of bricks and mortar and roads, it is still possible to obtain a fair idea of the lie of the ground. The Wallace Street and Thornhill Road intersection is thought to be the centre of the battlefield. (Falkirk) accordingly rode over to the English headquarters after dark. They told Edward that Wallace was planning to attack the English army by night while it was itself preparing the attack on the Scots for the next day. On the subsequent battle there has been much imaginative conjecture, not clarified by the fact that some of the accounts confuse this battle with the one which took place in 1746 on an entirely different terrain. Wallace, realizing by the absence of his treacherous earls that surprise had now been lost, decided against committing his outnumbered army to anything as speculative as a night attack. Instead he took up station where he knew Edward would accept the challenge. By deploying his army in the traditional three *schiltrons* (columns) he hoped that Edward would be induced to come straight to the charge. As his flanks were protected and there was a substantial piece of boggy ground in front of his position, he looked forward to events with reasonable confidence. Most of his army were infantry, however, and even after Stirling Bridge there was no certainty that they would be steady under prolonged attack. He also had 1,000 archers and a small cavalry reserve under John Comyn.

All went as expected – initially. The English horse, under Hereford, charged headlong into the boggy ground. As they endeavoured to extricate themselves the Scottish archers singled out the most important-looking targets.

The second wave of cavalry picked its route more carefully and was more successful. But even they found themselves in trouble when they reached the Scottish pikemen. An eighteen-foot pike held by a resolute man, flanked by others of equal steadiness, is an obstacle which is not easily ridden down – as would be proved on other fields. Wallace himself was giving his infantry a fine example. Swinging his great two-handed sword he seemed to be immortal, for arrows and spears fell all around him. At any moment the balance might be tipped in favour of the Scots. But, to everyone's amazement, the Scottish cavalry, which should now have hammered home an attack into the English second line, suddenly wheeled and rode off the field. This second act of treachery was a scandal which confirmed the opinion many Scots had of their aristocracy at that time. It was almost inconceivable that one nobleman after another could desert the country's army, which was fighting its English enemy, even though that army was led by a man of inferior rank.

But it happened. But, also, Wallace fought on. Realizing that they were unable to break that wall of spears by cavalry charges, the English commanders sent forward their archers and slingers. A sling is as deadly a weapon as a shotgun at short range. But, pounded though they were with stones and arrows, the Scots held on. Their own archers from Elrick died to a man, as did Grahame of Dundaff and the twenty-year-old Earl of Fife, and other aristocrats who had remained loyal to Wallace; by now the Scots were fighting behind a wall of dead bodies. Wallace had to be dragged from the battlefield and put on a horse, but even the horse was so wounded it could carry him only a short distance. It was a bitter day in Scottish history, a mixture of shame for the treachery which had lost the battle, and pride for the staunch resistance of those who proved that Scots could not merely fight in attacks or in loose order but could also hold on after betrayal and see the battle to the end, however grim that end might be. And the battle also said much for the qualities of the English, Welsh, and Irish of Edward's army who could fight with such relentless persistence after days of near starvation and nights of perpetual alarms. The casualties are not known; one chronicler gave them as 60,000 which is probably twice as many as the entire number of men in the field in both armies; they were probably about 2,000.

Wallace was never able to raise another field army. Soon after Falkirk he resigned his post as Guardian. His achievement was, nevertheless, considerable. He had shown that it was possible to raise a truly Scottish force, that he personally could triumph over almost any odds but treachery from his own side, and that Scots could fight in both offensive and defensive warfare. After Falkirk Edward laid the country waste but then withdrew. Comyn, de Soulis, Bruce, and Lamberton became Guardians. Wallace tried desperately to organize further resistance to English domination, even going to France to enlist support. But seven years after Falkirk the Guardians handed him over to Edward. Edward respected Wallace as a warrior but was in no doubt of the danger he constituted as a symbol of national resistance. In the barbaric custom of the day Wallace was hanged, drawn, and quartered. His offence was treason – although he had never sworn fealty. But he was too dangerous a man to live. And, of course, Edward could never forgive that raid in 1297 when, after Stirling Bridge, Wallace had devastated Northumberland.

mainly used for hunting, skinning animals, and woodcraft. The spearmen were no more and no less skilled in weapon-handling than were their opponents. When formed up in *schiltrons* (shield troops), infantrymen had weapons pointing in every direction, like an elongated hedgehog.

Edward's army was mustered and arrayed for battle at Wark on 17 June. It set off to march to Stirling, aiming at covering twenty miles a day. If Stirling castle was not to be surrendered by 24 June (Midsummer Day), the English army must be within three leagues (nine miles) of it. There was no time to waste, but the weather was hot and it was apparently an exhausting march. Nevertheless, the army maintained formation.

Bruce clearly could not welcome this encounter. He was heavily outnumbered and he had already called up all his reserves. He was, however, in a position to choose his ground and Edward's route between Falkirk and Stirling would take the English army through a number of places where the ground advantage might even out the disparity in numbers. And on this occasion, if there were any desertions, it seemed that they might occur on the English side, for numerous Scots had enrolled in the English army. Bruce's position, although not good, was by no means hopeless.

Although it was somewhat of a risk, Bruce decided to let the English army come close up to Stirling. The exact site of the battle is not known, because the countryside has changed considerably over the last five hundred years. Nevertheless, it is possible to be approximately right. The National Trust for Scotland has established a memorial in the battlefield area and in the nearby centre provides a most illuminating 'tableau vivant' of the event as it probably occurred. Although nobody claims to know exactly where the battle was fought, General Christison, former G.O.C. Scottish

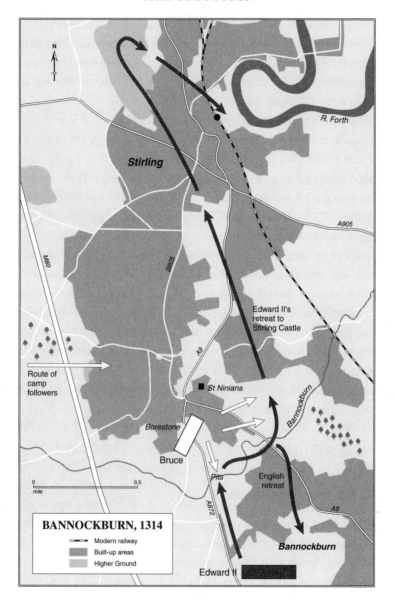

N

R. Forth

Stirling

A905

B805

Edward II's
retreat to
Stirling Castle

M80

Route of
camp
followers

A9

■ St Ninians

Borestone

Bannockburn

Bruce

Pits

English
retreat

A9

A872

BANNOCKBURN, 1314

Modern railway

Built-up areas

Higher Ground

Bannockburn

Edward II

0   0.5
mile

Command, studied the ground very carefully on his retirement and gave an opinion which is not likely to be bettered. There was incidentally no village of Bannockburn at the time of the battle, so even contemporary chroniclers must have had some difficulty in identifying the exact site. One vital additional piece of information came to hand during the last year, quite fortuitously, and this throws much light on the course of the fighting, but more of this later.

On Sunday, 23 June 1314, the English army, still in remarkably good condition in spite of its long march, came up the route of the A9 through Torwood, along the old Roman road and on to the route of the A872 towards Stirling. The castle can be seen along this road and it is possible that the English had become overconfident. Before reaching Stirling, however, they had to pass through a dangerous area which was a mixture of scrub and boggy land. The Bannock burn was partly responsible for the wet patches, but a more important contribution came from the River Forth, which is tidal and has a considerable effect on the texture of the adjoining soil. At certain times, apparently firm ground becomes not unlike quicksand, but less dangerous, an interesting fact which roadbuilders have learned recently. Possibly Bruce knew this but it seems unlikely; but he profited from it all the same. The Bannock itself flows west–east

Take the A872 out of Stirling. You will come to a National Trust property with the Rotunda and a statue of Bruce. The statue was set up in 1964 to commemorate the 650th anniversary of the battle. It probably stands where Bruce observed the advancing English army. The battlefield extended south and east of this position. The pits were south and south-east of the Borestone. A few were discovered and reopened in the nineteenth century. They were only eighteen inches deep but each had contained sharp hazel stakes. Fragments of weapons were discovered but soon taken away as mementoes. (Stirling) across this road and then curves north. To the left of the road along which Edward was travelling were quite dangerous bogs backed by scrub. This was in front of the Borestone; behind was a large swamp known as the Carse. Bruce deployed his army at the Borestone, protecting the front with concealed pits, and the flanks by resting the left against marshy ground and the right against a small hill (Gillies Hill).

Edward, realizing that the route immediately between himself and the castle would have been adequately prepared, decided on a dual form of attack. While the main body of his army continued to advance towards the castle, veering slightly to the right of Bruce's position, he sent a strong contingent to test the main defence of the Scottish army. This was the 'Great Van', a force composed of archers, cavalry, and infantry, under the Earl of Hereford. It was felt, not least by Hereford, that a sharp thrust in this quarter would send the enemy scurrying. The victory of de Warenne at Dunbar a few years ago had passed into legend and it was believed by many in Hereford's force that a similar triumph could be achieved by identical means.

But it was not to be. One of the first casualties was Sir Henry de Bohun. Sighting Bruce he spurred his horse forward in an exultant charge, hoping to end the battle then and there. Bruce was riding a Highland pony and was only lightly armoured. Seeing a heavily-mailed knight charging at him he quickly moved out of his path and, as de Bohun went by, dealt him a fearful blow with his battleaxe; it crushed de Bohun's skull and broke the axe. This was indeed a victory for morale. However, the 'Great Van' surged forward on to its task. Once in the pits, however, it was clearly in trouble. Between the pits themselves the ground was liberally covered with caltraps, three-pronged spikes so designed that whichever way they lay one spike would be uppermost. The effect of these and the pits on the English cavalry may be imagined, and, lacking effective leadership, it faltered and began to retire. Soon it was in disorder; but Bruce did not pursue.

On the right the main English body was still forcing its way forward. Along the only, but narrow, path open to it, it was easily checked, in spite of its greater numbers; the Scottish *schiltrons* were now proving their worth. Perhaps if the 'Great Van' had been launched in this quarter it might have forced a way through; but it was too late to think of that. The 'Great Van' no longer existed as a fighting force.

For several hours the fighting in this sector went on, cruel, bloody, and indecisive. The Scots fought with skill and tenacity on the narrow front; the English, equally determined but reckless with frustration, displayed similar energy. Both sides were now confident of victory. The Scots had faith in Bruce; the English doubted if their enemy would dare leave their prepared position if the threat to the right succeeded. At 3 p.m. Edward decided his weary army had done enough for that day. Now it needed rest and, above all, water. He gave orders to pitch camp nearer the castle, and, as it happened, nearer the Forth. The site was on the Carse, on the banks of a burn known as the Pelstream. Edward knew the area from his earlier campaign – but he did not know it well enough. The English cursed as they obeyed instructions to make a camp among the streams and bogs; not appreciating the tides which altered the terrain hourly, they became sceptical of the orders they received from above. But they camped.

It was a bad night. The English army was by no means sure it would not be attacked in the darkness. Food was lacking; the supply train had not found a way through the tidal rivulets. The only event in the Englishmen's favour that night was that the Earl of Atholl, who hated Bruce although he had taken service in his army, now attacked the supply depot at Cambuskenneth. He believed that when the English captured Stirling castle he would be rewarded.

At dawn on the 24th the English woke up to realize that the Scots were close at hand. Immediately they put in a charge using the remnants of the 'Great Van' which had been shattered the day before. As the survivors fell back they jammed the remainder of the English close together on slippery, treacherous, unknown ground. On to the packed mass the Scottish archers poured what arrows they had. A few English archers who broke away, formed up, and managed to retaliate were scattered by a Scottish cavalry charge. A great commander might yet have rallied the English and sent them forward. But de Bohun, who could have done it, was lying on the Borestone with his skull split in two, and Gloucester, who had tried, was now impaled on a Scottish spear; Edward was not the man for this situation. He had already left the battlefield and was on his way to Stirling Castle, with an escort of knights. Almost as his followers saw the Royal Standard leave the field they saw another terrifying sight – apparently a new Scottish army, streaming across from Gillies Hill. In fact it was a rabble of camp followers who, believing the battle won, felt sure there was plunder to be taken. But the sight was enough.

Like all beaten and demoralized armies, Edward's now began to flee. It was a hopeless endeavour. Many were drowned in the Forth; others hopelessly and desperately put up a last fight before being massacred. Few escaped.

Edward, of course, did. He rode to Stirling and asked for admission. Mowbray, however, being bound to surrender the castle on that very day, refused. Edward rode on and eventually reached

Dunbar. From Dunbar he travelled by boat to Berwick. He had lost the critical battle for Scotland. Later, when England and Scotland became united, it was dynastically, not militarily.

The visitor to Bannockburn will find everything easy except tracing the actual site of the battle. But he will find Bruce's commemorative statue, and excellent maps and a guide. It will not be difficult to visualize the events of 23/24 June 1314.

The aftermath of the battle was inevitable. The Scots acquired huge quantities of plunder and – perhaps even more important – gained a national identity. Soon they were raiding England again, and Anglo-Scottish relations, which had once seemed on the road to harmony, were now becoming increasingly bitter. Edward was now faced with so many problems nearer home that he did nothing to stop the Scots foraging. The crowning humiliation came in 1318 when Bruce captured Berwick. The following year a Scottish force under Randolph and Douglas drove far down into Yorkshire, where at Mytton-on-Swale they beat a motley force hastily assembled by the Archbishop of York. This battle was known in England as the 'White Battle' and by the Scots as 'The Chapter of Mytton'.

Contrary to popular belief, Bannockburn was not Edward's last foray into Scotland. In 1322 he took an army as far as Edinburgh only to find himself so short of provisions in a 'scorched earth' countryside that he had to retreat precipitously. But he made the attempt. Edward was not an attractive character and his reign was disastrous for Britain; his deposition and extremely cruel murder are the events best remembered about him. But, in his favour, it must be recorded that he did not give up lightly.

The Battle of Halidon Hill

19 July 1333

Edward II was murdered in 1327, and succeeded nominally by his fourteen-year-old son, who became Edward III. Robert Bruce's brother, Edward, who had been crowned King of Ireland, had been killed in battle at Dundalk in 1318. Bruce himself died of leprosy in 1329. His heart was taken on a crusade by his right-hand man, Sir James Douglas, the famous 'Black Douglas'. Douglas, however, was killed in Spain in 1330. New actors now came on to the stage, but the scenery was the same and the plot unchanged.

In the last year of his reign Bruce had sent the Black Douglas on one of the most devastating raids the border had ever known. Edward III in the dubious care of Mortimer, his mother's lover and father's murderer, was taken on the campaign against them. It was a time of chaos, confusion, and misery which ended with the 'Shameful Peace', in which England returned the Scottish crown, which Edward I had removed, and Edward III's sister was married to Bruce's eldest son, David – a boy of eight.

The Regency which now took control of Scottish affairs during the young king's minority could not have been set a more difficult task. Ostensibly the Regent was Randolph, Earl of Moray, but he was not entirely his own master. The recent 'Shameful Peace' had stipulated that a number of barons, known as 'the disinherited' were to be restored to their estates. As some of them were known to be

English adherents, Randolph refused. Among the disinherited was Edward Balliol, the son of John Balliol (Toom Tabard) who had had such a brief and disastrous reign. Edward Balliol now decided to claim the throne of Scotland and, aided by Edward III, who thought he might be a useful tool, raised an army. The first Regent, Randolph, had died in 1332 and had been succeeded by Donald, Earl of Mar. Balliol defeated and killed Mar at Dupplin Moor, captured Perth, and was crowned King at Scone all in the same year – 1332. He then acknowledged fealty to his backer, Edward III.

This was too much for the Scots. Reacting strongly, they appointed a new regent Sir Andrew Moray and with a hastily assembled force drove Balliol out of the country.

Clearly this meant full-scale war between England and Scotland again. In the early months of 1333 Balliol was busily preparing to regain the throne with the help of the army the English were prepared to supply. In the spring he reached Roxburgh and proceeded to put Berwick under siege. Edward joined in in person, laughed French protests to scorn, and scattered a French fleet which tried to supply the beleaguered garrison. This was an unlucky time for the Scots for they lost Sir William Douglas, famous as 'the Knight of Liddesdale', and Sir Andrew Moray, the Regent, in two separate skirmishes. But worse was to come. The new Regent was Sir Archibald Douglas and he decided that relieving Berwick was a task of the highest priority. Collecting all the men he could muster he set off to Northumberland in the early summer of 1333.

On arriving at the north side of Berwick, Douglas quickly realized he had set himself too large a task. For a while his not very substantial force tried to harry the besiegers who were pounding the walls with catapults. Their effect on the English army was negligible and partly out of frustration but partly in the hope of drawing the English army from the town they set off on a trail of devastation and burning through Northumberland. The English were not deceived, for it had already been agreed that, unless the town was relieved by a day which would later be specified, it would capitulate. Hostages were sent to ensure this.

With inexplicable stupidity – perhaps due to his youth and inexperience – Edward decided to try to frighten the town into a quick surrender, in spite of the presence of the Scottish army, by threatening to hang the son of Sir Andrew Seton, the Scottish Governor of Berwick. Seton had greatly annoyed him by resisting stubbornly and also by managing to burn part of the English blockading fleet. Seton was unmoved by the threat, and his son, young Thomas Seton, was hanged in full view of his defenders. This barbarous act did not hasten the surrender, but it caused 19 July to be specified as the agreed date.

The Scottish army, hearing this bad news, decided to call off its foraging and make one last attempt to relieve the town. It hastened back to Duns (the birthplace of Duns Scotus, the famous medieval scholar), where Douglas and the Scottish army were within easy reach of Berwick – or so it seemed. Meanwhile, Edward had posted the whole of his army, apart from a token siege force, on the hill two miles north-west of Berwick. As the A6105 runs straight through the middle of this battlefield which is also marked by a roadside plaque, it could not be much easier to find. Here Edward, who commanded the centre, was able to keep an eye both on Berwick and the approaches from Duns. The hill is 600 ft high and slopes gently, with a hollow just short of the road, down to a marsh. He was, of course, easily seen by Douglas as he advanced.

Douglas, sensibly enough, decided that if he moved straight across Edward's front, he would be asking for instant annihilation.

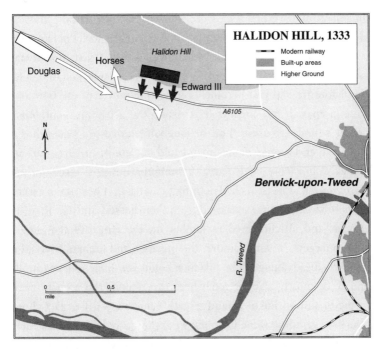

HALIDON HILL, 1333

Halidon Hill

Horses

Douglas

Edward III

A6105

Berwick-upon-Tweed

Modern railway
Built-up areas
Higher Ground

N

R. Tweed

0   0,5   1
mile

The battlefield is two miles out of Berwick-upon-Tweed along the A6105. There is a monument on the northern side of the road and the site is easily seen. No visitor should omit to take a good long look at Berwick, inspect the ruined castle, walk around the walls, and visit the museum. (Northumberland)

He therefore decided to pass in a wide skirting movement which would either avoid them – though this was unlikely – or tempt them down from the hill on to the flatter ground; what he did not know till he reached it was that this flatter ground was marshy. Once in the marsh – and it was, of course, the cavalry – there was no turning back. The English were still holding their fire and there was an air of unreality about the scene. The Scottish men-at-arms dismounted and were joined by the infantry who should have been more at home on soft ground. When they were well mixed together and moving slowly through the soggy country the English bowmen opened up.

It was not such a fusillade as would be seen later at Crécy, Poitiers, and Agincourt, but it was a foretaste, and it was enough. The English army had just become aware of the power of the bow and were prepared and organized to make the sacrifices – of other people's time – to use it. For the longbow needed practice; it had a 70 lb pull and a small or sick man could not use it. In later years an archer would loose twelve arrows a minute, but now three or four were enough. The Scots had nothing to match it. Their cavalry were immobilized by being separated from their horses, and as the men-at-arms and knights tried to lumber up the long hill they made superb targets. The remainder, the pikemen and archers, were at a hopeless disadvantage. The pikemen could not come to grips at all, and were mostly slaughtered where they stood; the archers were trying to aim up-hill at a blind target. A few Scots did in fact climb that long grinding slope but they were promptly killed for all their bravery and trouble. Finally with cruel precision the English knights, who had been waiting in the wings, thundered across the slope and speared the Scots who had struggled out of the swamp and were trying to rally for a final charge. It was less of a battle than a scene of slaughter. It avenged the defeat at Bannockburn, although the effects were much less far-reaching. Douglas himself was killed and – it is said – four thousand others; but the English casualties were very light, as they never broke formation.

Balliol was made king, and Berwick was surrendered. But the clock had not been stopped, only put back.

It has been suggested that the battle took place on the north-west side of the hill instead of the position described above. This theory is unrealistic for two reasons. Firstly, the Scots wished to relieve

Berwick and were hoping to slip by Edward, thereby getting between him and the town. If they had not been hindered by the marshy ground, they might well have succeeded; but Edward doubtless knew the route better than they did, and realized that they would be forced into arrow range by the marsh. Secondly, even the wildest medieval tactician would never have attacked directly up a slope unless cornered and desperate – as Douglas became. In normal circumstances he would try to skirt round the hill and lure the defenders out of their prepared position.

The Battle of Neville's Cross

13 October 1346

After Halidon Hill Scotland's identity as a nation seemed once again in jeopardy. Balliol was restored to the throne and in acknowledgement surrendered Berwick and a large tract of territory between the Tweed and the Forth. But the 'disinherited barons' now fell out among themselves and took sides, some supporting Balliol, others the exiled David II. With French support the latter party were now strong enough to drive Balliol out of the country. Edward III thereupon took an army back into Lothian and re-established him. One expedition was not enough, and there were subsequent demonstrations of military power. Scottish national resentment was not quelled; it merely watched and waited. Here and there the Scots retook a castle but Edward III was not unduly concerned. From 1327 onwards his main thoughts had been concerned with France, of which he now believed himself to be the rightful king. In 1337 he resolved to claim his right and for the next nine years was engaged on expeditions in France, a preoccupation which undoubtedly made life easier for the Scots who wished to eject the English. The castles of Stirling, Perth, and Edinburgh all fell to the Scots. On the other hand, at Dunbar in 1338, the Countess of March ('Black Agnes', from her swarthy complexion) defied an English army under the Earl of Salisbury for nineteen weeks. ('Black Agnes' had a habit of encouraging the garrison by standing on the battlements and jeering at her attackers.) By 1341 Scotland was thought safe enough for David II to return.

David, however, was not an unqualified success. He was described as being neither trustworthy nor likeable. Inevitably he felt bound to assert himself. For the first two or three years this attitude showed itself in probes towards the border. As it was clear that Edward was wholly preoccupied with France, the year 1346 seemed to offer a great chance of military glory – the defeat of an English army in the field and a really deep incursion southwards. Such a move would be welcomed by the King of France, to whom David felt he owed a considerable debt. The news of the French defeat at Crécy in late April 1346 gradually filtered back to Scotland, but its magnitude was discounted; nor from that distance were the Scots able or likely to take much notice of the way it had occurred. All they knew was that the French army had failed to stop an invading English army which was now laying siege to Calais; it seemed an opportune moment to intervene. It was believed that Edward III had taken every available man and weapon to France, with the exception of a few second-line troops left to guard the Channel ports, and every available man and ship would be needed to capture the fortress and port of Calais. David now mustered an army said to be 20,000 strong, which was small by exaggerated medieval standards but sounds reasonably probable. It was certainly good enough to clear away any opposition around the border and it marched on to Durham apparently invincible. Meanwhile an English defence force was hastily mustered, under the overall command of the Archbishop of York. Well might the Church at that time be called the Church Militant! The Archbishops of Durham, Carlisle, and Lincoln had all brought their contributory forces. The English force was said to number 15,000. It assembled at Bishop Auckland, eleven miles south of Durham. This

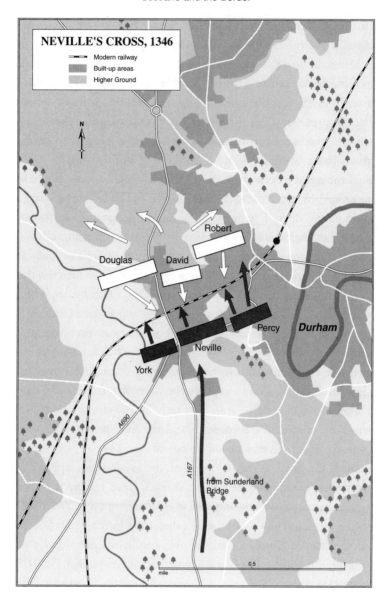

NEVILLE'S CROSS, 1346

Modern railway
Built-up areas
Higher Ground

N

Robert

Douglas   David

Percy   *Durham*

Neville

York

A690

A167

from Sunderland
Bridge

0   0,5   1
mile

was uncomfortably close to the Scots if they should make a sudden move, but they did not. The Archbishop had appointed an experienced soldier, Lord Ralph Neville of Raby, as the field commander; inevitably there was a Percy present and he commanded the right of the line.

The Scots had already probed south of Durham and set up a forward position at Sunderland Bridge, three miles south of the town. Here the Scottish army received a bloody nose from the English van led by Neville. The Scots were swept away as if they had never been there. Neville pushed on to a point believed to be just north of the Neville's Cross junction. There he was facing the Scots main army, and he was joined by Percy on the right wing and the Archbishop himself on the left. Remembering their experience at Halidon Hill, the English had a fan-shaped screen of archers in front of each division. Later the archers would be deployed in *herces*, wedge-shaped formations interspersed but jutting out of the front line – as they had already been at Crécy – but at this stage their dispositions were less sophisticated. The Scots were also in three divisions with David himself in the centre, and, slightly forward, Douglas on the right and Robert on the left. The area was rough and marshy and the Scots could well have taken note of that fact. However, in spite of the fate of the Sunderland Bridge detachment they were full of confidence and pushed forward to attack without making use of the ground. If a commander does not make use of irregularities in ground and adapt his tactics to them, he will soon

Although much built over, this site is not difficult to visualize. Take the point where the A167 crosses the railway line and you are in the centre of the beginning of the battle. Flass Bog was to the north-east of Robert's position. (Durham)

find himself at a disadvantage and this is what now happened to David. As they came forward to attack, Douglas's wing was constricted into the centre by the gully on their right. There, closely packed, it formed a target the English archers could not miss. The Scots, by impetuously charging forward, had contributed substantially to their own downfall. So cramped were they, they could hardly raise their arms to use their weapons, and from ahead and above poured that pitiless stream of arrows which for the next hundred years would make English armies more dreaded than Huns, Vandals, or Vikings had been. Previously it had always been felt that numbers and resolution might achieve victory or at least a cessation of attack; with the English archers it was felt that there was no trustworthy defence.

But the Scots had not forced their way south to be easily beaten. Battered and reeling from the arrow onslaught they still pressed forward. The left was less constricted and was able to drive in a part frontal, part diagonal attack. At the point now sombrely designated Red Hills they were checked. It is doubtful if they reached any further than the present line of the railway. At this stage the English cavalry, so far held in reserve, swept on to the field, entering diagonally from the right. The Scots now found that just as their advance had been constricted by the ravine so their retreat was hampered by the River Browney on one side and the Flass Bog on the other. Many were drowned in the river, while others were trapped in the bog. King David himself was caught at the river. Once again the Scottish pikes had never been properly employed because, by the time the English cavalry came in, the Scots were so disordered that no proper pike barrier could be arranged. The Scots had completely misread the ground tactically: they had no Wallace or Bruce to direct them and the result was unqualified disaster. Not only was King David taken, with four earls and the Archbishop of St Andrews, but the slaughter in the confined space crippled the Scots for many a year to come. The Earls of Menteith and Fife were captured, the former being executed as a traitor.

With David a prisoner, the Regency once more went to Robert the Steward. Robert the Steward, who had commanded the left wing at Neville's Cross, was the son of Robert Bruce's sister who had married a Norman noble named Walter Fitzalan. Fitzalan had been appointed hereditary High Steward of Scotland and his son Robert was known as Robert the Steward.[1] At the age of seventeen he had been appointed regent for his ten-year-old cousin, David, who had gone into exile after Halidon Hill. Robert was extremely able as had been shown when he commanded the Scottish army in its successful enterprises between 1333 and 1341. It was owing to Fitzalan's military skill that David was able to return from France and wear his crown, and he was not to blame for the Scots' defeat at Neville's Cross.

In 1347 something far more calamitous than warfare struck Europe, although it did not immediately reach Scotland. This was the infamous Black Death, which halved the population of England, France and Italy. Whole villages were wiped out, and even the monasteries, which at first tried to provide some medical care, lost all their inmates. It appears to have been a form of bubonic plague, characterized by large boils in the groins and armpits, violent fever, and death within a few days. Two hundred years elapsed before the population losses were made up but that did not stop men fighting

1 A steward was a ward of a 'stig' or 'ste', meaning a house or hall. It is still used as sty – the house of a pig, but this does not necessarily mean that stewards were sty wards and thus pig-minders. The word gradually changed its spelling and became (in most cases) Stewart or Stuart. It should be borne in mind that from a very early date the title of 'steward' denoted a very high and important office.

and killing each other in the meantime. Curiously, the Black Death did not reach Scotland till 1350, when it killed off a third of the people. The violent impact of the disease was enough to make England and France sign a truce which they kept for six years. It might have lasted longer, but, when Edward III offered to renounce all claims to the French throne if he were given Aquitaine free of ties (it had once been an English possession), the French king refused brusquely. In the circumstances, which are too complex to explain here, the offer was not unreasonable. Edward once again invaded France, this time through his new base at Calais. The relevance of this to the Scottish border was that in 1355, in order to take the pressure off the French, the Scots once more marched on Berwick, which they took, with French help. This time Edward was less preoccupied with France – which he felt could wait – and more interested in Scotland. He stormed back, halted at Roxburgh to give the Scots a chance to submit, and, when they did not, pushed on to Edinburgh.[1] The Scots tried to hinder him by clearing the country of foodstuffs, but this did not stop Edward: in revenge he burnt and destroyed every village and building in his path.

The following year (1356) the Black Prince was pursuing precisely the same policy through central France. At Poitiers he was intercepted by a huge but badly commanded French army, and the result was another devastating English victory. Even the French king was taken prisoner.

In 1357 David was released and restored to his Scottish throne. The English drove a hard bargain, for the Scots had to pay 90,000 marks (about £60,000) and cede Berwick and Roxburgh. David's eleven years' confinement in the English court had by no means

1 Berwick had already surrendered.

544

embittered him and in the subsequent fourteen years of his reign he sometimes appeared to be more in tune with the English than with his own subjects. His task was in any event beyond his limited capacities; Scotland simply had not the revenue to provide for the vast ransom which was never more than half paid. Eventually, in 1363, the Scots could stand it no longer and, led by the Earl of Douglas, Robert the Steward, and the Earl of March, broke out in rebellion. Unexpectedly and briefly David showed resolution worthy of his father. He captured Douglas and crushed the revolt. Eight years later he was dead, but not before arranging with Edward III that in the absence of a Scottish male heir the English king should inherit the Scottish throne.

Needless to say, the Scots were not prepared to accept the late king's private arrangement. The Scottish Parliament promptly rejected the scheme and invited Robert the Steward to be king. Thus Robert became the first Stuart king of Scotland. He was, however, Robert II; Robert I had been his famous great-uncle, who was not, of course, a Stuart.

Robert was, alas, a poor king, quite unlike what might have been expected from his record as a Regent. Scotland suffered anarchy nearly as much as England had in the reign of Stephen. Border warfare flourished independently and unrestrained. Its high point was the battle of Otterburn or Chevy Chase, between Percy and Douglas in 1388[1] (which the Scots won), but there were many other incidents nearly as bloody. In 1371 the Earl of March massacred the English in Roxburgh and burnt the town; the reprisals led by Henry Percy, were on no less a scale. Berwick was captured by the Scots in 1378 but soon lost again. A Scot, half merchant, half pirate, named

1 See *British Battlefields: the North.*

Andrew Mercer, took a mixed French, Spanish, and Scottish fleet to Scarborough and plundered it. He was counter-attacked by a similar freebooter, Philpot of London, who captured Mercer and his entire fleet. England was now reigned over by the ineffective Richard II, who before long had too many troubles near at home to give much thought to Scotland.

Robert II[1] died in 1390 and was succeeded by Robert III. Robert III was no more successful as a king than his father, well-meaning though he too was. In the very first year of his reign his brother, the Earl of Buchan, known very appropriately as the 'Wolf of Badenoch', burnt Elgin town and cathedral out of pure viciousness. The year 1396 also saw a remarkable clan feud between the Chattans and Kays settled in a spectacular manner. Thirty men from each clan fought to the death of the North Inch[2] of Perth. They were armed with bow, sword, knife, and axe. Twelve only survived. One of the Kays did not arrive in time and his place was taken by a Perth mechanic, known as Hal o' the Wynd. This blood-soaked spectacle had a cathartic effect on the passions of the thousands who watched and there was comparative peace for a few years. Today the visitor will notice a stone marking the occasion opposite Atholl Crescent, and will observe rather less bloodthirsty matches at tennis, cricket, or football, taking place on the same turf.

It was, however, clear that Scotland, like England, was now to be plagued with over-strong baronial factions. The mighty Douglas family could raise an army equivalent to that of the king – from their own lands. (The third Earl was known as Archibald the Grim.) The Macdonalds – the Lords of the Isles – thought no less of themselves. Meanwhile, in 1399, Henry of Lancaster deposed (and murdered)

1 He had six sons and eight daughters, all legitimate, and six illegitimate sons as well.
2 An 'inch' is an island.

his cousin Richard II and became Henry IV. Initially Henry IV tried a peaceful approach to Robert III to check the harrying of the border, but it was received with indifference. Henry therefore decided to settle the matter personally.

The Battle of Homildon Hill

14 September 1402

In July 1402 Henry IV, who had acquired the English throne by deposing and murdering his cousin Richard II, mustered his army at Lichfield with a view to dealing with the coming threat from Wales. Incompetent though Richard II had been, Henry IV had no illusions that his own usurpation of the throne would be widely welcomed. Already there had been an attempt to kill him while he was celebrating Christmas at Windsor and was presumably off his guard; the rebels had been betrayed by one of their number and were beheaded without trial. Large numbers of people persisted in believing that Richard II was still alive and even the macabre parade of a body said to be his, between Pontefract and London, failed to convince them; there were dark mutterings that this was a substitute who resembled Richard and had been killed for the purpose. They were grim days.

It was believed by the credulous that Richard had somehow escaped and found refuge in Scotland. Inevitably there was an impostor who, claiming to be Richard II, was well entertained by the Scottish court. A show of force was clearly needed in Scotland, but Wales came first. In Wales there was a guerrilla captain of exceptional ability, by name Owen Glendower, who had once been one of Richard II's squires. He had made himself master of North Wales, and was as legendary a figure as Bruce or Alfred the Great or

Bertrand du Guesclin. It would be a long campaign for, so far, Henry's probes into Wales had achieved nothing.

In the event, Wales did not come first. Henry's overtures to Richard III of Scotland had received a chilly reception; if the Scots did not come to pay fealty to the rightful King of England they cared even less to pay it to a usurper. Border raiding increased and the Douglases were foremost in the fray. French privateers were already operating in the Channel and, unless action were taken against Scotland soon, there would be French soldiers marauding in Northumberland as well as cattle-raiding Scots. Henry decided that the Scots must be taught a lesson.

It was the last expedition to Scotland ever led by an English king in person, but for all that it proved a failure. Henry set off in August with three divisions, one commanded by him, one by his son, young Henry, and the third by the Earl of Arundel. It was a disciplined expedition and did no unnecessary damage. Henry moved straight to Edinburgh; somewhat unaccountably he was not intercepted by a nearby Scottish army under Albany. But his task was hopeless. The weather was unseasonably bad, with a series of violent storms, and it was clearly impossible for him to reduce Edinburgh without a long and tedious siege. Showing sound military sense, he withdrew to deal with other more immediate problems. With him went the Earl of March, ready to betray his country to obtain revenge on the Douglases who had outbid him on a marriage settlement. March had planned to marry his daughter to the powerful Duke of Rothesay, son of the king, but instead Rothesay had taken a Douglas. Adding injury to insult, Douglas now captured Dunbar castle, the fortress of the Earls of March. Within the year Rothesay was dead, though whether from the debauchery for which he was renowned or from being murdered after unwise behaviour, is not known. All this favoured the Earl of Douglas who now led even fiercer raids into England. The English, stirred by the Earl of March, produced counter-raids, one of which accounted for 400 Scots at Nesbit Moor just south of Duns. Henry had allocated all the troops he could spare to the border regions but they failed to deter an army under Douglas which penetrated to Newcastle. It was said to number 10,000; be that as it may, it was a substantial force and was undoubtedly to be numbered in thousands rather than hundreds. Murdoch Stewart, the heir to the Duke of Albany, was with it, as was young Archibald, the 4th Earl of Douglas. Having had their fun with Newcastle they were now returning to the border, planning to cross the Tweed at Coldstream. It was a well-known route – an old Roman road; it had seen battles since the dawn of history and the earlier ones are marked by burial mounds and ancient fortifications. When the English, under Percy and the Earl of March, got wind of Douglas's return route, they moved quickly and efficiently to Milfield on the river Till. There they felt they might have a good effect on the Scots who were trying to get through the water with their plunder. The Scots, however, were not prepared to run obligingly into a trap. Their outriders reported the presence of an English army of unknown size and Douglas, showing unusual caution, decided to camp on Homildon Hill and take stock.

The visitor today may look in vain for Homildon Hill, but he will find Humbleton Hill, which is the same place, along the A697. As he comes out from Wooler he will find, two miles to the west, a terraced slope on his left, about 1,000 ft above sea level. On the right of the road he will see a large stone sticking up in the field, but he may not be able to go close to it if there are growing crops.

The battle which took place in September 1402 was extraordinary. The Scots, guarding their plunder, refused to be tempted out of

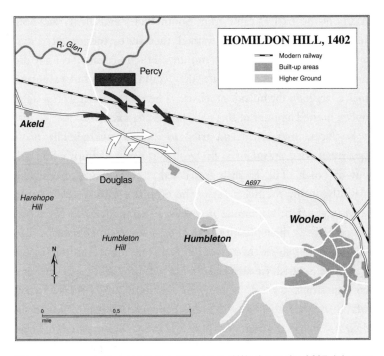

This is very easy to find as it is two miles west of Wooler on the A697. It is now called Humbleton. The Bendar stone is in the middle of the field to the north of the road. (Northumberland)

their strong position. It was very wise, though cautious and unlike the Scots. But the reputation of English arms at Crécy, Poitiers, and the like had induced caution, and Douglas thought it would be prudent to let them show themselves and decide on the attack then.

This unusual policy had not unpredictable effect. As the Scots huddled around their loot, the English army, which had now moved forward, gained confidence in spite of the disparity in numbers. Initially they were only skirmishing, but soon they grew bolder.

Many of the archers came from South Wales and plenty had seen service in France; they were trained, they were experienced in war, and they had a weapon which outranged their opponents. They did not even need to use fieldcraft; they could stand out of range and pick a target on the hillside at leisure. The Scots temper would stand only a limited amount of this passive elimination.

So far neither army had tried to use its cavalry. The Scots spearmen tried an infantry charge but it was cut down while still out of range. The English (or Welsh) bowmen were retreating skilfully, luring the Scots out of the positions, killing steadily, and staying apparently immune themselves. Soon the Scots were less concerned for their plunder than their lives; soon afterwards they were in doubt about their lives too and were making a dash for the Till. The Scottish cavalry had thundered into the attack but found no opposition. As they halted they too were picked off by arrows which smashed their way through helm and corselet. The horses died faster than the men, for they were even more vulnerable. Some staggered to Red Riggs where they were slaughtered wholesale; a few broke out and got to Scotland, but not many. Most of the slaughter probably took place in the field marked by that stone, known as Bendar. This is where Douglas himself was captured, wounded in five places and with an eye knocked out – he would not otherwise have been captured. There were a lot of prisoners – Murdoch Stewart, three earls, two barons, eighty knights, and even some Frenchmen. The dead far outnumbered them and included Sinclair, Gordon, Livingston, and Ramsay of Dalhousie. More were killed in the pursuit than on the battlefield.

Percy was jubilant. The ransoms of the distinguished prisoners would make them rich for years to come. It was a marvellous and unexpected victory. Henry should be grateful.

Henry, indeed, was. But, desperately pressed for money, he demanded that the prisoners should be handed over to him to refill the royal coffers, now perilously empty. With bad grace they were handed over, but the outcome was the rebellion which led to the battle of Shrewsbury in the following year. It was hard on the Percies; they had backed Henry IV in his own bid for the throne, and at Shrewsbury Harry Percy (Hotspur) was killed by an arrow in a rebellion he had been provoked into making. But what were death and misfortune to the Percies? There were others to fight and it was battle which mattered.

An Interim of Anarchy and Border Warfare

Certainly I must confess my own barbarousness. I never heard the old
song of Percy and Douglas that I found not my heart moved more
than with a trumpet; and yet is it sung by some blind Crouder with
no rougher voice than rude style; which being so evil apparelled in
the dust and cobwebs of that uncivil age what would it work trimmed
in the gorgeous eloquence of Pindar.

Sir Philip Sidney (1544–1586)

After Homildon Hill the border saw no major battle for over a
hundred years, but it was far from peaceful. Robert III died in
1406 and once again Scotland had a Regent. This time it was Albany,
appointed at the age of seventy and designed to hold office till he was
eighty-four; and to the satisfaction of all parties and ranks, with the
exception of James, Robert III's son. Albany had decided to send the
prince, then twelve, to be educated in France. Off Flamborough his
ship was intercepted and captured by the English. He was a prisoner
for eighteen years, though not an unhappy one. Of that, more later.

There was a brisk minor battle in 1409 when Jedburgh castle was
retaken from the English, who had held it since Neville's Cross; the
castle was so strong that its demolition was harder than its capture.
The raids went back and forth; Umphraville captured fourteen
Scottish vessels in the Forth, the Scots burnt Penrith. Some raiders

lost their way and achieved nothing. There was a battle of a different sort in 1411, at Harlaw. The Lord of the Isles decided to claim the Earldom of Ross; Albany refused it. The Lord of the Isles assembled an army, said to number 10,000, and marched on Aberdeen. Eighteen miles north of the town at Harlaw, he met Alexander Stewart, son of the Wolf of Badenoch. The Wolf was now a reformed character, and had acquired the Earldom of Mar; he had also soldiered in France in English service. There was apparently nothing subtle about this battle; it was just a murderous head-on clash which the Lord of the Isles lost. The cost in lives to both sides was appalling. Albany followed up, and drove deep into Ross.[1]

In 1424, for £40,000, James was allowed to return to Scotland. In his confinement in England he had clearly thought out how he would rule, and he soon put his thoughts into effect. He decided that the House of Albany was too powerful and too pleased with itself. An outburst of lawlessness by one of the younger sons, in which he burnt Dumbarton and killed thirty-five people, gave James the excuse he needed. The Duke and his two sons were held guilty and beheaded, in company with the Earl of Lennox, at Stirling. For a man of delicate poetic sensibilities James displayed an amazing forthrightness and lack of inhibition. He summoned a Parliament to Inverness in 1427 and, when the leading chiefs attended, he imprisoned forty and executed most of them. He confiscated the Lennox earldom and estates and followed it by appropriating that of the Earl of March, although the holder at the time was loyal and not like his renegade father. On even less pretext James took the Mar estate. Draconian though these and many of his other actions were, nobody could say that they were not merited, nor vital for the future

1 Against this background of battle and slaughter it is interesting to note that the University of St Andrews was founded in 1414. Scots were already at Paris university and Oxford and Cambridge.

well-being of Scotland. In 1436, for good measure, he led a border raid and besieged the English in Roxburgh castle.

But even the alert James was eventually caught unawares. On 20 February 1437 he was in Perth to receive a Papal legate. As the castle was being repaired he stayed in the insecure surroundings of the Blackfriars monastery, although warned of his danger. His own chamberlain was involved in the plot to murder him and had removed all the bolts from the doors. When, therefore, armed men appeared late at night – James was in his nightgown – there was no means of keeping them out. James prised up a flagstone and dropped into a cellar below, but there he was discovered, cornered, and stabbed to death; he made a brave fight of it. Although no friend to the English – he sent Scots to France to help Joan of Arc – he was an able king, making many reforms, and introducing a sensible Parliamentary system into Scotland.

His son, James II, was six. He reigned for twenty-three years (1437–1460). This coincided with chaotic conditions in France, and the Wars of the Roses in England; violent though both these were, they were matched in intensity though not in scale by events in Scotland. At first James was a pawn in the power struggle between Douglas and Stewart, with other minor actors such as Crichton and Livingston trying to take advantage of his youth and inexperience. The first stage of this conflict was brought to an end when James invited the young Earl of Douglas (apparently only sixteen) and his younger brother to dinner at Edinburgh castle. Hardly had they sat down before a black bull's head was put on the table – a sign of impending death. Then James stabbed both his guests personally. As he was only nine at the time it seems that he must have had some help in the deed. This was an outrage, even for those hardened times but nobody – not even the Douglases – saw fit to complain. Eight years and two earls later, the Douglases were back in turbulent power. The internal bloody feuds of this time are too complex to be set down in a book of this length – interesting and bizarre though they were – and we must confine ourselves to border warfare and major battles. A nine years' truce between England and Scotland terminated in 1448, and nobody regretted it. First the Percies and Sir Robert Ogle burnt Dunbar, then the Earl of Salisbury did the same for Dumfries. This was May. In June the Douglases burnt Alnwick, and in July they burnt Warkworth. In October the Percies set off with a substantial force to harry Dumfriesshire. It was intercepted by 5,000 Scots, some of them inevitably Douglases, at Gretna. Percy, the 3rd Earl of Northumberland, and one or two others were captured, but most of the English were killed or drowned in the river Sark. It is interesting to note that King James II was still only seventeen; the concept of children as we know it simply did not exist. Once able to walk and talk a person was treated as an adult, taken to battles, and given unsavoury tasks like choosing which prisoners should be killed and which spared. At sixteen young noblemen were commanding wings of armies – as the Black Prince did at Crécy. Surprisingly enough some of them lived to reach seventy or eighty in spite of debauchery, exposure, wounds, and accidents.

James was a soldier's king. He mixed with his men, sat on the ground or marched with them, ate the same food, and took the same risks. Nobody but he could have held the mighty Douglases at bay; with their military record, their vast estates, their enormous wealth they were virtually kings of the Border. They felt they had a better claim to the throne than James Stuart himself but they never bothered to press it; to be a Douglas was enough.

In 1451 it seemed though that James and the Douglases might still be able to live in harmony, although the Douglases were forging dangerous bonds with other powerful families. In February 1452 the Earl of Douglas was invited to Stirling to dine with the King. For a day and a night all went well, but on the second night James suddenly lost his temper and stabbed his guest in the neck. His servants then added another twenty-five wounds. Short of trying to depose the King there was little that the Douglases could do but what they could they did. The murdered Earl's brother rode into Stirling, blew twenty-four horn blasts (a sign of renouncing their allegiance to the throne), and burnt the town. In the north, their friend, the Tiger Earl of Crawford, laid the whole countryside waste until checked by James with a vastly larger force.

And so it went on. Periodically James took an army into the Douglas lands; periodically the Douglases set off a fresh string of troubles for James in a different area. One of these was in the Western Isles. Shortly after Douglas had paid a visit there, Donald Balloch took a huge fleet to Renfrewshire, burnt and plundered everything he could find, and then did the same for the Isle of Arran. James neither forgave nor forgot. In 1455 he was ready to settle the Douglases once and for all. With a large army he marched to Etrick Forest and then besieged the Douglas castle at Abercorn. Douglas quickly noted that this was not his day and disappeared over the English border. James cast his net far and wide. He demolished Strathavon castle, Douglas castle, and after a long siege the allegedly impregnable castle of Threave. Then he convened a Parliament which confiscated the Douglas estates permanently, outlawed the family, and removed from them the office of March Warden. And that for the moment was the end of the Black Douglases.

With his internal problems settled James turned to the external one – England. The time seemed appropriate to oust the old enemy from Roxburgh and Berwick. Berwick looked too difficult without French help so he marched on Roxburgh. In July 1460 he was besieging it with a well-equipped army; it had the very latest weapons – the firearms known as bombards. These were a great morale factor but erratic in performance. They were made of iron plates, bent to make a tube and welded together. As the king watched one, an unusually powerful charge of gunpowder was forced down the breech with the intention of impressing him, and the iron ball was rammed on top. The explosion split the barrel, killing all around instantly. James was twenty-nine. His son James III was nine and once again Scotland had a Regency.

For the time being Scotland prospered. James II's inspiration lived on. Roxburgh fell and was destroyed. Wark suffered a similar fate. A great triumph came unexpectedly. Henry VI had lost the great battle of Towton to Edward IV in 1461. The wretched Henry, half mad and never competent, took refuge in Scotland. In gratitude he handed over the castle and city of Berwick. The Scots could scarcely believe their good fortune. They even sent an army into England to embarrass Edward IV by attacking Carlisle. This was not, however, a very happy venture, for the Scots had to retreat hastily after losing two or three thousand men.

Edward was not much concerned about Carlisle but was considerably interested in relations with Scotland. He was aided by the exiled Douglas in establishing connexions over the border, while at the same time the Percies, staunch supporters of Henry VI's lost cause, were steadily defeated in one castle after another. Bamburgh, Alnwick, and Dunstanborough all fell in 1462; and Hedgeley Moor and Hexham in 1464, though minor battles were major defeats for Henry VI and the Lancastrian cause, and, of course, the Percies.

James III's reign, though not as disastrous as it is sometimes described, did nothing for Scotland. He was suspicious and secretive; he chose his friends from talented but flamboyant commoners in preference to the duller less cultured nobles on whose support he had to rely. By 1480 he was condoning border raids. These had continued on a small scale over the years but were now building up into something more significant. In the spring of 1480 one of the Red Douglases, Archibald, Earl of Angus, had raided as far down as Bamborough, which he burnt. He was known as 'Archibald, Bell-the-Cat'. James thought these activities would convince the English of the need for peaceful relations with Scotland; if anything they contributed to the reverse. On the Border they were thought of as normal practice.

In 1482 James was under pressures which he seemed unable to sustain. Albany, who had been imprisoned in Edinburgh castle in 1479 but had escaped down a rope, was now in England calling himself 'King of Scotland'. What was worse he was coming north with an English army to prove his claim. James set out to meet him. At Lauder the ill-fortuned Scottish king was surprised by a party of his own noblemen, led by Archibald Bell-the-Cat, who proceeded to hang the King's lowborn friends from Lauder Bridge. James was powerless; meekly he agreed to go to Edinburgh for discussions. Needless to say, Berwick promptly surrendered to the English, although the castle garrison remained defiant. But in August that too surrendered. Visiting Berwick today one has the feeling that all's well that ends well. It is clearly a Scottish town in England. The blood that flowed on the streets and walls of Berwick has somehow joined. Berwick, perhaps, may be likened to the boxing-ring where two fighters have pounded each other round after round and finally, on a points victory, shaken hands, smiled, and become friends. It is a town which no visitor is likely to forget.

But the end for James was not yet. Albany, his most feared opponent, crossed the Border to exile in England (although he left a garrison of English in his castle at Dunbar). Here and there James executed a suspected clan chieftain – about thirty in all. In 1486 Albany and Douglas rashly came into Scotland with a small band of supporters, hoping to find massive support. Not enough came, and Douglas was captured while Albany fled. The last of the Black Douglases was confined in the Abbey of Lindores, where he ended his days. Albany reached England and thence went to France. There, watching a tournament, he was killed by a splinter from a lance.

From 1486 onwards one plot succeeded another and James, faced with a minor civil war, took refuge in the north. Here he rallied considerable support and mustered an army which met the rebels at Blackness (close to the Forth Bridge on the south). After some ineffective skirmishing a truce was arranged; the armies parted but did not disperse. In June James felt he must now act decisively. On the 11th of the month he confronted his opponents at Sauchieburn, just south of Bannockburn, in a battle of which the records are too confused to be of value. James fled from the field leaving behind Robert Bruce's sword which he had hoped would be a talisman of victory. He hid in a nearby mill but was discovered and killed in cold blood (1488).

The new king, James IV, was fifteen. It was said that all his life he was plagued by the consciousness that he had been the tool of the conspirators who had murdered his father. However that did not make him any less forthright in dealing with any of his father's former supporters, even when they appeared in 1489 holding the late King's bloodstained shirt as a banner. In the second year of his reign national morale was stimulated by the remarkable exploits of an extraordinary adventurer and pirate, Sir Andrew Wood. Wood took steps against five English ships which were plaguing the Scots in the Firth of Forth – and captured the lot. England and Scotland were not at war but Henry vii of England could not let this pass so he sent one Stephen Bull, a similar type of freebooter, to reverse the account. After a two-day fight in which both sides suffered heavy damage the three English ships were captured and taken into harbour at Dundee.

Clan feuds did not, of course, merely exist on the border nor in the remoter areas. The Drummonds and Murrays, both of Perthshire, harboured a long-standing grudge against each other. In 1490 they clashed when one of the Murrays, an abbot, was levying a church tithe on Drummond land. They were attacked by the Drummonds and some 130 were then locked up in a church. As the Drummonds marched off, hugely pleased with themselves, a shot from the church killed one. The Drummonds promptly surrounded the church and set fire to it. They were soon brought to trial and executed for this mass murder but it did nothing to make the two families any friendlier. In an attempt to make another area a little more peaceful and law-abiding the Lordship of the Isles was abolished in 1493, but the contribution of this to law and order was not noticeable.

For some years Anglo-Scottish relations seemed likely to improve. This was mainly the work of James himself, although in England Henry vii could not be unenthusiastic to any proposal which would be likely to save him money. James, however, was a difficult man to deal with. He varied from boisterous high spirits to black depression; he was deeply religious yet practised and condoned every form of sensual debauchery at his court; he was handsome (it was said) though he never cut his hair or his beard;

and he wore an iron chain belt around his waist all his life in penance for the part he might have played in his father's death.

None of this stopped him from favouring Perkin Warbeck, the improbable claimant to the English throne. Backed by Maximilian of Austria, and beguiled by the promise that Henry VII would be toppled off his throne by the supporters of Warbeck, James assembled a considerable army on the border. His reward from Warbeck – when he achieved the English throne – was to be Berwick. His army, however, had no objective and was soon brought back to Scotland. In the meantime it had amused itself burning, plundering, and avenging every real or imaginary grievance it could find.

This was in 1496. Even parsimonious Henry could not tolerate such brigandage, but for the moment he had an anti-tax insurrection in Cornwall on his hands. Encouraged, the Scots invaded Northumberland again in February 1497, though on a lesser scale.

In July, as the English seemed to be feeble beyond measure, James mustered an army at Melrose, crossed the Tweed and besieged Norham castle. Norham, as the visitor will note, was not unprepared for such eventualities and held him off. While there he heard that the Earl of Surrey was coming north fast with an army of 20,000 – considerably stronger than his own; he hastily broke off the siege and returned to Scotland. Surrey came storming up, crossed the Tweed, demolished Coldstream castle – and many minor ones – and set off to Ayton. At this point it occurred to both sides to wonder what they were fighting about; in consequence they conferred and a seven-year truce was arranged. There was an unpleasant incident near Norham the following year, when a number of Scottish traders were killed by English soldiers, but Henry cooled James down and proposed a marriage between the Scottish king and his own daughter, Margaret.

Somewhat surprisingly this took place in 1503 (Margaret was fifteen) to the accompaniment of various optimistic treaties. The child of this marriage was James v; the only grandchild was the unfortunate Mary, Queen of Scots. From the latter's marriage with Darnley, later murdered, sprang James vi of Scotland and i of England. As a king, James vi was a pathetic, arrogant, and tiresome failure but his arrival in England in 1603 did at long last unite the two countries.

James iv was relieved when hostilities between England and Scotland abated, for it gave him time to attend to the Isles where troubles flourished as briskly as ever. As fast as he executed one malcontent, another rose in his place. Three successive annual expeditions eventually established royal rule by 1506 and in what seemed a form of miracle the next few years found the clans of the Western Isles respectful and loyal to their king. The spirits of Angus Og, of Black Donald, and of Donald Balloch walked no more.

But it would have been too much to expect the Border to remain peaceful. While they remained on a minor scale the raids worried no one. But raiding, like love or hate, never stands still, and here on the Border the raids would gradually increase in number and intensity until there was a mammoth bloodletting. There were also 'incidents' which inflamed passions. In 1508 Sir Robert Ker, Warden of the Middle Marches, was, by the terms of the truce in force, investigating certain grievances, when he was murdered by three Englishmen, Heron, Lilburn, and Starhead. Heron came from one of the most turbulent border families who lived at Ford castle. Lilburn was caught, but the others escaped, though the Scots were longing to get their hands on Heron. The Scots were now reviving their old alliance with France, and England did not fail to take note.

Henry viii who succeeded to the English throne in 1509 was of a very different temper from his father but was not at this stage anxious to fight the Scots. He saw greater gain and greater glory in a war with France. Margaret, James's wife, might have been expected to improve relations between her husband and her brother but she, believing that Henry VIII had not handed over certain jewels which were her right, showed no disposition to intervene. When Henry embarked for France, James decided that the time was ripe both to assist his French ally and to teach England a lesson.

In August 1513 Hume, Warden of the Marches, raided Northumberland with a force of some 6,000. On the way back, loaded with plunder, they were overtaken at Milfield by a force under Sir William Bulmer. In some ways the ensuing battle was a repetition of Homildon and the remaining Scots were glad to escape across the Border with their lives.

This was the 'Ill Raid', and it merely spurred James to greater efforts. In September he took his whole army to Flodden where in a completely unexpected disaster his army was cut to pieces and he himself was killed.[1] Without underrating the English achievement, the disaster was clearly in part due to James's casual attitude. The night before the battle he spent dallying with Lady Heron in Ford Castle and on the battlefield itself he fought on foot and gave impetuous orders. It is said that a major factor in the battle was the shooting of the Kendal archers, who were all too familiar with the tactics of Scottish raiders and cut them to pieces with deadly speed and accuracy.

Today the visitor to Selkirk may be lucky enough to witness the 'Common Riding'. One Scotsman was lucky enough to return from Flodden with a captured English banner, and he came from Selkirk. This antidote to a national catastrophe – it was never felt to be a

1 This battle was described in *British Battlefields: the North.*

disgrace, for it had been hard fought – was paraded around the town. The next year the ceremony was repeated, and continues annually to this day. Other Border towns have now introduced 'Common Ridings', but, as they will tell you in Selkirk, the honour really belongs to Selkirk – and to Selkirk alone.

The new Scottish king, James v, was one year old. Once more the clan feuds raged unchecked; once more trouble smouldered and occasionally flared up along the Marches. In 1523 a series of English raids surpassed in thoroughness everything which had gone before. The whole countryside was devastated. In September, Surrey, the son of the victor of Flodden, took 9,000 men to Jedburgh and sacked it; the Scots, however, aroused his admiration for the vigour and persistence with which they tried to block his path. Nor did the Scots omit to hit back when and where they were able.

At the age of seventeen, James v decided to put an end to the power of the Red Douglases, who up till then had dominated his life. He did this by proclamation from Stirling, and then tried to implement it by arms. At the latter he was less successful, being compelled to abandon the sieges of Coldingham and Tantallon (which no visitor to Scotland should omit to see); but time was on his side and the Douglases withdrew to England.

Two years later, in 1528, he decided to try once again to restore his authority on the border, and hanged forty-eight of his more turbulent subjects there. But it did not last. Soon both the Border and the Isles were doing much as they pleased.

In 1542 he made his last mistake. Not wishing to make a full-scale expedition against England, but determined on an exemplary raid, he launched some 10,000 men in the direction of Carlisle. They were opposed by a mere 3,000 but, as the armies sighted each other, Oliver Sinclair, one of James's favourites, read out a proclamation that he himself was commander-in-chief. The Scots nobility refused to accept the announcement; the result was that there was no supreme command and the Scottish army fought – bravely enough at first – as an uncoordinated host. Poor command is bad enough, but absence of command is fatal, and so it proved here. The Scots were pushed back to a narrow ford on the River Esk and thus on to Solway Moss. The result, with hundreds taken prisoner, was the greatest disgrace known to Scottish arms, although the fighting in the early stages had been nothing to be ashamed of. The news was taken to James at Falkland, and the shock and disgrace were too much for him. He went into a decline and died on 14 December. The heir to the throne was Mary, Queen of Scots, at that moment seven days old.

The Battle of Ancrum Moor

12 February 1545

The arrival of the infant Mary, daughter of James v and Mary of Guise, was bound to have a catastrophic effect on Anglo-Scottish relations; it was not likely to be conducive to internal harmony in Scotland either. She married in succession Francis ii of France; Henry, Lord Darnley, who was mysteriously murdered; and, finally, the suspected murderer, Bothwell. She was eventually executed on a flimsy pretext by her cousin Queen Elizabeth and died at Fotheringay Castle, Northamptonshire (now demolished); she met her death with great courage and dignity.

Initially Henry viii had plans for Mary; he decided she should be married to his son. The fact that Mary was an infant and a Catholic and that his son was a Protestant and nearly an adult did not affect his opinion of the suitability of the match; the fact that Edward was the victim of hereditary syphilis was also considered unimportant. The Scottish nobles who had been taken from Solway Moss agreed to the terms, and the treaty only needed ratification by the Scottish Parliament to become a fact. In December 1543, however, the Scottish Parliament, strongly influenced by Cardinal Beaton, repudiated the treaty and instead renewed the alliance with France.

Henry's fury was predictable and unprecedented. His instructions to the Earl of Hereford included the following: 'Put all to fire and sword, burn Edinburgh Town, raze and deface it so that it may remain for ever a perpetual memory of their falsity and disloyalty. Sack Leith and burn and subvert it, and all the rest, putting man, woman and child to the sword without exception . . .' And so it went on, giving detailed instructions as far as St Andrews. Hereford made two excursions in 1544, one in May, the other in September. Melrose, Kelso, Holyrood, Jedburgh, and numerous other towns and monasteries were burnt. These atrocities, apart from poisoning relations between England and Scotland for two centuries, were self-defeating for among the lands pillaged were many which belonged to Henry's Scottish supporters.

In 1545 the English were back again, this time with an even more mixed force than before. It was said to consist of 3,000 mercenaries, mainly German and Spanish, 1,500 English borderers, and 700 Scots who would do anything for money and found English money as acceptable as anyone else's. It was under the command of Sir Ralph Evers who had been on the previous expedition and distinguished himself for ruthless savagery.

At this point, the Earl of Angus, a Red Douglas whose estates had suffered badly, and the Earl of Arran, joined forces. Angus had raised 1,000 horse. The Scottish horse was small but extremely mobile and dexterous; he could even traverse boggy land by adroit jumping. The rider carried a long spear, a sword, or a battleaxe known as a 'Jedburgh staff'. With these troops Angus set off in pursuit of an English force which had plundered Melrose and was now moving on to Jedburgh. He was joined by a similar number under Lesley of Rothes. Even combined it was not a large force but it was enough to make the English think twice about crossing the Teviot without a preliminary battle. They, therefore, camped on Ancrum Moor, three and a half miles north-west of Jedburgh on 12 February.

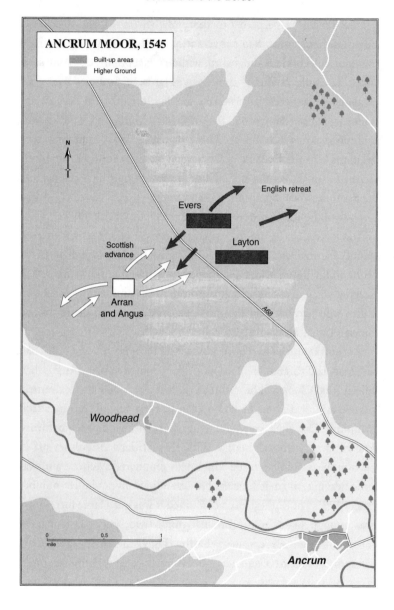

ANCRUM MOOR, 1545

Built-up areas
Higher Ground

N

English retreat

Evers

Scottish
advance

Layton

Arran
and Angus

A68

Woodhead

0   0.5   1
mile

Ancrum

Here Angus was joined by yet another force, under Sir Walter Scott of Buccleuch. Scott was burning for revenge, for in the previous year Evers had devastated his lands in Teviotdale, stormed two of his castles, killed many of his men, and carried off a great haul of plunder. Nevertheless, he did not allow his fury to affect his military judgement.

Ancrum Moor is easily found, for the A68 runs straight through the middle of the battlefield. The Scots initially took up station on Gersit Law overlooking the English camp, where they were in full view of their opponents. As the English settled down to their camping site, their scouts went out and inspected the Scottish position. This could be one of those occasions when the rival armies might inspect each other but not fight. The Scots were clearly outnumbered and, with memories of English archery, they might well decide to sheer off. But such was not their intention.

Instead, they performed the sort of subtle manoeuvre which occurred very rarely in those days. In clear view of the enemy scouts, who were allowed to remain unmolested, they sent followers and horses to the rear in the direction of Palace Hill. It looked, from a distance, as if they had decided that the English force was too large a nut to crack and that they would melt away to pick up reinforcements for an attack later. The sight was welcome enough to the English, who formed the opinion that a quick dash after them would destroy the basis of any possible danger on the return to the Border, and there might even be more plunder as well. Evers had a quick

Take the A68 (Melrose–Jedburgh); the battlefield is 3½ miles north-west of Jedburgh. This is some way from Ancrum itself. Some early accounts of this battle place it around Peniel Heugh (two miles north-west), which has Iron Age forts and was no doubt the scene of battles, but not this one. (Scottish Borders) conference with his captains; all were unanimous that an attack should be put on straight away. The men would not like it for they were weary from their march over bad tracks from Melrose, and were already weighed down and wearied with plunder, much of it as useless as it was cumbersome. But, with a hard core of mercenaries who were paid to obey and fight, there was no hesitation. The horses were quickly resaddled, the foot-soldiers made themselves ready for battle. The only factor which could beat them was the speed by which the Scots moved away. Taking no chances on this the men-at-arms put their horses to the gallop and the infantry broke into a run.

At the top of the hill there was no sign of the Scots; and as the English army puffed and looked around it seemed they had come too late. Suddenly a shout from one of the skirmishers attracted everyone's attention. He was pointing down the slope. There, indeed, were the Scots. They had not gone far and by the look of it they had decided they must try to put up some sort of fight. Down the slope the English rushed, scarcely listening for commands.

As they came on to the Scottish spearmen it was obvious that there were many more spears than had been expected. As the cavalry ran on to what looked like an impenetrable wall of points, horses threw their riders, both horses and riders rolling over in agony. Behind, the Scottish arquebuses were keeping up an intermittent fire, picking a man here and there. The smoke blew back into English eyes which were already dazzled by the rays of the late afternoon sun. Even so, these were no novices, they had seen a dozen and more battlefields, so they fell into line and now presented three ranks to the enemy. In the third line were the arquebusiers, with the latest hand-guns. The guns fired twice a minute – if all went well – but they needed careful handling and could be aimed only from the top of the long rest which each arquebusier carried.

Now, at this critical stage, with the English force breathless, unsighted, and confused, the Scots put in a charge. Those pikes, some up to eighteen feet long, were terrifying weapons, for it seemed impossible to dodge them. They were not always a success, for a pikeman needs to be well controlled if he is not to do more damage to his own side than the enemy, but properly used, and with the right conditions, they were superb. This was such a moment. They hit the English front rank like a wall of venomous snakes' heads, sending it reeling back into the second line, which, already half-blinded by smoke, gave way and blundered on to the arquebusiers, who had their rests knocked to the ground and their powder split. Under the shock all fell back on to the hilltop where they tried to regroup. But the ground was too uneven, so they tried again halfway down the slope.

It was hopeless. The Scots now came hurtling on to them, burning for vengeance, and looking like demons as they whirled their claymores.

At this moment the Scottish renegades with the English army decided this was an appropriate moment to change sides. All they had to do was to tear off the red badge they wore, shout a Scottish battlecry and plunge their swords into the nearest Englishmen. In the general tumult at the end of the battle no one would bother to question where they had come from. They were Scots and they had fought on the winning side. Who would want to challenge them?

The 'English', two-thirds of them being Spanish or German, were now in full flight. As evening drew in, for it was only February, the fugitives, singly or in bands, tried to make their escape. As usual, the local peasantry were hanging around the edges of the battlefield, happy to do business with the victors and finish off the wounded whichever side won. Now they had their chance. Some of the fiercest opponents of the flying Englishmen were the Scottish women. Although Scottish women's amiability had been commented on, with surprise, by both Roman and French, it did not extend to appreciating being raped by Border raiders. Now they took their revenge. One of the fiercest of the Scottish women, who took part in the battle itself when her lover was killed, was the 'Maiden of Lilliard', who gave her name to Lilliard's Wood, just to the northeast of the battlefield. Sir Ralph Evers was killed, as was also Sir George Layton, the cavalry commander; both were buried in Melrose Abbey with full military honours. Such was feudalism! Evers' stone coffin was discovered in 1813 near the altar, but the skeleton crumbled to dust when the lid was removed. Other English knights were taken prisoner and eventually ransomed. Although the slaughter around the battlefield was considerable, about 800 being killed, over 1,000 were taken prisoner as well.

The result of the battle was that all English raiders were cleared from the Border districts by the end of the year. It was a fine and well-planned victory and, although the English could not be expected to approve of it, they nevertheless admitted a certain admiration for the skill by which it was contrived.

The Battle of Pinkie

10 September 1547

The two years which elapsed between the surprising battle of Ancrum Moor and the even more remarkable one of Pinkie are notable for religious and political moves rather than military ones. The only key events which concern us here are the death of Henry VIII on 28 January 1547 and the adoption of supreme power by Edward Seymour, Earl of Hertford, brother-in-law to the late king. (His sister was Jane Seymour who had died in producing Henry's only male heir). The new king, Edward VI, was now ten, and Henry in his declining months had appointed a council of sixteen for the boy's minority. Seymour was President and it did not take him long to bribe his colleagues into letting him become 'Lord Protector' and adopting the title of Duke of Somerset. It then emerged that Somerset, as he was thenceforward known, was not a mild Anglo-Catholic but an intensely bigoted Protestant. Among his other activities was the destruction of much that was beautiful – and therefore presumably idolatrous – in English churches. Later it emerged that he was endowed with stupendous courage and fortitude as well. Life is never simple.

Within the year Somerset had contrived to plunge England into war with both Scotland and France. This was unfortunate but not disastrous, and Somerset was virtually above criticism so carefully had he distributed his favours. His brother, the Lord Admiral, became Lord Seymour of Sudeley and then married Henry VIII's widow, Catherine Parr. He had made immoral advances to the future Queen Elizabeth when she was only fifteen and even tried to propose marriage after Catherine died. However, his nefarious schemes, of one sort and another, ended with his execution two years later.

It was soon clear to Somerset that the French were in strength in Scotland, and unless the threat from the north was checked it would become very dangerous indeed. The Scots were unusually active at this time. Arran, the Regent, though naturally an idle man, bestirred himself to equip privateers, damp down internal feuds, establish a line of beacons with mounted sentinels nearby, and train and recruit by means of Wapinshaws – musters and inspections of local district forces.

Somerset arrived in Berwick in September 1547 with an army totalling 17,000, 14,000 of whom were English, the rest mercenaries. Lord Grey was overall cavalry commander, but Sir Ralph Vane commanded the men-at-arms (4,000) and Sir Francis Bryan the Light Horse (2,000). The German mercenary infantry were commanded by Sir Peter Mewtas and looked very impressive in their buff coats and pot helmets; each carried an arquebus and a sword. The cream of the army were the mounted Spanish arquebusiers, under the command of Don Pedro of Gamboa; they had had much battle experience. A colourful part of the army was Shelley's men-at-arms, who wore blue doublets slashed and faced with red. The army had fifteen heavy guns, 900 wagons of stores, and a contingent of archers and pikemen; there were also 1,500 pioneers, specially brought to clear the route. There were also in the English army 200 Scottish nobles and their followers, including the Earls of Bothwell and Cassilis, and there were known to be other waverers in Scotland who were waiting their moment to turn traitor. These renegades were the curse of Scotland, for they would betray their country in order to do a bad turn to an envied neighbour. This was the best English army which had ever entered Scotland. It is also one of the best documented, for the Judge-Marshall who accompanied the expedition left a diary giving the main dispositions and commanders. The army marched north up the coast, accompanied off shore by a fleet consisting of thirty warships and thirty-two transports. No opposition was encountered on the way, although there were various defiles where it might well have been badly mauled. The Earl of Warwick led the van, Somerset the centre, and Lord Dacre of Gillesland the rear. Each column had a cavalry screen at the side, pioneers out in front, and artillery at the rear. They were in no hurry and they burnt the countryside as they passed through it, in the mindless way that armies had at this time; such practices had no effect on the enemy but merely destroyed potential supplies which might have been needed later. At Longniddry, Somerset renewed contact with his fleet which was in Leith Roads; it then returned and stood off the Esk estuary. Somerset then moved down the west to Falside Hill (it was then Fawside) where he camped. Here he could see an enormous Scottish army which had taken station on the west of the Esk, on a slope known as Edmondstone Edge. The numbers in Arran's army were said to be 36,000; although probably not as large as this it was more numerous than Somerset's but not as well coordinated or armed; a fair estimate of its numbers would be 23,000. Somerset's first position had the left on the Forth estuary and the right on a dangerous bog. The Esk was deeper than it is now, broader and faster-flowing. The only means of crossing it was the old Roman bridge which may still be seen. The Scottish left flank had gun positions to cover attack from sea or land. It was an excellent position for barring an advance on Edinburgh.

But, as a Scotsman once sadly recorded, most of Scotland's lost battles have been due either to treason by their nobility or imbecility by their leaders. The latter was now paramount.

The day before the battle – the 9th – Lord Home rode out in front of the English camp at Falside with 1,500 troopers and taunted the English to attack. Lord Grey asked Somerset's permission to accept, and, when this was given, went out with 1,000 men-at-arms and 500 demi-lances (cavalry lancers) under Sir George Vane. In the end it was an unequal contest, for the English were fully armoured while the Scots had hardly a breastplate among them. Nevertheless, there was wholesale slaughter on both sides in a contest which would do little for morale. Home was mortally wounded; his son was unhorsed and taken prisoner. Somerset meanwhile had been casting a careful eye over the landscape. He noted that the Inveresk slopes overlooked the Scots position and, after a dusk reconnaissance, he sent some cannon up; from there the Scottish lines would be within range, which was not the case at Falside. It was, however, as a glance at the map will show, a dangerously exposed position.

At this time, late on the night before the battle, Somerset received a typically medieval-type challenge to stake the issue on a tournament of ten or twenty men, the Scots to be commanded by the Earl of Huntly. Warwick was eager to accept, but Somerset would not allow it. 'For,' he said, 'the Earl of Huntly is not the equal to your lordship.' It did not occur to anyone that saving the lives of thousands might perhaps offset the social solecism of a minor Earl having the effrontery to challenge a major Earl. Somerset had probably decided there was no alternative to a murderous battle, although he probably did not realize that the Scots were so confident that they were already gambling with the ransoms of the prisoners they planned to take the next day.

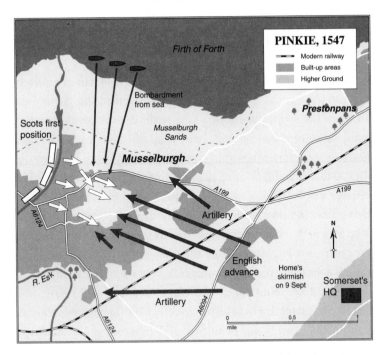

PINKIE, 1547

- Modern railway
- Built-up areas
- Higher Ground

Firth of Forth

Bombardment
from sea

Prestonpans

Scots first
position

*Musselburgh
Sands*

Musselburgh

A199

A199

Artillery

A6124

English
advance

Home's
skirmish
on 9 Sept

Somerset's
HQ

R. Esk

Artillery

A6094

A6124

N

0   0.5   1
mile

Cross the Esk on the A6124. Turn on to the A1, then turn left again on the
A6094. This will have taken you around the perimeter of the main battle. Note
the little Pinkie Burn, opposite Loretto, which became choked with bodies and a
major hazard. (East Lothian)

The 10th was clear and mild. Somerset now sent a second artillery
force on to the right flank to cover his advance and moved up
towards the Esk. To his surprise and pleasure he found the Scots
were advancing to meet him, having crossed the Roman bridge.
They were now deploying on the west bank of the Esk, on the plain
crossed by the Pinkie brook. This, incidentally, is a good mile from
the battle site marked on the ordnance survey maps and is just to the

west of Loretto School. (Loretto has subsequently contributed substantially to the defeat of many a Sassenach Rugby football team!)

On that fateful morning in September 1547 Arran completely misread the signs in front of him. He had assumed that Somerset's swing to the right, during which he positioned his artillery, was a panic move to reach the ships lying close off shore; in fact it was a move to draw the Scots within range of the ships' guns. Hardly were they in that exposed position than the English guns opened up. The carnage was appalling and the Scots had not yet been able to strike a blow. Their artillery, which was of poor quality, was far to the rear. The pick of the infantry, the Lowlanders (dressed in white) were in the centre, the Highlanders and the Islanders were on the right, and the left consisted of eastern county infantry under the Earl of Angus. This included a thousand monks, Black, Grey and Red Friars, who had come to the battlefield to strike a blow against the English Reformation; hardly one of them was alive at the end of the day, a fate which monkish militants had more than once known. The Scottish left flank soon began to take the entire fire from the ships; those who could therefore soon swung across into the centre to get out of range. Here things were not much better, for this was well within range of Somerset's artillery, firing over the heads of their own infantry. The Scots quickly realized the answer to standing and being slaughtered by gunfire and drove forward with tremendous force towards the heart of Somerset's position.

So far the English army had hardly been engaged but, seeing the rapid Scottish advance – far faster than could have been anticipated – Somerset ordered an immediate cavalry attack. It went in with vigour in spite of the soft ground, but, as it did so, the Scots spearmen took up position with their eighteen-foot spears and contemptuously held it off. Time and again the English men-at-arms crashed into the charge, time and again they stopped, wheeled, and regrouped. Behind that impregnable wall the Scots jeered at them as 'loons, tykes and heretics'. Grey was wounded in the cheek, Sir Andrew Flammoch all but lost the English standard, and upwards of 200 fallen men-at-arms were chopped to pieces by Highland 'whingers'. Grey received a spear thrust straight through his face, in through one cheek and out of the other. Nearly choked with blood, he reeled in the saddle, and his aides rushed to take him out of action; but he would have none of it. 'Give me a drink to wash this muck away,' he gulped. He was given a flask of beer, the only drink available, and he swallowed a quart. 'I'm all right now,' he said. (This scene was said to have taken place at Barbacklaw, the farthest point the Scots reached.)

Had the Scottish cavalry under Angus now put in a charge the day might have ended very differently. But Angus, uncertain of his infantry support, hesitated. Warwick turned the scale. Seeing that the cavalry charges could make no impact on the Scottish spearmen he ordered a triple cannonade. As the artillery began dropping shot into the Highland ranks, the bowmen sent in a steady stream of arrows and the Spanish arquebusiers galloped up, discharged their pistols into the Scottish forces, and galloped out again. They were followed by the German foot arquebusiers, known as *hackbuters*. As some of the spearmen had already broken ranks to plunder, this onslaught on a depleted line was more than flesh and blood could bear. As the weaker fell back, the stronger found their own position untenable. Suddenly, as a further English cavalry attack came in, the Scottish line broke. Now their only thought was of flight; it was, inevitably, a disaster. Some fled to the bridge where they were caught in the crossfire from the ships; others flung themselves into the river where they were drowned in thousands; yet others tried the Moss, where they were trapped. In some parts of this field there was no quarter, for in the earlier Scottish advance some wild cruelties had been perpetrated on the wounded; these were now discovered and triply avenged.

This was the 'Black Saturday of Pinkie', the Battle of Inveresk, or the Battle of Musselburgh. Whatever it was called it was a great triumph for English arms and equipment, and a sad memory for Scotland, although the Scots made a fine fight of it against impossible odds. They blamed their traitors.

> *Twas English gold and Scots traitors won*
> *Pinkie field but no Englishman.*

In fact it was the defeat of a medieval army, ill-equipped and badly commanded, by a well-drilled, well-equipped, balanced force. Unfortunately, just as cries of 'Revenge Ancrum' resounded on the fields of Pinkie, so would 'Revenge Pinkie' now be heard on other battlefields. It failed in its objective, for Mary, Queen of Scots was rushed off to France to marry the Dauphin, and French troops remained in Scotland.

The Battle of Newburn

28 August 1640

Newburn was a different sort of battle from those we have described earlier in this book. It was a preliminary to the fratricidal struggle known as the Civil War, which it preceded by two years. It was a battle for religious as much as political causes; such occasions, unfortunately, seem to incorporate the worst of each.

The causes of Newburn and subsequent battles in the north will be more readily understood and appreciated by those who have considered the earlier battles described in this book than by those who study them in isolation. Newburn and the great battles of the Civil War in Scotland are ostensibly conflicts between different religions allied to political parties. Newburn was a battle between fervent Scottish Convenanters who resented Charles I's attempts to impose on them an Anglican form of worship, and an ill-disciplined army of Royalist supporters who were in the field because their leaders had taken them there. Yet in both there were undertones of the old Border conflicts.

At Newburn the Scots were trying to preserve the religion that Somerset at Pinkie had tried but failed to impose on them. That was ninety-seven years before, and since then England had had a Catholic Queen (Mary) and a Protestant Queen (Elizabeth). For a time Scotland had had a Catholic Queen: Mary, Queen of Scots.

Many Scots disliked this distaff rule, and John Knox called it 'The monstrous regiment of women'. Any form of authority by women, he affirmed, was 'repugnant to nature, insult to God and the subversion of good order, equity and justice'. Knox had been dead for fifty years when yet another dangerous woman began to plague men's lives. This was Henrietta Maria, sister of that Louis XIII of France who was busy persecuting the Huguenots. She was Charles I's wife and doubtless behind his high-handed, religious schemes. This development was a great disappointment. After the death of Elizabeth, England and Scotland had been united under James I. He had been a misguided king but was too gutless to press his foolish ideas too far, but his son Charles was of different mettle. He not only thought he had a divine right to rule; he even acted on it. But the Scots would have none of it; noblemen and ministers and merchants all swore a 'National Covenant' to resist Popery and tyranny. Thus the Covenanters were born. Charles knew this meant business and began military preparations. So did the Covenanters; they raised an army of 20,000 and advanced to Duns, ready to defend the line of the Tweed.

This was clearly rebellion and Charles knew it. He mustered an army at York – and was appalled at the poor response. Desperate for money, he asked Parliament for supplies; Parliament refused. There was clearly only one thing to do – or so it seemed. He dissolved Parliament, illegally raised a few thousand pounds for vital equipment, and sent his men to tackle the Scots.

The English army which now marched north under the Earl of Northumberland numbered 21,000, of which 2,000 were cavalry. The infantry which made up the rest was organized in companies of 200. Each, unless depleted by desertion, had a captain, a lieutenant, an ensign, three sergeants, three corporals, three drummers, and 188

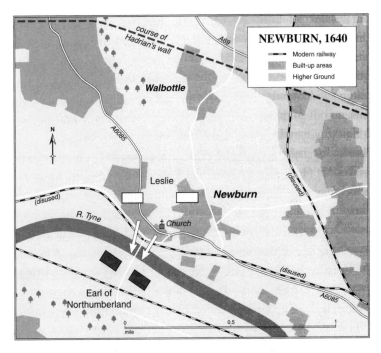

NEWBURN, 1640

- Modern railway
- Built-up areas
- Higher Ground

course of Hadrian's wall

A69

Walbottle

A6085

N

Leslie

Newburn

(disused)

(disused)

R. Tyne

✝ Church

Earl of Northumberland

(disused)

(disused)

A6085

0   0,5   1
mile

Take the A6085 out of Newcastle. The battle was by Newburn bridge. Note the church tower from which Leslie fired his cannon. (Tyne & Wear)

private soldiers. The army had swords and muskets; there is no record that it possessed artillery when it set off.

The Scots were initially vastly better equipped. They had 24- and 32-pounder guns which had been brought over from Holland, 4,000 horse, and a variety of arms. Their number was given as 25,000. They wore a 'uniform' of a Lowland bonnet with a knot of blue ribbons above the left ear. This is said to be the origin of the song, 'All the blue bonnets are bound for the Border'. A rather more valuable asset was the experience of their Commander-in-Chief, Sir

Alexander Leslie of Balgonie. He had served with Gustavus Adolphus, the brilliant Swedish General, and had brought back with him the tactics which served that dynamic figure so well in the Thirty Years War. One result was that the old, effective, but unwieldy pike was reduced from eighteen feet to fourteen; its bearers occupied the centre of every corps, where they were flanked by musketeers. They also had pistols and ball ammunition.

This Scottish army, led by Montrose, marched towards Coldstream on 17 August. Crossing the Tweed was a problem, for it was high. The Scots marched on, not plundering as their predecessors would have done, but so terrifying was the Scots reputation from past history that the countryfolk fled before them. Marching south along the line of the present A6085 with the intention of attacking Newcastle, the Scots came to Newburn. Just by Newburn Bridge there was a ford, where Lord Conway, the English General of Horse, had set up twelve cannon hastily removed from Newcastle. They were defended by breastworks and manned by 3,000 musketeers; behind were 2,500 horse. As dusk fell, a reckless Scottish officer rode to the Tyne to water his horse; the English did not care for such bravado and shot him dead.

During the night Leslie mounted a cannon on the top of Newburn church tower and drew nine pieces of ordnance to the riverbank where they were concealed amongst the bushes. The musketeers, under cover of darkness lined all the north bank, so that every foot of th south bank had a gun trained on it.

At first light the attack began. The Scottish marksmanship was deadly, particularly from the Newburn church cannon which was firing on the English redoubt. Under cover of this heavy fire, a small detachment of Scottish Life Guards, led by Major Ballantyne, forced their way across the river. Soon others followed. As they made their appearance on the south bank, men began to fall back without orders. Hoping to re-establish some sort of reorganization, Conway now sounded the retreat.

But it was not all over. A small body of English cavaliers, wild and boisterous throughout the march, now watched sneeringly as the musketeers withdrew. 'Scum of London,' they jeered, and then forming up, put in a charge against the advancing Scots which sent them reeling. Soon they were surrounded. Fighting on, first with pistol, then with rapier, they were overwhelmed. Even so the casualties they had inflicted before being killed or taken prisoner were alarming; it was impossible that a squadron or two of cavalry should check an army, but they nearly did.

After that it was all over. Losses on both sides were light, mainly because the main forces had not been engaged. Newburn, or as it is known, the Rout of Newburn Ford, was a victory for morale. The English on this occasion had no heart in the fight. Newcastle was now surrendered to Leslie, and shortly afterwards Durham capitulated to the Earl of Dunfermline. Perhaps the most notable aspect of these captures was the fact that the Scots behaved with the utmost propriety, plundering nothing and paying for everything except artillery and arms. Truly, times had changed.

The Battle of Kilsyth

15 August 1645

The main events of the Civil War have been covered elsewhere in this volume, principally in *British Battlefields: the Midlands*. By 1645 the two armies had acquired a certain professionalism from experience; both had been stirred by victories and tempered by stinging defeat. On 14 June the decisive battle of Naseby destroyed Charles's last hope of winning the war in England. His only hope lay in the north. Here James Graham, Marquis of Montrose, who had led the attack across the Tyne and Newburn, had broken with the Covenanters and raised the Royal Standard. He had already won five minor but important battles, such as that at Tippermuir in September 1644 when his cavalry consisted of three horses and his Irish supporters had one round each for their guns. Such deeds in such a manner gave hope indeed. Montrose was a leader of quite exceptional merit; even now he might turn the scale and win the war for his King.

In July 1645 General Baillie, the Scottish Parliamentary Commander, arranged a muster at Perth for an army of 10,000, and began to march south to link up with the forces of Lanark. This move would effectively frustrate any attempt by Montrose to march his successful army into England. Montrose, however, had other ideas. Fresh from victory at Alford (west of Aberdeen), he had come storming south, crossing the Forth at Frew, just above Stirling,

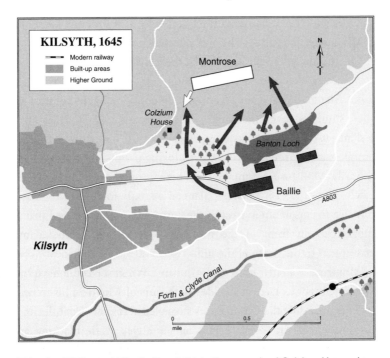

Take the A803 out of Kilsyth. Turn left into the grounds of Colzium House. In front of the house you will see the Montrose memorial. The battlefield area is to the east; some of it is now covered by an artificial lake. Relics occasionally come to light. As you look at the terrain you will probably be as surprised as Montrose was that he was offered battle here. (North Lanarkshire)

marching over Bannockburn, and was now, on 14 August, encamped by the side of the Colzium burn, a mile north-east of Kilsyth. Here he knew that Baillie, whom he had outmarched, must pass him here on his way south. Montrose had 5,000 men, including some good Irish infantry and some wild though warlike Highlanders. Among them were 700 men from the Hebrides, all called Maclean. These possessed a fervent hatred of the Campbells who were the keystone of the Covenanter army. His only deficiency was in cavalry.

On the morning of the 15th Baillie and his army were on the march early, determined to sweep Montrose out of their path. It was a hot August day and they were soon in considerable discomfort as they stumbled over the rough, boggy ground. Their thick buff jerkins, useful for protection against a sword cut, now proved a cumbersome burden. Nevertheless, singing psalms, they pressed on towards Montrose's camp on the high ground west of Colzium castle. Here the Convenanters planned not only to defeat Montrose but also to cut off any retreat to the north. Having discovered that a morass lay in front of the position, they set off in a skirting movement to the north of the hill.

Montrose watched with astonishment. Whatever the long-term strategy, this was tactical suicide. With difficulty he held his troops and his fire while the Covenanters struggled across his front, feeling no doubt that they were deploying for attack while blocking an escape route to the north. Then, when their flank was fully exposed, he gave the order. The clansmen went in first.

To men accustomed to leap over the rocky surface of hills and moors, the rough ground was no problem. What happened next is best described by a Scot:

In the headlong fury of the Highland charge alike to them were horse and foot, musketeer or cuirassier; with claymores and dirks and with heads down behind their targets they swept on with shrill hurrahs, high hoarse war cries, and the din of the pibroch in their ears. Like a living tide they went through the glen. Furiously, with their keen claymores and long dirks they fell upon the Covenanters, hewing down horse and foot with equal facility, many of the former having their thighs shorn off close to the saddle-lap, and, in a few moments the foe became an inextricable mob.

The Covenanters were not, of course, beaten by one charge. Gradually the steady front of the Covenanter pikemen, backed by withering fire from the musketeers, began to pull the battle round in their favour. As the line stabilized, Baillie quietly detached the uncommitted rear and wheeled it unobtrusively to put in an attack on Montrose's left flank.

The move was spotted by Montrose as it began. Attack for him was always the best form of defence. Detailing the Earl of Airlie (seventy years old) to put in a charge supporting the Highlanders who had now been checked and were in trouble, he turned his own attention to the flank attack. Here in a final devastating surge the battle was now won.

It was not, of course, the work of a moment. A charge might take an hour of hard fighting to win the day, but once the initiative had been gained the remainder was a struggle for victory by one and for survival by the other. Then the carnage began. The names of Slaughter How, Drum Burn, Kill-the-Mony Butts, and Slaughter Hollow tell the details. Even now occasional relics, such as bullets or pieces of armour, are turned up. There was littler mercy for those who could not flee. The Covenanters had mercilessly slaughtered wives and sweethearts of royalists after Methaven, branding them as 'whores, harlots and strumpets', which they were not. Civil War armies were followed by a considerable train of camp followers but by no means all were the whores whom the Scottish Puritans found so offensive. (The Parliamentarians at Naseby had been equally undiscriminating with the women they found there, but, perhaps, with more reason.)

Kilsyth was a devastating and brilliant victory. It destroyed Baillie's army and it roused Royalist hopes to the skies. But it led to that overconfidence which had often lost Scotland battles before and would do so again.

The Battle of Philiphaugh

13 September 1645

As a reward for his services at Kilsyth and before, Montrose was appointed Captain-General and Lieutenant Governor of Scotland. He had certainly deserved these honours. Within the year, from a start with no money, men, ammunition, weapons, or even reliable friends, he had become master of Scotland. He had outwitted and outfought his enemies at every point.

But, as Montrose knew, there were still problems. Victories need consolidation, even acceptance. This one had been secured by Highlanders over Lowlanders and that would produce its own reaction before long. Another danger was looting. In spite of warnings, there were outbreaks at Glasgow and he hanged a dozen offenders as an example. Soon there were other troubles. The Highlanders who had left their poverty-stricken homes in the hope of plunder and money now found they would not get the first and might not see much of the latter. Their families at home relied on them for food; if their men were away at the wars and could not send money home, how would they survive?

Gradually Montrose's army began to melt away. Men who had done a little private looting – and few had not – did not wait to be discovered and hanged, and headed for home. Even more serious was the departure of the Macleans, who feared that the Campbells would attack their homes and wished to destroy their old enemies first. Nevertheless, Montrose had no option but to continue campaigning and hope to pick up more recruits in the Border country. He acquired a few but they were poor quality. On 12 September he arrived at Philiphaugh, just south of Selkirk. There, on a flat meadow just below the junction of the Yarrow and the Ettrick, he pitched camp with the Ettrick on one side and a steep tree-covered hill on the other. It is a picturesque spot and easy to find, for the road runs through it. He sent out a scouting party but it reported that no enemy were in the district.

Seven days before, Lord Leven, who had been besieging Hereford, had been informed of the result of Kilsyth. The news ran through his army and caused great discontent; men asked what they were doing fighting in England while the Royalists were destroying their kin in Scotland. Leven acted promptly, raised the siege, and sent the able Major-General Sir David Leslie hastening north with 4,000 men. He moved at such a speed that if Montrose had come south with his army – as was his original intention – Leslie would have been caught at a disadvantage and easily beaten. But he was not intercepted and beaten; instead he picked up reinforcements on the way and soon had 6,000, of which 5,000 were cavalry. As he crossed the Border he was sent news of Montrose's latest moves and of the weakness of his army. He adapted his route accordingly, crossing the Tweed at Rae and marching straight to the junction of the Tweed and Ettrick; here he was a mere three miles from Montrose, and unsuspected.

The 13th was one of those foggy mornings which soon clear but make visibility negligible while the fog lasts. Montrose, who was in quarters in Selkirk two miles away, sent out scouts, but, not surprisingly, they saw nothing. The town was unfriendly to his cause but he felt he owed himself a little comfort. When the news of the disaster came to him he was at breakfast.

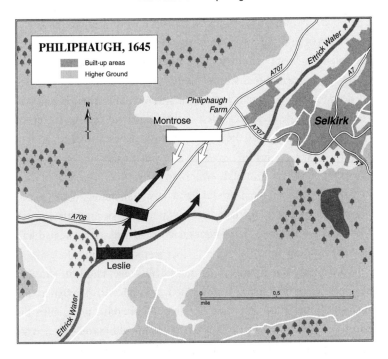

Take the A707 south from Selkirk. Turn left on to the A708. Philiphaugh Farm is on the immediate right of this junction; the rest of the battlefield is on your left and ahead of you. Newark Castle is two miles farther on and may be seen from the road. (Scottish Borders)

Leslie had divided his forces into two for this surprise attack. Coming up from Sunderland, the village where they had camped overnight, the two wings arrived completely undetected. Guided by local sympathizers, one came up the left bank of the Ettrick, the other along the road. They took the Royalists completely by surprise. Montrose's men had dug a few shallow trenches and these now became the scene of desperate fighting. The final resistance was

595

put up by Montrose's 500 Ulstermen, of whom 400 were killed. Gradually they fell back into the area now occupied by the Philiphaugh farm. Montrose had arrived within minutes of the alarm sounding and with a mere hundred horsemen put in an attack so desperately that for a moment 2,000 dragoons rocked back in confusion. In the same way a few determined men can send a crowd reeling backwards; but the crowd soon recovers and their weight tells.

On the field it was quickly over. Montrose would have died then and there – and perhaps should have been allowed to – but instead he was dragged out by his lieutenants and was soon spurring away from that scene where all his hopes had foundered. After he had left, the rest surrendered.

What happened then was an eternal disgrace to Leslie and his advisers. The prisoners were marched two miles to Newark Castle (still easily seen but not visible). Here they were herded into the courtyard and shot down by the dragoons in cold blood. They were buried at Slain Man's Lee, where their bones were discovered in 1810; there were said to be a thousand skeletons.

Nor, alas, was that all. Eighty wretched fugitives, all women and children, were overtaken by the Covenanters at Linlithgow Bridge. There they were flung into the Avon, fifty feet below. Those who struggled to the banks were pushed back into the water with pikes and, like the others, drowned. The Covenanters had been told that 'the curses which befell the enemies of God would fall on him who suffered one Amalekite to escape.'

As Mme Roland said witnessing the horrors of the French Revolution in 1793: 'O liberty, what crimes are committed in thy name.' As an afterthought she added, 'The more I see of men, the more I like dogs.'

The Battle of Dunbar

3 September 1650

The Civil War was drawing to an end in 1650 but, inevitably, after eight years, had taken courses and seen action which would never have been dreamed of in its early stages. King Charles had been executed as a tyrant, but the government which had replaced his was full of fanatics and aristocrats. In 1650, however, there was still royalist resistance in Ireland and Scotland.

Cromwell took an army to Ireland in August 1649. By the time he returned in May 1650 he had behaved with such ruthlessness that his name is still mentioned with hatred – over three hundred years later.

He would have stayed longer and completed his conquest of the whole country but the news from Scotland brought him hurrying home. Prince Charles, later to be Charles II, had 'taken the Covenant' and professed to be an ardent Presbyterian. (He was in fact a Catholic at heart and on his death-bed was officially received into that faith.) His return to Scotland followed a strong revulsion by the Scots against the highhandedness of the English Parliamentarians and their horror at the execution of the King. Cromwell, having conquered the Royalists in Ireland, now found himself confronted by a hostile Scotland with an army which might link up with the remaining English royalists at any moment. But he had no doubts about what he should do. On 22 July 1650 he was crossing the Border with 20,000 men.

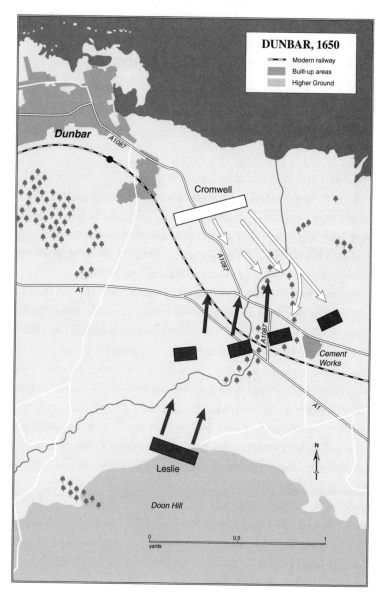

DUNBAR, 1650

Modern railway
Built-up areas
Higher Ground

Dunbar

A1087

Cromwell

A1087

A1

A1087

Cement
Works

A1

N

Leslie

Doon Hill

0   0.5   1
yards

The Scots easily foresaw what lay ahead and made preparations accordingly. Edinburgh castle was strengthened and garrisoned, as were many other castles. The countryside over which Cromwell would march was laid waste to deny him supplies, and an army of 30,000 was mustered to meet him. The army was then deployed on the outskirts of Edinburgh behind hastily but well-made fortifications. Against these Cromwell hurled his forces in vain. By 31 August his troops were short of supplies, frustrated, and full of sickness. Worse still his reputation as a general had been severely mauled. But facts are facts and on the evening of the 31st he gave the order to burn their huts and begin to withdraw.

The sight of the scourge of the Royalists beginning to retreat appears to have stirred Leslie to even greater efforts. As his previous victories – such as at Philiphaugh – had shown, he was quick to seize and hold the initiative. At this point he did so by marching his entire army of 23,000 at top speed to a point, three miles south of Dunbar, where Cromwell would have to pass between him and the sea. Leslie had taken up position on Doon Hill and with twice Cromwell's numbers looked forward with pleasure to the next day. It was now the evening of 2 September.

Unfortunately for Leslie, he was accompanied by a number of fanatical clergy who were extreme even by Civil War standards. On the next day, as dawn broke, they clustered around Leslie and urged him to charge down on the defenceless English, who were now well in the trap, and sweep them into the sea. 'The Lord hath delivered Antichrist into our hands and like Gideon you should descend on

Take the A1087 south of Dunbar. The battle took place where the A1087 approaches the A1. (East Lothian)

them and sweep them away before you,' they told him. With astonishing stupidity Leslie listened to what they said and apparently acted on it. Within a few minutes his army was moving down the slopes into the Brox Burn valley. There may, however, have been certain military considerations in his decision, for Cromwell was no novice and it was not out of the question that he might hold up Leslie's front line while the remainder of his army slipped past. This would no longer be possible. Cromwell observed Leslie's moves through his 'perspective glass', as the early telescope was called. 'They are coming down,' he exclaimed. 'The Lord hath delivered them into our hands.' All that day he watched as Leslie deployed his troops along the road leading to Berwick, and made his own dispositions accordingly. Even with this sudden dramatic turn of events, this would be no easy battle.

That night was stormy and wet. Morning broke through rain and mist. Leslie would clearly be poised for the attack so, to put him off balance, Cromwell launched a swift thrust on to the Scots' right, and weaker, flank. The advantage was momentary, for, almost as they came up, the Scottish cavalry put in their own attack in the same quarter. Within minutes the two wings were locked together. And so it stayed.

For an hour it was cut and thrust in this quarter, the English line giving slightly; then, as Cromwell poured in more and more men, the Scots began to be forced back. Equal pressure was now coming on the Scots centre, where the redoubtable Monk was directing the attack. The day had hardly begun, but the casualties were mounting fast. At one moment the Scots were hurling themselves into the attack, then, when the tide turned, were facing an English counterthrust until they were literally slashed to the ground by the cavalry. A whole brigade of Highlanders, whose reputation lay in making the charge, not holding it, nevertheless stood and perished to a man. In many places the soldiers were 'at push of pike', i.e. pikemen confronting pikemen.

At this stage, with the armies virtually deadlocked in a killing ground where the superior numbers of the Scots might tell, Cromwell showed his genius as a cavalry commander. It was impossible to get at Leslie's left flank, protected as it was by the ravine, so, taking out the cavalry reserve, he loosed it on Leslie's right with one final stunning shock.

It reeled, gave, and blundered on to the centre. As the disordered Scots fell back, some trying to turn and face the enemy, others trying to slip back away from those flashing swords, the centre too began to waver. And as the centre gave way the left, already under pressure, began to fall back to straighten the line.

In a moment, all was disaster. The English poured through, though many a man was cut down in the moment of triumph by a Scot who could fall back no more and took a man with him before he died. But soon it was all over, and the Scots were fleeing. At that moment Cromwell's trumpets sounded, his army halted, and all sang the 117th Psalm. It has two verses only:

> *O Praise the Lord, all ye nations: praise him, all ye people.*
> *For his merciful kindness is great toward us; and the truth*
> *of the Lord endureth for ever. Praise ye the Lord.*

But triumph, not mercy, was in their hearts. The trumpets sounded again and the pursuit and the killing, stretched over eight miles. The dead were perhaps luckier than the prisoners. The latter were stripped by their guards and then driven half-naked to Durham. No food was provided in eight days. The wretched captives ate leaves, twigs, raw cabbages, anything they could snatch up, as their guards jeered at them. Many fell out and were shot; half the original 5,000 reached Durham and many died on arrival. Of the survivors, 200 were sent to Virginia.

Such was the surprising but decisive Battle of Dunbar. It was not quite the end of Scottish resistance, for that would occur in 'the crowning mercy' of Worcester the following year. Whatever one thinks of Cromwell's sanctimoniousness and ruthless autocracy there can be no two ways about his generalship. Not only was he the architect of victory for his army but he was a superb field commander.

The Battle of Killiecrankie

27 July 1689

After Cromwell's unexpected but decisive victory at Dunbar came the even more fateful battle at Worcester the following year. Cromwell called Worcester 'the crowning mercy'; mercy was noticeably absent from the later stages of the Civil War, but what Cromwell doubtless thought was that all royalist resistance was completely and for ever crushed. His use of the word 'crowning' is interesting and perhaps reveals that he saw his Government as a natural successor to the monarchy. Politics, as Cromwell and his supporters soon realized, is the art of the possible. Ironically, the man who had sent his king to the scaffold in the cause of democracy soon found himself ruling more autocratically than Charles had ever done. Historians nowadays believe that Cromwell was less despotic than he is accused of being, but no one would claim that his rule was democratic. Surrounded by fanatics such as 'the Saints' and the Levellers, and frequently under the threat of assassination, he could scarcely be expected to behave like a benign caretaker.

After his death in 1658 the country lapsed into such chaos that the only solution seemed to be the restoration of the Stuarts. In consequence, in 1660, Charles II returned to sit on the English throne. Charles knew by bitter experience what it was like to be an exiled monarch and an unwelcome guest at foreign courts. Once back on the English throne he was determined never to lose it.

Nevertheless, he was secretly a Roman Catholic and would, if the opportunity had presented itself have restored both the Roman Catholic religion and an even more autocratic régime than his father.

His brother, James II, who succeeded him, lasted three years only. The best that can be said of him was that he was capable in military matters; the worst was that he was bigoted, obstinate, cruel, and stupid. Eventually he was toppled off the throne and allowed to escape to France. He was succeeded by William III, the Prince of Orange, and Mary. The Stuarts were once more in exile.

In view of the way James II and his brother had treated Scotland it was astonishing that there should have been any sympathy at all for the Stuarts. Both monarchs had put the Scottish Episcopalians in power and the Episcopalians had relentlessly suppressed the Covenanters. Goaded to desperation, the Covenanters had rebelled in 1679 and murdered the Archbishop of St Andrews. Their hopes came to a sudden end when the Duke of Monmouth, eldest of Charles II's illegitimate sons, scattered them in the Battle of Bothwell Bridge (June 1679). However, nine years later, when James II was pushed into exile, the Presbyterians rose again. The fact that the exiled king was a Scot had no influence on their actions; their prime motive was to revenge themselves on the Episcopalians who had treated them so harshly. This set the scene for the fastest decisive battle in British history.

One of James II's supporters was Colonel John Graham of Claverhouse, whom James had made Viscount Dundee. When the Convention of the Scottish Estates met at Edinburgh and pronounced that James II had forfeited the throne, Dundee dissociated himself from the motion, rode north and raised the clans. It was not an easy matter. The Marquis of Atholl stated that he was loyal to William III, even though the remainder of the inhabitants of the district sympathized with James (whom they referred to as James VIII) and his Jacobite followers. William had appointed General Hugh Mackay of Scourie to be Commander-in-Chief of his army in Scotland and Mackay was no novice. His first move was to blockade Edinburgh Castle which was held for the Jacobites by the Duke of Gordon; his next was to isolate Dundee from potential supporters.

Events moved faster than expected. While the Marquis of Atholl was away, his steward, Patrick Stewart of Ballechin, seized the castle of Blair Atholl and declared for the Jacobite cause. The move came as a surprise to Dundee – although a welcome one – and he decided to move south to support this new adherent to the cause.

Strategically the situation was evenly balanced. Mackay had left most of his infantry blockading Edinburgh Castle and his mixed force of 450 was scarcely a battle-winning factor. Equally, Dundee could not hope to use his newly recruited Macdonalds and Camerons until he controlled the vital passes of Dunkeld, Drumochter, and Killiecrankie. Neither general had a force large enough to make the moves necessary to the start of a campaign. For a few days both manoeuvred and marched waiting for an opportunity to present itself. Mackay occupied Inverness and garrisoned it with a small force; Dundee acquired another 300 Irish recruits. Suddenly, however, an opportunity opened up for Mackay. The Duke of Gordon surrendered Edinburgh Castle on 13 June, thereby releasing Mackay's infantry regiments. Mackay promptly returned to Edinburgh to reorganize and re-equip what was now undoubtedly the stronger force. Even so it had dangerous weaknesses. All his regiments were inexperienced and there was no certainty as to how they would behave if confronted with a Highland charge. A good number were recent recruits. Nevertheless, his numbers now totalled 4,500 and this enabled him to choose a plan by which

Dundee would be cut off and isolated. A first step was to recover Blair Atholl. Equally, Dundee was determined he should not do so, for it gave him control of access to Angus and Strathearn. While Mackay was no farther forward than Perth, therefore, Dundee moved towards Blair with a mixed force of Macdonalds, Camerons, and MacLeans, plus, of course, his recent Irish recruits. This army was roughly equivalent in numbers to that of Mackay, and probably a lot more spirited. Dundee reached Blair well in advance of Mackay's advance party which then had to make a rapid retreat down the awkward pass of Killiecrankie. However, once at Killiecrankie, Lord Murray, Mackay's vanguard commander, decided to stay and prevent Dundee's men filtering through. Mackay sent him reinforcements, bringing the total up to 400. This may not seem much to hold up an army of 4,000 but the Pass is three miles long, has precipitous sides, and offers numerous opportunities for ambush. Nevertheless, as Mackay knew, it was not sufficient to hold up Dundee; he had to be defeated in battle. On 27 July therefore he took his army through the pass and halted on the level ground along by the river Garry, near Aldclune. Mackay lacked experience of mountain warfare or he would have realized how vulnerable his position was. Scouts soon reported that Dundee's advance party was now very close. More ominous was the news that some of Dundee's men were positioned on Mackay's flank on higher ground. How many were there he did not know, but he quickly appreciated that he was now caught in a narrow pass with a river on one side and a formidable enemy on his right on higher ground. A further thought was that Dundee's men were thoroughly accustomed to fighting and movement in such terrain; his were not.

Action must now be swift if he were not to be annihilated. He turned his army to the right and faced the higher ground where, he

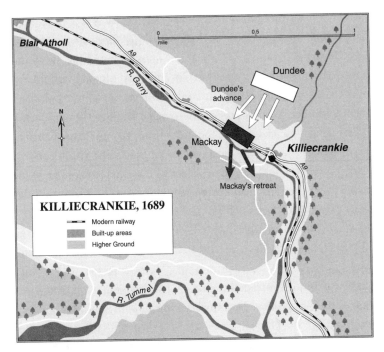

The A9 runs through the Pass and takes you by the National Trust Centre. Look up the slope past Urrard House to appreciate Mackay's position. The Soldier's Leap is also clearly marked. (Perth & Kinross)

suspected rightly, the main threat lay. He was able to reach the slope behind Urrard House, and decided to stay there, as it was a reasonable defensive position, though still exposed. His line from right to left was East Yorkshires, King's Own Scottish Borderers, Scots Fusiliers, and Royal Irish. To the rear, in reserve, were the Somerset Light Infantry. (None of them bore these names at the time, but that is what they later became.) Mackay was only too well aware that, if Dundee's men moved as adroitly as they undoubtedly could, they could cut in behind him and systematically chop his army to pieces. To prevent this happening, he lengthened his line, which was done by reducing it from six ranks to three. Dundee noted the move and balanced it by thinning his own line, thereby keeping his options open. Then they looked at each other. A few skirmishers clashed, mainly because Mackay was trying to make Dundee show his hand. A few shots bounced among the rocks from Mackay's three ancient guns. Mackay waited anxiously, knowing that if the attack came as darkness fell he could be in trouble, indeed. He gave a short harangue to his troops, letting them know what their fate would be if they did not fight vigorously enough to win. But no attack came.

At last, soon after 7 p.m. with dusk not far away, Dundee gave the order. His Highlanders, mostly naked to the waist, shoeless, and some dressed only in their weapons, leapt forward with a wild unearthly yell. As feared, they bore on Mackay's right who met them with steady musketry. But musketry needs time, and, before men could reload, the Highlanders were on to them with the broadsword. Desperate, Mackay's men tried to fend them off with their muskets. At this time the bayonet was plugged into the muzzle of the musket; thus it could not be put into position until after all firing had finished. The Highlanders charged so quickly that they were on to their opponents before they could plug in their bayonets, let alone use them. With their ammunition gone and equipped only with short bayonets, Mackay's troops were virtually helpless. In the dusk, with wild half-naked Highlanders leaping on to them, cutting and slashing, and with no leader in sight, it was all too much for the inexperienced recruits. As the line began to crumble and fall back Mackay made a last desperate effort. He ordered up his two troops of cavalry and, cursing roundly, rode forth himself to lead the counter-attack. Only one man followed him. His raw troops, bewildered and frightened, then did the very worst they could do for themselves: they ran. Stumbling and utterly confused, many of them got in each other's way and fell easily to the wild Highlanders. Mackay was lucky not to have shared their fate, but somehow in the general turmoil his presence was overlooked. He could, of course, easily have shared the fate of Dundee; but even the death of both the commanders could hardly have made this battle more bizarre. As it was Mackay now rode back through his lines to a point where the impetus of the Highland charge was spent. There he rallied 400 men and made his way back to Aberfeldy. But it was no bloodless victory for the Scots. In those fateful opening minutes Mackay's musketeers had taken a heavy toll; six hundred of Dundee's army died with him on the field. These casualties made the battle a loss for both sides; Mackay's army had been cut to pieces, but, with the death of Dundee and so many of his supporters, all hopes of a Jacobite revival were extinguished for the time being. Dundee was buried in his armour at Blair. Curiously enough, the effects of his death were not felt immediately. Elated by their victory his army stayed in the field, organized reinforcements which brought their numbers up to 5,000, and marched forward to Dunkeld. Reorganization had taken time and it was 21 August before they reached the little cathedral town. There they found the newly formed Cameronian regiment, commanded by Lieut.-Col. William Cleland, aged twenty-eight. Their numbers are said to have amounted to under 1,200, but they had established themselves in the houses and it was more than the Highlanders could do to move them. Cleland, who was a reputable poet as well as a brave soldier, was killed early in the fighting, but his men held on. Eventually the Highlanders wearied of this dull methodical battle of attrition which they would win – but to what purpose? To the surprise and joy of the Cameronians, they withdrew and returned to their homes. A more lasting effect of the battle came from Mackay's pondering on the reasons why he lost it. A year later he invented a type of bayonet which did not have to be plugged in to the muzzle of the rifle but could be clipped on to the side of the barrel and hence be ready immediately firing was no longer possible. Killiecrankie, which was a victory of sword over musket, was therefore unlikely ever to be imitated.

Killiecrankie has now become a famous beauty spot with a good road running through it. At the time of the battle it was merely a gloomy valley containing a single rough track. The battle itself took place outside the northern end of the pass, but the aftermath occurred in the pass itself along the banks of the Garry. The field where Mackay first stopped his advance is by the main road and is marked by a stone. It is said that he left his baggage here and that this fact saved many lives, for the Highlanders checked their slaughter in order to collect plunder. There is a stone in this field, but it has no inscription; furthermore this road is highly dangerous for motorists to park on. There are other stones which are said to have associations with incidents of the battle but it is difficult to believe in these convenient legends. The 'Soldier's Leap' is authentic. Donald MacBean, one of Mackay's troopers, was pursued by a Highlander who fired a pistol at him. Coming to the water, MacBean found it was about eighteen feet across, but, with a prodigious jump, he cleared it. He survived, and wrote his memoirs. In them he states that the troops fired three volleys in the battle before being overwhelmed; others say they fired only twice.

The visitor's best policy is to visit the National Trust for Scotland Centre on the pass where – as with Bannockburn – the battle is projected on a *tableau vivant*. Here he will be guided to the visible parts of the battlefield.

Glencoe

12 February 1692

References to Glencoe usually term it 'The Massacre of Glencoe' and this, unfortunately, is the correct description; it is, however, wrongly thought by many to have been a battle. It appears here so that it may be put into perspective in Scottish history and also that certain prevailing misconceptions about it may be rectified. It also belongs to this account as part of the sequel to Killiecrankie.

After the summer of 1689 public attention and military conflict shifted to Ireland. The deposed James II was already there with money, officers, and arms from France. The ensuing conflict reached its climax in the Battle of the Boyne (1 July 1690), when James's army was defeated by that of William III. Hard and bloody fighting continued until 1692, after which a repressive Irish Parliament had the country firmly held down.

While conflict had been raging over Ireland the situation in Scotland had passed virtually unnoticed. But in the Highlands there were chiefs who had supported Dundee and had fought at Killiecrankie and elsewhere. They were fiercely independent, and in remote areas felt they could continue to be so. Towards the end of 1691 William considered that the best way to establish law and order would be to grant an amnesty and let bygones be bygones. However, a condition of this amnesty was that all the clan chieftains who had not previously done so must acknowledge allegiance by 1 January

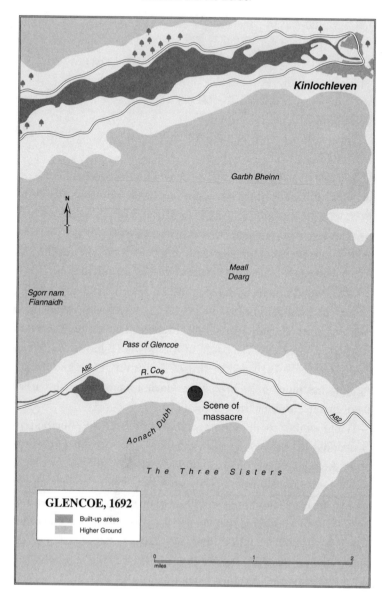

GLENCOE, 1692

Built-up areas

Higher Ground

Kinlochleven

Garbh Bheinn

Meall Dearg

Sgorr nam Fiannaidh

Pass of Glencoe

A82

R. Coe

Scene of massacre

Aonach Dubh

A82

The Three Sisters

0   1   2
miles

1692. All did except MacIan, chief of the Macdonalds of Glencoe. MacIan, partly as a joke and partly to preserve his diminished dignity, put off his submission – which involved taking the oath of allegiance, to the last possible moment. He then went to Fort William – which was not the place appointed for him – and found no magistrate there. His submission therefore could not be made till 6 January. What happened next was inexcusable, though perhaps understandable. The Secretary of State for Scotland was Sir John Dalrymple, Master of Stair, who detested the independent lawlessness of the Highlanders. Dalrymple therefore prevailed on William III to let him make an example of the Macdonalds; he did not, however, tell William that the Macdonalds had already submitted, albeit a few days late.

To understand Dalrymple's action, though not to condone it, it is necessary to have some idea of the Highlands at that time. Highland chiefs had absolute power and would occasionally execute members of the clan whom they felt had deserved the extreme penalty. This was only one aspect of their ancient barbarism; a more irritating one to their more settled neighbours was that they lived only for cattle-raiding and plunder. Many of their more industrious neighbours were paying an annual tribute to save their cattle from being 'lifted' – not always successfully. In the more remote parts of the Highlands it was reported that houses had no chimneys or lights, potatoes were still unknown, iron was too scarce to be used for anything but weapons, and horses dragged carts by their tails. Dalrymple perhaps thought that there was only one lesson such people would

The A82 passes through the glen on the way up to Oban. The scene of the massacre – as far as it is known – is on the northern slope of Aonach Dubh, south of the river Coe. (Highland)

understand and it would be the better for the rest of Scotland the sooner it was applied.

The treachery of the massacre, let alone its brutality, appals even now. Dalrymple despatched a regiment, commanded by Campbell of Glenlyon; many of its members came from areas which had experienced the depredations of the Macdonalds. MacIan gave them a traditional Highland welcome, with the best hospitality he could provide; doubtless he thought that this was a part of the ceremonial of oath-taking and allegiance. The glen was full of snow at the time. It says something for MacIan's goodwill that he could entertain a regiment commanded by one of the detested Campbells and not murder him and them; but he did so, and the regiment was with him a fortnight before it struck. At midnight on 12 February, when the Macdonalds were asleep, Campbell gave the order and the massacre began. The Macdonald himself was shot, and thirty-seven others – men, women, and children – were butchered. The remainder scattered into the snowy hills to survive if they could.

Today's visitor will probably visit Glencoe in the summer when the whole area will be strikingly beautiful and peaceful. The massacre took place somewhere between Signal Hill and Aonach Dubh, naturally enough the precise site is not exactly known. By the standards of other massacres, some preceded by battles, this was small indeed. It became notorious for its premeditated treachery, abusing one of the finest traditions of the Highlands – their hospitality – and astonishing all who heard of it by its cold-bloodedness. But, as we have seen above, deplorable though the massacre was it must be seen in the context of place and time. Perhaps the surviving Macdonalds took a grim pride in the fact that a regiment tried to kill a mere 200 men, women, and children, and that even with treachery, surprise and darkness it could only murder less than forty.

The Battle of Prestonpans

20 September 1745

At the beginning of the eighteenth century it seemed as if
Scotland and England were drawing much closer to each
other politically and further wars would be unthinkable. There
had, however, been setbacks. In 1698 a Scottish colonial company
had set off to colonize the area around Panama, at that time known
as Darien. This piece of enterprise was warmly approved by the
Scottish Parliament but William III looked coldly on the scheme,
refused to confirm its privileges or to give it English backing. The
Company, completely surprised by the tropical climate and diseases
– for the area was outwardly attractive – had a disastrous experience,
and all its settlers died. Appalled by this calamity, the Scots, looking
for a cause for the disaster, soon decided that it was due to English
envy, inspired by William. So high did feelings run that the Scots
began to talk of a separate kingdom again. The Prime Minister,
Godolphin, appreciating the dangers of the situation, pressed
quickly and strongly for an act of Union to ensure that relations did
not deteriorate further. The Bill was passed in 1707. It gave Scotland
forty-five members in the House of Commons and sixteen in the
Lords. The arms of the two countries were blended by combining
the white saltire of St Andrew with the red cross of St George. This
became known as the 'Union Jack', a jack being the flag on a ship by
which it shows its nationality. Nevertheless, plenty of Scots had

doubts about the alleged benefits of this union and the Jacobites lost no opportunities to deplore it. Hope of any positive and successful action was slim, until Queen Anne died in 1714 leaving no direct successor, and George of Hanover, descended from Sophie, daughter of James I, was invited to take the throne. James Stuart, the Old Pretender, the son of the exiled James II, could have had the English throne if he had agreed to become a Protestant, but he refused.

It looked, however, as if the time might be ripe for a Scottish bid for a restoration of the Stuart line. Few English people were pleased at the arrival of an unattractive fifty-four-year-old German who spoke no word of English and had apparently no desire to learn the language of his new subjects. In Scotland dislike of this new king was increased by the fact that he was strongly supported by the Campbell clan; any cause espoused by the Campbells was certain to be detested by their ancient rivals in the Highlands.

In consequence, a rebellion was planned by the Earl of Mar who was soon joined by Gordons, Murrays, Mackintoshes, Macphersons, Farquharsons, Stuarts, and Macdonalds (the last with Glencoe firmly in mind). When this force struck, similar risings were to take place elsewhere, in the Lowlands and on the Border, in Wales and in Devonshire. Unfortunately for the rebels' chances Mar was not the man to lead them, or anybody; he was a somewhat shifty character who had earned the nickname 'Bobbing John'. The risings in Wales and Devonshire were forestalled by swift action on the part of the government, which arrested the local Jacobites before they could put their plans into action. Even so it was a dangerous moment. There were less than 10,000 English troops available, and the rebels looked like putting many more into the field. Furthermore, French support had been promised.

But the 'Fifteen proved a fiasco. With Wales and Devonshire out of the fight, the only hope lay in vigorous action in the north; but vigour, alas, was absent. The northern counties force, under Thomas Forster, a Northumberland squire, was surrounded by a smaller cavalry force and tamely surrendered near Preston, Lancashire. Mar began well by capturing Perth, Aberdeen, and Dundee, but then halted, leaving Edinburgh and the surrounding area to his opponents. Not until 12 November 1715, two months after he had first raised the standard, did he move south from Perth. The next day he met his opponents at Sherriffmuir, just north of Stirling. The ensuing battle was as curious as it was indecisive. The left wing of each army scattered the opposing right. Then, not knowing whether it had won or lost each army retreated. Mar fell back to Perth, his supporters quarrelling among themselves and each blaming the other for the fact that the army had not managed to force a passage through to England. Even the belated arrival of the Old Pretender himself – a month later – failed to prevent them trickling back to the Highlands. With their hopes and plans in ruins, the leaders also soon went their separate ways. James and certain others went to France, whence no assistance was forthcoming now that Louis xiv was dead. The 'Fifteen, which could have altered history, quietly fizzled out. The rebel army was finally disbanded on 7 February 1716 at Aberdeen. Reprisals were not unduly severe in the conditions of the time. Thirty of the leading figures were hanged and a number were transported, but many kept out of the way and received a pardon later. Many, however, had their estates and property confiscated.

Even less successful was an attempt in 1719. This time three hundred Spanish soldiers were to land in Rossshire where they would find Jacobite allies. Five thousand more Spaniards were to follow. The three hundred landed and were joined by a thousand clansmen under the Marquis of Tullibardine. The five thousand never arrived at all because their transports were all destroyed in a storm. In consequence it was a relatively simple matter for government forces to scatter the insurgents at Glenshiel.

Two important and lasting results followed from these actions.

One was that General Wade, who had been appointed Commander-in-Chief for Scotland built a series of roads, small by modern standards, but large and impressive in their time. These, marked on the map as 'General Wade's military roads' were a ten-year programme which made the Highlands accessible, although they covered approximately only 250 miles. Not least of their benefits were the bridges which carried them over difficult watercourses.

A second result was the famous Black Watch regiment which was originally raised by Wade as a local police force. The Black Watch subsequently fought as the 42nd, distinguishing itself on the Alma Heights in the Crimea, and on many other battlefields.

After 1719 its English supporters lost interest in the Jacobite cause, but it lived on in Scotland. In 1745 Stuart fortunes suddenly revived, and for a time there was a genuine prospect that a Stuart might once again sit on the English throne. The circumstances were these.

The Old Pretender had two sons. The elder was Charles Edward, the younger Henry (later a Cardinal). Charles Edward was a complete contrast to his unlucky and depressing father. He was cheerful, adventurous, and energetic; he was clearly a born leader, and he looked like a prince of royal blood.

With England heavily involved in a war on the Continent, and thus denuded of troops, 1745 was an obvious time to pick for a bid for power. In the preceding year the French had assembled an invasion fleet at Dunkirk, with every intention of using it, but it had been, once more, destroyed by storms. This was a setback, but Charles was undeterred. He knew in his bones that he could and must win. The battle of Fontenoy on 11 May 1743 confirmed his opinion; the English were now in desperate trouble on the Continent, and all he had to do was to show his face in Scotland and the country would rise to support him.

Troubles began early. His little convoy was intercepted at sea and, when he landed in the Outer Hebrides on 2 August 1745, he had only seven supporters with him. On first landing, his reception was daunting, for none of his anticipated supporters wished to join him. He went on to Moidart, gaining a few, and thence to Glenfinnan. At Glenfinnan he raised the standard, declared his father was the rightful King of Scotland, and moved on to Edinburgh.

Glenfinnan had brought him a thousand supporters, and he was soon joined by another three thousand. With these he moved forward and took Perth. Thence he went to Edinburgh where the city was gained without a fight. It looked – and not only to him – as if success was in his grasp. The best of the English army was overseas and all that could be mustered to meet him was an army of less than three thousand, six battalions in all, of which two were very raw and new. Commanding them was the incompetent Sir John Cope who had already failed to intercept him on the road to Edinburgh. Cope had subsequently embarked his army and landed them at Dunbar, whence he had marched towards Edinburgh. Charles, full of heady triumph, was now moving south – and the two armies met, on 20 September 1745, at Prestonpans, East Lothian.

Cope, who had no alternative but to wait and see what his steadier regiments could do to a Highland charge, deployed his army between Preston Grange and Seaton House. He suspected (rightly) that Prince Charles had artillery and would be relying on traditional

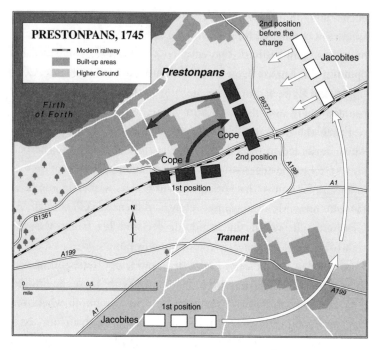

PRESTONPANS, 1745

- = Modern railway
- Built-up areas
- Higher Ground

Prestonpans

Firth of Forth

2nd position before the charge

Jacobites

Cope

2nd position

Cope

1st position

Tranent

N

0   0.5   1
mile

B1361

B6371

A198

A1

A199

A199

A1

1st position

Jacobites

Take the A1 from Edinburgh, then turn left along the A198. Ignore all signs directing to Prestonpans itself. A good starting point is the A198/B6371 junction from which you can have a look at Riggonhead farm and then follow the Highland charge. As the account of this battle shows, it covered a fairly wide area in spite of the small numbers engaged. (East Lothian)

weapons. By setting out his troops with their rear to the sea, but not too close, he had arranged that they could not be outflanked; ahead of him lay ditches and hedges which would take the edge off the fiercest and longest charge, he surmised. As the two armies closed, the Highlanders moved on to the higher ground around Tranent and took a long careful look at their opponents. The sight was not encouraging. Knowing their deficiencies in arms, without artillery, and mainly armed with broadsword or makeshift pike, the prospect of a successful charge over rough and unknown ground looked doubtful. Impetuous though they were, they were not suicidal.

Charles Edward, however, was burning for action. He rode restlessly here and there, hoping to hit on a plan which would convince the more cautious of his advisers. Luckily for him he encountered a man named Anderson, who lived near by and was a keen Jacobite. Anderson gave Charles Edward a vital piece of information: it was that a path ran through the bog which was partially protecting Cope's front. If the Young Pretender used this path he could take his whole army round to Cope's eastern flank, where, because of the protection of the bog, the latter's dispositions were thinnest. In the early hours of the next day, long before first light, Charles Edward had taken his army (it numbered only 2,500) along the path and close to Cope's position. At Riggonhead farm they were spotted by one of Cope's outposts and the alarm was given but it was too late for them to be checked here. Cope's army was facing south and the best he could do was to turn it to face east and give battle where the Highlanders chose to offer it. The latter, moving briskly towards the coast at Cockenzie, turned west along the line of the present B6371. Their achievement in crossing such rough country so easily is not now so well appreciated, as the long ditch which could have been such a formidable obstacle has been largely filled in; the presence of a road, a railway track, pylons, and a huge slag heap makes an appreciation of the 1745 terrain difficult though not impossible.

As the sun came up, and shone directly into the eyes of Cope's soldiers, he was still trying to make the best of his new position. On his right he had his artillery, all too close to the Jacobites. Behind were his raw dragoons whose task was to intercept any attack and break it up. Four hundred yards separated the two armies and, as the Jacobites checked their positioning, their whole army was gradually edging forward, closing the gap.

The battle began haphazardly. A range-finding shot from the English line found a target on the Scottish left. A man screamed. It was like a command to the Scots. They had not marched all this way to be picked off at will by the English; now they charged. The fury and impetus surprised even their own leaders. The English gunners got off five rounds and were overwhelmed. The dragoons behind, commanded by Colonel Gardiner, a brave old campaigner, saw the fate of the gunners ahead of them and without waiting for orders decided to avoid it for themselves. Gardiner tried desperately to rally them. Unfortunately they were in an excellent position for a cowardly dash from the battlefield, leaving their comrades in the lurch. On such a small area such a disaster was all too obvious, even to Cope's centre and left, which were now facing the fury of the Highland charge. Here again there was no chance to make use of their muskets before they too were overwhelmed; it was short bayonet against long pike and whirling claymore. Cope's men were like a skilled boxer who is trying to fight off a heavy puncher who is inside his guard. As they reeled back, the Macdonalds on the Highland right, a little late to begin but devastating now they were on the move, swept diagonally into Cope's army crumpling up its left wing as they went.

In minutes the battle was lost, but not over. The remainder of the dragoons also tried to escape but now found their way blocked by fallen or fleeing infantry. The Jacobites too were among them, unhorsing them and slashing them down with claymores. Colonel Gardiner, still fighting, fell with a dozen wounds. Cope made a desperate effort to rally some of the dragoons but the best he could do was to take some 400 men out of battle up the B1349, which was later mockingly christened 'Johnny Cope's road'. Inevitably English losses were as heavy as the Scots were light. Five hundred of Cope's army were killed and another 1,500 taken prisoner. In contrast, the Scots had less than fifty killed and about seventy-five wounded. Much of the slaughter must have taken place where the A198 is crossed by the B1349, for this is where burial pits were found later.

There are various memorials to Prestonpans. There is a large wooden outline of a Highlander and an English soldier, there is a memorial to Col. Gardiner which may be seen from the road, although it is on the other side of the parallel railway line, and there is another monument on the A198 junction immediately behind Cockenzie SSEB Power Station.

The Battle of Culloden

18 April 1746

After Bonnie Prince Charlie's devastating victory at Prestonpans it seemed as if not only Scotland but perhaps England too lay at his feet. 'They ran like rabets' he wrote of Prestonpans; clearly his chances were excellent.

Meanwhile, General Wade was sent to Newcastle with ten battalions to fend off the prospective invasion of England. This meant that 10,000 men of a different quality from those he had met before were now facing Charles Edward. Worse was to follow; the Duke of Cumberland was hastily summoned from Flanders with even more veterans, and the militia, lacking in experience but not in dash and courage, was called out.

Foolishly Charles waited five weeks before moving on from Prestonpans. Had he pressed forward at once he might well have reached London. But the delay was fatal, for, although he was rearming and re-equipping, his enemies were making even more strenuous and effective preparations. Even so, when he eventually marched he still had a chance of success, though a diminished one. Sweeping down the western side of England – to avoid Wade's army in Newcastle – he reached Derby. He was now a mere 125 miles from London.

At this moment, the dash and courage which had characterized his enterprise from the moment he landed in Scotland with seven supporters temporarily deserted him. His leading adviser, Lord George Murray, who had been largely responsible for the victory at Prestonpans, considered he was taking too great a risk with Wade on one side, Cumberland on the other, and an unspecified force of militia also to reckon with. Furthermore he was not getting the recruits he had hoped for, and desertions had reduced his numbers to 3,000. He took advice, and began to retreat; it was now 6 December.

But he was by no means beaten. His nimble Highlanders, although encumbered by plunder, made light work of the snowy road home. Neither Wade nor Cumberland could move fast enough to get near them. Once over the Border Charles paused and took stock. Recruits poured in; his numbers were now back to 10,000. It looked as if he was secure in Scotland at least, even if he had to forgo his visit to Westminster. The view was reinforced at Falkirk, where on 17 January 1746 his army inflicted a sharp and surprising defeat on an English army under General Hawley. Here again a Highland charge at the critical moment was the cause of Jacobite victory.

But now the tide was turning against him. Cumberland had mustered 30,000 men and more were still being called to the colours. Charles could not hope to match such a force, particularly as his army dwindled whenever there were periods of inactivity. His only real hope lay in French intervention. If the French either created a diversion on the southern coast of England or sent a substantial contingent of troops to Scotland, his fortunes could still revive. He was in the extraordinary position of losing a campaign though winning all his battles. But he still had 5,000 men.

Cumberland knew exactly what his task was. At best Prince Charles would have only 6,000 men, and it could well be a thousand less. He could engage these with a picked vanguard and still have superior numbers. He drew off 8,000 of his best troops and with these marched briskly forward after Charles, who was now retreating slowly towards the north-west. By the time he was pressing on to their heels, the Jacobites had had three months of slow retreat, a dispiriting process which had not been helped by shortage of food. Keeping a large army in the field is a hard enough task at the best of times, with its problems of feeding, morale, and supply, but it is doubly difficult in an area with limited supplies of foodstuffs. Nevertheless, cold and hungry though the Jacobites were, they had preserved their morale; after all they had a royal leader who could rough it with the hardest of them and win battles too. They did not know that Cumberland, mindful of the disgraceful defeats at Prestonpans and Falkirk, had been training his army to ensure that such scenes should not be repeated. His men were now thoroughly schooled in the technique of repulsing a Highland charge. The front rank would kneel with fixed bayonets; the rear would fire in volleys. The process employed may still sometimes be seen in ceremonial drill parades today, where it all looks very elegant. In eighteenth-century battle, however, it was entirely purposeful; for after the front rank fired, it would smartly step to the side and rear to reload while the rank from behind stepped forward and went through a similar action. By this means a line of soldiers with loaded muskets was constantly in a position to fire. The kneeling soldiers, after holding their fire till the last agonizing moment, would each lunge with the bayonet to the Highlander on his right front. The bayonet would go in on the Highlanders' unprotected side. This formation and procedure would be a very different matter from the shallow dispositions at Prestonpans. Behind and between the infantry were cannon whose fire would rake the Jacobite lines. Cumberland was probably well aware that, when Cope had arrived back in London after Prestonpans, he had laid bets that the next general sent against the Jacobites would be beaten. Men had laughed at him and accepted his odds. When Hawley was defeated at Falkirk in January, Cope became thousands of pounds richer. Cumberland smiled grimly when he heard of it. He had more than enough troops for his task and had trained them specially; furthermore he knew exactly what his problems were likely to be. Unlike his opponent, Cumberland, the second son of George II, was not a popular leader; he was known to be hasty-tempered, coarse, and tyrannical. He had been outgeneralled at Fontenoy and Lauffelt, but he was a methodical professional and learnt from his own and other people's defeats. He had been appointed commander in Scotland after the dismissal of Hawley. Even so, the full unpleasantness of his character had not yet been revealed.

On 14 April Cumberland reached Nairn. So far Charles's strategy had been to retreat slowly, leading Cumberland's army after him, inflicting a blow here and there, but eventually to lure the English into the hills where the ground would perplex them, the cavalry would be useless, their artillery could not follow, and the whole terrain would be disconcerting. Unfortunately he was completely crippled by lack of money, not merely to pay his troops – who had received nothing for weeks – but even to buy food wherever it might be obtainable. Even the most popular army finds food hard to come by if it has no money to pay for it. Many of Charles's men were now absenting themselves for long or short periods to scrounge for themselves. Morale was not high, for it was thought that the English should have been attacked at river crossings, such as on the Spey. It may have been good strategy to let the redcoats penetrate virtually unmolested right up to the Highlands, but to the Jacobite soldier it made no sense at all.

In fact, Charles too had now lost faith in his own strategy. Furthermore he had had enough of retreats. Admittedly, the withdrawal from Derby had been followed by the victory at Falkirk but this retreat had gone on too long. He decided to give battle.

The spot chosen was some rough ground, then known as Drummossie Moor, south-east of Culloden House. There on 15 April the Jacobite army took up position and waited. No English troops appeared. As time wore on the Scots, who were almost starving, took it in turns to creep away and find a few cabbage leaves or – if lucky – a little oatmeal. The staff looked around and appraised the battlefield, which had been reconnoitred and chosen by O'Sullivan the Quartermaster-General. They found it far from satisfactory. It was not rough enough to deter the English cavalry and its very openness made it ideal for English artillery fire. A less suitable site – for Prince Charle's army – could scarcely have been chosen.

Still no English appeared, and by late afternoon a morale-raising plan had been conceived. This was to make a swift night march to Nairn – eight miles away – and deliver a surprise night attack. Highland charges from close quarters in the dark or dawn could well produce a second Prestonpans. Departure was arranged for 7 p.m. But at 7 p.m., when the march was to begin, over a quarter of the army was absent, looking for food. Many refused to return till they had found it; it was decided to leave them behind. Even so, about 4,000 set off in the pitch dark, hungry and sullen, to pick their way through heather, bog, and hillock. Soon the column had straggled and gaps had opened up in it. Lord George Murray was in the van, Prince Charles at the rear. But as Murray approached Cumberland's camp he heard the alarm being raised. Alert sentries must have passed back waning of their approach. Murray, realizing that surprise had been lost and any further move forward would lead to a well-prepared reception, gave the order to retreat. As the rest of the column was still moving forward the confusion may be imagined and it would not have been surprising if Murray's men had been taken for enemy and fired on. However, they were not and for the rest of the night a disconsolate, bewildered, tired, and starving army was trailing back to Culloden. On arrival, dog-tired, they threw themselves on the ground to get some sleep. Prince Charles was as tired as any, but before he lay down himself he organized a final drive to obtain whatever food could be gathered from Inverness. The food was collected but few of his army ever managed to taste it.

Hardly were they asleep when they were roused again. The alarm came from Domhnall Macraonaill Mhic Aillen, Captain of the Men of Glencoe. He was with a party of scouts patrolling the front. 'The redcoats are on us,' he announced.

Charles, pale and hungry, rushed out of his headquarters at Culloden House on hearing the news. He had the recall sounded by a cannon shot, and, as if by a miracle, his followers appeared from bracken, wood, and ditch and fell in in two lines. On the right was the Atholl brigade, commanded by Murray and consisting of Camerons, Stewarts, Macintoshes, Frasers, and a few others. The Camerons thought they were entitled to the place of honour on the extreme right and were not pleased with the dispositions. The centre was commanded by Lord John Drummond and included the Farquharsons; the right had more Stewarts; and the left wing was Macdonald. This line had a few not very reliable guns of varying calibre. The second line contained some cavalry but much of this was now dismounted and serving as infantry. The dispositions extended from Culloden House to Culwinniac farm, and totalled 5,000.

Six hundred yards away Cumberland's army began to take up

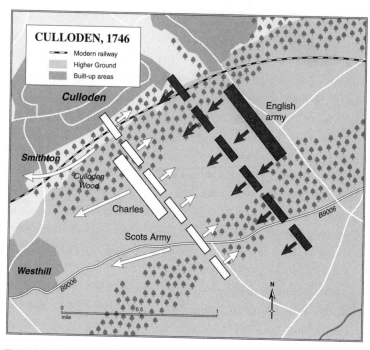

CULLODEN, 1746

Modern railway
Higher Ground
Built-up areas

Culloden

Smithton

Culloden Wood

Charles

Scots Army

Westhill

B9006

English army

B9006

N

0 0.5 1
mile

Take the A9 from Inverness; turn left on to the B9006, and seven miles from Inverness you may see the battlefield on each side of this road. The mass graves are marked by mounds and headstones. (Highland)

position. Curiously each army was too preoccupied with its own alignments to pay much attention to the enemy. This, as readers of other books in this volume will know, was not an unusual occurrence. Some battles begin as soon as the opponents come within range; others are preceded by hours of waiting or patient manoeuvring. This was one of the latter.

Cumberland's army was deployed in three lines. His front line consisted of Pulteney's, the Royal, Price's, Cholmondeley's,

Munro's, and Barrel's regiments, as well as the Royal Scots Fusiliers. The second line was Howard's, Battereau's, Fleming's, Bligh's, Semphill's, Ligonier's, and Wolfe's regiments. Artillery was positioned among the front line, and the cavalry was at the flanks and rear. It numbered 8,000.

Battle began with a burst of Jacobite artillery fire at 1 p.m. Cumberland had ten 3-pounders and they were soon replying. The Jacobite gunners did their best but their guns were poor and badly served; and they had few successes. As the 3-pounders ranged on to them, the Jacobite gun-crews, who were few and inexperienced, ceased firing and abandoned their guns. Still no troops moved. However, after the English artillery had been raking the Highland lines for half an hour, causing severe and increasing casualties, some of Prince Charles's army became restless. It was hardly surprising. Without food or sleep they had been required to stand for over four hours and now they were being steadily slaughtered by the English artillery. Charles, who had positioned himself at the rear, but not for lack of courage, was unaware of what was happening. Soon, however, he began to receive urgent requests for battle orders.

At 1.30 he at last gave the command to attack. The word passed along the line, but the Macdonalds, mortally affronted because they were on the left instead of the right of the line refused to move immediately. But others did. As they surged forward on to the cannon and muskets, fearful gaps appeared in their lines but they never hesitated. They covered the ground faster than anticipated and it was as well for the English infantry that they had kept their powder dry in spite of the rain, which was blowing hard into the Jacobite faces. Incredibly, all the old Highland magic was still there. Battered, starved, exhausted, the Prince's army, who were by no means all Highlanders, went into the charge as if they were fresh troops. Opposite were certain English regiments whose reputation had taken hard knocks in recent battles, and even earlier ones. This time, whatever happened, win or lose, they swore, they would not be disgraced. As the Jacobites came hurtling in the redcoats poured volley after volley at them. At once this had become a battle of heroes. Nobody in his senses could have predicted that the Scots would reach this far; nobody in his right mind would have dared speculate that, if they did, the English could hold them on their bayonets. The scene was unbelievable. Men were fighting on with half a dozen wounds, perhaps with an arm already lopped off, but slashing out with the other before they fell. It was, however, in the long run, a victory for the musket. By the time the regiments were hand-to-hand, the English had too great a numerical advantage to lose – unless a miracle occurred. Even so, neither army was fully committed; some Scots had never come into position, and the English reserve had scarcely been touched. But those who were committed fought with a frenzy and endurance that was almost superhuman. And in an hour it was all over.

The aftermath of this battle is perhaps too well known to need description here. Prince Charles escaped, and, with a price of £30,000 on his head, hid in the Western Highlands before he obtained a ship for France. Not a man attempted to betray him. He died in 1788. When his brother Henry died in 1807, the male Stuart line became extinct.

The sequel to Culloden was barbarous. Cumberland earned the nickname 'the Butcher' from the atrocities he unloosed on the Highlands, and the English Government which followed his cruelties with repressive measures were equally at fault. Cumberland's troops mercilessly hunted down the fugitives, dragging them out of cottages where they had found refuge and shooting them in cold blood. Equally brutal was the treatment of those suspected of aiding the escape of Prince Charles. It was entirely inexcusable even after the scare that the '45 had given to the English. Cumberland's attitude may perhaps be understood. He did not see the Scots as opponents such as the French to whom one might lose without great loss. He saw the Scots as a potential danger which might erupt again and destroy him and his line utterly. This he was determined to prevent. But no one, Scottish or English, will ever forgive or excuse him.

Much of the battlefield is now wooded over, but there is one clear strip from which the scene in 1746 may be visualized. It is now National Trust property and well signposted and preserved.

Index

Figures in **bold** refer to maps

Index

Index

St Albans, Second Battle of (1461) 94, 95–103, **98**, 104–105, 206, 207

Stafford, John 86

Stamford Bridge, Battle of (1066) 22, 157, 160–173, **167**

Standard, Battle of the (1138) 156, 174–181, **178**, 235

Stanley, Sir Edward **231**, 234, 235, 237

Stanley, Lord 141
  at the Battle of Bosworth Field 129, 130, **130**, 132–3

Stapylton, Sir Philip 441–442

Stephen, King of England 35, 174, 175

Stewart, Alexander 556

Stewart, Murdoch 550, 552

Stewart, Patrick 605

Stirling 517
  Castle 523, 530

Stirling Bridge, Battle of (1297) 506–513, **510**, 518

Stoke Field, Battle of (1487) 135–141, **138**, 227

strategy 13, 158–159

Strathavon Castle 558

Stuart, Charles Edward (Bonnie Prince Charlie) 618–622, 624, 625, 627–633

Stuf 295

Surrey, Earl of 186, 563, 566

Surrey, Thomas Howard, Earl of 228–238, **231**

tactics 13–14

Taillefer (Jester) 29

Tantollon, siege at 566

terrain 14–15

Tewkesbury, Battle of (1471) 114–126, **116**

Thurstan, Archbishop of York 176–177, 228, 235

Tillier, Colonel 253

Tippermuir, Battle of 588

Topham Hood, Colonel 59

Tostig, Earl of Northumbria 20, 21, 22, 162, 163, 167

Towton, Battle of (1461) 156, 205–216, **212**, 217, 218, 221, 223, 267, 559

Trollope, Andrew 102

Tudor, Jasper, Earl of Pembroke 115, 123–124, 127

Tudor, Owen 93

Twenge, Sir Marmaduke 511

Valence, William de 48

Vane, Sir George 578

Vane, Sir Ralph 576

Verney, Sir Edmund 385, 442

Wade, General 618, 624–5

Wakefield, Battle of (1460) 87–88, 89, 95, 100, 156, 198–204, **202**, 206, 209

Wallace, William 507–513
  death of 520, 521

Waller, Sir William 268, 389, 390, 401, 415, 422, 424, 456
  at the Battle of Cropredy Bridge 416–418, **417**
  at the Battle of Lansdown 103–107, 457–460
  at the Battle of Roundway Down 402–403, **404**, 405–406

Walters, Lucy 143

Wansdyke 324–325, 328, 403

Warbeck, Perkin 141, 563

Warenne, William de, first Earl 44–45

Warine of Bassingbourn 52

Warrenne, John de 40, 506–513, 514–20, 528

Wars of the Roses 64–141, 198–225, 352–374, 377

Warwick, Earl of, at the Battle of Pinkie 577, 578

Warwick, Edward, Earl of 136–137, 141

Warwick, Richard Neville, Earl of (the Kingmaker) 74, 78, 80, 84, 86, 183, 207, 209, 211, **212**, 217–225, 221, 226–227, 357, 358, 365, 366, 368–370, 374
  at the Battle of Barnet 107, 109
  at the Battle of Edgcote 106, 373–374
  at the Battle of Northampton 85
  death of 112–113, 114
  at the First Battle of St Albans 74, 75–78
  plotting against Edward IV 106
  at the Second Battle of St Albans 96, 98, 100–101, 104
  treaty with Queen Margaret 106–107

Wenlock, Sir John 80, 86, **116**, 119–121

Whitney, Sir Robert 60

Widdrington, General 239, **245**, 246, 247

William I, the Conqueror, King of England and Duke of Normandy 18, 19, 23, 25, 35, 160, 163, 165, 174
  at the Battle of Hastings **26**, 29–31

William II, Rufus, King of England 35, 174

William III, King of England 604, 613, 615

Wilmot, Lord **382**, 383, 384, 402–403, 405–406

Winceby, Battle of (1643) 157, 239–248, **245**, 264

Witgah 295

Wlencing 293

Woden's Barrow 313

Wood, Sir Andrew 562

Woodville, Elizabeth 226

Worcester, Marquis of 274

Worcester, Battle of (1651) **433**, 430–435

York, battle for 22

York, Richard, Duke of 78, 80, 199–204, 354, 356, 357, 364, 365–366
  death of 87–88, 89
  at the First Battle of St Albans 73–76, **74**
  as Protector 72, 87

Young, Brigadier Peter, DSO, MC 379, 444